Producing Excellence

Friends of the North Kingstown Free Library

In Honor of the Staff

2015

Producing Excellence

The Making of Virtuosos

IZABELA WAGNER

RUTGERS UNIVERSITY PRESS
NEW BRUNSWICK, NEW JERSEY, AND LONDON

Library of Congress Cataloging-in-Publication Data

Wagner, Izabela.
  Producing excellence : the making of virtuosos / Izabela Wagner.
    pages cm
  Includes bibliographical references and index.
  ISBN 978–0–8135–7006–8 (hardcover : alk. paper) — ISBN 978–0–8135–7005–1 (pbk. : alk. paper) — ISBN 978–0–8135–7007–5 (e-book (web pdf)) — ISBN 978–0–8135–7533–9 (e-book (epub))
  1. Violin—Instruction and study—Social aspects. 2. Music—Instruction and study—Social aspects. 3. Virtuosity in musical performance. I. Title.
  MT260.W25 2015
  787.2'193071—dc23

                                          2014046209

A British Cataloging-in-Publication record for this book is available from the British Library.

Visit our website: http://rutgerspress.rutgers.edu

Manufactured in the United States of America

For Filip and Ania
and all musicians I met during my life
and who still are in love with music

Contents

Acknowledgments

This book, like virtuoso playing, is the result of a sociological process; it is a collective work (like the art pieces analyzed by Howard S. Becker). Many people made this ethnographic study possible and helped me in the process of research and writing.

The book is based on participant observation, and as such requires thanks to all participants, who trusted me and spent many hours with me, discussing and confiding their hopes and fears. First, my son's contribution to this book should be mentioned. Without his involvement and patience, this book would not have been possible. Despite his youth, he is an exceptionally reflective and mature person; I am deeply grateful for the years we spent together on this project.

Some years after I started this study, my daughter began the violin and contributed as a second key informant to the observation process. Her sensitivity and spontaneous nature allowed me to explore this world from another perspective. I am deeply grateful for her help.

I am grateful to the dozen of young musicians who are close to our family. Knowing my sociological passion, they volunteered time and insight in the process of investigation and discussion. Living in our home sometimes for weeks or months, they shared with me their daily struggles, and I become a confidante and over time a specialist in their problems. I also wish to acknowledge all the adult participants who trusted me, despite the sensitive nature of the data. Without the time and attention of all these and other participants, this study could not have been carried out.

My work began as a PhD research project written in French under the supervision of Michel Chapoulie, a specialist of the Chicago school of sociology and a connoisseur of classical music, who was deeply involved in the process of analyzing the data. It was his idea to focus on violin virtuoso socialization. I would like to thank him not only for his supervision and for passionate discussions of sociology and music but for taking the risk of accepting me to the PhD group. I am also grateful for the amount of patience and the time he spent improving the French manuscript.

Before the PhD program, I had not done any writing in French. I was able to navigate this obstacle thanks to my husband, Philippe. His contribution to my study is incalculable. Philippe's tolerance of the constant presence of research participants in our home (for over ten years); his listening to unfinished stories and his contributions to endless discussions about the musical world; his logistical help with the organization of our family life; and his financial support of my study—all of these constituted an indispensable base for my work. For taking on all these responsibilities, and foremost for his emotional and intellectual support, I will always be deeply grateful to my husband.

Considering the international character my findings, I felt it would be vital to provide an English version of this work. Several persons corrected parts of the early drafts of the book; in particular I would like to thank Herbert Scott for his help.

The science journalist and author Arthur Allen and I developed a fruitful and fascinating collaboration that turned into a scientific friendship. Arthur transformed the text, bringing to it his mastery of English. In exchange I helped his research in Polish archives and with translations of Polish interviews and articles for his work. Our work will always remain in my memory as a happy example of scientific collaboration.

I would like to acknowledge the support of two reviewers, Howard Becker, who inspired my research and gave me positive and encouraging feedback, and Paul DiMaggio for his involvement and a detailed review of my book. I am certain that his helpful remarks improved my work, making the text clearer and integrating it more effectively with a wider circle of sociological thinkers. I also wish to thank my editor at Rutgers University Press, Peter Mickulas, for his professional and tolerant help. Working with a foreign author who has never published in an American house is certainly an experience that requires special skills. I was lucky to have had Peter's help. I was also lucky to benefit from the copyediting by a musician and professional editor—Dr. Helen Myers, who polished the text with deep field expertise—and Nicholas Humez, for indexing and proofreading.

Finally I wish to thank all the persons who read portions of the book—friends, sociologists, and others—for the time they spent reading the text and engaging in discussions about the work. Special thanks go to Josef Hermanowicz, Malgorzata Jacyno, Daniel Bizeul, Maciej Gdula, Adam Ostolski, and Sylwia Urbanska.

I wrote a book about the production of excellence, but this is also a book about passion. Passion for music, for violin, for perfection, for performance, for life. Thanks to all who contributed to the achievement of this book and to those who supported this passionate project and my passionate attitude toward my work.

Producing Excellence

Introduction

PRELUDE—SCANDAL ON THE STAGE

A European capital in the 1990s. A full concert hall in the closing hours of an international violin competition. Tonight, the finalists in the competition will each play a piece. Traditionally, the lowest-placed finisher takes the stage first, the grand-prize winner last. Tonight, the sixth-place finalist and the first to play is a sixteen-year-old Russian girl, Anastasia. Her selection is announced, a nineteenth-century piece for violin and piano. Anastasia, in a black evening gown, her violin in one hand, marches on stage with the confidence of her decade of experience as a soloist. Behind her is the competition's pianist, a woman of thirty, and the woman who will turn the pages of the score.

Anastasia takes her place at center stage, raises her violin to her shoulder, and nods for the A to be played in order to tune. Her accompanist gives the note; gradually the audience stops talking. The accompanist adjusts her bench, a ritual often done as the soloist tunes. Suddenly, with ardent passion and before the pianist can react, Anastasia attacks her violin with the first chord of a famous, expressive twentieth-century piece written for solo violin. The accompanist is shocked. Anastasia plays intently, as if possessed.

After the first bars, it is evident that the piece is not that which was announced on the program. Some in the audience cry in shock and anger: "How can she do that?" Others smile, openly or while staring at the ground. An amazed voice calls out, "What a character!" The discussion grows animated in the first rows, which are occupied by people invited from the music industry, the competition's jury members, and politicians and other public figures. Their furious comments do not cease throughout Anastasia's six-minute performance.

The majority of the audience does not understand the situation. Why this electric, nervous ambiance in the hall? Why isn't the pianist playing? Why are some people not listening? Is Anastasia playing poorly? Certainly not!

Her playing is filled with emotion and seems magical. It is clear to anyone listening that Anastasia is a wonderful violinist. When her piece concludes, the hall fills with applause. People call out: "She is wonderful! Amazing!" Nevertheless, some people refrain from clapping. Several scream "Scandal!" Low, resounding discussions stop only with the next competitor's performance.

The consequences of Anastasia's performance are immediate. A jury member, following her performance backstage, announces, "Her career is finished!" The performance is not shown on a public television special about the competition. A broadcasting presenter covers up the incident, saying there had been a "change of program . . . for unknown reasons." The next day, Anastasia receives news of the cancellation of two concerts that had been booked because of her high finish in the competition. "The sponsors," it is explained, "cannot tolerate this kind of behavior."

Why was this amazing performance by this beautiful young violinist described as a scandal? The public, after all, responded enthusiastically to Anastasia's playing. Nonmusicians and concertgoers liked the performance, and many felt that Anastasia was the best player that night—by far, some said.

This event was discussed by musicians for months. Other violinists I spoke with understood that by changing her program, Anastasia had demonstrated that she disagreed with the jury's verdict. As one said, "Musicians know that competitions are never fair. It is true that she deserved a much better place. But changing the program in order to protest—I do not know if that was a good decision. She really insulted the jury."

Others gave a positive review: "Everyone who was present in the concert hall knew that she deserved first place. That evening, nobody played like Anastasia— with that kind of talent, temperament, emotion, and fantastic musical maturity. At sixteen, to show in front of two thousand people that she doesn't agree with the jury statement? It was a fantastic act of bravery. She has the temperament and character to be a great soloist. I hope that this milieu doesn't destroy her."

On its surface, this might seem like a relatively minor affair: a high-strung, brilliant young musician defies her jurors. But within the culture of elite musicians, the event gave rise to endless discussions. Why did Anastasia play the other piece? Why did other musicians regard this as an act of extreme courage? Why did some find it potentially useful for a soloist's career, while others found it scandalous? Why must this sixteen-year-old suffer negative consequences after giving a performance of the highest quality?

To understand this event in its entirety, we need to learn how this rarefied musical culture functions. What values are obvious within this close-knit world, and how do individuals assimilate those specific values? In this book, I introduce this world of the musical elite, who live in the margin of our society, usually pursuing their activities in cities where creative milieus are developed. This book explains how, in the span of twenty years, the "talented child" (we will see what this expression means, and what consequences provoke this qualification) is transformed into a soloist through the process of socialization within this subset of society. I will explain how some people participate in the production of excellence.

In recent years, two books, Amy Chua's *Battle Hymn of the Tiger Mother* (2010) and Malcolm Gladwell's *Outliers: The Story of Success* (2008), have covered some of the terrain that I explore in this study. The success of both books shows the keen interest in the topic of training for virtuosity. Readers of the following study will find that, unlike Chua, who writes mainly about family dynamics and emotions, this book delineates the hidden mechanisms behind virtuoso education. I provide a step-by-step disclosure of the secrets of the process of creating excellence that Gladwell presents in an anecdotal way. What follows is a detailed, in-depth socio-logical examination of the development of an elite violinist, based on the study of dozens of classical musicians.

Certain categories of people are involved in this transformational process: music teachers, parents, juries, accompanists, and many other professionals participate at countless events to form a soloist. This education comprises a complex, lengthy process that passes through several stages, each determined by different—and sometimes opposing—factors. There are two very important theoretical points attached to this empirical study. First, this specific education involves a dual and interdependent hierarchy of teachers making reputations and students making careers, each using the other as rungs on their respective ladders. The second is that educating virtuosos is the job not only of teachers but also of complex informal networks and institutions.

Only the rare individual finishes the soloist education. Those who do com-plete it and become professional soloists at the international level are exceptions. Far more frequently, the soloist student becomes a violin teacher or orchestral musician, while maintaining a supplementary occupation as an occasional solo-ist. Infrequently, the soloist abandons music altogether, choosing a different career path. The prodigy who achieves a soloist career after undergoing all the socialization and overcoming the many stages of attrition on the path to success is perceived as enjoying great luck, divine intervention, or inherent genius, or perhaps all three.

I analyze this intensive process with sociological tools used in several studies of children's transformation (Adler and Adler 1991, 1998; Shaw 1930) and socializa-tion (Becker et al. 1961; Campbell 2003; Ferales and Fine 2005; Schnaiberg 2005; Shulman and Silver 2003; Traweek 1988) in order to understand and explicate the process of elite socialization in today's Western societies.

The soloist elite constitutes a small but significant part of the music world, and the artistic world in general.[1] This social group includes an ensemble of musicians who have attained a reputation as soloists in their professional careers. Other occupations engaged in the soloist's education include conductors, accompanists, concert organizers, producers, and agents. This soloist world is inscribed in the larger musician world, which is heterogeneous and structured by several cate-gories. Factors like the time of education (eighteen years minimum for pianists and violinists), beginning education at early childhood (four or five years old for violinists), the virtuosity of pieces played, and the soloist's visibility to the public contribute to the perception that violinists and pianists are elite musicians in the classical music world. (Parents considering a musical education for their children frequently choose these instruments.)

Competition is very strong—the race for privileged positions starts at the earliest stages of education. Pressure is great to mobilize power from a coalition of parents, teachers, and students. This is not exclusive to the soloist world: other professions where success is a product of extreme performance, ambition, and strong individuality function similarly. A paradigm is the world of scientists as described by Joseph Hermanowicz: "the scientist, like the artist or the athlete, follows a pantheon of immortals—figures who have achieved a place in history through exemplary performance. . . . Who aspires to be a mediocre Johnny Unitas, a second-rate Beethoven, or a watered-down Newton?" (Hermanowicz 1998: xiii).

Because greatness in classical music usually means to be known internationally, the race imposes an important geographic mobility. During a year's time, a young soloist typically takes part in at least one international competition,[2] gives several concerts, participates in a master class taught by other teachers, and attends his or her own teacher's master classes. These events may be organized throughout the world. European students take a master class at Keshet Eilon, Israel, or at the Summer Academy of Aspen, Colorado. American students participate in master classes in Sienna, Italy, or Tours, France. International violin competitions (the Geneva Guide for Competitions listed over three hundred in 2005) are held in Indianapolis, Montreal, Adelaide, and Pretoria, as well as Brussels, Moscow, London, Geneva, Hanover, and Poznan, Poland.[3]

This high-mobility and international activity is organized by networks of teachers who are powerful people in the classical music world. Without their support, no one could achieve a high-quality soloist education and embark on a soloist career. However, we should keep in mind that if for teachers the final goal is forming a virtuoso, the immediate goal is to hold on to their teacher's activity. Competitions for soloists, master classes, and other events bring participants together in a system of activities that generates the specific environments and nourishes several networks built around teachers. As we will see throughout the book, as the child's entourage believes in his or her exceptional talent, teachers never reveal the probability of success in such a long-lasting and exhausting education.

Because this education is a collective work, it is analyzed here as a process that the individual must go through to achieve a professional position. In this book, I consider this process a career path. I will use the concept of career in the interactionist tradition of the Chicago School (Becker 1970, chapter 11; Hughes 1971, chapter 14). This concept defines the course of professional life as a series of stages, which differ in the quality of interactions according to the individuals who play a relevant role in the professional environment. Following this approach, I will focus on the relationships between students and their teachers, parents, violin makers, and other persons significant in the career of future virtuosos. I distinguish three stages of the soloist student's career: the triad relationship of parent-teacher-student, for improvement in the student's playing ability; the relationship between teacher and student; and the relationship between categories of professionals who introduce young soloists to the adult market of classical music. As my results indicate, all soloists experience these three stages of education. The adult violinist's career depends heavily on this educational experience.

According to my interviews, musicians define "career" as the course of life that is directed at students from a very young age. The adult career is seen simply as the prolongation of the student career. The number of high-profile performances by the precocious child, and his or her early introduction in the professional milieu, are crucial to success. Other characteristics of this milieu include expensive immersion in this closely knit world and isolation from children of the same age. Finally, precocious soloists characteristically experience a strong merging of their professional and private ties and develop strong interactions with others at their career levels.

In October 1997, I started keeping ethnographic journals concerning the activities of the soloist class in Paris I had known six years earlier when my children were students in this class. The familial relationship with my field of research extends to my professional education—I have taught piano and music theory, and was raised in a family of musicians—and allowed me to act as a participant observer.[4] Observational experience continued with other soloist classes in France, Germany, and Poland. For nine years, I observed the work of a few soloist teachers with students from their classes, and in the master classes that constitute a central activity of soloist students. I have also observed eleven international competitions for violinists and two for pianists.

For all kinds of ethnographic studies, the characteristics of a researcher determine his or her access to particular fields and specific networks. For me, my Eastern European origin and profession of music teacher educated in Poland gave me a particular access to a mainly Russian network of violin teachers and their activity in Western Europe. Certainly a French sociologist investigating the violinist world in Paris would find another network of teachers (probably around the Conservatory of Paris) with another culture of work and a different organization of activities. There is no doubt that my particular positioning strongly determined the results; however, observed processes are specific for each and every field, especially when those differences are culture related (in the sense of ethnicity and geographic origin). Nevertheless, it is essential to be precise here that the results presented in following pages concerns the violin elite—the musicians on the top of the international market of classical music virtuosos.

For reasons that will be explained later, teachers educated in Eastern Europe are considered the best at training the young soloist at high levels of performance. The Parisian soloist classes that I principally observed were created by professors of Eastern European origin. Their students who were seriously engaged in this specific path were frequently came from Eastern Europe. Some—immigrants to France, or in residence there for the purpose of attending a master class or violin competition—shared our family life, and gave me crucial and precious information about their professional trajectories.

My observations focused on household activities of more than twenty young violinists who lived in my family home, sometimes with their parents, for periods from two weeks to one year. (We never accepted payment for their lodging.) Hosting musicians was not originally a research strategy; years before I began studying sociology, we shared our Paris flat with Eastern European musicians on tour. Hosting other musicians conforms to rules in the musicians' world, especially among those from Eastern Europe.

I recorded formal multipart interviews with students and parents. This method follows a first long biographical interview with later interviews focused on specific themes. These additional talks—frequently about topics chosen by my interviewees—were recorded in order to catch the dynamic of the participant's career perceptions. Countless informal talks with young soloists and their parents were not recorded; interrupting intimate conversation to plug in a recording device can destroy the rapport, even when the talk addressed key questions in my research.

What prompts young violinists to practice, and how does practice affect their success? The close proximity to families, in some instances over several months, provided conditions to observe this phenomenon in relations between parents and children. I became aware of the preoccupations of young musicians and their parents, and began to understand how they viewed their futures. Moments of crisis, joy, doubt, and anger—emotions I shared with the young performers—were of crucial importance. I was able to accumulate knowledge I partially had gained during my children's violin educations, but it would not have been sufficient to base a sociological analysis on auto-ethnography. Nevertheless, a deep understanding of the process of producing excellence would not have been accessible without personal experience as the mother of a future virtuoso.

I stayed in touch with the majority of my subjects via phone or e-mail correspondence. I traced those who did not provide updates or news through information received from other violinists and information collected on the Internet about their artistic activities.[5]

I have deeply analyzed the lives of ninety violinists. I have had frequent contact with nine violin professors and thirty parents of young virtuosos. Most of the time I was a participant observer, working "under cover," as the mother of a violinist. As Julius A. Roth remarked (1962: 283–284), the role of a "secret" observer is very important for research, because this role can provide access to confidential information and practices. In order to collect a wide array of information, I utilized different roles: I was known as "Michal's mother,"[6] but also as a "neutral" person who "researches the soloist students." I benefited from the support of my participants: several interviews were arranged by people that I had previously interviewed. One musician said, "You absolutely must speak with Laura. She has a lot of experience. . . . I asked her if she would like to do an interview with you and she agreed." Sociologists call this phenomenon the "snowball effect." I also played the role of concert organizer specializing in young performers, which I carried out at the heart of the family association.

During my years of involvement in this network, young musicians viewed me as a "curious" person available to listen to their problems and lend them support. Some of the young musicians and their parents viewed me as the mother of a successful musician who knew "how this milieu works." Some parents hesitated to share information because they viewed me as a competitor.

Between 1997 and 2004, I conducted more than one hundred formal, semi-open audio-taped interviews, and several hundred informal interviews (talks reported in my ethnographical journal). I recorded interviews with forty students from a soloist class, eleven teachers, fourteen parents, three accompanists, two concert organizers, two conductors, four teacher's assistants, four violin makers, and one sound engineer. Formal interviews lasted two- to four-and-a-half hours. After a short presentation of my research, I began with a question about the first violin lesson. Interviewees often relayed detailed stories regarding their musical and familial life; the soloist education, as we will see, is the family's life story. I asked them about their projects, competitions, concerts, about their accompanist if they had one, about sponsorship, scholarships, and, often, about changing teachers.

Speaking with teachers, I focused on their biographies, their work as a violinist and teacher, relationships with their own professors, relationships with their students, and their thoughts regarding the career of soloist. They knew that I had been a music teacher, which was helpful because I "understood how tough the job was." Some stressed that a scientific approach could provide better results in their work; they believed that socialization is the most important part of a soloist education. Another important topic that arose was that of relationships with their own teachers, showing how this relationship was a model for interactions with their students.

Interviews with other respondents—violin makers, agents—explored their roles in the education of young soloists. Their contribution was valuable, especially in the analysis of their support for soloist careers—frequently forgotten contributions to this career path. According to rules of anthropologists, whereby it is crucial to interview informants in their native languages, I conducted interviews in French, Russian, Polish, and English. In addition to my qualitative sample of ninety violinists (recorded and unrecorded interviews), I introduced participants from six international violin competitions to create a statistic sample that included 339 students. I have also accumulated documentation about the activities of forty violin teachers.

My research was carried out transnationally, mainly in France, Poland, and Germany, but also in Italy, Spain, and the United States. Within this elite milieu the actors know each other, or can quickly locate one another in their world. Thus, the examples cited omit information about circumstance and places, preserving the anonymity of the actors.

Opponents of ethnographic research underline that this method has negative consequences such as the lack of distance between observed processes, especially those perceived by participants as "new." To escape possible misinterpretation, I employed historical comparisons. This supplemental material verifies which phenomena are genuinely new and which have always been a part of the soloist world. As this study shows, the internationalization of careers, the decreasing age of "young talent," the international organization of master classes,[7] and strong backing by collaborative supporting networks (music world experts, agents, sponsors, media, politicians) are not new phenomena resulting from globalization. They are characteristics that have long existed in the soloist culture.

For a historical dimension, I supplement my data with material from biographies and memoirs of nineteenth- and twentieth-century soloist careers (W. Jouzefow-itch 1978; N. Milstein and Volkov 1990; J. Rawik 1993; I. Stern and Potok 2001). Barbara Lourie-Sand's book *Teaching Genius* (2000) relates the life of one of the best-known violin teachers of the twentieth century and provides a wealth of infor-mation. My principal source of historical information was the encyclopedic work of Boris Schwarz, *Great Masters of the Violin* (1983). From this book and *The Baker's Biographical Dictionary of 20th Century Classical Musicians* by Nicolas Slonimsky (1997), *Le dictionnaire des interpretes* by A. Pâris (1995), and *Zhizn' zamechatel'nykh skripachei* by L. Raaben (1967), I was able to produce a statistical sample of the cat-egory of "soloists of the twentieth century." I also used the professional journals in English (*Strad, String*), French (*Diapason, Le Monde de la musique*), Polish (*Ruch Muzyczny*), and Russian (*Muzika*).

The book is organized chronologically, following the three stages of soloist edu-cation followed by a description of soloist careers. However, all three stages are not strictly determined by age: I offer an example of a ten-year-old student who is at the end of the second stage of his career when the majority of the participants are on the first stage at this age. As for each individual training, an age should be an indicator and not a strict feature pointing at the student's career stage.

In the first part of this book, I present a historical introduction showing the birth of a musical specialty—the virtuoso. Then, I analyze the parental decision to have a child begin music lessons. Parents choose an instructor, or professor, to help the child with daily lessons, and participate in activities to advance the young soloist's skill. Intensive instrumental practice in early childhood is necessary to attain a level of virtuosity. I describe the specifics of organization in soloist teaching and the actions required to help the musician obtain the best results in his or her performances.

The most important component of this stage is collaboration between parent(s), teacher, and student. The essential events in this process are regular lessons and active participation of the parents between lessons (practice at home). I use the case of an eight-year-old prodigy to describe a typical soloist's violin lesson, showing each party's role in this first stage of collaboration. Depending on the student, the parental role changes after a number of years, and the relationship between teacher and student evolves.

Chapter 4 covers the second stage of a soloist education, which begins with the "crisis" period: a change in the teacher and student relationship. This stage, usually the teenage years, is frequently marked by instability—students change their teach-ers, play fewer concerts, become less satisfied with their performances, and express doubts concerning their career path as a soloist. At this stage, young violinists decide whether or not to conform to their parents' decisions. The most important events are participation in competitions and master classes. I describe and ana-lyze the master class lessons to understand the relationship between student and teacher. This period is crucial for the pursuit of a soloist career because the par-ticipants engage in the process of career coupling (Wagner 2006, 2010).

Career coupling is a social process characterized by parallel paths of actors collaborating during periods of time necessary to boost each other's positions in their professional worlds. This is a three-stage process: (1) matching; (2) active collaboration; and, (3) passive collaboration (Wagner 2006b). I describe how the students become well known through their collaboration with already well-known teachers—a process described in the sociological literature (for example, in descriptions of scientific researchers' socialization). I also show how teachers build their careers through the performances of their students, a new issue within the sociological literature. I explain why this interactional process is of interest and how musicians construct their reputations, which are the basis of their careers.

In chapter 5, I analyze the final stage of the socialization process, the relationships among students and other professionals active in the classical music business. At this stage, students build on the career-coupling relationship with their teachers. After intensive collaboration between these career-coupling partners, each undergoes a new stage of career interaction: passive collaboration. Their names are linked by joined reputations.

The duration of the socialization process is long—fifteen to twenty years—and the stages of soloist education are not exchangeable; thus, chronology is necessary to understand this process. The graduation from one stage to the next is not accompanied by a rite of passage, but each stage includes transitions through significant life events. Upon the completion of these stages, a violin student is transformed into a candidate as an international soloist professional. Competitions and concert performances are of the greatest importance and are necessary to open the door to the international concert scene. After presenting this lengthy socialization process, I list and analyze the characteristics that determine a successful education.

Frequently in this book, I use the personal testimonies of soloists from today and earlier eras to illustrate my observations. The histories of famous performers are an important tool for understanding the socialization process of new soloists, and such chronicles play a critical role in the transmission of professional memory.

In chapter 6, I relay the trajectories of the students who do not follow the conventional path of socialization, but readjusted their goals to the reality of their career. Several occupational conversions are analyzed, and alternative paths are described. I provide examples of the lives of students who failed to achieve their goal of becoming soloists. In my conclusion, I stress the ideal trajectory that enables students to attain the status of a soloist, giving them hope of entering into the elite classical music market. This optimal trajectory is a model for producing excellence in this highly competitive, transnational environment.

I hope that the analysis of soloist student careers and their relationships with professionals from their world will inspire other researchers working on socialization and career-making in the professional worlds of artists and intellectuals. Writing this book, I tried to follow Clifford Geertz's statement: "ethnographers need to convince us . . . not only that they were truly there, but also, that in their place, we would see exactly what they saw, improve the same as they improved, and conclude the same as they concluded" (1996: 26).

CHAPTER 1

A Short History of the Violin Virtuoso Profession

To understand the socialization process of the virtuoso we must first examine the history of the profession. This history plays a crucial role in the education of virtuosos, who are nourished daily on the biographies of famous musicians during their training. This history is an integral part of the virtuoso's professional knowledge. Some of its elements are transmitted orally from teacher to student, along with the violin lessons, the secrets of instrumental technique and interpretation. This chapter describes that history and what it means to people working in the soloist world; in part this is a story of the origin and the development of a profession—the violinist interpreter.

The musicologist Alberto Cantu has highlighted the ephemeral character of the interpreter's fame (Cantu 1997: 180). The names engraved permanently in the collective memory of generations of musicians are usually the composers and performers—the great masters of the violin. To trace their history I mainly employed Boris Schwarz's 1983 *Dictionary of Performers and Musical Interpretation in the Twentieth Century*, filling in late-century data with the *Dictionnaire des interprètes* (A. Paris 1995). The second important publication about violin virtuosos is *Baker's Biographical Dictionary of Twentieth-Century Classical Musicians*, by the famous musicologist, pianist, and composer Nicolas Slonimsky (1997). Schwarz himself was a virtuoso and teacher, and the author's lack of distance from the biographies he describes can be felt. While the book is very informative, its portrayal of professional violists is sometimes romanticized. Schwarz, who was Russian-trained, spent his life in the soloist milieu, which may explain his lack of distance or critical viewpoint, and a tendency to line up with the profession's ideology. I use virtuosos biographies here in order to supplement Schwarz and filter his professional myth-making.

We find the first traces of the violin in Italy and Poland in the sixteenth century, represented in paintings and contemporary texts. In the seventeenth century, France and Germany followed. In the eighteenth century, musicians typically played several instruments and performed their own compositions on violin. Two centuries later, virtuoso musicians focused on a single instrument and dedicated their lives mainly to the works of others. Changes in the violin's place in music can be divided into four periods.

The first period features the musicians who preceded Niccolò Paganini, whose life was a turning point in the history of music (we could compare this change to the paradigm shift as presented by Kuhn 1960). The second part is the career of Niccolò Paganini and his imitators. The third part features the "new type of virtuosos." The great twentieth-century performers are the subject of the last part. No clear dividing line exists between the second and third period, or between the third and fourth. The current stage of the history of the soloist begins with the first years of twenty-first century, in which virtuoso teachers work around the world.

Versatile Musicians, Multi-Instrumentalists, and Composers

Initially, violins were used to accompany the human voice. The oldest preserved scores for violin date to 1582. During the period of development of baroque music, through 1750, the violin was used as a part of an ensemble. During this early period, violinists played several instruments: viola, cello, and harpsichord. They were musicians and composers whose knowledge and musical practice always included composition. Musicians at that time were always teachers, and some led musical ensembles such as orchestras and choirs. Musical performances were mainly held in churches and aristocratic residences; musicians were employed by ecclesiastical insti-tutions or private patrons. Versatility was a requirement of the profession. J. S. Bach's activities—playing several instruments, singing, directing, teaching, composing— were typical of musicians at the time. Perhaps the first famous violinist and teacher was the Italian Arcangelo Corelli (1653–1713). "During his lifetime," writes Schwarz, "he was called 'master of masters.' On each anniversary of his death, his students and admirers gathered at his burial place in the Roman Pantheon to perform his concerti grossi, a ceremony that continued as long as his students were alive. His reputation spanned Europe, from Rome to Paris and London" (Schwarz 1983: 29).

Corelli was also the first violin teacher to win international recognition, and it is possible that the practice of venerating violin teachers was born with him. That phenomenon continues today, a testimony to the crucial role of teachers in the socialization of the virtuoso and in all activities in the soloist world. Since the time of Corelli, certain traditions for the soloist's classes have crystallized; for example, the assignation of a high-level student with the sobriquet "student of X." Music historians note that these designations establish the virtuoso's ped-igree and maintain genealogical trees—"student of X, who was a student of Y."[1] In the world of musicians this classification is also practiced by musicologists, who use the term "school" to refer to "teacher to student" lineages (Travers R-C. in Parîs 1995: 20). There are several ways to play the violin, and violinists recognize the influence of each "school" in the way the violin and bow are used. In the history of the violin, we can distinguish several schools (named according to their geographical origin), and these schools are sometimes linked.

Among the other famous early violinists—who were all polyvalent musicians and whose names remain in history mostly because of their activity as composers—are Antonio Vivaldi (1678–1741), Giuseppe Tartini (1692–1770), and Giovanni Battista Viotti (1753–1824). Their works constitute part of the repertoire of soloist class students. Tartini's student Pietro Locatelli is considered the "father of violin virtuosity" (Schwarz 1983: 92). Outside Italy other composers developed the violin repertoire during this era: Johann Sebastian Bach, Leopold Mozart, and Wolfgang Amadeus Mozart were all violinists. In the life of Mozart two major changes occurred that would affect the careers of musicians: the release of the artist from the exclusive authority of the patron (the musician became independent) and the popularization of the phenomenon of "child prodigy."[2] The figure of the born-genius musician became desirable for a beginner in a virtuoso career pattern. The course of many violinists inscribed in music history begins with a period as a "child prodigy." Parallel to this phenomenon, the growing interest in education through a master pushed students to follow a great teacher. Gradually, soloist classes were organized around the best performers and most famous violin teachers.

In France, Jean-Marie Leclair (called the "French Corelli") is considered the founder of the French school of violin. G. B. Viotti was an important figure of the Italian school, which influenced the French school. The career of Niccolò Paganini arose within this landscape of national schools (Italian and French), each seeking famous violin teachers, at a time of growing interest in classical music among the bourgeois and aristocratic public. Paganini revolutionized violin technique and modernized the occupation of the musician-performer, in the process becoming the embodiment of virtuosity.

PAGANINI AND OTHER VIRTUOSOS

"Paganini (1782–1840) was a phenomenal virtuoso. He invented a new style of spectacular violin playing, which he employed in his own compositions. He also had the good fortune to begin his career in an excellent historical period, and was the first virtuoso to take advantage of these excellent conditions for performing" (Muchenberg 1991: 33, part 2).

The technical innovations introduced by Paganini influenced the style of music writing at his time, adding emphasis to dozens for virtuoso playing. This influence remains visible in artistic performances to this day.[3] Paganini's romantic personality gave birth to myths that Paganini himself carefully spread and maintained.[4] He knew how to work the publicity specialists and concert agents of his time and was the first instrumentalist to follow the path of opera singers by hiring an impresario. These elements were fundamental to the development of Paganini's career and gave him a singularity compared to his virtuoso contemporaries. His career then became a model for other virtuosos to follow—violinists but also other instrumentalists, such as pianists, for example, Liszt. Starting with Paganini, instrumentalist virtuosos could become "stars," a pinnacle perceived by musicians themselves as the highest professional achievement. The public loved Paganini and other romantic virtuosos, who become celebrities and heroes.[5]

If Paganini was the first of romantic virtuosos, he was the last to gain equal fame as a composer. This was so because his followers gave priority to their performing careers, although not a few of them remain known to posterity as composers of violin music. These individuals include Heinrich Wilhelm Ernst (1814–1865), Charles-Auguste de Bériot (1802–1870), and Henri Vieuxtemps (1820–1881).

The impact of Paganini's career on the education of the generations of violinists who performed after him is astonishing. To be known as "the Paganini of . . ." was the highest accolade—thus Ole Bull, "Paganini of the North" or Henry Lipinski, "the Polish Paganini." Other "reincarnations" of Paganini included Jan Kubelik, August Wilhelmj, Willy Burmester, and Jascha Heifetz. Jan Kubelic was called the "second Paganini" as were the Pole Henryk Wieniawski and the Spanish performer Pablo Sarasate. Wieniawski developed the virtuoso technique further and passed into history as a founder of the Russian school of violin. He was a "child prodigy," then a virtuoso performer and composer. His pieces are as difficult as those of Paganini. As a composer, Wieniawski is considered a member of the Polish national school for violin in the way that Chopin was for the piano.

In the nineteenth century, some violinists scorned the model of the romantic virtuoso and reproached Paganini and his imitators as "charlatans" (Schwarz 1983: 243). A generation of Vienna-educated Austrian violinists including Louis Spohr and Joseph Joachim created a countercurrent to Paganini, focusing on the quality of their sound and the beauty of their melodies rather than on acrobatic passages. Joachim was the first performer to devote his public performances to the music of other composers. In addition to his soloist activity he was a famous professor and violin master, teaching many European soloists while working in Hanover and Berlin (1867–1907).

"The New Style of Virtuoso"

Technical advances by Paganini and Wieniawski, along with research on interpretations done by Joseph Joachim (1831–1907) modernized the violin vocabulary and allowed the emergence of what Schwarz calls a "new style of virtuosos" (1983: 279), musicians with excellent technique and great musical and creative talents, combining intellect and instinctive sensitivity. The main representatives of this type are the Belgian virtuoso Eugène Ysaÿe (1858–1931) and the Austrian Fritz Kreisler (1875–1962). Although these two violinists helped define the new virtuoso style, their personalities, careers, and style of play could not have been more different. Kreisler had a slow start finding a place on the European scene, which at the time was dominated by a "titanic force"—Ysaÿe. The romantic journey of the latter, a son of musicians and "child prodigy" with an explosive and unpredictable personality, contrasted sharply with Kreisler, an elegant, beloved virtuoso always referred to as a "gentleman."

Similar oppositions occur throughout the long history of musical interpreters. George Kulenkampf (1898–1948) the "less German" German violinist, had a playing style influenced by Slavic and French schools of interpretation. His opposite was Adolf Busch (1891–1952), an "ideal type" German violinist. In Berlin, the Hungarian Carl Flesch (1873–1944) led an influential class of soloists starting in the early twentieth century. Flesch, who switched to teaching after the failure of his own virtuoso career, was the prototype of the twentieth-century master. He taught first in Bucharest, then in Amsterdam before taking a position in Berlin. During World War I, the Germans interned Flesch because of his Hungarian citizenship, and in 1923 he left for the United States, where he taught at the Curtis Institute in Philadelphia. Five years later, he returned to Europe to teach again in Berlin and Baden-Baden, with sporadic teaching stints in London and Lucerne. Flesch developed a new method that was opposed to the teachings of the Parisian Conservatory, which he called "mummified, and limiting the repertoire of violinists" (B. Schwarz 1983: 332). He wrote several books on his violin technique, which differed from other teachers because of the position of the right hand and the bowing technique: Flesch's students could be recognized by the upward position of their elbows while playing. They included Henryk Szeryng, Ida Haendel, and many other violinists, including the students of teachers influenced by his teaching, such as Dorothy DeLay. Flesch also established a model of internationalism: his students came from all over the world, especially Eastern Europe, and the diversity of his class is exemplary of later periods in the soloist culture as a whole. Writes Schwarz,

> After World War I, Berlin became a Mecca for the arts, especially for modernism and experimentation. There was a considerable immigration from Eastern Europe. Particularly noticeable was an influx of gifted young Polish violinists, most of whom were poor and needed scholarships. Their idol was their compatriot Huberman, who recommended Flesch as a teacher, and so they wound up in Flesch's studio in Berlin. Initially, the climate in Berlin was not ideally suited for those young Poles: they had to contend with a foreign language, a sophisticated culture, German haughtiness, and latent anti-Semitism. As for Flesch, his intellectual approach to the violin was diametrically opposed to their "gutsy" concept of fiddling. But they survived and learned; they became remarkably well acclimatized to the Germanic surroundings; and most of them prospered during years of the Weimar Republic. All dispersed when Nazis came to power in 1933. The young Polish group in Flesch's studio included Szymon Goldberg, Stefan Frenkel, Bronislaw Gimpel, Roman Totenberg, Henryk Szeryng, and Ida Hendel. All had played the violin since early childhood and had concertized as prodigies; some studied in Warsaw with Michalowicz, a fine teacher. But by Flesch's standards, all had to be reschooled, and retrained. Not every remodelling process went smoothly, there were personality clashes between teacher and student, but on the whole Flesch's iron discipline was beneficial. (B. Schwarz 1983: 343–344)

The combination of the following elements: coexistence of different cultures (Slavonic, Hungarian, German), an experienced teacher with a strong reputation in the training of young virtuosos, and a specific geo-historical context (Berlin in 1920–1933) allowed many young violinists to launch international careers.[6] Berlin before 1933 was the world center for classical music, but there were other places for violinist training: Hanover, Munich, Vienna, Prague (the Bohemian school with Otkar Sevcik, Jan Kubelik, Vasa Prihoda and Josef Suk), Budapest (the Hungarian school represented by Otkar Sevcik, Jan Kubelik,[7] Vasa Prihoda, and Josef Szigeti), and Warsaw (Michalowicz).

After World War II, France lost her dominant position in the field of violin playing: "After Ysaÿe left the concert stage, Thibaud alone remained to uphold French fame, though he was past his prime" (B. Schwarz 1983: 356). Jacques Thibaud became the most important violinist of French school, a status that accompanied him through life. There is a facetious anecdote told by the Russian American violinist Elman: "Twenty years ago I came to Paris and I asked, 'Who is the greatest French violinist?' The answer was 'Thibaud.' Now I come back, I ask again, and the answer is still 'Thibaud!' What happened to France?" (B. Schwarz 1983: 374).

Another famous violinist and composer based in Paris at the time was George Enesco, who was of Romanian origin but considered both a universal artist and a representative of the French school (Pâris 1995: 383). A new wave of virtuosos emanating from the French school included Zino Francescatti, Ginette Neveu, Arthur Grumiaux, and Christian Ferras. According to Schwarz, they were good musicians but "not designated to achieve the summit of celebrity" (1983: 374). French musicologist Roger-Claude Travers, however, believes the violinists of the French-Belgian school were the leading violin performers in the world at that time.[8]

Nevertheless, it is clear that Russian musicians occupied the top places of the virtuoso violin world in the twentieth century. Schwarz attributes this leadership position to the strong centers of virtuoso training and music lovers' preference for the Russian style of performing classical music. "The French style of violin playing, with its elegance, refinement, and charm, was being displaced in public favour by the Russian style, stressing sweep, brilliance, and sensuality," Schwarz writes. "Heifetz became king, and every newcomer was measured by his towering standards. Milstein fitted into this framework, and later Oistrakh. The first Ysaÿe competition of 1937 was swept by Soviet violinists" (B. Schwarz 1983: 374).

GREAT PERFORMERS OF THE TWENTIETH-CENTURY
RUSSIAN SCHOOL OF VIOLIN

The Russian School is the most important twentieth-century tradition of teaching and interpretation of the violin repertoire. In fact the school should properly be divided, because of political changes provoked by the 1917 Revolution, into two working schools: the Russian and the Soviet. The development of the Russian school began with the activity of four masters: Auer, Stolyarski, Yampolsky, and Yankelevich. Although teaching was done mainly in St. Petersburg, Odessa, and Moscow, students were recruited largely from the Russian Jewish community. This culturally homogeneous recruitment is a significant topic of discussion in the soloist world: on many occasions I heard violinists speak of the relationship between career development and cultural origins. A specific profile was seen as the key to becoming a virtuoso: "You must be born a Jew in Eastern Europe, and become a student of a great teacher representing the Russian school." This widespread belief, especially among students and soloists of Eastern European origin, is discussed by Schwarz, though he warns against oversimplification: "The initial success of the Russian school was not entirely due to the teaching of one man but the result of a variety of favourable circumstances, such as a vast reservoir of native talent (especially among the Jewish population), unified teaching methods, generous public support of the arts, and an unbroken tradition of excellence and high standards" (1983: 409).

These factors certainly did come together to create masterful violinists. As Schwarz points out, teaching conditions depend on place: the Russian school students learned in cities that had an intense musical and cultural life, a public that supported young virtuosos, and institutions that provided them with the basic means for their specific training. Another important factor was the reserve of violin masters found in the Jewish population of Russia at that time. Features such as the high level of interest in music in Jewish bourgeois families, their traditional investment in the education of their children, and especially their connection to an international culture, with geographical mobility and knowledge of foreign languages, were crucial factors in the virtuoso's training. The high status of conservatory students helped entire Jewish families of gifted pupils escape life in the ghetto,[9] enabling them to obtain permission to live in city centers where they were protected from pogroms. As Nathan Milstein (1990) pointed out, the success of Jews who followed this educational path encouraged parental enthusiasm for early violin (piano, cello) lessons. The non-Jewish Russian bourgeoisie, intelligentsia, or nobility had other patterns of education and career plans for its progeny. These upper-class Russian parents did not dream that their children would become professional musicians.

The pattern of early twentieth-century virtuoso education was similar to the contemporary model: before becoming pupils of a famous professor, young students were initiated to the violin by their parents—Yascha Heifetz began studying with his father Ruvin at age three—or by local teachers (Nathan Milstein began work with an unknown before coming under the wing of Piotr Solomonovitch Stolyarski). Then, after several years of hard work, performed under strict parental supervision, the masters sent their best students to conquer the European stages. For many violinists of the twentieth century, Berlin was the place to launch a European career, but young virtuosos traveled around the continent performing concerts and presenting themselves to the famous violinists of the time. Their parents accompanied them on these trips or used familial connections in provide care for the virtuoso youngster on his travels. Adaptability and skill with languages and foreign customs were important additional strong points that helped the virtuoso conduct this kind of artistic life.

The biographies of the great performers almost always revolve around a relationship with a great teacher. The genealogy of the great violin masters can thus help us understand the contemporary world map of virtuoso training.

The first master considered by musicologists to be the successor of Henryk Wieniawski was Leopold Auer (1845–1930). This Hungarian-born violinist unsuccessfully attempted a solo career after his training in Budapest and Vienna (Schwarz attributes his failure to a physical defect; Auer's hands were "too weak.") At the age of twenty-three, Auer accepted a professorship at the conservatory in St. Petersburg, where he went on to teach for forty-nine years. Soloist class teachers consider Auer the model of the virtuoso violin teacher, and the teacher-pupil relationships in his school were also emblematic of a type. "Auer's procedure was one of near hypnosis," Schwarz writes.

> Auer's teaching began where technique ended: he guided the students' interpretation and concept of music, he shaped their personalities, he gave them style, taste, musical breeding. He also broadened their horizons, made them read books, guided their behaviour, career, and social graces. . . . He insisted that his students learn a foreign language if an international career was in the offing. . . . Auer was also solicitous of the material needs of his students; he helped to obtain the scholarships, to enlist patrons, to get better instruments. He made every effort to obtain residence permits for his Jewish students, using his influence in high government circles. Even after a student had started a career, he followed his path with a fatherly eye. He wrote countless letters of recommendation to conductors and concerts agents. When little Misha Elman was about to make his London debut, Auer travelled there to coach him. He continued to work with Zimbalist and Parlow after their debuts. (B. Schwarz 1983: 420)

Auer's whirlwind activities established a prototype for the virtuoso teacher: while teaching in St. Petersburg he also held master classes in Dresden, Germany, London, and Norway. In 1917, at the age of seventy-three, he decided to leave for the United States. After giving some concerts as a soloist he moved to Manhattan's West Side and gave private lessons. In 1926, Auer accepted a teaching position at the Institute of Musical Art (now the Juilliard School of Music) and two years later, succeeded Flesch at the Curtis Institute in Philadelphia. Among his many students (more than five hundred between 1868 and 1917) were six violinists who experienced worldwide fame and came to represent the "St. Petersburg School": Mischa Elman, Efrem Zimbalist, Eddy Brown, Jascha Heifetz, Mischel Piastro, and Toscha Seidel. Another famous virtuoso, Nathan Milstein, was Auer's pupil for a short period but is considered the student of Stolyarsky, another virtuoso master. All of these musicians were native to Russia with the exception of Brown, born in Chicago. The others left their birth country following their education, in most cases because of the October Revolution. They immigrated to the United States, where they had successful careers.[10]

Piotr Stolyarski (1871–1944), whose teaching was based in Odessa on the Black Sea, shaped many violinists who enjoyed important careers on the international scene. Stolyarsky was trained by his father, then by Barcewicz in Warsaw and Mlynarski Karbulka in Odessa. In 1911, Stolyarski created his own private school, which soon came to be known as "the talent factory." One of Stolyarski's students,

Jalagin, described his master's method as consisting of "instil[ling] confidence in the young pupil by assuring him that he had extraordinary talent. . . . The child worked with enthusiasm" (Jalagin 1951: 204). Stolyarsky knew how to handle children to get them to work hard, and he knew how to master the ambitions of their parents, Schwarz notes. Following the institutional changes after the October Revolution (nationalization of private institutions), Stolyarski's school joined the Odessa Conservatory, but he continued to teach there. This continued until one of Stolyarski's best pupils, David Oistrakh, became a world-renowned virtuoso and organized Stolyarski's transfer to Sverdlovsk,[11] in order to ensure the violin education of his son, Igor Oistrakh (who also became a famous virtuoso). Soon after the old master's arrival, however, he died. Some of his students emigrated to the West, and the reputation of his school gradually spread, strengthening the position of the "Russian school" in the world of classical musicians.

The movement of musicians of Russian-Jewish descent onto the world stage at the beginning of the twentieth century constitutes an important moment in the history of professional violinists.[12] This history is often used in virtuoso teaching, as summed up in the following excerpt by Yehudi Menuhin:

> It was the Russian Jewish community, rooted in a universal philosophy, literate and urban, skilled in commerce, driven by passionate, intense feelings and ambitions for liberation, which became the main interpreter to the world. . . . One must bear in mind that the Russian Jew of the village ghetto had, as well as the example of the village folk fiddler, that of the gypsy fiddler, whose melodies he also shared, to say nothing of the unique treasure of traditional local heritage from the cantors and the Chassidic rabbis. It was the Jewish fiddler who always played the violin to express the joys and sorrows of the Russian villages; thus he had both played and listened to the Russian folksongs and those of the gypsies. . . . For the Russian Jew, highly motivated, highly literate, and yet ever destined to start life anew, the violin was the passport, purse, and path to the summits of society. From the southern warm-water port of Odessa . . . many of the best Russian violinists came. I well remember my amused amazement when, after the first concert I gave there, the people who flocked backstage made no comment whatsoever on the music, but one and all asked me specifically what fingering I had used in such and such a passage. It was more like being engulfed by a gigantic crowd composed of students, ex-students, and professors than by the heterogeneous audiences of any other city I have ever played in. Indeed, there was barely a Jewish family that did not have its young, budding violinist. (Menuhin qtd. in B. Schwarz 1983: 16–17)

After several years, the communist regime put the brakes on the emigration of musicians, limiting the issuance of passports needed to leave the USSR. Thus, in the thirties and during World War II, the artistic activity of the country developed almost in isolation. The greatest virtuosos of that period were David Oistrakh (1908–1974) and Leonid Kogan (1924–1982). The latter was a student, in Moscow, of Abram Yampolsky (1890–1936), considered by musicologists to be the third "great master" of the Russian violin school. The last of the masters of the Russian school, prior to the 1980s, was Yuri Yankelevich, who formed the virtuosos of the generation that followed that of David Oistrakh. They included many winners of international competitions, as these events became an increasingly popular part of virtuoso training. Mikhail Vaiman (born 1953), Igor Besrodny (1930), Mikhail Bezverkhny (1947), Victor Tretyakov (1946), Victor Pikaisen (1933), Vladimir Spivakov (1944), Gidon Kremer (1947), Tatiana Grindenko (1946), and Viktoria Mullova (1959) represent the generation of violin virtuosos active on the stage after World War II. Most of these virtuosos won the "Queen Elisabeth" competition in Brussels, beginning with Oistrakh in 1937. The Russian-born violinists reigned supreme in the solo violin world (sometimes sharing the pinnacle with soloists born in other Eastern European countries, who were taught by teachers trained in the Russian school).

Prior to 1980, musicians could emigrate only in exceptional cases (one way out of the USSR was to apply for the visa emigration as a Jew). However, some escaped on tour or while visiting the West to compete in musical competitions. The opening of borders that followed perestroika in the late 1980s enabled a massive wave of Russian musical emigration to the West. These violinists in turn created or re-created famous soloist classes, which produced the winners of competitions for virtuosos. In the early twentieth century, the term "Russian school of violin" signified a certain style of playing technique (contrasted with the Franco-Belgian school) and a way of interpreting works. With the proliferation of virtuoso education centers around the world in the second half of the twentieth century, the meaning of "the Russian school" changed. For participants in my study (violinists and their teachers) "the Russian school" is rarely synonymous with technique, but does refer to a particular approach to violin teaching—a specific relationship between master and disciple involving major commitments to daily practice and special requirements concerning quality of playing. In my study, which primarily involved students who see themselves as representatives of this school, I use the term in accordance with the perceptions of those involved in the process. It refers to the relationships among the participants in this training, their common origin and networks, trained in a closed space within similar geopolitical environments (the countries of Eastern Europe and especially the Soviet Union, and then Russia), in which artistic activity was highly valued by society.

AMERICAN VIOLINISTS

Musicologist Boris Schwarz places the appearance of the American school of violin in the early twentieth century. The activity of virtuoso teaching was implemented mainly in four cities: New York (Juilliard School of Music), Philadelphia (Curtis Institute), and Rochester (Eastman School), and beginning in the 1970s, Bloomington (Indiana University). Instrumental teaching at the virtuoso level is done at universities in the United States. Students become soloists frequently after taking lessons from musicians born and educated in Europe. At the beginning of the twentieth century, virtuosos such as Maud Powell (1868–1920), Albert Spalding

(1888–1953), Franz Kneisel (1880–1926), David Mannes (1866–1959), and Louis Persinger (1887–1966) were some of the leading North Americans performers. Franz Kneisel, born in Bucharest and trained in Germany, was known for his chamber music activity (the Kneisel Quartet). David Mannes, born in Manhattan to German-Polish parents, taught in addition to his career as a soloist and orchestra conductor. With his wife Clara (pianist and niece of the famous conductor Walter Damrosch), Mannes created a music school. The couple were philanthropists, and their school made accessible high-quality instrumental education to children from disadvantaged backgrounds. Louis Persinger, born in Rochester and trained in Germany, is currently known in the world of musicians as "Yehudi Menuhin's teacher." In 1930, he succeeded Leopold Auer at the Juilliard School of Music, and for thirty-six years trained virtuoso violinists, giving violin and chamber music lessons. His most famous students included Ruggiero Ricci (1918), Bustabo Gulia (1919), and Miriam Soloviev (1921). Schwarz reports that Persinger was known for his kindness, his patience, and his accompanist talents. As teachers, Mannes, Kneisel, and Persinger followed in the footsteps of Auer and Flesch. Many of their students came from families who had emigrated from Eastern Europe. Yehudi Menuhin told the following anecdote, as reported by Schwarz: "Rabbi de Sola Pool, an old friend of my parents when they first emigrated to New York, told me that following the pogroms of 1905, Jews arrived at that time in Palestine with almost every child carrying a violin case" (Schwarz 1983: 16–17).

Yehudi Menuhin (1916–2001) made an international career for himself before the start of World War II, becoming a major presence on European stages. Ruggiero Ricci (1918) and Isaac Stern (1920–2002) became well known first in the United States, then in Europe, in the process popularizing the American school. Although the U.S. and European concert markets for classical music are quite different, some virtuosos manage to become famous on both continents. After the Great Depression and World War II, the activity of teaching virtuosos in America was mainly concentrated around Ivan Galamian (1902–1981), Dorothy DeLay (1917–2003), and Josef Gingold (1909–1995). Gingold, born in Brest-Litovsk (on the border between Belarus and Poland), arrived in the United States at the age of eleven to study with Vladimir Graffman, a former student of Auer. Like most virtuosos living in the United States at this time, Gingold went to Western Europe to perfect his studies, under Ysaÿe in Belgium. In addition to working as a soloist musician, Gingold was concertmaster of the largest U.S. orchestras and worked with, among others, Arturo Toscanini. He also performed as a chamber musician as a member of the famous Primrose Quartet. After several years of teaching at the University of Cleveland, Gingold in 1960 became a professor of violin at Indiana University in Bloomington, where he taught almost until his death. Among his students were Joseph Silverstein, Jaime Laredo, Miriam Fried, Isidor Saslav, and Ulf Hoelscher.

Another great master of virtuoso teaching was Ivan Galamian, born in Armenia and trained in Russia and Paris. Galamian taught in the United States beginning in 1937, first from his apartment in Manhattan, then at the Curtis Institute in Philadelphia and the Juilliard School of Music in New York. Galamian was often

considered the top virtuoso coach, and his young students took impressive num-
bers of awards at international violin competitions. He was known as well for his
personality. Former students describe Galamian as a severe, even austere, teacher.
Galamian was a master at inspiring fear, but passage through his class was a key
to success in the soloist market. Among his famous students are Itzhak Perlman,
Pinchas Zukerman, Sergiu Luca, Eugene Fodor, Glenn Dicterow, Miriam Fried,
Jaime Laredo, Peter Zazofsky, Paul Zukovsky, Michael Rabin, Berl Sanovsky, and
Ani and Ida Kavafian. For twenty years, Galamian's assistant was Dorothy DeLay,
whose personality strongly contrasted with that of her boss. After a long collabo-
ration punctuated by misunderstandings mainly about DeLay's relationship with
the students, she opened her own soloist class at the Juilliard School. Beginning in
the 1970s this class became the top destination for virtuoso violinists in the United
States. The list of former DeLay students includes Perlman, Shlomo Mintz, Mark
Kaplan, Mark Peskanov, Cho-Liang Lin, Nigel Kennedy, Ida Levin, Nadja Salerno-
Sonnenberg, Dimitri Sitkovetsky, Midori, Sarah Chang, and Gil Shaham. The
virtuosos trained by DeLay, Galamian, and Gingold constitute the major American
artists of the late twentieth century.

Violinists of Israel

Israel plays an important role in the history of classical music, especially that of
violinists. Long before the creation of the state of Israel, beginning in the 1920s,
Jewish musicians immigrated to Palestine where they created orchestras,[13] ensembles, and instrumental teaching classes. The emigration of musicians from Eastern
Europe continues with diminished intensity even today. In 1983, Yehudi Menuhin
remarked: "Today, so it would seem, it is only thanks to the Russian Jews emigrating to Israel that the string ranks, particularly the violins, of the Israel Philharmonic
and the Jerusalem Symphony can be maintained" (Menuhin in Schwarz 1983: 17).
    Israeli students with the potential to become soloists continue their education
mainly in the United States. The America-Israel Cultural Foundation, created by
Isaac Stern, plays an important role by providing scholarships for studying at the
Juilliard School of Music in New York and other universities. Three main factors
contribute to the liveliness of the Israeli school,[14] which Schwarz considers "an
offshoot of the Russian school" created through the recruitment of Ashkenazi
emigrant students.[15] As in many Eastern European Jewish communities, significant family investment stands behind many Israeli soloist careers. For virtuoso
children brought up on the kibbutz, huge support from the community at large
was critical during long years of intensive training. But the country lacked ade-
quate infrastructures to ensure the promotion and production of soloists of international dimension. To obtain this support, young virtuosos usually went to the
United States—two famous examples being Shmuel Ashkenasi and Rony Rogoff,
both born in Palestine in the 1940s. A few violinists, such as Ivry Gitlis (1922),
who was born in Palestine and trained in France, obtained formal training in
Europe. The obligatory two-year military service that has been required of young

men and women since the creation of the state of Israel is one of the factors that pushes virtuosos to emigrate. Two years without formal instrumental practice can be seriously detrimental to a virtuoso violinist. The violinist Shlomo Mintz, an exceptional soloist, was able to complete his military obligations by arranging tours of duty while living and working in the United States. Passage through three countries (birth in Eastern Europe, early childhood training in Israel, master training and career commencement in the United States) is a typical trajectory of Israeli musicians such as Zvi Zeiltlin, Miriam Fried, Pinchas Zukerman, Sergiu Luca, and Shlomo Mintz. Since the 1970s some Eastern European-trained musicians have immigrated to Israel, among them Philip Hirshhorn, Dora Schwarzberg, Silvia Marcovici, and Liba Shacht.

Asian Violinists

Beginning in the 1960s, Japanese violinists in growing numbers took part in the international competitions for young virtuosos. Many Western soloists touring in Japan, among them Nathan Milstein, were struck by the level of interest in classical music. Milstein was surprised to hear classical music played in cafes, bars, and taxis, places where popular music is typically heard in the West. The popularization of classical music in Japan coincided with a decline of interest in Western Europe and in the United States. This "classical music fad" stimulated Japanese music schools. A new method of learning violin basics was developed by the Japanese educator Shinischi Suzuki (1898–1998), with great success. In 1950, the Suzuki School trained 196 advanced students—by 1972 it had 2,321. Today, the method is known around the world and is used for various classical instruments.[16]

Interest in Western classical music also expanded in China and South Korea. Many Korean emigrants pursue virtuoso training in American universities, while the interest in classical music is a more recent occurrence in China, dating, perhaps, to Yehudi Menuhin's visit to the country in the late 1970s, following the Cultural Revolution. Young Asian violinists' training is similar to that of young Israelis— first at home, then in Western Europe and the United States. They emigrate early to start their soloist careers at a young age. However, many have had difficulty permanently maintaining their positions as soloists in the international market of violin virtuosos.

Training Environments: Soloists at the End of the Twentieth Century

In the 1980s and 1990s, soloist training took place in different parts of the world and in different institutions: universities, academies, and private and public schools. Some teachers provided education through private classes and private lessons; others mixed private lessons with public ones. From a sociological perspective, what was interesting about this situation was the lack of connection between the prestige of the institution and its rank as a place of virtuoso training. Unless it had a master in residence, the name of an institution such as the Juilliard School of Music or the Conservatory of Paris provided no value in and of itself. The superiority of a virtuoso training site was entirely linked to the teacher in residence.

This reputation (as a "soloist stable") tended to be dynamic and to vary from one decade to another. The style of the institution depends on the activity of the master (or masters), but economic and historical conditions also have their influence. But the master is crucial. When a master leaves an institution—whether by emigration or some other departure—its reputation can be lost. The political or economic situation in a given country can cause the massive departure of teachers and thereby contribute to a school's loss of reputation.[17] This instability can be illustrated by comparing Boris Schwarz's list of violin instruction centers with the current soloist training map. In 1983, Schwarz noted that "New York, Philadelphia, Moscow and Leningrad are the centres of gravity" for violin instruction. Twenty years later, the layout of soloist education has changed: conservatories in Moscow and St. Petersburg (former Leningrad) no longer provide as many winners in competitions. Most reputable teachers have left these places, and those who remain on the staffs are frequently absent, guest-teaching in Western Europe and Asia. Many violin teachers have taken advantage of the border openings to settle in the western part of the European Union or in the United States.

Western cities have offered better working conditions for masters specializing in the training of soloists. The most striking example is Zürich, whose famous conservatory during most of the twentieth century hosted master classes by the greatest musicians (N. Milstein, H. Szeryng, V. Spiakov). Switzerland also houses the School of Young Virtuosos in Sion—created by Tibor Varga (1921–2003), a Hungarian-born naturalized Briton who lived in Switzerland. But after Varga's death, this institution lost its reputation as a "factory of young talents." London is another training center for violinists. While the Yehudi Menuhin School in Folkestone previously attracted young violinists, London's Royal Academy of Music is currently training "successful" virtuosos. New cities have appeared on the European map of training centers—Madrid, Karlsruhe, Cologne—building solid reputations for their virtuoso training schools. Vienna has managed to maintain a high position, with several renowned masters. On the basis of attendance at competitions by students trained in the United States, four U.S. cities predominate: New York and Philadelphia, followed by Bloomington and Boston.

Obviously it is difficult to create an exhaustive map of violin virtuoso training places, because the situation is dynamic. The process of instrumental education and the reputation of a master—as well as that of the institution where he or she works—take years to build. The knowledge of these centers of excellence is critical to young students and to parents concerned with creating a virtuoso. As we will see in the following chapters, the biggest problem for students traveling over this long, arduous path is "being in good hands, in the right place, at the right time."

CHAPTER 2

Before Entering the Soloist Class

EARLY SOCIALIZATION OF SOLOIST STUDENTS

What can I tell you about a violinist's education? I have observed them for more than twenty years now. Each day they come into my workshop, and I can only say one thing: It is crazy stuff, this system, and has nothing to do with music. This is a factory that creates so-called "musicians" and all that is born out of this is crazy parental ambition. They are sick, all sick of this incurable illness—known as ambition.

—a forty-one-year-old violin master at a school for talented youngsters

For students in a soloist class, violin playing is the principal activity of life. In addressing the questions "How do young children become violin students?" and "How at an adolescent age do they find this activity 'natural' and indispensable?" I am primarily interested in the family environment. Before a child enters a soloist class, parents must set in motion specific events: deciding their child will take up the violin, then choosing the violin teacher. Understanding why parents project this future for their children is of interest. The main question, however, is who the parents are.

SOCIAL ORIGIN OF EUROPEAN SOLOIST CLASS STUDENTS

In the European soloist class, more than eight of ten students have at least one parent who is a musician (Wagner 2006a). In the category of parent-musician, I include fathers or mothers who are professional musicians and parents who are amateurs. For more than half of the students in my sample, both parents were musicians. I separate parent-musicians into two groups. Parents belonging to the professional music world—instrumentalists, violin makers, sound engineers—constitute 64 percent of the sample. The second group, amateur musicians, account for 16 percent. These results confirm "professional heredity" in the music world, as noted in previous studies on the origin of musicians (Defoort-Lafourcade 1996; Dupuis 1993).

For parents who are orchestral musicians or music teachers, the role of soloist constitutes the road to excellence in their professional universe and gives their child the possibility of joining the musical elite. Parent-musicians decide their child will learn violin because they project a future in their own world, not just as a member but at a high position.

Musician-parents may feel that the "capital" of their professional relationships can be converted into ascendant mobility. As Pinçon and Pinçon-Charlot (1997a) suggest, this relational capital can be fruitful only if transmitted. The child of a musician who becomes a math teacher does not reap rewards from the professional (musical) relationships of his parents. This transmission of capital may be a motivating factor when parents push children to follow their professional path, as exemplified in the words of a violin soloist and teacher who is married to a piano teacher and himself the son of a violinist and music theory teacher. Of his daughter, seventeen, and son, ten, the father said: "My two children will be musicians. Because of our position . . . and all our professional ties, we are in a position to enter them into this milieu. The [children] manage very well with their instruments. It will be not very difficult for them to become professionals."

Numerous occupations offer important degrees of "professional heredity"; the literature includes studies of this effect in physicians (Thélot 1982), notaries, and auctioneers (Quemin 1997). The early socialization of children into a specific culture favors the child that is compatible with the parents' projections. Families of numerous generations practicing in the same field constitute dynasties, both in the familial and professional sense. Musical dynasties were well known in the past; an apogee was the Bach family, with three centuries of musicians. Twentieth-century musical dynasties include the Menuhins and the Sterns, violinists with children who became pianists or conductors.

PARENTAL INVOLVEMENT

Young children in such settings often start their violin education before the age of five. Many such children remember learning to read and write, but do not remember their first violin lesson. They have the impression of "always having played." The immersion is so deep that it is perceived by soloist-class students as "something natural." Pinchas Zukerman, the renowned violin soloist and son of a violinist, is a typical of these "inheritors": "I was born to play the fiddle. It's so natural for me" (Schwarz 1983: 608). For musician-parents, the motivation for introducing a child to violin education seems different from that of nonmusician parents. Hilary Levey-Friedman (2013) examined parental involvement in the high-level training of dancers, soccer players, chess players, and beauty competitors, presenting their attitudes as outgrowths of the competitive culture and the seeking of winning positions in American society. For professional parents who introduce their progeny into their own profession, the situation is different.

As Becker and Carper (1956) show in their study of professions, parental occupation indirectly influences the offspring's orientation. Parents working as technicians, for example, often expect that their child's best future lies in earning an engineering degree. Another degree at the same level, such as an MA in philosophy, would not satisfy them. Most parents of soloist students were never soloists themselves, yet for them, soloist education constitutes the path to excellence.

The students that I interviewed were "plunged into the family ambiance, which was centered around music," as one student put it. Music was a financial resource, and a leisurely activity and was practiced actively or passively by at least one family member. This relationship to music was described as "passionate," "very important," "vital." The majority of students I interviewed felt they were self-motivated, at least at first. "It is normal to practice an instrument," a typical student said. This general feeling seems to be understood within musician families, but exceptional students aged fifteen or older who do not come from a musical family made similar statements, probably because of the strong socialization received during their violin studies.

The adjective "normal" is frequently used by the students. They do not see the musical life as they lead it as worthy of discussion, moving quickly on to other questions. Perhaps this is not surprising, given how young they have been socialized into this role. But parents are eager to discuss the subject. They often insist that it is the child who desires to play, and that the family only encourages this desire: "I am a music-lover, and I sing in a choir. We have three children and we proposed that they choose an instrument to play. Both sons first played the piano, and afterward, they changed to the saxophone and drums. Our young daughter, who always listens to music in our house, loves the violin."

The importance of instrumental practice, the vitality of music as a vocation, and especially the veneration of famous artists, are all aspects of family culture that may play important roles in the child's turn toward becoming a musician. Subtler aspects later stimulate violin students in their involvement: hearing stories about successful musicians, admiring those who play in renowned concert halls, getting to know those who collaborate with well-known musicians, meeting famous artists. These factors are specific to the musician's world. One must be initiated into their significance in order to share them—among soloist students and soloists, it is difficult to find children of businesspeople, manual workers, or farmers.

One famous American soloist seems to be an exception: Elmar Oliveira, son of a Portuguese immigrant carpenter. But his father's fascination with Stradivarius, the famous violin maker, confirms my argument that a family culture steeped in the values of the musical world is a principal factor in the education of the soloist. Almost all soloist students who do not originate from a musical family—less than 10 percent of the sample—have parents in intellectual occupations who are passionate about music. They are music lovers and share with parent-musicians one strong ambition: their child will become a virtuoso. Family influence on the young violinist thus comes directly, through parental enforcement of training programs, and indirectly, through family culture and values.

A family's decision as to which instrument the child should study depends on a variety of factors. But in hindsight—after the child's education is completed—parents of violin soloists generally give two explanations for the choice: violinists rank high in the hierarchy of the musician's world, and they have relatively good employment possibilities because of the large repertoire for violinists within orchestras and chamber ensembles and as soloists. The large percentage of violin students who are children of pianists may indicate that nonviolinist parents perceive the violin as a better specialization. Parent violinists reported that they wanted their child to learn to play "their" instrument. It is a very convenient decision, because as experts they can assess the quality of the child's instrumental education. Parent-violinists hoped their child would benefit from the parent's experience to emerge with a more brilliant career. In almost all cases, parent-violinists who were interviewed had not achieved an international solo career. As we will see, an availability of parents, or at least one of them, is necessary in order to help the child in this very intensive training. A soloist with an international career spends the majority of his or her time out of the home; it is difficult for them to help their kids with their daily practice. In addition, successful soloists frequently say that their profession is "hard" (the life of travel, a high level of stress, and a certain instability). Children of famous violin virtuosos are frequently musicians: composers, conductors, pianists. Nevertheless, the orientation of daughters and sons of a first-rank virtuoso is rarely a simple "reproduction." Exceptions, such as David Oistrakh and his son Igor—both international virtuosos—are rare.

The peer environment of a young candidate beginning his or her musical education also plays a role in the choice of instrument, as this interview with an eighteen-year-old soloist student illustrates: "When I was very little, my parents sent me to music school to learn the piano. I had a friend who started violin lessons, and I wanted a violin, because on the street, when we walked through the town you could see that everyone was thinking, 'There goes a young violinist.'"

In his autobiography, Isaac Stern—one of the most famous violinists of the twentieth century—relates a friend's influence on his thoughts:

> I started piano lessons when I was six, shortly before my sister Eva was born. At that time, we were living on a street about three blocks from the northern side of Golden Gate Park. Across the street from us lived a family named Koblick, with whom my parents were friendly. They had a son named Nathan. When I was eight years old, Nathan was already playing the violin. I've often said that I didn't return home from a concert one day and plead for a violin. . . . My friend Nathan Koblick was playing the violin; therefore I wanted to play the violin. . . . I insisted on continuing with the violin, not because I thought I was musical but because Nathan Koblick was still playing. (Stern and Potok 2001: 10)

Parents seldom recognize that they desire the path of a "child prodigy." Yet when "little virtuoso" crazes sweep society, violin teachers observe an increase in students. Violinists Mischa Elman, Jascha Heifetz, Yehudi Menuhin, Sarah Chang, and even Matilda May (not a pure classical musician), as prodigy performers, stimulated many students, parents, and teachers. A lot of parents dreamed about such a career path for their child.

STARTING INSTRUMENTAL EDUCATION

Most parents decide which instrument their child will play; in general they seek to give the child at least nominal choice but often provide a nudge, such as by giving a violin as a Christmas or birthday present, or taking the child to a star violinist's concert.

Sometimes other, coercive mechanisms are employed. The daughter of an orchestra musician recalled: "We are four children born within one year of each other. When we were between the ages of five and eight years old, my father called us and said, 'Listen, you will learn this song. The one who learns first will play violin; the second the cello; the third the viola; and the last, the piano.'" Within this family, the gateway to musical education was constructed as a competition, with violin study as the grand prize.

As this example demonstrates, early in instrumental education there are various ways parents can inspire the child's interest and commitment. Parenting mechanisms may differ, but the age at which children start their education is generally homogeneous.[1]

The age of the child during his or her first lesson is easily ascertained; the question is frequently posed to violinists and it is contained in resumés and published biographies. In my study group, 69 percent of students started their violin education between the ages of four and six, 10 percent before the age of four, and 21 percent at the age of seven or eight.

I compared this sample with a group of famous twentieth-century soloists, and the results overlapped. I found one exception: a soloist of Polish origin who started at the age of eleven. This data suggests that for those who started their violin education after the age of eight, achieving an international soloist career is nearly impossible. The solo violin career is one of the few professions that starts when the person chosen for it is barely out of diapers.

Not only soloists get such a young start. Westby (1960), in his study of orchestra musicians, estimates the average age for the first violin lesson is about three or four. Dominique Villemin, in her book about parents who want their child to play an instrument (Villemin 1997), made a table with the optimal age to start on each instrument. Professors specializing in the Suzuki method work with children at the age of three, and sometimes younger. Most teachers state that the older a student is when he or she begins lessons, the lower the chance of attaining a high technical level. In interviews, it was not exceptional to hear that it is "useful to start at the age of three years old, in order to have an advantage over other students." In general, parents are advised to "put their child into violin" by the age of five or six.

Precocity is an important criterion for teachers, one of whom was observed telling parents that their child "doesn't use vibrato,[2] and he doesn't play in the high positions,[3] because he started at the age of eight. That's a little late to become a student in my class. Perhaps one day, when he gets up to speed."

But not all violin teachers find that starting before the age of seven makes sense and is fruitful. One teacher stated:

Why put them to work so early? The age advantage gets lost after a few years as the effects of talent and practice gain importance. . . . My friends—musicians but not violinists—insisted that I take on their five-year-old daughter. . . . She's nine years old today, and it is true that at the age of seven, when other kids were starting, she was already playing very well, but today there is not a big difference between her and the others.

Despite various opinions concerning the optimal age, however, teachers were unanimous that a child had no chance to become an elite violinist unless he or she began study by the age of nine. This particular knowledge, even if not shared by all participants, constitutes an aspect of what Robert Merton called socially expected durations, the phenomenon related to the timing of a given social activity, negotiated and transmitted in the practice of a given group. While the age of debut is important, unwritten rules circulate among participants (Merton 1984).

In contrast, parents interviewed for this study set a younger age barrier. They began their children's lessons—at home, in the case of violinists, or with a violin teacher—before the child reached the age of six.

When I conducted interviews with both parents at the same time, they frequently did not agree on the exact age of the first violin lesson. When interviewed separately, the responses varied more widely. The responses of parents differed from those of their child. One father, a pianist, suggested that certain parents pretended that their children's lessons had started later, in order to show "that in such a short time, he/she reached such a high level of violin skill." Others give an earlier starting age, to show that their child was able to play when almost nobody could play. Both types of fib are designed to support the exceptional brilliance of their child. However, I think mistaken responses are more frequently unintentional.

Imprecision among the interviewees may suggest that they wished to initiate their child at a very early age, but were sensitive to criticism. During a meeting of string-instrument teachers organized by the International Association for Music Teachers' French chapter, the participants—about fifty music teachers, almost all of them women—asked about methods in a child's musical education. Among the three presenters, a specialist in educating young children in violin was the center of attention. Almost all questions related to the teachers' own children, not their students. One woman asked, "Can I start working with the violin with my daughter who is eighteen months old?" The presenter was visibly flabbergasted. This age pressure on precocious violinists is seen in the example of the mother of a toddler nearly two years old. The woman, a pianist and Russian immigrant living in Italy, planned to move to Germany because her son needed an excellent violin teacher. For a child his age, the best one lived in Germany.

How Do Parents Choose Violin Teachers?

The choice of the teacher and the soloist's school (that is Russian school, French school, etc.) is of great importance for violin education. The child will develop within this violin class and not others, and will be socialized into this support net-work and not another. It is a strategic decision similar to the choice of university for young people on more conventional career paths. In almost all cases, the choice of instrument is made before the choice of teacher, though some parents choose a teacher before an instrument, or make the choices simultaneously.

In considering these choices, I divide parents into two categories. The first and most important category is the "parent-musician," composed from two subgroups: violinists and other musicians. Criteria for the choice of teacher are the most diverse among parent-violinists. The second category is the "nonmusician" parent. Among them we can also find two subcategories. The first is the "parent-novice," parents who do not have professional or personal relationships with musicians, and the second, "parent-insiders," who have experience as soloist parents though they are not musicians themselves. The latter group's immersion in the solo violinist world is similar to that of musicians who are not violinists: they know the terrain but lack technical playing knowledge.

Parent-Novice: Choosing the Institution Rather the Individual

Parent-novices recounted that, at the beginning of violin education, they did not have "professional projects" planned for their child. Two elements were frequently cited in the choice of the first teacher: the proximity of the violin lessons and avail-ability of parents and teacher to make the family schedule compatible with lessons.

The price of lessons could be an important variable. In countries with a devel-oped infrastructure of music schools or conservatories, parents prefer to enroll their child in a violin class rather than having private lessons. However, systems of music education can impose age minimums. Some French schools allow violin lessons only to children who are six or seven years of age. Other parents start with private lessons; when the child reaches school age, he or she integrates into the music school at which the teacher gives lessons.

For some parent-novices, the professional skill of the teacher is confirmed by the given institution. One mother, an artistic director of a publishing house, states: "I saw the list of the conservatory teachers, and I called one up. . . . This is how my son started his violin education at four and not at seven [the age limit at the conservatory]."

Parent-novices share a belief that a teacher working in a conservatory or music school will be "better" than a teacher giving only private lessons. Another crite-rion of choice is the quality of the relationship between the teacher and student. An exceptional situation occurs when parents do not have the option of choosing the teacher within the conservatory—here, parents speak about connections that occur "by chance."

Parent-novices do not discriminate between the choices of an athletic coach or violin teacher. None spoke about the technique of playing or interpretation of music; they gather information regarding the quality of teachers by word of mouth, and they ask people who seem to be experts in the discipline. Other categories of parents use the same method, with one distinct difference: the "expert" is not the same. For the parent-novice, a music teacher in a general school could be this expert. For the parent-insider, the only expert is a violinist or violin accompanist working in the soloist class.

The Parent-Insider: Following the Familiar Path

Parent-insiders usually take advice from more than one person before deciding which teacher should educate their child. They profit from their knowledge of a musical education, following the familiar path they went through with their first child. They usually follow the advice of the first child's teacher, whether the next child plays the same instrument or a different one.

The Parent-Musician: A Highly Strategic Decision

The majority of parent-musicians state that the choice of teacher is very important; some are thinking about it by the time their child is born. They want to give them a maximum amount of support to optimize their career path. It is a similar approach to choosing the perfect preschool that leads to the "right" middle school and the "right" high school, and eventually to a prestigious university (Chin 2000).

In the parents' remarks, one observes that all their knowledge is mobilized in the choice of violin teacher. They use the expression "placing into" (the hands of)— also used when apprentices are entrusted into the handicraft world. The choice of teacher seems more complex for parent-musicians than for parent-novices or parent-insiders. This complexity is related to their knowledge of the multitude of options and consequences.

We can identify two subcategories among parent-musicians: violinists and non-violinists. The first seem to favor quality of education and acquisition of good technical background over relationships within their professional world. The mother of a nine-year-old violinist, who is a pianist and whose father is a cellist, illustrates this position: "When dealing with the career of your child, you don't care about your friends [who are violin teachers]. After my daughter's first year of education, I stopped lessons with my friend, because the bow technique was not good at all." A father who is a guitarist provides another example: "I put my daughter into the hands of Dana. She has a good position and plays very well."

Involvement in the complex networks and relationships of the musical world can make the choice of a teacher difficult. Among some "parent-violinists," the choice of teacher can be complicated by relationships with people in this milieu.

Some parent-musicians described a feeling of "having no choice." "I couldn't do anything else other than to put him [his son] in Claude's hands. I play with [Claude] in the same quartet." Family relationships can determine the decision: "The choice? It was obviously going to be his uncle. . . . In fact . . . he is one of the best teachers in the area."

This decision can be strategic: the child is "placed" in the teacher's class, and the parents access new networks and reinforce existing ones. These parents try to compensate for the teacher's weaknesses, working with the child or with another teacher. But the latter teacher stays in the shadow of the principal teacher, as this story illustrates:

> We put our daughter into Michel's hands because he is Boris's assistant. So, when she gets older, she'll go directly to Boris's class. . . . His students play everywhere, and many important people gravitate toward his class.
>
> The important people?
>
> These are the people who organize the concerts, the violin makers, the media, and others. As for technique, we will teach that to our daughter ourselves.

This argument is characteristic of parents convinced that they have excellent violin technique that can be transmitted to their children, and that it is vital for the children to enter into particular networks of relationships. By doing this, the parents confirm their own membership in the networks.

A small group of parent-violinists decide to teach their children on their own. This happens most often with a child younger than the age of eight. Such cases are difficult to study, as the parents find this topic not worth discussing. Convenience in organizing this education may be a major factor; responses suggest that, above all, teaching one's own child is done in the name of "good quality." Most parent-violinists work with their child only in the initial stage, "just to see how the child manages with the violin." When lessons become "serious," they search for a "good teacher." Children of parent-violinists are most likely to change their teacher at a young age. Some parent-violinists, dissatisfied with the work of their colleagues, end up teaching their child themselves.

Auditioning and Joining a Soloist Class

The group active around the teacher and students of a soloist class include parents, piano accompanists, and in some instances teaching assistants. The teacher is the key person and his or her teaching the main activity. The teacher's name is an important reference for those in the music world, who use it to situate a given student. "Who is your teacher?" is a frequently asked question. Later I will discuss the consequences of belonging to one or another class. Here, I will focus on what distinguishes a soloist violin class from a normal violin class.[4]

The first peculiarity of a soloist's life is the main activity: learning to play the violin. The second is that in a soloist class, children and their parents already have a career in mind. In a regular violin class, children learn to play, but few consider it a means to a professional career. In the soloist class, becoming a soloist is the main aim of life. Regular education becomes a secondary investment in terms of time, energy, and involvement.

The teacher holds a central position during the first two stages of the soloist's education. Normally, the career of virtuoso professors has three stages (as a criterion for differentiation of each stage, I am using the principal tasks of their activity). The main occupation of the violin teacher in the first phase is based on teaching pupils.

The second stage consists of having been recognized as a good professional in the world of violin teachers and, by consequence, changing the amount of time spent on their principal activity—teaching regular students. The second stage involves teaching violinists at a high level and acquiring the status of a member of competition juries and of a professor at master classes. It is also the position that allows them to select the future members of this elite. The third stage of a successful route into the milieu of soloists evolves to almost total withdrawal from the initial day-to-day activities (teaching a regular class of students), so as to assume the role of star-professor, with teaching of several students under the organization of master classes. These star-teachers take strategic positions: they take part in, organize, or preside over competitions and festivals.

From the start, the teacher attempts to win the student's commitment to his or her transformation into a soloist. Teachers bring up the example of "professional idols" to motivate their pupils. Robert Faulkner described this phenomenon after analyzing the effects of professional-idol projections in an orchestral musician's life: "Heifetz, Stern, Menuhin, Piatigorski, and other great artists . . . become the standards by which personal success in music is evaluated" (Faulkner 1971: 54).

There are a variety of roles played by people contributing to the functioning of the soloist class. Parents are obligatory assistants of the teacher and concert agents for their child. Other professionals who contribute include accompanists, sound engineers, concert organizers, violin makers, and conductors. My observations suggest that the absence of these professionals and patrons, music lovers, and amateur organizers indicate that a violin class lacks elite character. When children satisfy their first teacher and parents, the parents consider placing their child in a soloist class. A strong conviction runs through the violin soloist's world that children who join soloist classes earliest have the best chance of professional success. This is confirmed by statistics: almost 90 percent of twentieth-century violinists educated in the United States prior to 1930 were students of four famous soloist teachers: Persinger, Galamian, DeLay, and Gingold.[5]

If a child comes to the elite teacher too late, he or she will find a less receptive audience. "Gulia Bustabo[6] . . . came to Persinger when she was eleven or twelve, already with a reputation as a prodigy. Persinger listened to her and said, 'Very good,' but then shook his head sadly and muttered, 'but too old'" (Schwarz 1983: 543).

To be considered for the chosen teacher's class, parents make audition appointments, the crucial selection criterion among soloist class candidates. Information about these classes is not easily obtained; they may function inside conservatories or music schools or within the system of private lessons. A given violin class may be a soloist class, or an "ordinary" one (the vast majority of violin classes in conservatories and music schools).[7]

Differences between ordinary and soloist classes are informal. In ordinary classes, children learn for pleasure with an eventual aim of amateur playing; in soloist classes, the goal is to educate professional musicians and endow them with the highest level of skill. A soloist class is a group of students, their parents, and other music professionals who gravitate around a violin teacher at the center. Education into the soloist class requires several years of socialization, which is an immersion in the professional world. Proximity to specialists of the music world and the specific relationship with the teacher play decisive roles in the soloist's education.

For the children of parent-novices, entrance into a soloist class most frequently takes place during or after a competition, when one or more jury members congratulate the parents and offer to take care of their child, accepting him or her into the soloist class.

As the parents of young Wladek recall, their son's first teacher prepared him for a competition, after which Wladek received an invitation to join a soloist class. Both parents are physicians; the first teacher convinced them that Wladek had talent that they were obliged to support. The first teacher eventually urged Wladek's parents to pay for supplementary lessons and intensive preparation for the audition, where Wladek earned high marks from the jury and was chosen as a soloist student. The parents' decision was difficult: they lived two hours by train from the city where the soloist class took place. From the age of nine, Wladek lived in a dormitory with other children and saw his parents once a week.

Parents may find their lives in the hands of teachers, whose ability to recognize talent is beyond their own. "It was the first teacher of my daughter who said we needed to show Vera to Mme Lwowa. She told us that our daughter had amazing abilities [at violin]. . . . Despite the fact that Vera lacked solfege lessons,[8] Mme Lwowa accepted her immediately. . . . Our first teacher probably thought this well-known teacher would be better for our daughter than she could be."

After a few months spent with the first teacher—and sometimes a few years—the parents contact a soloist teacher and ask him or her to audition their child. Often the parent-violinists select the teacher after attending concerts of his or her current and past students, checking these students for "good playing posture," and virtuosity. (Musical interpretation of the pieces is typically the last point of interest.) Most parents make contact by phone, mentioning an intermediary: a common relative, or the people who recommended their child.[9]

The child attends the audition accompanied by one parent, rarely both. Two or more pieces are prepared and played in most cases. After the first performance, the teacher provides feedback to see how quickly the child can alter his or her playing. After this test—free of charge in almost all cases that I observed—the teacher provides his or her expertise about the performance and the young violinist's potential. In more than thirty cases I observed, the child was present and listened in on the discussion between the parent(s) and the teacher.

The audition can have two types of outcomes. Infrequently, the teacher's decision is positive, and what follows is a discussion of the soloist class and future collaborations between the teacher and parents. If the teacher finds that the candidate is not ready, the teacher may advise that the child work with his or her assistant or collaborator to further prepare the young violinist for entrance into the class.

I saw another situation many times with violin masters. The teacher, bored and listless, listened with anger and impatience to a candidate, then gave his judgment to the parents about the young student's unreadiness. In the interviews I conducted, teachers share the feeling of "wasting their time" with inferior talents.

This form of selection applies to students of a soloist class until the age of twelve or thirteen. The oldest students need to participate in the master class—usually very expensive—to offer the teacher and students time to see if future collaboration is possible.

Becoming a "Talented Child"

The label "talented" is crucial for soloist students because, much like the deviant categories analyzed by Howard Becker (1963), a principal condition of appurtenance to the soloist-student category is labeling. The difference between both types of labeling is that the Beckerian "deviant" is a negative label, while "talented child" is a positive one. This process is similar to the phenomenon analyzed by Pierre Bourdieu in his work on artistic consecration in literary fields (Bourdieu 1995). The difference is that in the virtuoso world we do not have the original products of creation—the musicians perform pieces composed by others.

The students become soloist students because someone stated that they had "talent." It is important who attributes this label to a young violinist. Most students in a soloist class have been labeled "very talented" since the start of their musical education. Equivalent valuations are "particularly gifted" or "a child prodigy"—though the latter is less often used by musicians.

The phrase "he/she is a very talented violinist" is introduced by the violin teacher, or by a violinist to whom the child was "shown." (The expression "to be shown" is frequently used by parent-musicians, who choose to audition their child before violinists that they view as capable of discerning the child's potential evolution.) This label is then enforced through the child's subsequent education. It can be used, for example, by the director of a music school, other teachers, conductors, and adult violin soloists.

Evaluating the quality of performance and performer is complex. It is useful to remember that this evaluation is built on various informal criteria based on a subjective judgment of performance and on comparing performances of other soloist students. It is not a normative comparison, but a relative one. For example, for certain teachers a child could be "very gifted" because the teacher predicts this child will play better than other children. Other teachers may disagree; they may work with another child who plays "better."[10]

The power of this label is proportionate to the position of the expert who expresses it. When an unknown violin teacher expresses admiration for a student, it obviously doesn't hold the same water as an attestation from Yehudi Menuhin.

Once the child enters the "talented" category, he or she benefits from special treatment. Violin lessons become more frequent and intensive, time spent on daily instrumental work lengthens, and the number of public performances grows. Parents make "sacrifices," focusing family life on the soloist's education. General schooling is put in second place; often the child stops attending traditional school altogether.

The parents accompany the child to violin lessons, concerts, and competitions, activities that optimize the conditions of education and make it possible for the child to "develop his or her talent." The child's activities become the same as other "talented children," and through this he or she gradually integrates into the world of soloist students, learning behaviors that may conform to the soloist's role.

Vasia was born into a family of two violinists and was regarded by his parents from early in life as a "very gifted" child. His parents gave him his first violin lessons at the age of six; they showed Vasia to a famous children's teaching specialist in Moscow. According to them, the specialist stated that he was "the most talented she had ever seen, even more than her best student," who is one of the most recognized violinists in the world.

Vasia's family left Russia, and the parents decided to take up Vasia's violin education themselves. Numerous musicians found Vasia very gifted, promising to support his career, but no concrete actions followed. Vasia was in contact with prominent people, the elite of the musician world: violinists, conductors, agents. They invited him to come back after finishing his studies and winning competitions.

When Vasia was twelve years old, during his performance on a popular television program, the parents presented him to a violinist, one of the important people in the music world. This old virtuoso was on the program to encourage children to play classical music and, specifically, the violin. (Vasia's mother played in the orchestra that was regularly hired for the broadcast.) In front of the camera, on a program aimed at a large public, the old virtuoso declared that Vasia "has a lot of talent." The comment was then transported into the professional soloist world and accompanied Vasia's career until his entrance into the adult violinist market. Vasia's biographical notes contained it, and it was highlighted on his first CD (produced six years later). The declaration helped Vasia borrow a prestigious violin; concert-hall performances were organized by amateur agents impressed by this one sentence.[11]

Vasia said that the sentence helped him through moments of doubt and became a strong element of motivation. It remained useful when, three years after the program, Vasia failed in a competition presided over by the old virtuoso. Vasia competed against sixty other soloist-class students considered, like him, to be "very talented." His failure was kept hidden, and the famous sentence was always used, waiting for future successes.

Vasia's story illustrates the mechanism of labeling in the case of the soloist student. Teachers announce to parents and young violinists that their students have "rare talent." This "talent" is presented by teachers as if it were a supernatural attribute that could be lost if the parents do not "invest" in a soloist education. In soloist classes, all students have this label: it is the sine qua non of belonging to this category. Parental reaction to this sentence, in all observed situations, was similar. They never doubted the "exceptional" character of their child's talent. For nonmusician parents to adopt without reservations the opinion of teachers or other music experts is not surprising. It is surprising, however, that parent-musicians always believe their child possesses "extraordinary talent."

Numerous factors may help explain this phenomenon. Soloist classes bring together students from the age of six to twenty-four.[12] Frequently the newcomer is the youngest, making it easier for his or her parents to believe their child is "better" than the others, who are older. Parents are apt to believe their child is exceptional, and the moment somebody pinpoints their child's talent, they accept this comment. Also, most parent musicians were not soloists, and thus lack the background elements of comparison to judge just how exceptional their child is.

One day the moment of disappointment arrives, and the parents of soloist students realize that "talented children" are quite numerous. An interview illustrates one father's point of view: "You know, there are a lot of prodigy children. But ones like my daughter are rare—she was very young and played as a soloist with an orchestra and the public is crazy about her. And even for her, it is very difficult to reach a high position. Even for such a huge talent!"

According to my observations, parents in all categories tend to believe that their child's talent will enable them to prevail in the struggle that is the consequence of a saturated market. This conviction is shared by others in the direct environment of young soloists. The "aura" of a "talented child" mobilized the parents to pursue the path indicated by the teacher in the first stage of education. At that moment, and beyond, these expressions meant that their child had the potential to become a soloist.

CHAPTER 3

Triad Collaboration—
Teacher, Parents, and Child

THE FIRST STAGE OF SOLOIST EDUCATION

"I do not need prodigy pupils, only gifted mothers."

—Violin teacher

This phrase, above, is well known within the world of violinists, illustrating as it does the importance of the parent in creating a path of communication between teacher and child. The central activity of this career stage is the violin lesson with the master, whose goal is to quickly accelerate the child's virtuosity. The lesson is where knowledge and expectations are transmitted from teacher to student; parents assist the child by taking notes and sometimes recording the lesson to work with the child at home.

In my work I observed a triad relationship that replaced the traditional bilateral relationship between parents and children that constitutes family education in our culture. Instead of having one parental authority, the soloist child has two: parent and teacher. The soloist teacher establishes the life-project for the child, and parents adhere to his or her decisions and advice. The teacher's first objective is to establish a good collaboration with parents, because parents translate the teacher's expectations to the child. A thirty-one-year-old soloist describes the role of her mother, a pianist: "She explained everything to me because my teacher didn't have the time and patience to explain it in 'little girl's words.' It was she who said that my playing was very good; my teacher simply said 'okay' . . . For him, the program I played was . . . the best proof that my violin skills had progressed. . . . I did not understand that!"

If communication between the three parties is effective, codes of behavior concerning each individual's role are known and respected. Lessons are set according to convention concerning soloist lessons, in the sense of Becker's conventions, as presented in *Art Worlds* (Becker 1983), including rules of collaboration. The child knows to listen to the teacher's advice, when to play, when to repeat, and when to stop.

The following example is based on recorded and written observation of a lesson with a nine-year-old girl, Margot. The lesson took place in the teacher's Paris flat one month before an international competition. Margot was fluent in the specific codes and language necessary to accomplish instrumental practice worthy of an adult violinist, although the teacher's reactions could suggest she was not prepared for the lesson.

The teacher, Vera, in her early thirties, opens the door, and immediately asks with a strong Russian accent: "How has Margot practiced since her last lesson?"

"Well," the girl responds.

She takes her violin from the case, remarking that she has forgotten her rosin.[1] The teacher opens her own violin case, takes her rosin, and rubs it on Margot's bow. The girl's mother sits and prepares her notebook. The teacher speaks: "Okay, go, the open strings!"[2]

Margot plays, and the teacher speaks: "In the middle." Vera stands, approaches, touches her right hand to help Margot drive her bow, speaking in a monotonous voice: "Perpendicularly . . . with the entire sound . . . caress the string." The teacher raises the violin with a gentle movement. "All the sounds of bow . . . touch the violin string . . ." She raises her voice: "Without accents!" The teacher moves Margot's head position on the violin. This sequence takes seven minutes, with Margot playing continuously.

"Now the scale.[3] What scale did you play?" "A-major," the student replies. "So, go up four times as we did together. When going down, slide on the first finger." The child seems to have difficulties following these instructions, and slides on the second finger.

The teacher takes Margot's bow, annoyance in her voice: "When you move up it is always the second finger and when you go down it is the first finger! One more time, go down with the first finger," Vera repeats, nearly screaming, pointing a finger next to Margot's head. "You need to see the first finger; it needs to slide ten times! Slower! Why didn't you play here?" exclaims Vera, pointing to part of the violin. "Play with your bow correctly! Stop! The same thing with the supplemental notes again!"

Margot plays without pausing. Vera takes her own violin to show how to play the scale.

Both play together and Vera stops. She places her violin on the table, touches Margot's elbow to position it under the violin, picks up her violin, and begins playing again with her student.

When the scale is finished, Margot seems happy to play another piece and prepares her scores. Vera glares at her. "The same thing," she insists. The student replays the scale; her teacher repeats the command. After the fourth time, Vera states: "The first time was correct. Your thumb was never up! Now we can take out the additional note! The bow in one whole piece, four legato, the same things! There! You continue on the E-string."

Vera takes a metronome and starts it, the dining room filling with steady tock-tocks. "The articulation, the pretty sound, the regular beat. . . . If you have two fingers on that, it means that you have a jump of a third. We play the supplemental note. Now we play, but with exactly the same bowing. Stay focused!"

This sequence lasts thirty minutes. Margot has been playing for almost forty minutes, her arms in a high position. Vera restarts instantly: "The bow exercise in first position!"

Two minutes later, Vera interrupts, "You completely forgot. In order to obtain détaché[4] it is not necessary to do that [she demonstrates with a gesture]. There's nothing to do here, just look at your bow!" Vera shows how to do it correctly. She makes a movement with Margot's arm; one string is touched badly, the bow skids off its mark.

"Control your bow," Vera exclaims. "No, no, no! This is done with the hand!" She gestures, then looks at how Margot makes the same gesture. "Quicker! Quicker!" After two minutes, Vera states: "So, the bow technique was very good."

The teacher looks in Margot's bag and finds the piece she will play in the competition. After the Margot finishes the first part, the teacher says, "It was very, very, very beautiful . . . just some nuances, so I will play the phrase and you will repeat it. There [the teacher points in the score] the first mordent[5] is tararara . . ." She sings; Margot repeats by playing. Vera takes her violin to show how the section needs to be played, "My turn," and the teacher plays. "Your turn," and Margot repeats. "My turn. Your turn. And more discretely, with a very light bow on C . . . a high C[6] . . . the bow . . . you see? So if you play a little lightly and caress the accents a bit more . . . there [Vera points to the score]. It was not bad. It was okay, but the sixteenths, the little notes, use less bow. Yes, it's perfect!" Vera seems to be very glad.

At the moment Vera stops, Margot repeats the section being worked on. "It is not bad," Vera says, "but you need to hide the G, the becare[7] is very close. Give more bow on the high D. Bow! Listen to the difference between this phrase and this one." Vera plays twice, differently. Margot plays and seems to have difficulties applying the corrections. "And no slower. . . . This is not forte![8] . . . It is very deep. . . . We need to spare the bow. Here, we will already have rallentando."[9] Vera indicates it in the score, but Margot does not stop playing.

Vera picks up other pages of scores and gives the command: "The second part now!"

And Margot plays. "You stop this note. You can't make the trill[10] shorter. It is good, but don't panic on the trill. You need to articulate on the mordant. . . . This is crescendo.[11] And this is forte." The teacher points to the score. "You want to stop the lesson?" Vera seems to be very angry. With sadness in her voice, Margot responds, "No."

"So, play correctly." Vera takes the metronome. "Play with it on. These are the sixteenths. This is slower . . . slower. . . . This is slower! Pay attention. See? I beg you, the notes."

"It is hard to hold the bow," Margot says.

"No, you need to take the bow like before. Show me! And you need to practice like that all day: two times with the metronome, then seventy-two [beats per minute], and then eighty. OK, that's enough for today. You can put your violin into its case." Vera turns to Margot's mother: "She needs to practice very seriously, each day like always, for a minimum of two-and-a-half hours."

I present this scene at length to provide a sense of this central activity in the soloist student's life. We observe that the level of the teacher's technical expectations was high in relationship to the age of the student. At the age of nine, Margot needed the following skills: the capacity to carry out the details of a performance, the knowledge of specific vocabulary, a high level of concentration to accomplish complex, simultaneously assigned tasks, and the endurance for long sessions of instrumental practice. This last skill requires a level of physical fitness enabling the student to stand with both hands in a high position for over an hour.

Students must submit to the authority of their teacher, which is evident during the lesson excerpt above. This relationship explains why Margot's mother did not say a word during the lesson. The lesson setting is characterized by the unequal status of the people in it.[12]

It is a triad relationship between the teacher, student, and parents, whose success depends on a fruitful collaboration between the adult parties. Teachers mobilize parents to play the role of their assistants, but during the lesson, parents rarely intervene. Their role is played outside the physical space where the lesson takes place.

PARENTS AS ASSISTANTS

Between two lessons, parents interpret the teacher's remarks and orders to the child, and educate the child to conform to the teacher's expectations (parent-musicians know these expectations very well). Before the first class, a mother speaks to her seven-year-old daughter in the music school corridor: "You must be focused and you must react very quickly. . . . Please, be good, but like at home—full of energy!" This mother, a pianist who was a soloist student, is convinced that the teacher will perceive her daughter as someone with talent, "potentially able to become a soloist" (an expression used by teachers of soloist classes).

Some teachers and musician's parents consider whether the child has an "artistic personality"—here taken to mean an extroverted child who works quickly and is interested in various subjects: "good in mathematics and chess." Personality plays an important role in the selection process, as indicated by this quote about a soloist class at the Juilliard School in New York City: "DeLay hears about 250 auditions for Juilliard each year and has described that meeting as being akin to a first conversation, since it reveals not only performance ability, but also the crucial aspects of intelligence, humor, and personality" (Lourie-Sand 2000: 95–96).

Parents pay attention to other features specific for a soloist performer: good physical form and excellent health. The violinist-father tells his nine-year-old boy to "forget" his headache: "You know, when you play a concert, the public must be happy listening to your music, and your professor will not work with a child who is in bad health!" During his lesson, the teacher remarked that the boy was ill: "You know, a soloist must be strong. Go on! Forget everything and play!"

As we have seen in the lesson above, as a rule the soloist student does not speak, with parents providing the teacher with necessary information about the student.

The child's role is to play, react to corrections and orders, and respond to questions about performance. In my observations, parents excused their child's weak performance when the child had not practiced, explaining that the child had been ill or busy. These explanations are infrequent, because a soloist cannot be ill or busy. As one teacher said to an eight-year-old girl: "At 3 a.m. if you need to play, you must play the best you can. You know, seven-year-old Vengerov practiced at 1 a.m. because his parents couldn't work with him earlier—they were orchestral players!"[13]

The child often listens to stories about other child-violinists who perform well, in the opinion of their teachers, under difficult conditions. Famous violinists are used as examples, including success stories of the teacher's former students. Parents adopt this education model: "At your age, Menuhin played Mendelssohn's Concerto!"

Parents are indispensable intermediaries in the soloist's education, motivating both the student and the teacher to maintain fruitful collaboration. The parent makes enormous sacrifices to enable the child's musical training; the teacher also seeks to influence the child's nonmusical education, as this teacher's comment to a mother illustrates: "I have taken care of your son for more than three years . . . but . . . he needs to visit museums, to read literature, you know, not only play the violin." This teacher provides the child with free lessons and use of his $15,000 violin.

This closeness teaches children that private relationships are mixed with professional ones; the emotionality of the relationship surpasses that of most professional teaching. An important supplement to parental authority is integrated into the children's lives. In turn, the child adapts his or her behavior to this division of roles. Lessons with the master are the most important element of the violin student's life, at least on a par with family relations. Student and parents closely attend to the teacher's reactions. If a lesson "is good," the teacher is glad, and so is the family. If the lesson sours and the teacher is grumpy, the family becomes frustrated.

Let's Play . . . Ambition

At the beginning of a young soloist's career, he or she encounters the parent's ambition. Parent-musicians hope their child will become a soloist. This parental ambition interacts with the teacher's ambition, which is to demonstrate excellence through his or her musical offspring. Among violin soloists, it is said that masters play through their students. Ambition increases the master's engagement in furthering a promising child's career. Thus engaged, the teacher calls in favors through his or her network: an accompanist focuses on working with the student; a sound engineer prepares a free recording; an organizer puts the student on important concert bills.

The teacher, a powerful person,[14] does not give the same level of attention or favors to all students. Only those deemed to have soloist potential benefit from special treatment. This constitutes the first condition of a successful soloist education: the student must have a privileged position with the teacher that merits special educational treatment.

When parents and teacher share an ambition for the student, they awaken a similar ambition in the student. The children I have observed like to play on stage and enjoy their adult public's applause. Yet while performance is a source of satisfaction, hours of daily instrumental practice can be tedious. Practice at home between lessons determines a musician's progress. Parents and teacher may share a desire for the child to practice intensively, but the young virtuoso is less enthusiastic.

Thus, an important goal of parents, teacher, and student is to find pleasure in daily instrumental practice as well as in performance. This is crucial if the young musician is to be motivated to the necessary work. Gratification comes when he or she is able to play Paganini's Caprice No. 5 before the age of ten, for example.

Though parent-musicians and teachers share the same ambition, they may clash. I have observed conflicts between parent-musicians and teachers over issues such as program choice, concert preparation, competitions, and even technical aspects of violin practice. I have observed children who never took more than one month of lessons from the same teacher, because the parents felt no one was good enough. Young soloists taught by their parents may face rejection in the soloist world. Lack of collaboration within this triad relationship constitutes a huge obstacle, and can lead to the end of a promising path toward a solo career.

Parental Investment

Ruggiero Ricci, the American violinist, said, "When you find a prodigy, you find an ambitious parent in the background" (in Schwarz 1983: 534).[15]

In addition to monitoring and coaching the child's day-to-day studies, the parent of a prospective soloist has many other tasks, such as buying, borrowing, or photocopying scores, copying fingering,[16] and acquiring CDs of violin pieces. Parent-musicians, unsurprisingly, are the most effective at completing these tasks. A soloist-student's mother, a violinist and graduate of a famous Soviet school of music, explained: "In Moscow, in the music schools, the best of them [teachers] take only children from musician families, in order to have better results. . . . The nonmusicians don't understand the role of the teacher. . . . It is necessary to make these sacrifices: you have to lose money, you have to go with your child for long-distance trips, and if you don't do that, [the child] loses."

Except in a few states where music education is free—such as the Soviet Union before perestroika[17]—parents pay almost all the costs of a soloist education.[18] Expenditures include lessons (music school and/or private tuition), the student's individual work (general schooling), and specific events (concerts, competitions, master classes). Parent-novices, even if they are wealthy, are less inclined than parent-musicians to pay travel and lesson costs. Some parents invest all their savings in soloist education and/or a prestigious violin. Almost all young virtuosos and those known as "prodigies" in their youth mentioned "sacrifices" their parents underwent for their careers. Vadim Repin reported in an interview how he obtained his bow: "I have a beautiful Kittel, which I got at the age of thirteen. My mother invested all our capital in order to buy me this bow."[19]

Several parent-novices told me they had declined to enroll their child with a particular master because excessive fees were requested. Parent-musicians never made such comments. As they are socialized into the musical milieu, parent-novices acquire perspective and gradually conform to the actions of parent-musicians.

Family members may help finance the soloist's education, but even parent-musicians never anticipate the full expenses. They do not have a "financial plan" for the future, and rely on support from various institutions or private sponsors. Parents I have observed arranged their lives step by step.[20]

In interviews, parents avoided evaluating education costs, stating that they "have no choice," and "aren't entitled to refuse" financing their child's soloist education. They are entirely committed to that specific education. "When the chance of having a very gifted child is present, you need to do everything possible to make sure that talent isn't frittered away," said a scientific researcher, the mother of a soloist.

In exceptional cases, when a child was considered very gifted by the teacher and his or her parents but could not pay, the teacher gave free lessons. One of these teachers, Misha, said to me: "You know, my teacher told me there are two categories of students: those who need to pay and those who have talent."[21] Misha calculated that his less-gifted students subsidized the talented ones. Another teacher had a contract specifying that lessons were to be without fee, but demanding a significant part of the student's income from competition prizes or future concerts.

In order to better understand the situation of parental choices regarding specific educational investments we should keep in mind that the European system of education offers access to the best schooling without paying, and that includes higher education (this system is maintained mainly in EU but in the past it was the rule in Eastern Europe—and still remains in some countries). In addition to this, health insurance is also covered in several countries by the system of social security, which is working well and is efficient. This is why most families are not obliged to cover the general education or health insurance. In such a friendly social support system, savings are devoted to musical education. (Obviously, among virtuoso students it is difficult to find the children of the unemployed and those on minimum wage; the nature of the classical music practice and the parent's focus on young children's education eliminates students from families of limited means.)

Parental investment is an important element of selection, and students who drop out are commonly obliged to do so because their parents are not able to invest enough in virtuoso education. To some extent all parent-novices have difficulty paying the requested amount of money and adapting their family life according to the teacher's expectations. This is not a simple issue of money but also of nonmaterial values. Not all parents who pay large amounts of money are in an excellent financial situation. Even if they belong to the upper middle class, those who will pursue their children's training will do it because they believe their children's education as essential. This is not only about general culture that includes instrumental practice and classical music culture (typical for Western middle-class parents). This is about huge investment in the extreme development of a specific "talent" of their children. Parents mobilize all kind of resources, focusing on their progeny's future career. A huge majority of those who persist are the children of parent-musicians.

It is relatively easy to analyze parental financial involvement; parental investment of time, however, is more difficult to analyze. Parents typically use one of two
systems to enable the training of a child aspiring to soloist.

At first, young soloists (the same is true of children who are dancers, actors,
figure skaters, or other athletes) attend special schools for students who require
reduced time for general education.[22] They spend half the day in school and half on
instrumental practice. Twice a week or more, they go to violin lessons and sometimes to other music courses. Some parents, to save transportation time, change
residences to be closer to the teacher's apartment or school.

In the second type of organization, children are essentially home-schooled
through a correspondence program. This option is favored by soloist families. These
young soloists spend most of their time at home practicing or learning general
subjects. Some children remain enrolled in school but are absent much of the time.
An eleven-year-old student, living in a Paris suburb and taking lessons through
correspondence school, has two daily routines during the week. Most of the week
(Monday, Tuesday, Thursday, Friday), he is supervised at home:

> 8:30–9:30, French; 9:40–10:40, violin practice (scales, open strings, studies);[23]
> 10:40–11:10, break; 11:10–12:10, mathematics; 12:10–1:30, lunch; 1:30–2:30,
> violin practice (pieces); 2:30–2:45, break; 2:45–3:30, history (or geography
> or natural science); 3:30–4:00, snack break; 4:00–5:00, violin (pieces, sight-
> reading);[24] 5:30, dance lessons (or theory of music or choir); 7:30–9:00, dinner
> and free time.

Break times are laid out by the student. Free time is devoted to a short walk, book
reading, dancing, and educational computer games. On Wednesday and Saturday,
the student goes to the city with a parent to take violin lessons, which last one-and-
a-half to two hours. Travel time is about four hours. The student plays one hour
before the lesson and an hour upon returning home. On the days of violin lessons,
the student is free from school obligations. Sunday is a free day, with "only" three
hours of violin practice.

Parents of children enrolled in correspondence school devote much more time
to their child than those of children in regular school. Few occupations are compatible with the typical schedule of soloist parents. Madame Dupond provided
accommodation and a small salary to a twenty-year-old violin soloist student in
return for the student's supervision of her twelve-year-old daughter's instrumental
work. It is very exceptional to find a soloist student attending a general school. I
met only one such student, the son of a Japanese pianist living in Paris. He worked
on his violin each morning before school, beginning at six in the morning.[25]

Interviews with parent-musicians indicate that their knowledge of the social rules
of the musicians' world is a most useful contribution to their child's soloist education.[26] But even those ready to invest significant resources in the preparation of their
children's careers have difficulty spending each day supervising the child's instrumental practice. Some take extraordinary measures to supervise their child's education,
as with Maxim Vengerov's parents. According to a biographical TV broadcast, when

Vengerov was only seven years old, his parents would return home after nocturnal concerts and work with him until 2 a.m.[27]

But most parent-musicians lack this kind of commitment or time. A forty-one-year-old violinist and soloist, married to a violinist concertmaster of a national orchestra, told me that the couple's lack of time was the decisive factor in abandoning the instrumental education of their first child (of four): "My daughter played the violin. . . . She was very talented, but we both were busy with our activities: concert tours, different projects, and our other children. . . . It's a pity, but we aren't available to push her and supervise more."

INSTRUMENTAL PRACTICE

The famous violinist George Enesco once said, "Poor devils! They are just like convicts (condemned to hard labor), martyrs . . . sometimes saints" (quoted in Schwarz 1983: 360*).*[28]

Verbal terms for instrumental practice vary. French violinists use the words *travailler* for working, *jouer* for playing, and, sometimes, *s'exercer* for exercising. Polish violinists use *ćwiczyć* for training and the Russian *zanimatsia* for making themselves busy. Instrumental practice signifies the day-to-day maintenance and improvement of technique, improving current repertoire, and learning new pieces. Practice is indispensable for the violinist at a high level, as it is with a high-level athlete: even virtuosos at the peak of their careers are constrained to practice. For the student soloist, daily instrumental practice is undertaken without the teacher, but parents are generally present, at least early on.

Teachers advocate minimum practice periods of an hour to an hour and a half for three- to five-year-old students; two to three hours for six year olds, four or more hours daily by the age of eight. The famous twentieth-century teacher Stolyarsky Piotr Solomonovitch "demanded that his student take the violin out of its case immediately after breakfast and put it away just before going to sleep at night. All other activities, including general education, were expected to be cut to a minimum" (Schwarz 1983: 458).

Teachers in the Russian tradition follow this model. They use a quote attributed to famous pianist Arthur Rubinstein: "When I stop practicing for one day, nobody notices, the second day I hear the difference, and the third, my public hears it too." During an early lesson with a new soloist student, teachers familiar with the Russian tradition often relate the following anecdote,[29] which I first heard while observing an eight-year-old student taught by a renowned teacher from the Moscow Gnesina School:

> You know who Niccolò Paganini was? The most important virtuoso of the nine-teenth century. You know why he was so famous, so great, and the best violinist of his time? People say that he offered his soul to the devil in exchange for such magical skill that [his instrument] was a magic wand! Niccolò, at your age, had

already worked very hard. From the beginning of each day, his father confined his little son to a small empty room and ordered him to play violin. After one hour of work, Niccolò earned the right to breakfast. Then again, he worked until lunchtime. When the father had estimated that Niccolò played badly, he wouldn't let him eat anything. In that manner the boy worked all day. This is the big secret of his excellent technique. Nothing came by itself—it was necessary to work at it. So you, after returning home today, need to practice for one hour. And then, until the next lesson, for three hours each day.

Some teachers speak directly to their students; others point out the necessity of work with the parents. Said one teacher during the formal interview, "I know all these stories told by parents about 'young prodigies,' about their child who never works hard and who does everything immediately. These are pure lies. They make up the story in order to show that their child is very gifted. . . . It is necessary to practice a lot to play very well, and there is no other option!"

Teachers argue that the parents do not have the right to slack off on the child, thereby denying him or her the chance to develop exceptional talent. A teacher addressed the parent of an eight-year-old girl: "This child is extremely talented! She came to the lesson and I worked with her, and by the end of the lesson, she had already played very well. Three days after . . . she lost everything. . . . Hire a coach, or work with her every day at least for two hours. . . . I can't work seriously in such a way!"

Often a metronome is used to organize instrumental practice. A teacher instructed a seven-year-old's parent: "He needs to start with the eighth [note] at 100 [per minute] and do this first part ten times. If it is without errors, increase the tempo, by two or four notches[30] each time, until he is at 180 for the eighth. He must play at each speed several times, at least six times, and after, he should reduce the tempo [i.e., the metronome setting] to 90, but for the quarter note. . . . This exercise will take nearly one hour, but his problem with the beat should be resolved by doing this." One teacher frequently says to his student: "And don't forget your best friend: the metronome."

Practice

The implantation of work habits is hard, and young violinists experience difficulties applying their teacher's advice. Teachers can pressure students in a humorous or sarcastic manner, or lose patience and explode in anger.[31] In interviews, three teachers said strict supervision was more effective than screaming or threatening, so they placed students in rooms near their own, then checked to see if they were practicing. This approach was confirmed in interviews with former students: "When I was seven or eight, or older, my teacher closed me inside a class near hers, and told me, 'practice!' The first time you look out the window, the second time you stare at the wall, and after, what else can you do in an empty classroom? So, you start to practice."

Some teachers work in this manner with their entire class: "You go very early in the morning and each student, one after the other, plays one piece. After that, the teacher says what you need to work on and how to work on it. And you hear this holy sentence: 'Now, you go to practice; come back after you've finished.'"

In interviews, parents stated that as motivation they most often used rewards such as candy, toys, or going out with friends. Some parents declared that they used their authority and simply expected the child to practice. I never witnessed physical abuse by parents, and have only twice collected testimonies of it. A thirty-two-year-old woman who had stopped her violin training at nineteen told me that her amateur-violinist father, of Ukrainian origin and himself the son of a violinist, would strike her on the head or hands with his bow. In another case, the parents of a child were said to have given him slaps on the head, or pulled his ears or hair. Public revelations concerning such practices are rare, yet Ruggiero Ricci, the American violinist, is convinced that numerous child virtuosos are victims of parental pressure or abuse. According to Schwartz, "Ricci was speaking from experience. He describes his father as 'some kind of musical maniac.' He had all seven children playing an instrument. 'I wanted to be pianist, but my parents got me off that jig. They bribed me with fiddles.' On the whole, Ricci had an unhappy childhood. His father did not hesitate to put pressure on the boy" (Schwarz 1983: 534).

Many adult violinists told me they had been subjected to psychological pressure from the parents, such as threats, screaming, and various punishments, such as limiting freedom to leave the house or banning the use of computer games or television if they did not finish their work. For almost all of my interviewees, this behavior was considered an unpleasant but necessary disciplinary strategy similar to those encouraging children to progress in school.[32]

I observed one family using a kind of indirect tool: frequent public performances, which gave their son continual motivation to practice intensively.[33] Only one interviewed violinist said that she had been motivated entirely "by herself," without parents, teacher, or close family pressure. Violette is a thirty-year-old French violinist, whose father is a concertmaster, her mother a piano teacher, with three older siblings who were music conservatory students. "I remember that at the age of five, I think, I had put on the door of my room a big notice: 'DO NOT ENTER! I'm practicing!' . . . Even today, I need to be alone for practicing, and never—even when I was little—has anyone helped me in my instrumental work. Okay, my mother accompanied me on the piano, but it was only for the rehearsals before concerts."

According to some teachers, culture of origin can influence students' submissive attitudes. Some state that Asian students have a better work attitude than other students. "I think that in the near future, I will take in my class only students from Japan, China, and Korea," one teacher said. "They are already focused and involved in their work. . . . I am like God for them!"[34]

It is safe to say that most students at the start of their soloist education have serious difficulties meeting their teachers' and parents' demands for instrumental practice.[35] The great majority of violinists I interviewed testified to their resistance to work during childhood. Some common resistance ploys included pretending to have a headache, a fever, or hand or finger pain. More subtle forms include "automatic practice," which consists of playing without focus. Violinists call this "playing without the head," and consider this "lost time."

According to current and former soloist students, when parents are absent, young violinists sometimes give themselves long and frequent breaks. They resort to other forms of work resistance in situations where they are supervised. When someone supervises them without seeing, only hearing—because this person is in another room—some students read while playing—usually comics. Some described watching television while playing. A ten-year-old student living in front of a garage described focusing on the activities of a mechanic while he played; he later described all the car repairs he witnessed. One student told me she spent more than half of her time on her own compositions; the cleaning lady hired to supervise her was unaware she was cheating.

Resistance is most difficult in front of parents who are musicians. In this case, resistance to practice can take the form of sabotage, with the violinist damaging the instrument. A ten-year-old girl knew how to put her fingernail or other tool on a string, loosening it to the point that the string threatened to break. A broken string could hurt the violinist's finger, which made it necessary to stop playing. This "accident" happened only on Saturday evenings, when it was impossible to buy another string. The violin shop did not open until Wednesday, thus she had a three-day break from practice.

Another demonstration of "how to have a practice-free weekend" was provided by a teenage violinist who tended to "forget" her violin at school on Friday afternoons. Another young violinist, the son of a pianist and a violinist, decided to stop playing definitively. As a protest against the imposition of practice, he broke the violin's fingerboard, telling his parents it was an accident. When the same "accident" happened two months later, his parents, after a long discussion with their son, decided to stop his soloist and musical education.

During the first stage, students who rebel can be transformed into do-or-die workers who invest their entire lives in playing the violin. The teacher, with parental help, teaches the student to find pleasure in reaching difficult goals. Each new piece of work is presented as a bonus. The teacher says, for example: "You should play this piece by Ernst. This is very difficult, very virtuoso. Even though you are very young, you will be able to work it!" Step by step, students adopt the values of the soloist world, finding gratifications that are only understood within this world. Their interests meld with those of their parents and teacher: to attain as quickly as possible virtuosity and mastery of their instrument.

Biographies of famous soloists of the twentieth century show that their childhoods were given over to intensive instrumental practice. An extract from the biography of Polish soloist Wanda Wilkomirska, born in 1929, shows how this need for instrumental work inspired soloist students and their parents. In her book, Joanna Rawik writes of Wilkomirska:

When she came back from the factory [in the last days of German occupation, winter 1945, in Lodz, Poland] Wanda heard her father tune the violin. "You wouldn't play a little?" he asked. "Have mercy upon her," said Wanda's mother. "After twelve hours of hard labor!" . . . He started, as in Wanda's childhood, with sequences of five minutes. Her fingers were frozen and hurt. . . . Wanda buckled down to playing without her father forcing her. The music took her. She prolonged the practice time for herself. (Rawik 1993: 23)

Once they have become famous musicians, the practice levels of soloists are frequently kept deliberately in the shadows. Some intimate that they do not need any more practice, since they have already mastered playing. Others suggest that they continue to practice intensively. Kubelik's biographers reported that he worked twelve hours each day before concerts; on the evening when he performed, his fingers would bleed. Heifetz described his practice as two hours each day, exercises and scales, and several hours of repertoire. Only Kreutzer, to my knowledge, devoted little time to instrumental practice. Schwarz (1983: 304) explains that Kreutzer, due to the specific morphology of his hands, found it possible to avoid the constraint of daily training.[36]

The relationship between teachers and parents is rich in conflicts and negotiations, most often regarding the child. In a situation of conflict, parent-musicians, knowing the rules in the soloist world, are able to collaborate more effectively than parent-novices, who need to be initiated.

Teachers say the particulars of collaboration with parent-musicians are sometimes vague. "I prefer parents who are involved in their child's musical education, but who aren't musicians. And above all, no violinists! . . . Other parents—those who are violinists—are never here. They are absent . . . but they know better than I do: when to play, what to play, and how to play. . . . I need homemakers, who have the time to devote to their child." Soloist teachers often feel that parent-musicians bring them their children because they lack the time or inclination to school them themselves. One teacher recalled: "A father comes with his daughter and asks me if I can take care of her. . . . She is eleven years old, and both parents are violinists. Her mother is even a soloist, and their daughter is . . . pitiful! . . . In short, she doesn't work! . . . She stayed in my class a few weeks, and afterward, they changed the teacher."

Recognizing the quality of peers' work is crucial for people in most professional worlds.[37] In the musician world, recognition of quality by one's peers is the basis of careers.[38] For classical musicians, evaluation of professional production is reserved for specialists. According to this precept, only a violinist can give an opinion about the performance of another violinist. Despite difficulties in the relationship between parent-musicians and teacher, teachers appreciate material investment such as the purchase of a violin or the proximity between class and family culture, because these factors make it more possible to fix goals.

Teachers have to lecture parent-novices against dangerous sports activities such as skiing, skating, horseback riding, volleyball, or judo, and against time-consuming activities such as dance or theater. All of these activities that reduce the intensity of practice can become subjects of conflict, as in the case of this teacher, speaking to the mother of an eight-year-old student: "Monique must not go on holiday without her violin, as she did last year.[39] She must practice every day. If not, she will fall behind!" Most parent-novices plan family holidays with their child differently than would the teacher or parent-musician. For the latter, two weeks without practice is regarded as "lost time."

An important point of disagreement for the parent-novices and teachers is the question of schooling. For some teachers, going to regular school is also "lost time." As a teacher explains, "The future soloist needs to practice a lot and make progress—and what is learning chemistry and physics for? . . . Other things are not useful for a violinist! Playing chess, learning English, and music analysis, yes!"

The majority of parent-novices and some parent-musicians do not agree. Kathy's mother, who gave her testimony in a tired voice, said,

> From the beginning, since Kathy was in second grade, [Mme Zvonov, the teacher] insisted on a special school for musician children. Kathy had no desire to join this musician's school because all her young friends went to the district's school; so she whined, and got to be with her friends. Two years later, however, we were obligated to change and enroll in this specific school. Now, Mme Zvonov insists on correspondence school, and again, Kathy doesn't want to leave her present school because she is afraid she will lose all her friends. But she can't continue like before. . . . All the violinists in Mme Zvonov's class are forced to attend correspondence school, because if not, there are so many tales . . .

A few months after this interview, Kathy was enrolled in correspondence school. Accepting that regular school is incompatible with the soloist education constitutes an important element of the socialization of soloist students. Refusal to change to the special musicians' school is frequently a factor in abandoning the soloist path.

Relocation

Several students from my sample took classes with teachers who taught in another city, in a few cases in a different country.[40] Following a teacher who frequently changes locations requires travel on the part of the soloist family and potentially a change in place of residence. If this change involves a young child, sometimes the entire family moves. As a consequence, the parents modify their lifestyle, and even their professional life.

At the age of eleven, Juliette earned a place in a soloist class. She needed to move from one European capital to another. Her father, an attorney, stayed in their family home, and Juliette's mother moved along with Juliette's sister. The family met every two weeks. After two years, the parents divorced. Juliette's mother was a concert agent, but then she took a job as a commercial agent in real estate.

Sometimes both parents move with their child, but following a soloist student with the entire family is very difficult. Such was the case with twelve-year-old Zaria's family, who left their home in Kazakhstan. The parents quit jobs, left their house, and moved to Vienna with their three children because Zaria entered a soloist class there. When I interviewed Zaria's mother, the family had been in Austria for more than a year, living off a sponsorship. Their sponsor decided it was crucial for Zaria's career to move to the United States to enroll in lessons with a specific teacher at the Juilliard School. This plan would not include the living costs of a five-person family: Zaria would have to go with her mother, and her father and two brothers would stay behind in Vienna. The family hesitated about this separation.

In the majority of these cases, the mother moves with the child until the moment when the child is old enough to go by himself or herself. The expression "old enough" is not at all precise, as it is up to parents to judge if their child could stay without their family in a boarding school or with a host family, without dropping intensive instrumental practice. According to my observations some parents reject propositions of placing their kids in an environment other than familial before the age of sixteen. Most often it is the mother who takes care of a young virtuoso and their specialized education. Such arrangement is seemingly common also in other cases when women put their work on hold to take care of their child, returning to their occupation when the child is in primary or secondary school. For the soloist's mother, it is different. They stop working for longer periods, risking a loss of their skills. I have met many women in this situation. Their investment in the career of their child is huge. Some pay by dropping their professions, other by having a crisis in marriages (caused by the frequent separations due to the child's travel). Some parents even divorce. Fathers seem more distant and less engaged in this challenging pathway. Why? Probably, for many women who stayed at home rising family, a child's career is a way of completing their life, a way of satisfying their own ambitions. Fathers are working and earning money, which will cover the fees of that education. Mothers, at least some of them, seem to have a unique raison d'être, a major goal in their life: to have their child become a virtuoso, as in the following story.

Sonia sacrificed her professional life for the soloist education of her daughters. She was an engineer, but limited her working hours in a big factory when her first daughter started violin lessons at the age of six. One year after her debut, Sonia's daughter began lessons with a soloist teacher in a city 400 kilometers from their small town. The second daughter also took up violin lessons (according to Sonia, "because it was convenient for both children to have a similar occupation"). Sonia stopped working to help her daughters in their soloist student lives, homeschooling their general education and supervising instrumental practice. Today, her daughters are violinists, both near thirty years old. The three women reside in different European countries. Sonia, having moved twice because her daughters changed their soloist teacher, now lives alone. She has not found a steady job, and her engineering skills have disappeared over time. She remains in a very difficult financial situation, earning money through small jobs. Her daughters help her financially and this is what Sonia gets for her sacrifices. Both daughters feel in debt to their mother.

Another example comes from an only child of parents who invested their whole life in the career of their daughter. They succeeded and this young woman—a well-known soloist—declares to be acutely aware that she is in charge now of both her parents; they live in a country with an excellent social security system. However, she feels an obligation to support them both emotionally and financially.

THE SPECIFIC CIRCUMSTANCES OF EMIGRANT STUDENTS ORIGINATING FROM EASTERN EUROPE

Emigrant families from Eastern Europe, especially the former Soviet republics, state that "almost all good teachers" emigrated after perestroika. These families came West following their teachers. Rarely are the families of such young soloists financially supported by sponsors. Their lives seem similar to the lives of other immigrants. One of my interviewees, who immigrated to France fifteen years ago, reported:

> After one lesson, my son's teacher announced that he had a request for me. He knew that we had recently moved into our big house. He asked me, "Do you have a lot of renovation work with your new house? Do you have someone to help?" I responded, "No, I did not." He knew very well that we were quite broke after making such an expensive investment and he also knew very well that we were in the process of paying for the violin, which he bought in our name from his violin master. "So, I have an idea," he announced to me. "Right now, in my home (a Paris flat of three rooms) there is a man, very kind and gentle, who came here from Turkmenistan. He is Russian and he is here with his daughter, a violinist. He himself was a choir conductor. His wife is an opera singer, but she stayed in Turkmenistan. . . . He wants to stay here with his daughter. She is eleven and plays very well. . . . He knows how to do a lot of things; but in Paris, he can't find a job, because he doesn't speak French. . . . He could come in very useful for you, and you could help him with his housing problem." . . . The day after this talk, Fima and his daughter arrived in our house and stayed with us for months.

Anna's family had lived with different German families for two years. Vasia's family shared a home with a French family for one-and-a-half years, until they obtained their long-term visa and an apartment from social services, where social workers, touched by Vasia's performances, wanted to support the career of a "young violin prodigy."[41]

While it is not always clear whether the soloist education of a child was the primary reason for emigration, parents in this sample denied being motivated by economic reasons. All said they were following an emigrating teacher.

Mobility is also a concern for students originating from the West. One example is a French violinist, Sarah, the younger sister of Pierre, also a violinist. When Pierre entered a soloist class in Switzerland at age fifteen, their mother became a parent-insider, devoting her life to the preparation of her soloist children. Over ten years, they traveled over 500 kilometers per week between France and Switzerland.

Years spent traveling, as in the case of Sarah's mother, or moving to another city or country, as in other cases, is characteristic of the "sacrifice" made by almost all soloist families.[42] Introduction into a soloist world encourages geographic mobility of families, for whom soloist education is a priority. Geographic mobility is not a new phenomenon for soloist musicians, though it has increased in tandem with global communication and political changes, such as the creation of the European Union and the fall of communism, the system that isolated Eastern European countries' citizens.

Isaac Stern, born in 1920, moved at the age of eleven with his mother to New York for six months, leaving the rest of their family in San Francisco (Stern and Potok 2000). Yehudi Menuhin, born in 1916 in New York, moved to Europe for six months with his family. Some young soloist students have similar experiences to that of Nathan Milstein, who describes leaving Odessa, his city of birth, to study with Leopold Auer:

> After a long family discussion it was decided that I had to go study with Auer in Petersburg. I went with Mama. First we stayed in the Abelsons' house at 28 Mokhovaya Street. The three Abelson brothers were wealthy financiers. One of them was even chairman of the stock exchange committee. His wife was from Odessa and was the sister of the engineer Vurdgaft, a friend of my father's. . . . We got up early, at seven. We had breakfast: bread and butter, and tea. . . . After that, I would go to my music stand and practice the violin. Mama would sew, embroider, or write long letters home to Odessa with detailed instructions for all contingencies. (Milstein and Volkov 1983: 13–16)

The alternative to family mobility is placing the child in a dormitory or with a host family. Menuhin, upon creating his school for soloists at Folkestone, opened a dormitory run by nuns. When a famous soloist teacher, Zakhar Bron, moved from Novosibirsk, Russia, to Lubeck, Germany, he took some of his best students and opened a dormitory. But for some parents, the child's mental balance depends on parental presence. Also, the parent is required to enforce instrument practice.[43]

THE ETHNIC ORIGINS OF VIOLIN STUDENTS

A soloist teacher from Moscow once said, "If you have this mixture of blood— Russian, Polish, Slavic—with Jewish culture, an occidental passport, and you live in a Western metropolis, you have many chances of becoming a soloist. All great violinists have that." In fact, most participants in the soloist world believe in a causal link between place of origin and potential success. "Russian" origins, meaning Eastern European, are traditionally perceived as "good origins." A twenty-nine-year-old soloist recalled: "When I participated in competitions fifteen years ago, I had a strong and truly obsessive fear of Russian passports. . . . All those [violinists] who they [the Soviet regime] allow to participate were strongly selected and very good."

Some European teachers are fascinated by Asian students. A teacher told me, "Now, I take almost only Asian students. . . . They listen to me and immediately execute my advice; they have this extraordinary work ethic and outstanding focus." National culture in this milieu is important.

Mobility is illustrated in its most striking form in cases of international mobility. To generate a ratio of students who changed countries of residence, I compiled statistics on participants in six international competitions.

My sample comprises 336 participants in competitions that took place in Europe between 1996 and 2001.[44] I distinguished a subcategory of finalists—those who had the best potential to become a soloist. The data on the participants' nationalities shows the prevalence of Eastern European soloist students in numbers; the finalist data correlates with relatively small variations.

Israeli students show strong chances of becoming finalists relative to their absolute numbers, but the small size of the Israeli sample makes it hard to draw conclusions. However, if we consider the population of Israel we should admit that the representation of Israeli violinists among winners is significant (this is, among others, the effect of the historical importance accorded to the musical practice in this society). The ratio between participants and finalists is generally consistent. Eastern European students in the full group and subgroup are quite significant: one in two originates from this part of Europe.

Violinists originating from the former USSR or other Eastern European countries, and educated by teachers representing the Russian tradition (Wagner 2006a), are prominent in the classical music market. This fact is related to significant emigration of musicians in the 1920s from Russia and the Soviet satellites, a wave that recurred at the end of 1980s.[45] Between these two waves of emigrants, visiting participants at competitions or concerts frequently had defected from the Soviet Union.[46] The majority of current soloist classes in Western Europe and in the United States were created by members of the recent emigration after the 1980s. Their students win many prestigious international competitions.

In the early twentieth century, the label Russian school corresponded to the specific playing posture—distinct from that of violinists from the French-Belgian school—and a particular interpretation of musical pieces. For violinists educated in the late 1990s and for their teachers, the Russian school is now seen as a specific

TABLE 3.1

COMPETITION PARTICIPANTS BY NATIONAL ORIGIN

	Total Participants N = 336	Participants in Finals N = 38
Eastern Europe	48%	50%
Western Europe	23%	21%
Asia	19%	21%
United States	3%	0%
Other	5%	4%
Israel	2%	4%
TOTAL	100%	100%

approach to instrumental teaching: the model of a particular relationship between master and disciple, with strong involvement of teachers in their students' instrumental practice, and particular expectations for the quality of instrumental play.

Current trends suggest that Asian musicians in the twenty-first century will probably have a far more important presence on the international stages than in the twentieth century. The increase of their presence in the competitions as well as their success (increasing number of finalists) are the consequences of the popularity of classical music in Asia (Japan since 1950, then South Korea, and recently China). Statistics from the Jacques Thibaud International Violin Competition 2005 in Paris show 58 percent of the competitors originating from Asia.

Statistics on the geographic origin of students are becoming difficult to compile as it becomes increasingly rare that a musician can give a simple response to this question. Students are frequently mobile. Many are educated in various countries. Some come from immigrant or mixed families. I have prepared a specific category of students with dual citizenship or in process of acquiring a new citizenship.

Obtaining this information about competition participants was not easy for several reasons. Some students had administrative, political, or strategic personal reasons for not disclosing this information. Some mentioned only the country of their study and not their place of origin, or vice versa, depending on the advantages that disclosure would provide them. In a competition in Paris, the candidate who has dual French and Romanian citizenships announced only his French nationality, because the French competitor who obtained the best result in that competition won a special prize.

Sixteen violinists, representing 41 percent of the competition winners group (n = 38) possess dual citizenship when only 20 percent (sixty-one musicians) of participants in the competition (n = 336) are in the same situation. It is certain that the number of students who had moved outside their country of birth was higher than the 20 percent cited in the official information booklet for the competition.[47] It was nearly impossible to determine just how many students belonged to this category. The same question in relation to the finalist category was easily answered: their biographies were known. Forty-one percent had emigrated, the majority from Eastern Europe. This same phenomenon is reflected in the U.S. soloist class, and this is not a new tendency.

Barbara Lourie-Sand, the author of Dorothy DeLay's biography (2000),[48] describes this immigration phenomenon:

> As the new century begins, the great majority of the children at Juilliard are from the Far East, and the younger they are, the higher the proportion. This is particularly true for the piano and violin students, most of whom are hoping for solo careers. If you sit in the lobby of the school on a Saturday, when Pre-College[49] is in session, you might easily be in China, Japan, or Korea. When DeLay started teaching at Juilliard in the mid-1940s, virtually all of her students were Jewish. They were children of the great wave of immigrants who fled Russia and Eastern

Europe at the beginning of the century for either America or what was then Palestine. However, in the next generation—in the 1960s and 1970s—many of the gifted violinists at Juilliard were Jews coming from Israel, not like their predecessors, as refugees, but as young artists in search of larger musical opportunities. Itzhak Perlman, Pinchas Zukerman, and Shlomo Mintz came to the United States specifically to study with DeLay and Galamian. . . . The early 1980s saw the beginning of another cultural shift at Juilliard, as well as at many other educational institutions, as students from the Far East began arriving in the United States in ever-increasing numbers. . . . The article [*Time*, August 31, 1987, "Those Asian-American Whiz Kids"] estimated the number of Asian and Asian American children at Juilliard at that time (1987) to be twenty-five percent of all students. Ten years later, this number more than doubled. . . . However, William Parrish, the assistant director of the Pre-College Division at Juilliard, suggested in a conversation we had in 1998, "today we are starting to see an increase in the number of students coming from Eastern Europe." (Lourie-Sand 2000: 74–76)

The mobility of young musicians depends largely on a network of hosts, such as those that often exist for Jewish students and others from cultures with ethnic diasporas (Armenians, Russians). This crucial factor contributes to the high mobility of young children, which can lead to success in a soloist career.

THE SOLOIST CLASS: SOCIALIZATION WITHIN THE ELITE MUSICAL WORLD

The group active around the teacher and students of a soloist class includes parents, piano accompanists, and in some instances teaching assistants. The teacher is the key figure. For soloist students their master is like a god. It's not surprising that the instructor represents a model to follow and stands as a professional idol for students to admire. The master's biography is subject of constant storytelling, a very popular activity among both parents and students. The teacher's childhood is related in detail. Often the hero of these stories provides the material to share among his disciples. In particular, the first years of violin training are under constant discussion, as are the master's parents and their involvement in violin training. The teacher's relationships with mentors, as well as the whole context of his education, even if the events took place many years ago, frequently in another country, are constantly evoked. The past constitutes the background of present activity of the soloist class. Why this past is so important? Why the need and curiosity for information about the past?

What people are looking for in the past, in their roots, is frequently perennation; they hope to belong to a "lineage." The importance of the past and history reinforces their belief that they belong to an elite—a phenomenon similar to the feeling of being a part of an ancient noble family (Pincon and Pincon-Charlot 1997b). The "longue durée" appears especially important when one takes into consideration the uncertainty of student's present and future status in the soloist milieu. The violinist-soloists belong to a professional world in which uncertainty and precariousness is very high. This is due to the individual character of performance (rarely a group activity) and the freelance nature of soloist employment (few permanent positions). In the particular context of careers not evolving within an established institution such as an orchestra, concert ensemble, or academic institution or conservatory, the soloist class is particularly important to students' identities. This is their frame of reference and their "longue durée" perspective—inscription in the tradition of their mentor and their teacher's mentor serves not only as access into the elite environment that underlines the highest professional value, but also gives the students stability that only old and famous institutions can provide.

To paint the backdrop for this story of complex professional education, I will begin by describing where soloist teaching is conducted, then discuss the activities and strategies involved in the first stage of soloist socialization.

Observation of the soloist class suggests that the particular space in which this activity is conducted influences soloist education.[50] This is not specific for soloists. Jazz musicians studied by Howard S. Becker (2002) were influenced by places in which they performed. This holds true outside the music world. Spradley and Mann in their book about work in bars remark that "Wherever people work, live, or play, they stake claims on space and attach meanings to them" (Spradley and Mann 1975: 102). Anne Monjaret, in her analysis of offices, states: "The equipment of a space informs us about the function, as well as the hierarchical status of the occupant" (1996: 131).

I will analyze several interiors, showing how these places influence the young virtuosos' socialization. Soloist students have their lessons in three major types of places: (1) at an institution (conservatory, music school, or university), (2) in various sites in which the master classes are arranged (manor house, palace, concert, or conference hall or cultural institute), or (3) a private space (most often the teacher's apartment). Each type of space plays a role in the relationship between teacher and student.

Soloist classes bear the seal of the master. Interior decoration is personalized with photos of the master, especially with students who have become famous. The class of Madame Katz is typical. The classroom is part of a music university, in a chateau built in the beginning of the twentieth century. The space is about one hundred square meters, with a ceiling more than five meters high. The room is well lit, with huge windows in two walls. The Bechstein piano, one of the best at the university, is placed in the middle.[51] The teacher's writing desk is under a mirror between two windows, the remaining walls lined with numerous chairs for visitors and students. A tea kettle sits on a small table near the writing desk; some coffee cups and pieces of cake are always there. Framed photos show the teacher at about twenty-five years of age, on stage with a violin, and students at ages ranging from seven to thirty, years after departure from the class. Almost all the photos have an inscription addressed to the teacher, and copies of competition diplomas are on the walls.

In music schools, violin classes are frequently named after composers or performers (Mozart, Paganini, Heifetz), given musical names (sonata, allegro, waltz), or simply numbered. But spaces that are, or were occupied by a soloist teacher, with rare exceptions,[52] are rebaptized with unofficial appellations: Madame Katz's class, for example. The caretakers of music schools frequently transmit this unofficial name, contributing to the maintenance of tradition.[53]

Master Classes

The majority of master classes take place during holidays, most often in summer. Buildings devoted to this activity frequently offer accommodations for teachers and students. I have observed master classes in transformed castles, manor houses, hostels, and old farms. The master class organizer tries to find a prestigious place so that technical conditions for teaching can be very good.[54] Rarely does a famous teacher work in a place with poor technical conditions, but there are exceptions. A teacher well known in the soloist world teaches for one week in winter in a European capital. Lessons take place in a classroom that is a part of a private music school belonging to the Russian embassy. The space is small: inside are some chairs, old tables, and an old piano of low quality. Tickets are required to visit, and are sold by the music school director. The teacher, accustomed to prestigious places, has difficulty moving in the restricted space. Nevertheless, lessons are done according to schedule, and he does not complain during the week of his visit. The final concert takes place in the embassy's better hall.

I later observed the same teacher in a more exemplary setting, a private hall near the city's most famous concert hall. At the center of the stage was the grand piano, illuminated by spotlights. Some students' parents and other students observed the lesson, some taking notes. The teacher acted as if he were playing in a theater: "Was this version better?" he asked the audience of about ten people.

A few weeks later, the teacher gave public lessons in the UNESCO concert hall, with television and radio participation. About one hundred people attended this event. The students performed in conditions similar to those of the important concerts. This type of master class venue is reserved only for the best teachers.

In one master class, in a castle close to Paris, several violin teachers participate. Students learn in halls open to castle visitors taking guided tours. They practice in rooms high in the castle, and in parts reserved for employees. Lessons are not public here, due to security, but each day concerts are open to the public, sometimes commented upon by a teacher. Concerts by teachers and the best students take place in the castle's reception hall.

Teaching at home is a common practice among soloist teachers. Lessons done in conjunction with a conservatory or music school can also take place in the teacher's home. During my fieldwork, especially in France, I met teachers who complained that their available institutional time was too light. Consequently, young virtuosos almost always had supplementary lessons, paid or free. Music school schedules do not permit ad hoc prolongations of lessons (a recurrent practice), another reason that teachers choose to teach in their homes. Some teachers find conservatory classrooms ill suited for "elite teaching": the small rooms that are sometimes changed; the parents, students, and others who come and go; pianos that are not well tuned.

> For years I had a classroom with excellent acoustics, a high ceiling, and a beautiful piano, but when a new director came, he installed his office in my classroom (it was the best one in the conservatory), and now I need to work with my students in the practice room in the attic. . . . The ceiling is so low that my students touch it with their bows. . . . Therefore, I decided to work from my apartment.

This teacher, as with other emigrants from Eastern European countries to France, gave a negative comparison of his current workspaces to those he had in the past. In Eastern Europe, such teachers had their "own" classroom, with free access seven days a week, without a fixed schedule of class occupation, as in French music schools. Time saving, better working conditions, and the tradition of students being received at a teacher's private space are factors in the difference. In the tradition of Eastern European violinists, teaching at home is a sign of celebrity and a practice influencing student-teacher relationships.

Lessons taught at home take place in the living room or a specially arranged room. I provide three descriptions of these spaces.

The first is a three-room Paris apartment. The teacher is a fifty-year-old woman, situated in a building constructed around 1930, in an artistic area of the city. Lessons take place in a twelve-square-meter room, with a sofa-bed on which parents sit. Thick drapes cover the door to "create better acoustics." In front of a bookcase with scores and CDs, the teacher sits on her chair at a low table with a huge digital clock-radio. There are no paintings or photos on the walls.

The second place is that of a fifty-five-year-old soloist and teacher, situated in a modern building in an immigrant district. Lessons take place in the living room. Big windows allow light to enter, which strikes a wall decorated by paintings dedicated to the teacher. In the center are a black piano and a wooden music stand; in front of the windows is a low table strewn with CDs, concert documents, and other papers and scores. To the right, is a bookcase with many books, largely in Cyrillic, classics of Russian literature. Photos of the teacher with a violin are on the wall and the bookcase. There is a sofa where parents sit and observe. The workings of a giant digital watch attract attention. This second example is a typical performer's practice room, a musician's space that students are invited into, filled with personal objects.

The third setting is a flat in an old building with a resplendent entrance. Lessons take place in a double living room, separated by double doors closed during lessons. The room is spacious, more than five meters high, with over a hundred square meters of space. Between huge windows, bookcases reach up to the ceiling, filled with CDs, LPs, scores, and music books in several languages. In the middle of the room are a grand piano and two armchairs. A Persian carpet is on the floor.

Diplomas of students and numerous photos (famous violinists, pianists, conductors) hang on the wall. Between these is a photo of the teacher—the owner of this apartment—with a well-known Russian politician.

If the first room is a model of a soloist-class space, the last is characteristic of an elite class space, similar to descriptions by soloists of former generations: Auer's class in St. Petersburg,[55] for example. Ivan Galamian's students described his apartment in Manhattan as a true music school. A photograph in Barbara Lourie-Sand's book shows the old man sitting before a grand piano, a violin in his hand, the wall behind him covered with photos. The caption reads: "Ivan Galamian, in 1977, in his Manhattan studio, where pictures of history's greatest violinists glared down upon his students" (Lourie-Sand 2000: 46).

According to my interviews and informal discussions, the perception of these places is individual, yet nobody remains neutral to the messages springing from the walls. Parents and older students recognize the famous figures in photographs. Younger students do not attach importance to the places of their lessons at first, but gradually become attentive to this aspect, and eventually feel a strong attachment to their lesson environment.

Soloists are not alone in perceiving feeling emanating from specific places. In Joseph Hermanowicz's study of physicists' careers (Hermanowicz 1998), researchers educated in prestigious universities describe the power of corridors decorated with photos of famous scientists, and strong feelings from the knowledge that these spaces were used by the greatest names of science.

Soloists' descriptions are similar.[56] In the soloist classroom, students experience the most intense activity of their education. This activity, during which they are constantly evaluated, is at the center of their young lives. One specificity of this education is the fact of individual lessons with the same teacher over many years. In my discussions with students and former students, the interior decor of a music theory class, or other musical classes, never comes up. All remembrances are related to the violin lessons.

The kinds of decoration in teachers' classes are also found in the shops and ateliers of violin makers—photos of famous clients: violinists, cellists, and violists. Autographs may include grateful sentences where performers thank the violin maker for working on their instrument.

In a violin class, there are photos of the teacher's former students and master, and often a picture of the master of the master. This indicates the "violin school" to which the teacher belongs, and demonstrates the continuity of musical dynasties.[57] Also essential are the teacher's early photos, often as a child playing the violin, always at the peak of the performer's career. This model of exhibition is similar to interiors of noble manors in which a family demonstrates affiliations with other prestigious families, with genealogical trees surrounded by portraits and photos.[58]

The following description comes from a student at the first stage of his collaboration with a new teacher: the matching stage of career coupling.

> When you enter into his class, you immediately see with whom you are dealing: the photo of Maazel, smiles, hugs, shaking the hand with R [former leader of Russia], and the photos with his students, always before or after concerts or final concerts of a competition. For example, this photo taken with Queen Elizabeth of Belgium. And this photo with Oistrakh! You say to yourself: "Well, I am here with someone!" And immediately you have the jitters.

Anne Monjaret describes and analyzes similarities in other workplaces: "The elements of decoration reveal the networks of acquaintance and the relationships maintained with others" (Monjaret 1996: 133).

The second goal of this classroom decoration is to testify to the teacher's position within the elite. Photos can show the master and his disciples with personalities in the music world, or with politicians. Former students recounted how these interiors influenced their feelings of being a part of the same world as the most famous violinists. Perhaps, one day, their photo would be up on the wall. Feelings of belonging to the elite also have been expressed by students in other fields who patronize prestigious places. Hermanowicz cites a physics student: "The names that one sees on the doors, for me, are the names of heroes" (Hermanowicz 1998: 48). Corridors with pictures of former students and teachers of this university, who later became Nobel Prize laureates, instill feelings of distinction among students taking their turn at learning in these spaces.

Young musicians, through the photos of "heroes," sense that they are entering the world of their role models. Their goal, of becoming a soloist, seems within reach.[59] Some of these spaces are "sanctuaries" venerated by musicians. The most famous violin class from the early twentieth century, in the Stoliarsky School at Odessa, is described thus:[60]

> Today's Stoliarsky School, in its fine though dilapidated building near the Potemkin steps and the harbor, is still presided over by Stoliarsky. His picture hangs on the main staircase rising from the entrance hall. . . . It is, however, in the small hall where Stoliarsky taught that his presence is most strongly felt. Here, photographs of him are surrounded floor to ceiling by pictures of students—including Oistrakh, Richter, and Elizaveta Gilels[61]—together with opera and concert notices. During our five-day stay, there was always a bunch of fresh flowers in the corner, informally stuffed into a jar in a touching tribute to the national hero. ("Measures," in *The Strad* 111 [December 2000]: 1344)

These particular spaces and decorations play a role in the formation of young violinists.[62] In some soloist classes, the presence of public observers modifies the lesson into a kind of concert. As a student of Yuri Yankelevich recalled in *Yuri Yankelevitch et l'Ecole Russe du Violon*:

> In general, the class was full: friends, assistants, soloists of orchestras, students; visitors from different institutions, nationals or foreigners, most often attended during his lessons. . . . He transformed his individual lessons into a sort of "action" in which the framework was a passionate process of education of a

young professional, an initiation into the understanding of Music. (Qtd. in Brussilovsky 1999: 250)

These public lessons allow a professional audience to observe the methods of this teacher. Some students had traveled from afar (Israel, the United States) to meet the master.[63] During the era of the Iron Curtain, students came to Moscow to take lessons or observe the work of famous teachers (though Russian students could not travel outside the USSR). Former students bore witness to a particular ambiance: "During Yankelevitch's lessons . . . a lot of people attended: students, teachers, and outside visitors. These things made playing more similar to a performance on stage and increased the sense of the student's responsibility" (Testimony of Arkady Fouter, a former student of Y. Yankelevich, in Brussilovski 1999: 333).

The final aspect reinforcing distinctions between soloist students and their peers is accessibility of places including manors, castles, and some concert halls. The students' access to these spaces is specific to their status. When in the teacher's apartment, they are not visitors. At master classes in the manor, they are not tourists. Soloist students are guided by their entourage in the proper use of these spaces as a part of their professional education. This progressive early socialization—early in comparison to other occupations—constitutes an important particularity of the young soloist's life.

Hierarchy of Students in the Soloist Class

The hierarchy of students within the master class constitutes an important element of professional soloist culture. This hierarchy is built in large part by the teacher, who evaluates a student's "potential" and establishes a prognosis, treating their students differently depending on where they stand in his or her musical judgment. The different ages of the students complicates the measurement of their standing. The rating is not explicit. The rules are not clear and it seems that it is a structural mechanism that could prevent huge competition between students and by consequence, conflicts between their parents. Moreover, this kind of rat-race ambiance is welcome by some teachers.

Soloist students achieve excellent grades on music school exams, but when they enter soloist classes, only a few are considered "stars," as a few teachers describe their leading pupils. During a formal interview in her home, one teacher told me: "I have numerous students who are very strong, maybe even too many. . . . I now have four star students in my class, and before their concerts, before international competitions, I must give them lessons each day. . . . Do you know how long one violin lesson, at maximum, lasts? . . . Eight hours!"

Rifts can develop between stars and the other students. When I was the mother of a young virtuoso who came before teachers as a potential client, the teachers acted as if they were impartial toward all their students. Even after I had interviewed them as a sociologist, most claimed (with two exceptions) that insider hierarchy was a figment of parents' imaginations. But they would have at least two reasons to conceal any ranking system within their classes. First, ranking implies that the class contains poor students; the best teachers are only supposed to have extraordinary students. The second reason is related to the pedagogy of instrumental teaching;[64] categorization of students is contrary to the consideration of each student's development as a unique individual. Because organization of a hierarchy is complex, teachers prefer to show themselves as not having favorites. However, my observations contradict such affirmations.

The duration of a lesson and the number of lessons per week are good indications of unequal treatment. Teachers prolong lessons in recognition of the student's position within the class, and student stars benefit from long, intensive lessons. Some teachers reduce the time they give to students they consider poor. "He's not as good, so it is necessary to abridge his lesson in order to make time for prolonging other lessons," said one. "What is always worrisome with Grigori's lessons is that he comes to Splendidcity only twice a month, and we have one lesson each time. If you can't play very well . . . your lesson could take only five minutes and that's all!" Students notice the differences and can become unhappy about them. Some teachers respond by making a gesture of equality. One teacher said, "I stopped prolonging lessons, because I had realized that my students were creating many tall stories: 'You are better than me, because your lesson is always thirty minutes longer than mine.' Or 'How was your lesson?' 'OK, fifteen minutes of prolongation!' Now, it is finished. Each one has an hour and that's it!"

A more subtle way to favor certain students—one for which musical knowledge is necessary to decode—involves the distribution of pieces to be played. Some students receive music that is complex for their age; others get technically easier programs. Performances, participation in the media, prestigious musical events, and international competitions are other determiners of distinction, and easily decoded by violinists and their entourages. One soloist-class student prepares for an international competition; another student of the same age will participate in a less prestigious competition. Students told me that their teacher taught only star students in his or her home. Other students took lessons at the music school where the teacher worked.

Student positions within the soloist class are dynamic: An "average" student can rise to become a star, and the reverse is also possible. The uncertainty involved in judging the quality of violin performances constitutes one of the important problems for students. The instability favors competition and the maintenance of competitive relationships among students and among other participants—parents, for example.

According to formal and informal interviews, parents seem to be the category of participants most preoccupied with hierarchy practice inside the soloist class. Their point of view about "favoritism" practiced by teachers depends on the status of their child. Parents of star students, for example, are less concerned about the teacher's preferential treatment. They may consider their child very talented, find it legitimate that the teacher takes better care of their child, and complain about the "jealousy of other parents." The mother of a sixteen-year-old student said: "Marie is a little particular in her violin class, but she was always the student who was the most advanced, most mature, and who performed her programs with the most seriousness and organization."

Parents who did not have a child atop the hierarchy frequently expressed discontent, finding it "dishonest" that the teacher took better care of other children than their own. "Now, in class, something has changed," said one mother in an interview. Her daughter had been at the top of her class until a new student arrived. "The 'new' Laura is a star. . . . The lessons, the concerts, the projects and everything else revolve around her." I observed conflicts between parents and teachers, and sometimes between parents and students, based on hierarchy and favoritism.

I have also seen projects collapse because of such conflicts. During a meeting of parents of Madame Malina's class to consider funding for master classes and travel to competitions, one parent suggested raising money by creating a CD of each student playing a solo piece. Other parents approved of the idea, but the teacher declared that only the star student could produce a record of high quality. The other parents would not support a recording project involving only a single student.

Student views about hierarchy are different from those of their parents. Teachers classify them into gifted and nongifted categories. If they are the star, teachers treat them as special and set them as examples for others. Stars often make this clear to their colleagues: "See how you play? You came to this competition for nothing." With time, though, students learn codes of behavior, saying "good luck" to competitor-colleagues who are preparing for public performance, for example.

Students are used to unequal treatment by teachers and give the impression that they consider it "natural." Those not at the top of the ranking do not seem to feel any injustice, but hope to become star students themselves. Star students, on the other hand, tend to see the hierarchy as stable and irreversible. Internal hierarchy prepares students for life in the highly competitive soloist world.

COMPETITIONS

Participation in competitions sets the soloist class apart; competitions play different roles in different stages of the soloist education. We can divide competitions by age: junior competitions for young violinists, and those for soloists starting their adult careers. However there is generally no strict age limit for entrance to the adult competition. If a thirteen-year-old violinist can perform the repertoire well, he or she can participate in contests for adult virtuosos.

Competitions are further distinguished by their importance, which is based on reputation and prestige.[65] The prizes awarded in highly regarded competitions range from a few hundred to several thousand euros. First place in the Wieniawski competition in Poland in 2001 was 20,000 euros; the Thibaud in France in 2002 was 30,500 euros; in 2002 in Indianapolis the prize was $30,000. Winners are selected to play concerts (one or several), for which they are usually also remunerated. The violinists can receive more than one prize and accumulate several distinctions (best interpretation of Bach pieces; best violinist from Russia; best performance of Paganini's Capriccio). Junior competitions lack these levels of distinction, and the number and quality of concerts related to the competition are less prestigious.

Competition procedures are the same for junior and senior competitions. Applications may include recommendation letters and CVs, audio or video recordings of performances, a list of chosen pieces, and a fee (usually ranging from 25 to more than 100 euros). Each competition has several selections over several days, organized in three or four stages. Pieces played in each stage are imposed; some can be chosen from a list, while for others the violinist has no choice at all. Some pieces have been written expressly for the competition. (To give time for preparation, the list of pieces is announced about a year before the competition.)

The technical level of the pieces requires intensive practice over months and even years. For example, a twenty-four-year-old, three-time winner of second place in big senior competitions had presented the same program for seven years. The selections are frequently open to the public. Participants find competition performances much more stressful than concerts because they are judged by other violinists. The performer must correspond to expectations of each jury member (which is virtually impossible) in technique, interpretation, and stage behavior.

In countries with centralized systems of state-supported musical training such as Eastern European countries before 1990, competitors had to win national contests to enter international competitions, much in the way that high-level athletes go through regional and national selections to compete on the world stage. This pyramidal selection process socializes players to the high demands of the big competitions.

Junior competitions give young students and their families opportunities to broaden their knowledge of the world of soloists in preparation for senior international competitions.[66] One of the two most prestigious junior competitions in Europe takes place in Lublin, Poland, and is called the Little Wieniawski, in reference to the "big" Wieniawski Competition, the oldest in the world, which takes place in Poznan, Poland. Another important junior competition was created by Yehudi Menuhin in Folkestone, Great Britain, and now takes place in Boulogne sur Mer, France. Other prestigious competitions are in Italy, Germany, and other European countries. These events are organized by an informal hierarchy, and some are an intense focus for local media.

Students attend competitions with their teacher or their parents, and sometimes both. Stays vary according to the competition—three days to two weeks for small events—and finalists stay longer. Competitions constitute a tool for comparing the soloist's performance with that of others, and an opportunity to set deadlines for preparation of repertoire. Some within the soloist world down play the significance of these events to students. Others find that participation focuses the soloists and spurs along the "stable of young horses" in the rest of the class. When the teacher judges that a student is ready, he or she is prepared for a young-soloist competition.

The following field notes concern a typical competition, in Germany in the 1990s, and serve as an introduction for the analysis of certain aspects concerning the event.[67] The competition is bienniel, with a twenty-year history, and was created by a local music school with support from the ministry of culture, local associations, media, and private sponsors. Participants are between the ages of eight (no minimum age limit) and twenty-four, and choose three programs adapted to their skills and, by consequence, age. The first group involves students up to the age of fourteen; the second, to eighteen; the third, to the age of twenty-six. The competition is organized in three stages. Auditions at the first stage take place according to a schedule that is generally alphabetical, although the first player is selected at random. Results are announced when all participants have played. At each selection, about 50 percent of participants are eliminated. In the final stage, six to ten musicians participate for each group.

Before the competition and during tests, violinists, their parents, and teachers play games around predicting the results, studying the program booklet and sharing information about competitors, guessing which candidate has the best potential to please jury members. In doing so, they apply their knowledge about the professional world of soloists. Teachers make a similar evaluation before sending their student to participate in a given competition. This is always a strategic decision. The composition of the jury is important, as is suggested in the following statement by a teacher: "This year I refused to send my students to K. [the city in which the competition takes place], because this jury is hostile to me."

This competition, as with many others, is named unofficially after the organizer: "Starski's competition." In fact, many violin teachers told me they refused to prepare students for this competition because, in the words of one teacher, "The prizes are distributed before the performances." In the competition I observed—and this is not exceptional—all of the competitors who ended up as finalists were students of members of the jury. As we will see, the subjective nature of judging constitutes one of the most discussed issues in the entire soloist education.[68]

The choice of jury members depends on the competition's organizer. For the majority of competitions, the jury changes from one event to the next. Two kinds of jury configurations are usually practiced: a jury made up of musicians educated in the same conservatory or belonging to the same educational tradition, or one made up of individuals who represent opposing schools.[69] Exceptions occur in young-soloist competitions, in which some jury members are not teachers. In important competitions for soloists, composers and conductors may be invited to participate in the jury. Diversity within a jury can reduce the number of teachers who have prepared competitors and can vote to support their candidates. In some competitions, teachers on the jury are not allowed to present their students; in other competitions, when teachers prepare a competitor, they may not give points to that student.[70] However, this applies largely to students who have taken lessons for years from that teacher, and students from master classes are not subject to the rule.

Competitors try to have a master class with at least one jury member. In the case of the observed competition, its organizer created a master class with a jury member just before the event, to allow competitors to "better prepare their performance," as a jurist explained in his opening speech. For this master class, lessons and accommodation cost over 300 euros. Not all competitors were able to pay this, but all competition finalists had participated in this master class.

Variety on an international jury may certify openness and impartiality. But first impressions can be deceiving, as with the jurists of the Starski competition. These violinists, men with an average age of fifty-five, are well known within the soloist world. This is the seventh time that they have met at this competition (each also judges other competitions). The organizer and jury president, Roman, is from Eastern Europe and is a professor at the Superior School of Music in a large German city (in this province this institution is supported by the federal state Staatliche Hochschule fur Musik; other schools of music are led by local governments). Out of eight jurists, one is German and four others work in Germany. Others are professors in superior conservatories in the capitals of Russia, Poland, the former East Germany, and Romania. Their social positions in Germany and in Eastern Europe are comparable to those of university professors. Each is connected with Roman in some way. The oldest member, at seventy years old, is his teacher. The violinist representing the United States was a student of this same teacher in the soloist class with Roman. Another jurist, about sixty-five years old and from Moscow, is a friend of Roman's teacher. Four of the jurists are the main organizers of competitions in their respective countries and had invited Roman to participate on those juries.

The jury makes successive selections of violinists according to certain criteria that are seldom discussed openly.[71] Each member makes his or her assessment according to his or her preferences. Unlike athletic competitions,[72] in music and other areas of the arts, judgment of production quality is largely subjective. The absence of objective measurement raises the question of arrangements and negotiations among jurists. To attract the jury's attention, young violinists try to establish relationships with jurors. They know that for a juror considering perhaps twenty performers in a day, it will be easier to focus on a student who worked with him or her, even for a short time, for example in a master class. This interview extract is from a teacher who frequently works in competitions:

> They will be playing their worst before the jury. This is normal. They have the jitters, that's all. But if we have heard them during their lessons . . . we know at this same moment that they have played a thousand times better! . . . And after this guy who you know so well comes another, someone unknown, and he makes an error while playing. Maybe it's an even more minor mistake than your student made, but you say to yourself, "He plays badly, he doesn't know enough."

Negotiations of the jury are secret; according to testimonies, discussions are sometimes stormy. According to a teacher who participates in juries, it is always possible to "sway the vote." Three jurists working together, he says, can control and influence competition results. "I don't know of any competitions which aren't backhanded. It is always possible to support or throw out someone before the finale." An accompanist, speaking with a competitor's parent on the first day of selections, expressed discontent: "Here, the prizes have already been distributed.

It's a pity, because I have accompanied children who have played very well. For them it is so hard, but you know, they don't despair. The main thing is to play. And everybody knows what this competition is about."

Competitions play an important role in the soloist education. The crucial factor in success is social position and position in the strategic network of the competitor's teacher and/or his or her parents. And despite widespread knowledge about the backhanded behavior, students consider competition winners "good violinists," and those not selected "bad ones." Other people from the soloist world, who believe that artistic competition is not a completely satisfactory concept, still recognize competition finalists as "better violinists on the market of classical music."[73]

Parental responsibilities include moral support of their child, day-to-day organization, supervising daily practice, and helping to find practice space (competitions rarely provide enough training rooms for the candidates). Parent-novices learn roles from parent-insiders and parent-musicians during competitions. Teachers also indicate tasks to increase the students' chances of winning.

When the teacher is absent, parents make sure that rehearsals take place with the piano.[74] They help assure that exams go according to schedule, making sure their child's name is not skipped or forgotten. Parents also make sure the child gets food and rest; the stress of competition frequently disrupts both. Finally, parents organize free time: a walk, a trip to the swimming pool, ping pong, or chess. During the competition, the children are at the center of parental attention, far from home, housework, and professional occupations, and focused on winning the competition. Novice participants learn that final results can depend on power relationships within the jury or their teacher's relationship with the jury.

The following example describes family strategies. Maria, twelve, was enrolled by her family in a juror's master class. Another jury member is a friend of her father, who is a violinist, and a third was once his teacher. From the start of the competition, parents at the master class perceive Maria as a potential finalist: in addition to playing a prestigious violin exceptionally well, she combines all non-musical assets. Her father, mother, brother, and grandmother support her during performances. She seems relaxed, walking in the park with family members. Each evening after exams, she takes a lesson with one of two members of the jury. This is criticized by parents and some competitors, who perceive a transgression of the unwritten rules. Maria's parents pay for rehearsals with a pianist (competition rehearsals are limited to twenty minutes before the test performance).

In comparison, another student has come from Russia without her parents, who could not afford the travel costs. She has not taken violin lessons for two weeks, and spends her time with a soloist classmate from Russia, with no adult supervision or support. She does not get a single rehearsal with the piano during the competition.

Maria, who other parents had predicted as a first-place winner, finishes second, and her parents are happy that their efforts brought results. The rule about lessons with jurists during competition was ignored. Nor was that unique at this competition: other parents tried to break prohibitions against direct contact with jury members, inviting jurists for a beer or dinner outside the place of competition, seeking information about their child's chances. At competitions, the parents tell me, "relationships" are the most important thing.[75]

The only informal transgression I heard about that resulted in negative consequences occurred in the case of Nastia. This girl was a finalist in a competition where first place went to a candidate who changed her program at the last minute, which is prohibited by competition regulations. Nastia's parents pointed out this fact, nobody reacted, and they took the matter to court and won the case. The winner was eliminated, Nastia took a higher place, and the parents seemed to have won. But their daughter was never accepted to another competition—as a young violinist said, "she was burned in the soloist milieu." Her parents had broken the informal rule concerning obedience and compliance with the jury—whose dicta apparently supersede the actual rules of the competition.

Competition judges, as this informal rule acknowledges, impose a code of law and authorize themselves to transgress the rules they created. The majority of parents, after their first experience of competition, know these rules. Even if they share the conviction that competition selections depend on factors not related to musical performance, almost all continue to enter their children in these events. In the soloist milieu, they argue, competitions offer a unique opportunity to "build a career."

In this highly competitive world, winners are few, losers are numerous. An important parental task is to assist their child in managing failure. (Failure by the "child prodigy" is also difficult to accept for parents, who are convinced of the child's unique talent.) Young competitors frequently perceive not being selected as a catastrophe. When results are posted—often in the hall where the competition took place—sad sobs mix with cries of joy from the few selected candidates. Most parents are left to try to comfort their child. The results were rigged, they say, "everyone knew that." Others attribute the failure to bad preparation or insufficient practice.

Walking through a corridor during the first round of a competition, I heard a child screaming behind closed doors: "I'm very tired. I am exhausted." A moment later, I saw the mother of an eight-year-old Russian girl with her teacher. I observed this little girl at practice in the following days, from early morning to late evening, with only short breaks. Her mother reproached her that she had worked badly and, because of that, they would have to return to Russia early.

Reactions of a winner's parents are interesting. Before the results, many express the widespread opinion that competitions are unfair, that private relationships and connections skew the results. Immediately after learning that their child has made the final selection, they state that the competitions were fair, and that this kind of event is useful to their child's career.

Although they involve very young violinists, competitions create visibility for winners within the soloist world. All participants learn from the winners' performances. They learn to adapt (an indispensable skill when working with different teachers) and to detect effective networks available to support young violinists.[76] An illustration is provided by the following story, which took place during the described competition, in which the finalists were all students of jury members.

After the competition, the parent of a losing candidate asked two jurists separately for reasons they did not select his child. Both men responded that the young violinist was very talented and a soloist career was at his fingertips, but that he should change his teacher. Both suggested the young musician would be welcome in their classes.[77]

Conclusion—First Stage of the Soloist Education: Mutual Dependencies

Relationships between participants in this period are of a specific nature, with the teacher giving time and knowledge to those students evaluated as promising, in exchange for money or, sometimes, a parental service (help in organizing concerts, babysitting, writing official papers, translating). When the teacher gives free lessons, this is perceived in the soloist world as recognition of the student's potential and as important compensation for the student's hard work.

Another compensation is to prepare the student for taking part in international contests. Students who participate in these competitions become a sort of business card for their teachers. Barbara Lourie-Sand, in the biography of Dorothy DeLay, writes that "teachers owe their reputations to their successful students. Even the greatest pedagogues are usually known only within the music world" (Lourie-Sand 2000: 41).

Such dependency is illustrated by the case of Eastern European violin teachers who emigrated in the 1990s. They struggled to take their best students to Europe or to the United States. Without these "imported star students," the teachers' careers could easily have collapsed. These immigrant teachers had to build up new soloist classes; otherwise they could have lost their reputations and regressed to previous career stages.

Young performers build the reputations of their teachers and their own reputations, which form the bases of their soloist student careers. Competitions serve as an opportunity for young soloists to take their place in the soloist world. During these violin competitions, all-important actors of the young soloist world are present: famous teachers (as jury members), students (future soloists), accompanists, and sometimes agents and conductors. Participation in competitions from an early age is intrinsic to the soloist's class and provides excellent opportunities for students to learn the practice of creating and maintaining ties, as in the following example.

The evening before the departure of a student for a competition, his teacher gives him this last piece of advice: "Say 'hello' from me to J. [a member of the jury]. He has been my friend for a long time. You will play for him before your official performance at the competition starts. I will call and tell him that you are my student." The tie between the teacher and his colleague is not only professional: they have been friends for a long time. This is typical in the soloist world. The teacher puts his students in touch with a jury member, indicating how he or she can take part in such relationship-building in the social venue of competition.

Teachers do not hide that competitions are a place where the selection of the "best" violinists are not solely determined by quality of performance (Wagner 2006a). In six competitions I observed, finalists have always been students of jury members (soloist class or master class). From their first competition, the young participants learn that, in order to win, it is important to be close with a teacher who holds a degree of power in the professional world. This mechanism also explains why, for teachers, being on a jury is important, an opportunity to show their importance and to push their students forward.

In the first stage of soloist education, the student depends on executive decisions made by adults. His or her universe consists largely of hard daily instrumental work. The young soloist is enclosed in a sort of cell, built by the parents and the teacher. This is how the system works until he or she reaches the next stage.

The End of the Transformation Process: Novice-Parents Become Insiders

At the first stage of soloist education, success depends on collaboration between parents and teacher, with both sides making strong efforts to adjust expectations and actions. The teacher initiates the parents into the world of the soloist: even parents who are musicians need this initiation because, like the majority of parents, they have never played the role of a soloist parent. The teacher introduces the parents into their role of assistant. It is not in the interest of the teachers that parents know the complex functioning of this specific education—especially the low chances of achieving a successful position after more than fifteen years of professional training. The success in the passage to the next stage (and prevention of drop out) is related to the capacity of the teacher to persuade parents to persist, even if their child is not a competition winner. An effective impression management[78] is in this relation of the highest importance.

For parent-novices, new knowledge entails information about violin technique, about coaching children, and about functioning in the soloist world. The socialization of parent-novices includes such information as the teachers care to transmit. Parent-novices, and parent-musicians who are not close to the soloist world, are not informed about the numerous failures that occur after this long-lasting, intensive, exclusive (in that the child does not prepare for other professional avenues), and expensive education. The parents, typically, are ignorant of the difficulties of the soloist market in the world of classical music. If they truly knew the competitive reality, the investments they make in their child's future could seem highly risky. Parent-musicians, who are more familiar with the soloist world, hope that their knowledge will protect their child from failure.

In order to achieve this first stage of education, each category of parents needs to modify its attitudes and adhere to the teacher's expectations. Nonmusician parents need to put aside expectations concerning general education. Without these adaptations, parents may renounce their child's soloist education, as in the case of this piano soloist and mother.

My son . . . screamed at each lesson, and afterward he refused to practice at home. I met the teacher to discuss this and she said, "Your boy has huge talent, but you need to take care of him seriously. Your own career as a pianist is a small career in comparison to his future. Drop it all, and take care of your son. . . . In three years, he will make a living for your whole family." After this talk, I took my son out of the class. He continues to play as an amateur, only for his pleasure, without screaming.

Accomplishing the first stage of a soloist education depends on the capacity of parents to assume their soloist-parent role. When, after many conflicts and negotiations, the triad team starts to function well, the child progresses in this stimulating unit and develops his or her soloist skill. It is only after this collaboration has been attained that a new crisis arises.

CHAPTER 4

Crisis and Career Coupling

THE SECOND STAGE OF SOLOIST EDUCATION

Partial Student Emancipation from Parents

The second stage of soloist education, usually in the teenage years,[1] starts with the striking diminishment of the parental role. Previously docile and submissive, the soloists begin to assert their right to independent choices. As before, parents pay for the child's lessons and other fees, and in some families, the parents remain booking agents while managing all the activities ordered by the teacher. The sharpest changes occur around parental involvement in the student's musical education and training. Parents usually stop attending the child's lessons and no longer supervise practice. Young musicians start to disagree with their parents' opinions about work methods and strategic decisions concerning their education.

The first type of conflict arises with the supervision of practice. The future soloists no longer want their parents to work with and supervise them. Children of nonviolinists typically begin to make sarcastic remarks about their parents' ability to offer oversight, like the thirteen-year-old girl who said to her father, "You don't even know how to hold the violin, let alone play it."

Emancipation from parental guardianship is expressed not only at home but also in regard to lessons, competitions, or master classes. At this stage, young violinists emphasize their desire to become independent and gain control over their education. Most parents adapt to their child's expectations. A mother, waiting in a cafe for her thirteen-year-old daughter in front of the teacher's Paris home, remarked: "Now, she forbids to me to go to the lessons. She wants to go alone and she says I know nothing about it. It's true that I'm not a musician, but I was able to help her a little at home. But, what can you do? (sigh). She doesn't want my presence there anymore, and that's it! She's a teenager! So I'm basically a taxi driver."

Parental attendance at competitions, which usually take place far from home, diminishes. Even if parents do accompany their children to these events, they spend their time there in the company of other parents, rather than with their child. The young musicians keep their distance. There are some exceptions to this distancing, especially among some Asian musicians who, even after finishing their education, come to competitions accompanied by their mothers. Also, the break is less pronounced in families in which parents play multiple roles (such as accompanist, teacher, manager, concert agent). This was the case with both Anastasia and Sasha, whose parents' activities were almost entirely focused on the child's career.

Anastasia struggled with her father—who was also her violin teacher, as was Anastasia's mother—but only over musical interpretations. Father and child worked closely together in discussing and negotiating her concert and competition arrangements. According to Anastasia's mother, her father was skilled at winning Anastasia over to his ideas about her projects. Whereas many students start to become "difficult" as young as thirteen, in Anastasia's case the break did not occur until she was nineteen, when she left home to study in a city 600 kilometers away. Even then, her parents continued to manage her career, though they lost control of her schedule and could no longer monitor her instrumental practice.

At the age of sixteen, Sasha was always in the presence of his parents. His mother was his accompanist in all concerts and competitions; his father was his concert agent and manager. Musically, Sasha gained his freedom at a very early age. From the age of ten he practiced without close supervision from his parents, who were pianists (he was the only violinist in the family). Sasha's continued close collaboration with his parents was based on professional convenience and need.

THE PERIOD OF CRISIS

For the majority of students, the second stage begins between the ages of thirteen and nineteen.[2] Teachers and others close to the soloist world call it "the period of crisis." We can find exceptional examples of students who went through this stage earlier than age thirteen. Virtuoso education is individual and contrary to the regular school rules, and the age and the stage of education are not the same for all students. This is why in the following chapters I will cite instances of teenagers as well as children before they are ten years old in my examples of opinions of students in the crisis period.

The students' physical and psychological changes have obvious consequences on their violin playing. Their arms and fingers become longer, but also thicker, which sometimes results in a temporary loss of virtuosity. As their bodies change, the students need to move up in violin sizes. Having started with one-eighth violins (one-sixteenth in rare cases) and moved through quarter, half, three-quarter, and rarely seven/eighth sizes, they attain the full-size violin. The young musicians are happy when they change violin size, because it means that they have reached the next stage of their education. But the new violin creates new playing challenges, though these resolve quickly in most cases.

Perhaps more important, the teen years are typically a period of fewer public performances. Numerous famous soloists of the twentieth century experienced a break in their concert schedules between the ages of about fourteen and twenty.[3] Due to the lack of sources, I am not able to provide an exhaustive list of the causes of that break. To some extent, my own data, which concerns participants of my study, can bring some information about the break in public performances that occurs in the life of future soloists when they are teenagers.

For a large majority of students, the second stage of soloist education is a tough period. Students frequently express feelings of anxiety. As they grasp the competitiveness of the soloist world, they worry about their ability to make it. They become aware of their parents' heavy investment in their careers and the built-up expectations. They feel a duty to become soloists to fulfill the dreams of their parents and extended family. Some are attacked by feelings of guilt. And at this phase of acute psychological and physical stress, they are generally under a growing load of general schoolwork as they prepare for college.[4] All these factors create frequent jitters on stage.

It is no wonder, then, that all the students I interviewed said that at this stage they had questioned their continuation on the professional path. A small number considered abandoning the soloist path, but I am not sure that they did it in the short time after this declaration. I am not able to provide statistics about those who drop out at this stage. Some students changed teachers, and by consequence moved to another city or even country. They left my fieldwork and those networks with which I was familiar; they never participated in important competitions for virtuosos. But did they stop their music education and, if yes, when? This is a process that can take several years. The students interviewed are most often dissatisfied with their performance. None of these students escaped moments of doubt and hesitation concerning their education and the validity of their work as an instrumentalist. Their doubts about the pertinence of their involvement in the violinist virtuoso life increases, and the hope for a glorious future, which was supported by their entourage in the first stage, decreases. The following extract from an interview with a twenty-year-old student illustrates this:

Q: What are your plans?
A: At the moment I don't have any. I wouldn't want to be disillusioned.
Q: Why?
A: Because, among my peers, there are a lot of people who have created plans and had hopes based on nothing. So, I don't know who I am. I don't know what my own value is . . . I won't pretend that I will do better than others.

Even those rare violinists who are always competition finalists, regarded as the shiniest of stars, state that they have had doubt regarding their careers. For the ex-"child prodigy," this crisis stage is especially difficult. After they reach the age of sixteen, they lose the indulgence of the public, which is reserved for the "instrumentalists in short pants."[5] The public is tolerant with the little children, dressed as children, who play the solo violin like adults. When the musician starts to look like an adult, expectations change. Other participants declare that they should redouble their efforts in order to regain the old feeling of mastery of their instrument and to achieve a higher level of skill; this stage is marked by the quest for technical perfection and sharper individual interpretation.

Musicians, too, become more critical of their own performance. The feeling of certainty and conviction that "I play very well and show my mastery" is no longer there. Said an eighteen-year-old former "child prodigy":

> When I left my first teacher I was fifteen. I spent six months correcting my playing position and a lot of time improving psychologically. The last two years have been very difficult. I had major jitters—me, who never had jitters even before a more important public than this one. And I had this horrific feeling of being a nobody who didn't know how to play one single note, a feeling of going backward. I wanted to stop several times and I didn't touch the violin for two months. Fortunately, this time has almost passed, but I feel fragile still, and I have a problem with playing before people . . . It's not like before.

For "ex-prodigy" children it is very difficult to regain trust in themselves. Some students, ex post facto, call this a period of being "down and out."

> It is a normal phenomenon everyone goes through, but not all of them speak about it. We find ourselves no good, straight out crappy, and we don't progress anymore. We don't progress because we don't work, because we don't believe anymore, because we don't feel up to it, because we're growing, because we are tired and fed up with working like a madman for so many years! We want to do stuff like everyone else: cinema, girls, parties! The good life, you see! At that time, I was in a master class and I was really down and out—a few dozen violinists, all excellent, all better than me. And on top of that, a Japanese girl was staying in the room next to mine. It was horrible! I slept for days because I was so bad that I wasn't able to practice, and she played from early morning until late at night! More than ten hours per day. I went crazy! I did nothing during that master class! . . . Everyone goes through this. Some of them drop the violin . . . others continue.

This account about crisis is a typical example of narration about the teenage period. In our Western culture, focused on individual self-reflection, we are used to asking the question about the future, choice of life, profession. This "crisis time" is expected by parents and teachers independently from educational training or area of activity in which young people are involved. This is a general attitude that is considered "natural" at that age. However, in the case of violinists we have the physical aspect of a growing body, which influences in an important way the quality of performance. Moreover, the emotional "fragility" (whatever origin would be— cultural, psychological, or biological) could be an important obstacle to pursuing high activity on the stage and in consequence to continue virtuoso education as a successful student.

Young soloists go through this crisis alone: they push their parents aside and have no one to lean on. It is no wonder they feel so fragile and deeply in doubt, but this phase is necessary if they are to make a soloist career their own. The time in which parents dictated their lives has ended. The decision on whether to go forward with this life must be theirs alone.

The fire that animated the students in the first stage of their education has been quenched, which is typical aspect of "being in the crisis"—the lack of passion for violin training. The students doubt that their placement in the soloist class was appropriate. Some students rail at their parents for having chosen such a difficult path for them. During a rehearsal for an international competition performance, a young student lashes out at her mother: "It's you who got me into the violin, and you don't know how difficult it is! It is not like the piano! I have had enough! And I'm not so wonderful as you say! They are much better! Why should I kill myself, working like a slave?!"

In his or her own manner, each student takes charge of the decisions previously made by parents. I observed five different attitudes. The most frequent one was the confirmation of the parental decision by appropriation: "Everyone decides for himself if he will or will not become a violinist. OK, in the beginning, it's the parents who say, 'practice.' But there comes a time when they are no longer around, and one must make this decision alone. We work alone with our violin, and we may or may not have the desire to play the violin. That's all. Those who don't want to play, drop it. We aren't obliged to play. When we were little, yes, but no longer!"

Some students take a more passive approach. They follow the path traced by their parents, waiting for circumstances to decide for them whether they become soloists. Typically, these students seek another plan of action as a possible alternative "if the soloist career doesn't work out." Typically, such students' "safety net" is a job in a prestigious ensemble (such as the Berlin Philharmonic or the Philadelphia Orchestra) or a chamber music group.

The third type of attitude, which is less common, involves shifting to a nonmusical career. I do not have any data to prove that those declarations bring people to change their professional world or not. However, it is interesting to observe that at this stage of virtuoso education, only a few students take into account the opportunity of a professional future not related to music. This is a rare attitude while the option of not becoming a musician requires the training in other than music fields (mathematics, biology, genetics). Rare are those who have the resources (a good level of knowledge in those disciplines) to plan such a career reorientation. One student wants to become a genetics researcher in case his soloist career fails. Another student wants to become a psychologist. These students are cautious, because they see the need to have a career backup, but if they gain success on the soloist path, the security options would be tossed out.

The fourth type of attitude (also rare) is illustrated by this nine-year-old student, who without hesitation pursued the way chosen by her parents:

> I've always liked the violin, and I had no one specific moment when I decided that I wanted to become a professional. My mother really hesitated to start [violin education] with my brother, because she knew that it is so difficult and that for playing well, it is necessary to practice it seriously, professionally, and if not, it would be easy to lose the pleasure in playing. I've always gotten pleasure from playing. . . . I was lucky to have a very motivating teacher. And after a certain time, when I found that he [the teacher] didn't give me correct lessons, I went looking for someone else.

This violinist, today a successful soloist, represents a small group of students who never had doubts about their parental choices. The instability so characteristic of this second stage of education affects these violinists only in their concerns about playing technique or teaching methods. These students never question their future as violinists.

The fifth attitude is one of strong opposition to the parents leading to abandonment of violin education. This is also rarely observed among students in the soloist class.

It is not easy to find students who have changed their professional path, because in the soloist world, the rejection of the soloist career is perceived as a failure. The students who leave the path disappear from the musical universe, regardless of their one-time fame.[6] Teachers, parents, and students typically keep silent about them. Silence preserves faith in the soloist career of the students who continue.

Although it is difficult to interview students who have abandoned the soloist career, I met three of them. The first had dropped all musical education and finished his studies in computer science. Sometimes, he plays guitar (self-taught). This comment, provoked by the concert performance of a twenty-three-year-old violinist, explains his renunciation of the violin, and his regrets:

> This is the first time in my life that I have regretted my decision—just today—and because of this concert! They are both wonderful [the violinist and the pianist]. When I think that I could play as he [the violinist] does today, I am pissed off! But I never wanted to work a lot throughout my life with the violin, so I stopped at thirteen. My parents couldn't force me any longer. Two years of screaming and negotiations was enough. I didn't work . . . not enough . . . although it seems that I was made for the violin.

Abandonment of violin education does not always mean a definitive exit from the musical world. Another former soloist student, the son of an orchestra conductor and a pharmacist, learned how to play another instrument and became a pop/jazz professional. Classical training can help prepare for other genres:[7]

> I was enrolled in the class of Warecki [a famous class in Poland], and I was one of his best students. . . . But around fourteen I'd had enough of working like a crazy man, and everyone knew that Warecki went off on his students so hard that it was even difficult to imagine. I had no more desire to be terrified before and during each lesson. Then some friends and I started a band, and I tried to play bass guitar; and, it was so easy for me! The music came by itself . . . no problem! So I said to myself, "You have to be crazy to continue playing such a difficult instrument, if so many others exist that can be played more easily and without much work." Some months after my father had immigrated to South America, I dropped the violin and became a bass player. I don't regret anything.

The third former soloist student dropped out to become a medical student. At a time when instrumental practice and scholarly studies were increasingly at odds with one another, he decided that soloist violin was incompatible with a more general education.

GO TO SCHOOL OR STUDY AT HOME?

In most of Europe, legal school obligations end at age sixteen. Nearly all students taught in Eastern Europe benefit from special schooling in institutions that combine modified general teaching with intense musical education. These kinds of schools, especially the Central School in Moscow, are a model for Yehudi Menuhin's school in Folkestone in Great Britain and the Pre-College Division of the Juilliard School of Music in New York. Young students at this latter institution attend a general school part time.

In Europe, the completion of school obligations varies depending on the country and the system of musical education. In Eastern Europe (Poland, Hungary, Romania, Russsia, etc.), musician-students have obligatory general education classes until they pass an SAT-equivalent exam at the age of eighteen or nineteen. They require this degree to pursue their studies, because musical teaching is organized in university institutions where all students are required to pass an entrance test after the SAT type of exam. For this reason, Eastern European violinists all attend special schools for gifted children. They have no choice, unlike their colleagues in Western European countries.

Western European students have more options. In France, special public schools have schedules that provide general education while preparing students for a music diploma. However, soloist teachers still advise their students against attending such schools, because their busy schedules hinder intensive violin practice.[8] A second possibility is to pursue an education through correspondence (the equivalent of today's online colleges). Two famous French violinists, Gérard Poulet and Patrice Fontanarosa, studied in this system (Hattemer Cours—a private school—was the first French school to adopt this system). Most soloist students living in France take general courses through correspondence with the state institution, CNED (National Center for Homeschooling).

This system allows students the freedom to organize their schedules and prepare for national exams in general disciplines in an individual manner, without the constraints of long school hours. This system also has a supplementary advantage: the students can choose their own major. They may prepare for a music degree, but that diploma does not have a good reputation and precludes later study of several specialties. After receiving a musical diploma (F11—the "musical bac"), students usually find careers in music teaching. I met only one student who remained at school and attained her degree in literature. She missed many courses, so her mother, a teacher, negotiated with the principal and teachers to excuse her for long absences. This student was alone in pursuing a soloist education in conjunction with a "typical" education. For the majority of soloists, the decision to pursue a general education in a full-time system decreases their availability. This forces them to abandon soloist training, as a former soloist class student, who became a medical student, reports:

> I was good in violin, and I was at a good technical level. Before high school, I was
> in a violin class in which all students were excellent. I followed the master classes;
> I played virtuoso pieces at a very early age: Bazzini, Paganini, the "Devil's Trill"

Sonata . . . and then my parents were opposed to my enrollment in the CNED [correspondence school], and when I started high school, the violin was finished for me. I didn't play anymore because with my work in medical school, I had no free time. It's a pity, but with this instrument . . . if you stop practicing, you lose your skill very quickly and it becomes very difficult.

Soloist teachers are usually opposed to anything other than "correspondence" school, and push their students in this direction. Most soloist students try to limit the amount of time spent in general school education. But they insist that the choice be theirs:

It was I who decided about my school. They [his parents] have always supported me, guided me, because they are musicians and know the system well. For example, when I entered to the Conservatory of Paris, I told my parents that I would stop school because I really wanted to work on my violin. I wanted to take up lessons by correspondence. They thought it was too early to drop school, but I said, "I need to practice in the morning, from 8 A.M. to 12 P.M., and after from 2 P.M. to 5 P.M." I was very motivated to work on my violin, and I didn't see myself attending school. So it was I who made the choice.

This student was thirteen when she enrolled in correspondence school. She finished school at sixteen, without obtaining her French baccalaureate diploma. Violinists who choose the correspondence route cite the reduced time to graduation from general education. Said another soloist, who obtained a baccalaureate in math (both parents are mathematicians and musician-amateurs):

I always wanted to play the violin, and since the time I found out that you must earn money to live, I wanted to become a violinist—not necessarily as a soloist. It could be as an orchestral musician, and I thought that I could also teach. I wanted to do correspondence school because it saved me time, and I was enrolled in a math field because math was so easy for me![9] I didn't have to work a lot for the exam; I have a lot of skill when it comes to science.

Not all students who took correspondence school did so because they were committed to a soloist career. In fact, many saw this route as one that kept other options open. Said a violinist who had not determined a final career path:

Even when I lived in Paris, which has special general schools for artists, I never wanted to enroll in that kind of school. They prepare you for the F11 exam [musical specialization], which for me is not a true [baccalaureate] exam. Yes, OK, I'm a musician, and that's good, but one day I may not be able to play violin as a soloist. If that were the case I'd prefer another job, and because I'm passionate about the sciences, above all microbiology and genetics, I wanted to do the "bac spe-bio" [state exam in science—specialty of biology]. With my schedule—seven or eight hours per day of violin practice, it is not possible to go to high school. So, starting from the sixth grade, I was enrolled in a correspondence school.

Other students attended a general school until they received their baccalaureate, thanks to modifications of their programs that allowed them schedule classes "à la carte." This French student, despite a strong involvement in her soloist project, wanted to pass the general school system:

> I had two very difficult periods when it was hard to do both things at once, and everyone asked me how I could manage it. OK, it was difficult, but I worked very quickly at school. I did my schoolwork really fast, and afterward I worked on my violin. At that time, I was in a general school in Marseilles. I had never been enrolled in a special music school, because in Marseilles this kind of school works with a conservatory, and I was not a conservatory student—my teacher lived 500 kilometers from my city. I also liked literature, and I wanted to have a baccalaureate of literature. My mother also said that having a free afternoon at the age of twelve or thirteen was not a good option. School was never an obstacle for my violin work; the year of my baccalaureate exam I started working most intensively on my violin, because I had begun lessons with Madam Lubov. I was very motivated and school came easily. Science was not my thing, maybe because it would have taken too much time. I finished secondary school at seventeen, a year ahead of everyone else, because I had skipped second grade. That was a huge advantage. At seventeen, I had my baccalaureate, and was free to work on my violin. That was the main goal: to finish school as quickly as possible in order to play the violin more.

This student's experience was unusual; her mother, a schoolteacher, was able to organize her schedule, negotiating free time during competition periods.[10] Also, two of the girl's violinist brothers had earlier been enrolled in correspondence school and ended up never finishing secondary school. The mother blamed this on weak supervision, which is characteristic for correspondence schools. Sometimes, however, students have no choice but to enroll in correspondence schools, as in the case of this immigrant student:

> I had a lot of problems with the school in France. From my first day there, I was already behind. I didn't know the language, neither did my parents, so nobody could help me. I was in a class with children younger than me, and because of concerts and violin practice, I missed a lot of lessons. So my father enrolled me in this correspondence school, but the level was very high and I got more and more behind. I had more and more concerts. The bottom line is, I was enrolled to obtain a document showing that I went to school, but I did the minimum.

The experience of this soloist student, who did not finish primary school, shows that emigration can play an important role in how general studies are pursued.

Other students avoid correspondence school because they feel it isolates them from their peers. This was the case with Marion, whose mother said:

> For a long time now, I've wanted Marion to attend CNED and Regina [her teacher] agrees. I was thinking about this other famous private school; they have excellent teachers, and with lessons once a week, they have rigor that is lacking in

CNED. But Marion didn't want to hear that, because in her class [for gifted children] there was a good atmosphere, she had friends and all that. She was scared that if she went to CNED, she'd miss party invitations. This is very important at her age. But her friends are not involved in soloist classes. They take ordinary classes in a conservatory, so they don't work as much on their violins. Next year, I think Regina will force Marion into the CNED.

It would be overly simplistic to assume that the most dedicated soloist students choose one type or another of general education.[11] I found general school students among the very determined soloists, and students who doubted their soloist careers taking correspondence courses. Entry into a particular school system could result from unusual circumstances, as with immigrant students, or particular personal values, such as Marion, who wished to stick with her general classes for social reasons.

There is no typical general school experience for soloist class students because each country has its own system. In France, it is not exceptional for students to leave general school without receiving a baccalaureate diploma. Some students within my sample quit general study between the ages of fourteen and sixteen. A French soloist explains,

I stopped in the second class [at sixteen] because I was in CNED, and at that time I was studying in the US, so it was hard for me. The American [school] required me to pass the exam for their musical diploma, because they did not recognize my certificates from the Parisian conservatory, since I was very young. It was interesting; everything was in English, such as music theory. I don't consider that a waste of my time, but I dropped my general school in France [she never was graduated from general education in the United States either].

Most dropouts were fifteen or older, but I encountered some much younger, such as Vasia, a Russian violinist. He came to France at the age of seven but "escaped" (as his father put it) the French educational system for one year (school obligation begins at age six). He then began ordinary public school but remained only a few months. His parents, shocked that French children remained in school until 4:30 and not until 12:30, as in Russia, withdrew him. The parents then moved Vasia into a private school, where he had an individual schedule, attending school only once a week. But at that time, Vasia was already behind in comparison to other French pupils: he spoke French fluently, but his writing was very poor. As a consequence, he was put into a class of children three or four years his junior. The family had little interest in general study and were of little assistance at home (neither parent spoke French fluently), so Vasia left school before receiving a primary school certificate (at fourteen). In the French system, this deficiency is not an obstacle for pursuing a professional musical education. At twenty-three, when I interviewed him, Vasia was a successful performer.

As both stories suggest, a change in the country of residence, system of education, and language of learning contribute to the abandonment of general study. However, not only immigrant students are prone to this course. Some natives abandon general school because, as one student explained, "they want to be free from the shackles which general study imposes," in order to devote more time to instrumental practice.

A survey of soloists' biographies shows that they usually put general education in second place, after violin practice. However, the context was different in the early twentieth century, when bourgeois families still frequently hired private tutors, and it was common for mothers to take the entire responsibility for their children's education. Nathan Milstein in Russia and Yehudi Menuhin in the United States were home schooled. Isaac Stern, in his autobiography, states that the school administrator forced him to take an IQ test to determine his level of backwardness from having missed regular schooling. After scoring well on the test, he was relieved from attending school altogether (Stern and Potok 2000: 20–21).

Two other well-known violinists in the twentieth century did, however, finish their higher study in a domain other than music or the arts. Fritz Kreisler (1875–1962) was a medical student; Gil Shaham (born in 1971) studied mathematics. Kreisler pursued his study thanks to private tutors; in doing so, he was able to practice violin as well. Gil Shaham, like so many soloist students, attended a special school for gifted children and then became a rare example of someone who pursued another specialty.

Soloist students have a highly specific lifestyle that includes violin lessons, competitions, concerts, and individual practice, along with a structured reward system (e.g. competition prizes, scholarships, support from "well-known individuals in the milieu"). Early on, young students become part of a professional milieu, and this professional investment is important, as Becker and Strauss (1956) remarked in their study of careers.

When an unexpected event disturbs the ordinary life of a soloist student, the peculiarity of his or her lifestyle shows up very clearly, as in this anecdote:

> It happened when I had hand surgery. Nothing serious, but I realized that my days were completely empty! Nothing to do! No more six hours of work, no lessons, no rehearsals with my pianist, no commuting. I found myself struck at how many free days I'd have. But instead of being happy the whole time and taking advantage of these free days by living like other young people my age—going to movies, or parties, I was scared to death. How will I do it? I will die of boredom! Two months without the violin! I will lose everything!

This exceptional situation brings to light the degree of personal commitment made by these young musicians. Their style of life is very different from peers whose activities consist of general school studies and the life of a teenager: sports, games, friends, young love, and pleasure. Young violinists, who lived through the first stage of their education in a closed box created by their parents and teacher, modify the box (when they are teenagers), distancing themselves from their parents but remaining in isolation. They continued on a path in this specific world thanks to the support and guidance of their teachers. Now they try to find a perfect master.

If they think that their teacher is that person, they look to that teacher as a model, believing that this path, so well known and so deeply communicated to them through the years, exists for them. They would like to see the master as the perfect realization of the model set out for them as the goal of their lives.

THE MASTERS AND THEIR CLASSES

The teacher's style influences his or her relationships with students and is a crucial element in the development of the soloist. My observations of lessons suggest that different teachers follow a particular model of teaching that exists in their discourse. There are also deviations from the model. Each professor, it appears, imposes a style of teaching and a type of relationship with students. I will first examine the "idealized" model that is common among the soloist milieu and the present variants I observed. This will make up the framework for analyzing the teacher-student relationship. Believing in the importance of interaction, I show how this typology is dynamic. Students also influence the quality of teaching relationship. This is why, after the typology analyzed below, I will provide an account of three lessons with the same teacher. There it will be clear that even a charismatic teacher with his or her own style of working is dependent on the student. We will see how those relationships are complex and far from models presented in the interviews by professors.

In the idealized representation of the master-student relationship, frequently glorified in narratives (for example in artists' biographies), the term "family" is frequently used. A good example comes from Arcady Fouter: "The class of Yuri Yankelevich was a big, working and unified family. The accompanists were complete members of the class and profoundly respected. Yankelevich never broke off a relationship with a student who had finished their education. He remained their advisor and friend in ordinary life" (Fouter in Brusillovsky 1999: 331).[12]

The underlining of the familial character of the special class is common to specialized education (sports, theater, dance, etc.). The characterization of the class as a family evokes the patriarchal role of the teacher, modeled on the head of family. In the soloist class, as in a large family, the children of different ages are together (this is not always the case in a school class or instrumental class of music school, in which the children are grouped together based on age). The soloist class students spend their time together, even outside of their instrumental activities. In some cases, they live in a boarding school or away from their own families. Finally, the teachers, who work with their students several times a week in the music school and in their homes, create a group that functions much like a family.

In his evocation, Arcady Fouter underlines the adjective "working" for this class. This trait differentiates the soloist class from the typical family, which, in most cases (farming may be an exception) in modern Western society no longer centers around common work. This contradiction does not disturb the soloists and teachers. They devote their time to reaching the main goal—attaining a high level of instrumental performance. Another particular aspect of a soloist class that Fouter notes, and which teachers like to point out, is the sustenance of teacher-student ties long after the lessons have finished.

Promoting the familial image, the teachers involved in the activity of young soloists reinforce the distinction between the ordinary violin class and the elite class. This ideal vision of the class and its teamwork is not shared by students and their parents. The conflicts among the three categories (teacher-students-parents) concerns the hierarchy. While the teacher speaks about the class using the word "family," students and their parents use other terms. Some compare the class to a "camp" in the military sense, or a "network."

The homogeneity of teachers' discourse is similar to the homogeneity of students' statements that their teachers determine the relationship and mood within the class entourage. The soloist class is perceived and categorized on the basis of this important person. The students' narratives mix comments about the teacher's pedagogical practices, behavior, and matters such as the decor of the classroom. The various aspects of soloist education overlap into what students call the "ambiance" of the class.

Through the following examples, I show how the model presented by teachers contrasts with the situations found in the field. I also show how the "ambiance" features influence the soloist's education. Several types of classes presented below give a specific frame for performing a lesson provided by a master. Because of the elite aspects of this teaching, the frame should be different from a normal class. This is more than marketing tool; this is the seal of the excellence, transmitted by previous generations of famous teachers directly or via biographical books and numerous insiders talks. This is the part of the virtuoso culture. The style of teaching, or rather (in the case of public teaching) presenting the art of transformation from a violin student into a virtuoso, from an adolescent into an artist, is made in different styles.

The Class as a Theater

This first type of style exemplifies common beliefs about a certain artistic education, and revolves around teachers who already have a strong reputation in the world of violinists.[13] These famous masters give lessons attended by public audiences; they work in a way so as to satisfy this public. This teaching style involves continuous looks in the direction of the public, discussions with the audience, and explanations of the pedagogical work. The teacher walks on stage and plays his own violin to give an example. Then he plays on a student's violin, making noticeable gestures that may be aimed at the student but are exaggerated so that the public can also follow along.

Boris is a teacher who likes to dazzle with his talent as a teacher and to demonstrate that he is a polyglot. He cares a great deal about his public image. Each visitor who drops by his class as a guest is questioned during a short break in the lesson. Each visitor needs to explain the reason for his or her presence.[14] Sometimes, in my observation, he pointed his commentaries in the direction of the spectators. When, without knowing Russian, an Israeli teacher attended several lessons taught in Russian, Boris translated a part of his comments and advice into German (which the Israeli teacher understood). To each sentence, he added an explanation. Afterward, he looked at me and asked, "You follow me? You didn't need a translation?" He expressed his feelings in a very theatrical manner; he became upset if the students were not able to make the proper corrections immediately. Once, he stomped his foot and screamed very loudly, "No, no! It is not like that. You need play like this! I told you already!" When he was satisfied, he smiled and congratulated the student.

N. Ijevskaïa—an accompanist of the famous Russian teacher Y. Yankelevich—described his classes in a similar vein: "Like all artists, he liked the public and he appreciated when a talented student with whom he had the pleasure of working would come when his class was filled with an audience. If something was particularly well done, he would glance at the audience to read the emotions that the performance provoked. It was a look that seemed to ask, 'It is well done, no?'" (N. Ijevskaïa in Brussilovsky 1999: 337).

For this category of teachers, the class is a sort of theater in which the master creates a stage to aid in the art of teaching. The master makes the students participate in this environment, which strongly influences the manner of play. Thanks to this practice, the students become familiar with having an audience and accustomed to being on stage. Many years after their education, Yankelevich students who became well known in the soloist world described their lessons as a time of joy and pleasure: "Y. Yankelevich was so invested in the work of his students that he forgot himself. Each lesson became a celebration, and the particular ambiance was transmitted to each student, and each violinist played in a different manner" (Brussilovsky 1999: 284).

These recollections from a former student of a famous master contrast with the testimonies I collected from young soloists. For a future virtuoso, to be part of a famous class performing in front of a public stimulates the perception that one is being evaluated. Consequently, the students become fearful that they may not be good enough, and they work hard for their public lessons. The "personality" of their teacher, who creates a theatrical drama, impresses them, as suggested by the following extract from an interview:

It is not easy to play in these circumstances. It's theater! The TV often records the classes and the concert hall is nearly full. The teacher walks on stage and makes important movements. That's it—a show! For example, last week he said to a student who was just before me: "How can it be? It is not possible anymore in western Ukraine to learn how to play in tune?" And he ended by saying: "Come back when you are ready." After that, it was my turn with the sonata. I needed to be relaxed and it was very hard to do so before him—one of the most important violinists in the world—and before this audience. This is not a violin lesson! And then he said, "Relax," and he showed me how. He spoke half to me and half to the public. And when I played well, he was proud, as if it were he who was playing.

While this type of theater-class creates an intense emotional strain on the students, it helps prepare students for their professional lives. The teachers' expectations, expressed in demands for immediate correction, compel students to have an excellent mastery of their instrument and exceptional self-control. Such lessons are good for preparing students for competitions. By experiencing "class-theater"-style lessons, violinists learn how to adapt to public performances and competitions.

The Office-Class: Death from Boredom

I observed another example of class style with two teachers. Based on informal talks with students, I call this style "office-class." It is completely different from the previous model in terms of the teacher's investment and the staging of attendance. According to his students, the teacher of the "office-class" is not motivating: he appears uninvolved, distant, and boring; the teaching is ordered and repetitive, and the teacher acts the same toward each student. An example of such a class comes from observation of a forty-three-year-old teacher with a reputation of giving serious and solid lessons. The students who join this class desire regular lessons throughout the school year. Although the lessons are open to the public, spectators are few. The teacher speaks in a monotonous voice, without gestures or addressing the public, such as it is. He sits on the chair, puts the violin on his knee and gives advice. He always starts and finishes on time, never prolonging the lesson. It is as if he has had a similar plan for each student, past and present; only the pieces played change. In the world in which individual approach and passionate involvement is highly valued, this kind of teaching is not really appreciated.

Some students find that this class is boring and dull: "Everything here is similar: the fingering, his voice, and his investment is similar for each one of us. However, what is good is that he gives regular lessons, and I think that this is why he has good students. But we fret. . . . It is not at all a good ambiance for work."

Boredom is usually a stranger in the world of the musical elite, but this teacher is doing his part to create it. Students of this class have some success in violin competitions, but at the time of my study, no one had experienced the goal they all hoped to achieve—a first-place award in a competition and the pursuit of a soloist's career. While students join this class because of the teacher's reputation for "serious work," many will abandon it because they feel a lack of motivation to do the work that the students insist is necessary for soloist education.

Cafeteria-Class

In the third class type I observed, the environment was similar to that of a cafeteria at a university, a place of convivial meetings from which the smell of coffee and cookies emanated. The door of this class opened frequently: people entered and exited freely; some spoke with students from other classes or observed another student's lesson. Students described the ambiance of this class as stress-free and easygoing, but sloppy, because the lessons were frequently interrupted. The students rarely knew when their lessons would begin because the master (a woman of more than sixty) instructed them to come "a little later and then we'll see." According to a former student (her current assistant), the number of interruptions greatly increased after the invention of cell phones.

These conditions make learning during the lesson difficult, and the students complain of the teacher's lack of involvement.

> People constantly open the door and enter to say "hello" and gossip while you are playing. . . . It is a souk![15] Also, it is necessary to come several times a day, and in that case it is you who disturbs other lessons, because you always need to ask at what time your lesson begins, and the lessons never start on time anyway! This is a hard environment if you want to work seriously, even if it is "cool." It's a pity because she [the teacher] gives good advice . . . when she wants to.

Although all students complained about the lessons' organization, this teacher has continually retained students because of the teacher's soloist past and her reputation as a powerful woman in the music world. The "cool" style attracts students, but only for a short time; students who abandon such lessons are numerous. According to participants, this type of class is not exceptional: I assembled similar testimonies about the ambiance of other classes. One of them is well known throughout the soloist world, and is conducted by a woman, age seventy, who seems to be a grandmother with a gentle voice. She is not only interested in her students' music, but also in their private lives. Her entourage is very large, and "she knows everything about her students." The lessons take place in a relaxed environment with plenty of coffee and cookie scents. The teacher encourages the students; she is very protective, and they seem calm, but despite this idyllic picture, they live in a continuous state of stress.

The biggest problem with this teacher, many students said, is not the quality of the lesson. The students in this class swim in the ambiance of mastery and virtuoso music in the presence of a large public under the famous teacher's eye. That is all well and good. But this revered teacher, at the last stage of her career, unfortunately operates in a way that is typical of famous music teachers: she recruits more students than her schedule allows. She overbooks. In addition to paying her, students need good "savoir vivre" and negotiating skills to reserve their lessons, which are organized by the music school (a famous institution). These negotiations are not easy and they are recurrent. The students are constantly preempted by colleagues or parents of young violinists, who, in either a direct or indirect manner, make arrangements in order to enter the class. Several students complained: "It is difficult to battle for each lesson. The atmosphere among students is very bad." As a consequence of the teacher's reputation, she continually attracts new streams of candidates, creating new hitches in her schedule. And thus in spite of the excellent and relaxed relationships among the teacher and her students, some of them quit the class. They tire of the conditions associated with being her pupil: a poor learning environment and competition for access.

The Sporting-Class

Just as preparatory classes for high-level performers are organized for competitions, so are some soloist classes. In the fourth type of soloist class, which I call "sporting class," the teacher places the students in a permanent competition inside their own class, in which they are compared not only to each other but to previous students. During a lesson, I heard the following remarks expressed many times to a student: "At your age, Franceska had already played the 24th cappricio of Paganini, and how she played it!!! . . . at your age, Carla won the competition in Zurich. She was only twelve years old and played better than those who were twenty-two!"

Contrary to the "cool and relaxed manner" of some teachers, the masters of a "sporting class" are not looking to establish a family atmosphere. Their students are there only to give everything of themselves and to prove that they can win. The teacher treats each student with a similar approach, but works longer with those who are potentially closer to victory in a competition.

Lessons are done before a public, always in the presence of parents (until adolescence). At each lesson, the students receive goals precisely set: "You need to play the 36th measure with the metronome at 120 on a quarter note, fifteen times" or "You have two weeks to prepare the concerto at the final speed." This means the student needs to prepare very important pieces, which are new to them, at the speed imposed by the composer, which is frequently very difficult to achieve in a few days.

The teacher plays very little during the lessons, whose feeling of ironbound discipline evokes a military drill field. This strict disciplinary atmosphere seems quite contrary to the ideal of a soloist education that nurtures creativity and independence in an artist.

The Team Soloist Class

In another type of class, the teacher seeks to introduce the competitive spirit to his students, but with a different approach. This class type is extracted from the testimony of Stoliarsky's students, who worked with him in Odessa in the beginning of the twentieth century. This violinist worked with numerous children simultaneously, strongly encouraging their efforts, but also placing them in a competition. Some of his students—those who became soloists (Nathan Milstein and David Oistrakh) as adults—judged that this class ambiance was not incapacitating for them.

> The pupils took lessons at Stolyarsky's apartment. Every day, ten to fifteen little kids came to him. The professor had four rooms, and musical squeaks and noises came from each of them. Often Stolyarsky brought us together and we would play in unison. . . . Stolyarsky selected pieces for his pupils that could be played in unison—not only because it was easier for him to control the horde but because it was good for us: by playing together we learned from each other. We would glance around to see who was doing what and who was better. (Milstein and Volkov 1983: 6)

The author called his class "a musical kolkhoz." This type of organization was partially employed by Suzuki, the creator of a method of violin teaching based on the simultaneous playing of numerous violin students. This approach is usually employed for children, and the example given by Milstein above concerned kids. However, the spirit of collective enterprise characteristic of "team soloist class" is certainly perceived in classes where teenage students are working. The specificity of soloist training includes the rule of no age limits at entrance. A famous professor for soloists could have children younger than ten years old in his class as well as a twenty-year-old violinist.

The "Torture Chamber"

To round out the possible class types one must mention Ivan Galamian's class, which one student described as the "torture chamber" (Lourie-Sand 2000: 48). An ambiance of fear reigned during the lessons, and students were scared. Teachers in Galamian's school gave lessons in a very authoritarian manner, exercising pressure on their disciples. I have observed similar classes where it was not rare to see students, facing an audience of other children, crying in fear before and during the lesson. The stressful character of certain teachers' lessons is the subject of much talk among students' parents. A fifty-year-old pianist, the mother of a sixteen year-old violinist, told me that her son had an asthma attack during a violin lesson. She attributed this incident to the tension provoked by the lesson. Her son needed to take drugs in order to stop the attack and continue: "It was simple. I knew that in advance. Jules begins the lesson and he immediately has an attack. I always had the Ventoline [an asthma drug] in my handbag, and it was impossible to take lessons without it. He was afraid of his teacher. When we changed the class, the attacks became very rare."

Many parents worry about the pressures their children undergo during their violin education. However, such feelings rarely compel them to change teachers. In interviews and informal talks, parents were convinced that pressure is part of soloist education. Nathan Milstein, a former student of Leopold Auer, well known for his emotional austerity, affirms that the stress imposed by the teacher improves the student's quality of play: "It's important for the teacher to be unpredictable and potentially explosive. Then the pupil tries harder to avert a scene and subsequent punishment. In the final analysis, this instinct for survival improves the quality of playing" (Milstein and Volkov 1983: 26).

I observed numerous lessons with teachers who exercised pressure on their students. If for North American parents this situation could be surprising (we can see the reaction of the public to Amy Chua's book and her account about pressure experienced by her daughters—music students; Chua 2011). Why do young virtuoso parents accept this? In Europe it is common that parents express a similar opinion that the hostility of a teacher is necessary to the virtuoso education (actually in France similar expectations could be formulated toward general education institutions—learning something is related to effort, hard work, and sometimes suffering of students). Moreover, this kind of unpleasant approach is perceived as a sign of excellence in violin teaching—not only by parents but also by students. Following lessons with a strict and exacting teacher, the young violinists find themselves in a situation that, because of the tension, resembles the environment of competitions, exams, or concerts. These events are customary for the elite of the musical world.

The "Ideal Class"

During many conversations with students in the last stage of their education, they spoke longingly of a particular famous teacher's class. This teacher never missed lessons and had a particular style. In his class, the lesson frequently lasted much longer than expected, with few breaks. In a class I observed, the teacher spoke slowly. His gestures were kind. He smiled and was in a good mood. In this class, it seemed that only the teacher and his students existed. He was not there to play a theatrical piece, nor did he show concern for the public. Students waiting for a lesson listen to the previous one. No one speaks except for the teacher and the student. Only between two lessons can questions about organization be raised. No one knows how long the lesson will last. The teacher explains this to his new student: "The lesson runs as long as necessary: sometimes five minutes, and sometimes five hours. If a student comes with ten hours' worth of work, the lesson lasts ten hours."

This teacher is considered exceptional in the soloist milieu, because he works in a very assiduous manner, never missing classes because of events such as competitions and master classes, which are the principal activity of some soloist teachers. His class, in a superior music school, contains ten students. They never pay for supplementary lessons, although some receive four times more instruction than is scheduled.

Several students from his class became soloists, and three of them became well known before finishing their education. One of the students, now a soloist and also a teacher, has his own class and tries to adopt a similar organization and dedication, but he finds it difficult. Conducting two careers simultaneously (as a soloist and a teacher) is too hard.

Dissonance between the "Ideal Class" and Observed Situations

Clearly, there is dissonance between the image of a soloist class that some teachers and former students diffuse, and the reality as described by current students. This difference may partly be due to the changing structure of soloist education. Around 1980, starting with political changes in Eastern Europe, the work environment for the best teachers changed, and so did the operation of their classes. Many top-flight teachers now work in a few cities and sometimes in more than one country, maintaining a stable of dozens of students in each locale. Under these conditions, their classes function much like master classes: the lessons are intensive and occur close in time (for example every two days). The teachers' absences are frequent, and very often an assistant replaces the teacher. The majority of the teachers with the best reputations are engaged in several teaching projects at one time (more than one soloist class in different cities, several master classes, and competitions to prepare and to participate as a judge). It is difficult for such teachers to focus on the principal activity: giving violin lessons.

RELATIONSHIP BETWEEN TEACHER AND STUDENT: THE CAREER COUPLING PROCESS

No soloist can create a successful career without a successful relationship with his or her teacher. Soloist students search for a teacher who can provide them with total expertise in the art of playing. Young virtuosos are unanimous about the necessity of studying with a "great master." In response to the question, is it necessary to study with a master to become a soloist? this young virtuoso, the student of a very famous teacher, states "Yes, absolutely! We need someone that we can copy . . . the teacher's advice is one thing, but to have someone we can imitate is necessary."

Another student, whose parents turned down an opportunity for him to study under Brilov, felt this had been a fatal mistake in his career path:

> If my parents (when I was twelve), had accepted the proposition of Brilov, I would not be at the same moment in my career that I am now. At the age of eighteen, I would probably have participated in important competitions and I would have finished in the finale. But I was not with Brilov and now, I am still always at the stage of technical correction, because since the age of fourteen I have changed my teacher four times. OK, now I am finally in good hands, but my parents made a huge mistake six years earlier when they opposed enrolling me in Brilov's class. It is a pity and probably irretrievable for my career.

In the light of this study, the suppositions of cited student are correct. His parents replied that Brilov's teaching led several students into troubles. Too much pressure in conjunction with absence of family and the ambiance of the "rat race" were responsible for all kinds of psychological and personality difficulties, which, as numerous anecdotes provide, were frequently observed among Brilov students.

The process of career coupling involves interactions between the careers of the initiator and the newcomer. The two categories must work together. Young people, obviously, are socialized into elite circles through the education and introductions they get from members of the elite. For the elite, collaborations with the young are key to furthering their own careers. Most violin soloist teachers no longer do intensive violin practice (six to eight hours per day) or tour, and thus the professional activity of their students is, by extension, their own.

Such dependency is best illustrated by the case of Eastern European violin teachers who emigrated in the 1990s. They struggled to take their best students, who were their "business cards," to Europe or to the United States. Without these imported star students, the teachers' careers would have collapsed, because these immigrant teachers would have had to build up new soloist classes just as their earlier reputations were slipping away. To create a good impression, a soloist teacher must always appear very busy and never seem to be hunting for new students. Of course, he or she is always ready to hear and assess a new candidate for career coupling.

We can distinguish three main stages in the career coupling process: matching, active cooperation, and passive collaboration. The following section is devoted to the deep analysis of this social process.

Collaboration is the basis of the career coupling process. Here, I use the term "collaboration" to define the work between teacher and student, emphasizing that teachers and not just students benefit from the master/disciple relationship. This fact has rarely been pointed out in studies of elite education (for an exception, see Wagner 2006b).

By joining the stable of an elite teacher, the student not only learns how to play, but also benefits from the master's label of excellence. This label is the "trademark" (an expression used by the students) or the "master's seal" or "master's mark" (expressions employed by teachers). The student's performances are the final work product of teacher and student—the result of their collaboration. In becoming excellent, the young soloists who perform on stage confirm (or create) the reputation of the teacher. The performances of the student are continually credited to both the student and his or her teacher. The commonly heard expression "The master played through his students" reflects the fact that the career of a soloist teacher depends heavily on the students' careers.

The "matching process" consists of the selection of collaborators and the trial period of their collaboration. When the student finds a teacher who seems to correspond to his or her expectations, and the teacher accepts this student into his or her class, the parties enter into a matching period in which they try to adapt to reciprocal expectations. The master class system is an ideal setting in which to determine whether a longer partnership is possible.

In order to illustrate the relationships between teacher and student in the different stages, in the following section I will describe three lessons I observed. The first student is at the selection stage—just before the first stage of the career coupling process. The second student is at the matching stage—the first stage of the career coupling—in the trial period. The third student is in the stage of active collaboration. After a very detailed description of these three lessons and their analyses, it will be clear how this career coupling process works in the soloist world.

Master-Disciple Relationships

At the second stage of soloist education, the master class lesson is similar to an ordinary soloist lesson of the type taken by students year-round with their principal teacher. For some students, the difference between both types of lessons (master class lesson and ordinary soloist lesson) is related to their status. The students who work all year long (or over several years) with this master do not have the same position as students who work only sporadically (during the master class). The following examples relate to both cases. The first student takes lessons with this teacher from time to time, and the third is a year-round student. The second lesson concerns a student who wants to apply to the soloist class conducted by this teacher; she takes up lessons with him only during the master class. These three examples clearly show all the specific elements frequently observed in the soloist world.

All the teacher's actions during the lessons, especially the public lessons, are specific to the second stage of education. The master plays his role with theatrical carriage, which conforms to the tradition of the virtuoso world. In the following observation, the master lesson corresponds to the situation described by Goffman (1973: 40–41):

> It may be noted that in the case of some statuses, dramatization presents no problem, since some of the acts which are instrumentally essential for the completion of the core task of the status are at the same time wonderfully adapted, from the point of view of communication, as means of vividly conveying the qualities and attributes claimed by the performer. The roles of prizefighters, surgeons, violinists, and policemen are cases in point. These activities allow for so much dramatic self-expression that exemplary practitioners—whether real or fictional—become famous and are given a special place in the commercially organized fantasies of the nation.

In the soloist world, this tradition has been maintained for many years. Here, I introduce this theatrical presentation, conducted by a famous practitioner in his discipline, who possesses the mastery of soloist teaching. In ensuring the commercial prosperity of his enterprise, he becomes an authority in the soloist world.

Three Lessons

The three following lessons take place with the same teacher, on the same day, in the same environment, with the same pianist—a good "control" situation in which to observe the varying levels of collaboration. It is winter, late 1990s, in a European capital with many Russian artists, on the top floor of an early twentieth-century building. The forty-square-meter classroom is usually occupied by a local private music school. In this small space stands a piano of low quality, some old school benches, a bureau, and some chairs. Half the space stays empty in order to make room for the violinist. Next to the piano, there is a metal music stand. The interior is exceptional for a master class. Usually, in Europe, the master class takes place in luxurious or prestigious places (such as a chateau or an old abbey).

For one lesson of sixty minutes, each student is expected to pay 150 euros. The schedule is put up the day before on the entrance door. To take lessons, the new students need to play a short audition before the teacher. In an interview with this teacher, which I conducted two years after this observation, he told me that he never parts with his notebook, and he writes notes (the program played, the technique difficulties, and other remarks) only about those students whom he finds have soloist potential. It is no wonder that this notebook was the subject of conversation among the students. When the teacher wrote something, it signified the recognition of their potential, because this teacher enjoyed an important reputation in the soloist world.

The teacher, fifty-five-year-old Andriej, was born in Russia but has been living in Germany for several years. This morning, as always, he dresses in a suit, a white shirt, and a necktie. Andriej is a good-sized man, with a bon-vivant build.

He speaks with speed, a strong voice, and expressive, rapid gestures. He gives the impression of being in a hurry. Andriej comes in with Eva, his forty-five-year-old accompanist. Like Andriej, Eva is Russian but resides in Germany. She has been working with Andriej for several years now. During the lessons, she is almost always in front of the piano, and when the students play, she accompanies them. The public is not numerous, which is exceptional for a master class of this reputation. The reason was poor organization and no advertising; this place was a replacement of another beautiful interior, which was cancelled in the last minute. The public consists mainly of another violin teacher—a woman of thirty-five who is Andriej's assistant in her country. She is constantly making notes, jotting down remarks and advice of the teacher.

Family members accompany most of the violinists. Only the first student comes in alone. The second violinist is accompanied by her mother and her aunt, and the third student comes in with her aunt. I sit among the public as a specialist in the pedagogy of music and sociology; my activity (taking notes) is unobtrusive.[16] In other master classes, students frequently observe the lessons of their peers. Visitors can watch the class, paying 15 euros for half a day. But because of the humble setting and the lack of publicity, there's no audience today.[17]

Lesson One: 10:00 A.M. The first student is eighteen-year-old Irina, originally from Bulgaria but living in Austria. For years she has been studying at the high school, specialized in music, and is at second stage of her virtuoso education. After the lesson, I learn that this is the third time she has taken master classes with this teacher so we can consider that she is at the first stage of career coupling process—in the selection stage. She comes in ten minutes before her lesson, opens the violin case and after tuning her violin, lays the instrument on the desk and installs her video-camera.[18] At 9:55 A.M., Eva is in front of the piano, drinking her tea. Three minutes later, Andriej enters the classroom, nearly running. He takes off his coat and greets everyone, opens his violin case, and puts it on the desk. The teacher explains to Eva that the first lesson of his day, which took place in his hotel room, ran late. Andriej opens his schedule and invites the violinist to start. He speaks to Irina in German: "What will you play today?" "'Carmen,' by Wax-mann,"[19] responds the girl in a soft voice. She is visibly scared and stressed. "So, I'm listening now . . . please . . ."

Irina takes her place in the center of the room. Standing, she starts to play accompanied by the piano. As soon as the first note sounds, Adriej becomes tense, sighs, and begins tapping his foot at an accelerated tempo. Irina isn't playing fast enough. He takes off his jacket and listens until the end of the piece. When Irina finishes, Andriej speaks in a low and tired voice: "One more time!" After a few notes he stops her: "No, not like that! You need to play: la . . . la . . . mh . . . (he sings the phrase, gesturing with his arms to imitate playing the violin). And with character!" he shrieks. "This is a Spanish piece!"

By now Andriej has become irritated. He rapidly describes an image of the opera: he speaks of a *torero*, a bullfight, the love story of Carmen. He is annoyed, and sings the themes of the piece while pretending to play the violin. His voice is strong and he seems excited. Irina observes him, nodding to show that she understands. Her gestures are slow, as if she has lost her nerve. Visibly, she is both impressed and at the same time not surprised the lesson has developed in this way. She puts her violin on her shoulder and continues to play. As soon as she plays a few notes, the teacher stops her. He takes his own violin and plays one phrase in order for Irina to follow him. Irina replays; Andriej stops her after a few minutes and asks her to replay again. Each phrase is repeated in this way at least twenty times.

The teacher's corrections concern only the musical interpretation, not the tune or technique, although Irina has technical problems with certain passages. Andriej only shows how he wants her to play this piece. After around ten minutes, although Irina has not entirely corrected her performance, he switches to another part of the piece. Then, he states with a very tired voice: "You truly play completely the opposite of how you're supposed to!"

Eva seems to be very tired too. She follows the violinist, playing her part for the piano, but she stops each time Andriej speaks. Sometimes she plays only with one hand even if the score is written for two. Eva stares at her other hand and doesn't seem to be very interested in this lesson. At one point she stands up, gives a signal with her head to Andriej, and leaves the classroom.

Without interruption, the teacher works with his student on these passages, which are written for a violin solo. Five minutes later, Eva comes back with a glass of hot tea in her hand. She sits before her piano and plays with her left hand, lifting the glass with the right. She places the glass down when Andriej picks up his violin and plays a long passage from "Carmen" while explaining to Irina how it should be interpreted. Then Irina repeats this part. Andriej sings during certain sections, and in other moments he bites his fingernails, and again sings in order to give more energy to the performance. Then, suddenly, Eva does not follow the violinist and Andriej speaks to her in Russian: "Perhaps you can focus in order not to get lost in the music." Retorts Eva, "It was the girl who jumped a passage, which you modified last time!" All three are visibly irritated.

Andriej explains to Irina the modification and adds advice in German. Suddenly, the assistant puts her hand up and asks what the word "ruhe"[20] means in German, and Andriej responds, sounding tired (in German): "nicht so laut."[21] At 10:40, the next student—a fourteen-year-old girl—enters the room with two forty-year-old women. Andriej smiles at them. Sighing, he glances at his watch. He stands up, takes his violin, and starts to play with the pianist in order to show an example to Irina, in the presence of his now slightly larger audience.

Like a gunshot, an argument suddenly breaks out in Russian between Eva and Andriej. "I told you to play 'forte!'" Andriej shouts. "I play what's written in the scores! It's 'piano'!" responds Eva.

After stopping and starting on the piece three times, Adriej angrily shoves his violin into its case without playing the passage at the end. Eva continues to play alone. After a minute, Andriej quietly asks Irina to play for the last time. The pianist reapplies a bandage to her fifth finger (Eva bites her fingernails, and, she says, frequently suffers infections). Suddenly, the assistant, who has been taking notes the whole time, stands up and looks at something in the score of the pianist. At the end of the lesson Andriej says: "the tune."[22]

Then he explains: "In order to play pizzicato, you need to be free!" His voice is dry and unkind. Andriej begins playing his violin, looking at his student while screaming an explanation at her in a mixture of German and English. Then he slouches into his armchair and says in German: "Is this clear? So, thank you and next, please!"

Irina puts her violin in the violin case, stops her video-camera and leaves the room, saying goodbye. The time of this first lesson was divided into three, nearly equal parts: the student's performance, the teacher's performance, and his oral explanations.

Lesson Two—11:00 A.M. This lesson is with a fourteen-year-old Spanish student, Fabiola, who enters with her mother and aunt. Fabiola's mother is a Spanish violinist married to a Russian violinist. The family resides in Spain. Fabiola's aunt, her father's sister, speaks Russian, but not Spanish, so she translates from Russian into English. Fabiola's mother then translates from English into Spanish. Both women are dressed with elegance and they smile a lot. They do not record this lesson or take notes. Fabiola is not yet a student of Andriej's class. She is working with him in the master class in order to determine whether a long-lasting collaboration will be possible. Three additional persons enter the class. They have no connection with Fabiola; it seems they are violin students living in this city and coming to watch a lesson with a famous teacher.

Fabiola stands in the middle of the classroom with a serious face, showing strong focus. She plays the "Valse Scherzo" of Tchaikovsky. Her gestures are fast, and she seems to be more sure of herself than the previous student. As she performs a small smile appears on her face. During this first performance, Andriej progressively relaxes in his armchair. His face becomes less tense and more luminous, showing that he feels pleasure listening to Fabiola's playing.

When she finishes, the teacher says in Russian:

> Today it is much better. Your mother is not yet satisfied [he looks at Fabiola's mother, smiling], but today is much, much better. Now we can organize your interpretation. This is my first remark. Second, the cantilena[23] is better, but sometimes there appear to be problems with vibrato [he approaches Fabiola and points to one measure in the score]. Here, the cadence was no better, because you badly used the distribution of the bow, and the character of the stretto[24] was modified.

Fabiola's aunt translates one part of this advice into English and then nobody translates his remarks, so at one moment Andriej says: "Who is translating the following part? Both of you speak Russian. What?" Turning to Fabiola's mother, he says, "You don't understand anything? I see that you understand everything!" Andriej bursts into laughter, and at the same time, shows in the score, "This point, here, we already did yesterday." Then he touches the finger of Fabiola's left hand, takes her bow, and makes a movement with her finger, pushing Fabiola's bow himself. In doing so, Andriej shows her which movement she needs in order to reach vibrato. He smiles the whole time and says: "Yes! Much better! How to say that in Spanish? Mucho? Muskitos?" Fabiola has difficulty restraining her laughter.

Observing this situation, it seems evident that the teacher has enjoyed working with Fabiola, that he is happy to see she understands his advice and applies his recommendations without effort. She plays almost without pausing, and suddenly Andriej says loudly, while laughing, "Not so abruptly! Not 'When mom looks at me I'll go faster!'" He walks around Fabiola and touches her shoulder in order to correct her playing position—something he did not do with his previous student. He speaks directly in English to Fabiola, asking her to be more relaxed, and to replay a phrase. When she realizes what he asked her, Andriej says: "Here you start scherzo, and now . . . [as Fabiola plays] you see that you can!!! [He laughs joyfully.] Your mother will tighten the buckle on you day by day, and we will soon see huge progress!" He laughs again, then switches from English into Spanish and says: "Your hand cool . . . and continue like that!" Each musical phrase is reworked several times, but in contrast to Irina, Andriej speaks continually while Fabiola plays, giving encouragement and advice.

Suddenly, Andriej cuts the performance and speaks in German (he gives the impression of someone who has just woken up), "It is played badly. We have chaos!" Fabiola's mother translates into Spanish. The young violinist tries to correct her playing, and the pianist struggles to catch up (it can be difficult for an accompanist to find where the soloist is playing if she begins in the middle of a piece without warning). The teacher enjoys it—this version is noticeably better, "Muchos buenas! How is my Spanish?" he asks in Russian. "Better than your mother's Russian?" Fabiola does not understand that the teacher has attempted to speak to her in Spanish—his Spanish is not so good. Andriej jests, "See her, now she doesn't understand Spanish anymore!" The public in the classroom laughs, and it seems to be a good lesson for the teacher. Fabiola continues to play, and the teacher continues to work. "Don't mix the notes. Organize your scherzo!" He touches Fabiola's right hand to correct her position, and the girl screams, "aie!" while continuing to play.

Now Andriej picks up his violin and parodies her playing, showing with facial expressions how she should interpret this section. When Fabiola tries to correct herself, he adds, "Sad. It needs to be sad . . . Yes! Like that! More heartfelt!" He sings as the student plays. "Here, yesterday it was good and today it needs to be similar— the crescendo. Like yesterday. Ah! It is good, today, like yesterday! Here you have quintuple piano," he says, showing her the score and switching into English (up to now, Fabiola had followed his Russian advice without any translation). Fabiola's aunt translates Andriej's earlier advice to the assistant. Andriej speaks to the accompanist with a very gentle voice, "Eva, please, did you want to start here?" and indicates to her the place in the score. Then he stops Fabiola, "Please, more deeply." Andriej works on the details. Fabiola repeats, usually five to ten times, the same passage, and when Andriej's advice has been executed (or when he judges that Fabiola understands that she needs more practice than is possible during the lesson), they move on.

At one moment, the teacher points to the score and says, "Here, it is necessary to play like that . . ." and he plays. Suddenly, he is screaming, "Here, rubato,[25] please! And no accelerando[26] . . ." He screams suddenly, "The rhythm!" and he beats the rhythm with his bow on the desk. Fabiola continues to play and Andriej walks around her, sometimes singing, sometimes dancing, and suddenly she plays out of tune. The teacher makes a face like a clown, showing that he is completely disconsolate. Then he sits at his desk and plays his violin, demonstrating this passage. While speaking at the same time, he plays, "Here is leggiero[27] and not hippopotamo!" Then in the next phrase, "and here, not so fast." Fabiola replays the passage again and he buries his head in his hands and shuts his ears: "Aie! The half-tones." At twelve o'clock, Andriej glances down at his watch and says simply, "Thank you very much." It is the next student's turn. This lesson was an excellent example of the "theatrical"-type lesson.

Lesson Three—12:00 Noon. As Fabiola's lesson ends, Jane, a fourteen-year-old girl, enters. She is Irish, but resides in Germany in order to follow her education in Andriej's famous soloist class. Jane also follows her teacher's master class around the world, because she does not want to miss a single lesson. Her father, a rich entrepreneur and music lover, finances this expensive education, and her aunt accompanies Jane during all of her travels and lives with her in Germany. Jane's aunt takes advantage of their time in this city to find a concert dress for the young violinist. "It is much cheaper and prettier than in Dublin," she says. Jane takes her place in the center of the classroom and, very self-assured, turns on the recorder in order to make a record of her lesson.

She plays "La Campanella" by Niccolò Paganini from beginning to end. For all his students, Andriej uses the same method: first, he listens to the entire piece. Andriej listens, smiling. He exchanges some remarks with his assistant and explains that he is very proud of this student, and listens again. When Jane plays a difficult passage, she accelerates and plays without precision. The teacher laughs and reclines on the bureau in order to watch from a different angle. He laughs again, and makes a face in order to show that the passage was not in tune. But he stays visibly satisfied. When Jane finishes playing, he speaks in German, "Good, but if you want to attain a superior level, we need to organize better than this." Then he explains in detail, with musical slang, much as he would speak with an adult, how she needs to play and when. It takes four minutes to give this advice, which concerns interpretation of the piece. Then she plays again, but the sections between Adriej's interruptions are much longer than those of the previous students. The door opens, and the director of the music school, who often works in this classroom, enters with a glass of hot tea for Andriej. At the same time, two fifty-year-old women (maybe violin teachers?) take their place in the audience.

The teacher drinks his tea, listens to Jane's performance, and says, "It is much, much better, but you need to find another character." He stands up and touches her shoulder, "It doesn't need to be fast, but it must sing." Then he takes Jane's violin in his hand and tunes it. This is the first time that I see the teacher tuning the violin of a student in the master class. This practice is reserved rather for the young students. Through this act, we can infer a certain intimacy: this is a student enrolled in his soloist class, who works with him at least three times a week. Jane is certainly not a simple student-in-passing. The teacher gives back her violin and continues to explain: "It needs to be played with more fantasy."

He works on a one-minute sequence for about ten minutes. "It's good, but here [and he shows in the score]–not so loud!" Each time when she starts to play, he starts to go to the desk to sip his tea, and each time he does not get there, because he turns back and corrects Jane: "Vibration! We can see inside your Irish accent!" and he tickles his student.[28]

Jane laughs but does not stop her performance and Andriej adds: "You have a big problem with your first finger." In comparison to the previous lesson, the teacher seems much more involved; we see this through his focus on the music, the rapidity of the corrections, and the fact that he cannot manage to drink his tea. Attentively listening, he passes next to the pianist and, visibly fascinated by Jane's performance, speaks to the accompanist in Russian: "You see, Eva? What a temperament! Sounds like Eugen Onegin!" Eva responds with a tired voice: "No, I don't know."

Suddenly, in the middle of the lesson, Jane speaks to her teacher with fear in her voice. This morning (and this is not exceptional) it is the first sentence formulated by a student that is directed at her teacher: "Do you find that a little better than the last time?" Andriej exclaims, very surprised, "Sure! What a question?!" Then, he takes her bow, stands next to Jane, and replaces her right arm, while at the same time she continues to play only with her left hand. Doing so, they play together on the same violin and Andriej speaks to her: "Don't accelerate . . . slowly . . ." and he returns her bow and Jane continues to play alone, Andriej corrects only the position of the right hand. Then Andriej stops her and shows: "Look! I'll show you: when you play 'forte,' the accents are not the same as when you play 'piano' [Jane plays, underlining the difference to show that she understands.] Great!!!! This is passion 'a-la-Irish' that you're playing now! Oh, look, your string is broken!" Jane has not noticed that her string has come unstrung, which can risk an injury. There is a break of a few minutes for Jane to change her string; the teacher finally finds time for his tea.

Jane returns to the middle of the classroom and tunes her violin. Immediately, Andriej takes his violin and plays, speaking, "Listen, this is better, one thousand times better, but not yet 'good.' This is exactly the same problem that you had in 'Caprice Basque.'" Jane starts to play, despite the fact that the teacher is still playing, but she plays badly—not in tune, so the teacher stops her and says, "Now I need to hear adagio."

Holding the violin in her right hand, with her left Jane places the score on the music stand. She does it awkwardly and drops the score. Gathering the pages of music, Andriej says, "Sit on it." Jane is uncertain whether she has understood his German and looks at the teacher with a puzzled expression, as does Eva the pianist. Andriej explains in Russian (directing himself mostly to the pianist, but with gestures so that Jane and the public can understand), that she needs to sit on the score, because of the old superstition that if a musician does not sit on a score that has fallen, a bad concert will follow. The assistant says that when bread drops on the floor, it is necessary to kiss it to prevent starvation, but she's never heard this custom applied to a musical score. Nor has anyone else in the classroom, much to the teacher's surprise.

After quickly sitting on the score, Jane starts playing the adagio. A young sixteen-year-old boy enters the classroom, and Andriej tells him in Russian: "I told you to call me before coming!" Clearly, the intruder is one of the students from Andriej's class. He has a violin case in his hand. "But your cell phone doesn't work!" The teacher responds, "That's normal! When I'm giving lessons, I turn it off! You need to call me before 9 A.M. and after 9 P.M. You know that. I can't listen to you now. Come back after 3 P.M."

During this discussion, Jane continues to play adagio. "OK, now the cadence," says the teacher. At the same time, he puts on his jacket and prepares to leave, packing up his violin while he gives advice for interpreting the cadence. He finishes the lesson saying, "You must continue like that. After some time, it will be better!" Andriej leaves the room, followed by his assistant, the student who was late, and the director of the music school. He's in a hurry for lunch. Jane falls into the arms of her aunt, who kisses her, saying that it was very, very good. Her aunt is not a musician; however, she followed Jane since years and assisted in hundred of classes. She recognizes that teacher was happy about Jane's performance. We can say that it was an example of an "ideal lesson."

Starting from these observations, filled out with other empirical data, I propose to analyze the teacher-student relationships. Three different lessons gave several data for the investigation of mutual expectations of both teacher and student, as well as the basis for the comparison of different aspects of work. The lessons were dynamic, full of emotions between main participants (teacher and students, as well as pianist and family members). It was easy to note the nature of those emotions: admiration of the teacher, the teacher's involvement in his work, the impatience to obtain a positive result after corrections, and the anger when the performance was judged not good enough. If the last lesson was certainly the example of successful collaboration, the first gave us the possibility to follow the lesson full of tensions, anger, stress, and frustration. Those negatives feelings signify the conflict between master and student. For a sociologist of work, the analysis of the conflicts and their origins provides more information and gives a better insight into observed processes than the account of a peaceful collaboration. This is why, taking into account all three examples of lessons, I focus below on conflicts between two main actors in this study.

Many conflicts arise between masters and students because of the different expectations one party has of another. All three students observed during this lesson-day were capable of meeting the teacher's basic expectations. While of different ages and from different cultures and countries, the three behaved similarly during their lessons because of prior socialization. Though small differences of temperament were visible, all three musicians spoke little. They knew when to play and when to listen to advice, and their attitudes toward the teacher were similar. However, their capacity to follow the teaching of the master was different, and this aspect determined the relationship between the teacher and his students.

The teacher expects students to conform to his or her expectations within the following two types of norms: (1) technical norms, meaning technical mastery of violin; (2) attitudinal norms; behavior during the lesson and in the student's musical interpretation and within the soloist world.

Technical Demands

As a first requirement, soloist teachers demand that their students master the instrument. Students in the second stage of their soloist educations need to have excellent technique, which teachers say must be acquired in the first years of education. Among the teachers I observed, teaching technique, including playing position and handling of the bow, is not interesting. Using the vocabulary of specialists in the sociology of work, we could call this technical training "dirty work" (Hughes 1971).

Though these tasks can be part of their jobs, masters do not consider such teaching noble and gratifying activity.[29] They prefer to delegate such duties to assistants. Sometimes permanent teachers (full-year teachers) handle the particular technical correction. But sometimes a student takes classes with a master without his permanent teacher knowing and agreeing with this choice. This act could be seen by a long-term teacher as a betrayal and will be the source of conflict or even rupture. Virtuoso teaching is so individualistic that it is difficult to pursue a musical education with two masters who do not agree on the same technical style of playing or pedagogical approaches. This is why the majority of the observed students took the master class with the professor advised by the full-term teacher.

The elaboration of interpretation and the polishing of musical expression are usually the specialties of soloist teachers. This is why the students who take soloist lessons only during a master class perform a piece they can handle with utmost technical mastery. Soloist teachers say they prefer to do "the art and not the handiwork," and that the "true duty of a soloist teacher is working on music." This attitude is widespread among teachers, though there are exceptions. One teacher adopted a similar attitude toward technical and interpretation problems. For such teachers, the technical problems constitute an integral part of soloist education, regardless of the age of the pupil.[30]

Most teachers expect students who join their classes to be free of significant technical problems. Those who show defects in their playing position or have other problems do not meet up to expectations. Before the teacher can work on interpretation—a "noble" task—he or she must correct the student's playing position with a so-called "change of technique." This work, which can last for months, is considered painful, time-consuming, and not at all interesting.

Teachers evaluating whether to accept a student are likely to factor in the time that will be required for technical corrections. In some cases, the teacher decides to undertake this "dirty work," depending on various factors. The first is the duration of the relationship. The teacher does not have as much time to work with a master class student who comes for a few lessons each year (such as Irina) as with a longtime soloist student (Jane). The first student was eighteen when she began working with Andriej. This is considered in the virtuoso world as too late if the student does not have an excellent technique and does not know much of the virtuoso repertoire. Even if she could pay regular lessons during whole year, it is only a narrow possibility to enter into a similar relationship to Jane's. The age barrier crossed with the level of performance is an important factor of teacher's assessment, strongly related with evaluation of student's potential. This is the second factor. If the student seems likely to make technical changes speedily or seems to be a promising soloist, the teacher may decide that his or her potential merits the time required for technical corrections. Finally, the teacher's plans related to this student, such as participation in concerts and competitions, play an important role the relationship.

In the three lessons described here, the status of each student was different. The first, Irina, was a transient student. Her slow reactions, timidity, and lack of violin mastery did not satisfy Andriej. He did not change Irina's playing position, and did not begin technical corrections.[31] The teacher focused only on the interpretation and was constantly frustrated because the student was not able to implement the expected corrections. Sighs, grimaces, and gestures, such as ostentatiously glancing at his watch, showed that Andriej felt his time was being wasted.

In contrast, Andriej clearly felt Fabiola was worthy of teaching some technical improvements, as demonstrated his gestures related to the technical playing of vibrato. He became involved in this work because he could obtain good results quickly. The correction did not take time, and Andriej could also work with Fabiola on the interpretation of the piece. His patience with Fabiola also reflected the fact that the family planned to enroll her in Andriej's class. Thus, she was in the process of changing her status, from master-class student to regular soloist class student. If for several violinists becoming a regular soloist student is related with important financial investment (social class and financial status of parents are crucial here), some students (those who are seen by teachers as violinists having the highest potential to become a virtuoso) will have support (scholarship, financial help, solution for living in the city in which professor teaches, free lessons within an institution—conservatory of music or music university). This is why we cannot simply conclude that the financial status of the parents determines the access to the highest level of soloist education. It is the case for the majority of students, but those perceived as "the best," will benefit from different types of resources, which will supplement the familial financial involvement.

It is not uncommon for newcomers to require some technical adaptation. During the master class, Andriej had already started this kind of work with Fabiola. He had already developed projects for Fabiola because he was opening a new soloist class in her country, and she would be among his first new indigenous students. Andriej knows that the students who are natives of the country in which the class functions have the highest probability of obtaining funding from private and public sources. In fact, several months later, Fabiola became Andriej's regular student.

The last student, Jane, received only a few pieces of technical advice, because during the previous year, when she had worked several times a week with Andriej, she had probably had sufficient time to correct her technique. From the teacher's point of view, Jane was the best of the three at meeting his expectations in the matter of playing technique.

Teachers' Expectations for Student Behavior

The second aspect that influences the teacher-student relationship is student behavior. This is different from what has been described in literature on general primary and secondary schools (Becker 1951; Masson 1996), because soloist education is characterized by a two-way relationship, rather than a teacher interacting with a group of students. The behavior expected by soloist teachers is, in a word, obedience. The student has no part in discussing his or her education. The previous socialization (first stage) imposes an identical behavior on the students, which we can observe during these three lessons. This behavior can lead the external observer into error; because of the student's apparent obedience, conflicts are hardly visible to uninitiated people.

Consider, for example, a case in which the teacher yells at student for playing *forte* when the teacher demanded *piano*. To the outsider this may seem like a simple mistake, but in the musical world it may be viewed as a discipline problem. In the soloist class, all students know how to play *forte* and *piano*. Perhaps the student is playing *forte* on purpose, a transgression of the obedience rule that demands the student follow all the teacher's wishes, no questions asked. At the second stage of the soloist education, conflicts about obedience are very common. Sometimes, the teacher throws up his or her hands, as seen in the following extract: "I do not know what to do with him. He doesn't listen to me. I told him to play like this. He plays another way, whereas he knows very well how to play as I expect. He doesn't obey anymore! When I was a student, I never dared to do something like that to my teacher. It's not possible to do it any other way. And he, it seems he knows better how to play than I do! I can't do anything with him!"

The student must learn to adopt an attitude that combines confidence on stage with docility toward the teacher. This behavior needs to be precisely titrated: the student cannot be too timid, because a soloist must be sure of him- or herself. At the same time, he or she cannot appear to be too much at ease. The student needs to adapt during lessons but also on stage. A young teacher complained to two parents about other teachers who had criticized her student's performance in a year-end test.[32]

> They [other teachers who work with my respondent in the music school] said to me that Liuba played very well, almost perfectly, but she "made a movie," she behaved like an actor, and she looked directly into the eyes of the judges! For ten minutes this was all they could talk about, without saying a word about

the playing itself, and they forgot that Liuba is only nine years old. With her program, she plays three years ahead of other students. What is wrong with her feeling very comfortable on stage?! For them, it's not like that. They think, "A student should not behave like a star." Ida Haendel [a great soloist] always looked her public right in the eye, but what is allowable to her is forbidden for my student. Liuba played perfectly, and the judges gave her only fifteen out of twenty, because she played "like an adult."

Perhaps because of her age (under thirty) and lack of professional experience as a soloist teacher, this teacher has an unorthodox view of student behavior on stage. For her, the performance itself is the most important, nearly the sole criterion for evaluating a student's playing. In her view, if Liuba applied all her teacher's advice on the piece, she would have satisfied the teacher's expectations, and she should have obtained the highest grade. Perhaps because of her lack of experience, the teacher did not prepare Liuba to meet the jury's expectations of attitude during tests. The little violinist attracted the jury's attention because she transgressed the unwritten behavior rules for such performances.

When teachers speak about the behavior of students they employ the term of "personality." Insiders of the soloist world understand "personality" as a set of student behaviors—on stage, during lessons, and outside of work time. The teacher expects the student to possess a "temper," but also that the student not show "too much personality" during lessons. Frequently, I heard the following critique from teachers: "He/she plays as if he/she is already a soloist, but he/she is only a student," or "During the competition the participant shouldn't play as if he/she was already a soloist."

However, in the soloist world this lack of "personality" is perceived as an obstacle. A student "without personality," teachers say, will bore the audience with a flat and unexciting performance. One component of "personality" is the capacity to endure stress. Fragile and sensitive students have trouble bearing the pressure of lessons and tense relationships with their teachers—Irina being a case in point. This is frowned upon. Unfortunately, participants are used to the behavior of teachers which will be certainly negatively perceived in other settings—Andriej's pressure on Irina is not seen among virtuoso students as an example of a particular abuse but as a case of a "not-good-lesson." A famous master "has a right" to be authoritarian and not "nice." He is the star teacher and becomes angry quickly if the student is not showing improvement on the spot.

Generally, teachers consider it impossible to change the "personality" of their students. The teacher gives technical corrections if need be, but changes of attitude (not the same as musical interpretation style) are not their responsibility, say the teachers, as illustrated in the following quote, from an informal discussion: "I don't have time to be a shrink. Our profession is tough, the milieu is not easy, and you have to be strong. Me, I take care of playing and I haven't enough time to do it all. When my students play badly, I tell them, and it is up to them to do it correctly, so I don't repeat it."

The soloist student should not show psychological or emotional weakness, because the soloist ideal corresponds to individuals who are psychologically resistant. A teacher may lose interest and become detached from a student who is too thin-skinned, especially a master teacher who has a large portfolio of students and also busy giving the master classes in different parts of the world. Soloist professors justify their attitude by common inside-of-a-virtuoso-world opinion, that a soloist student cannot be emotionally fragile, scared, or self-effacing. Working with students who present these characteristics, like Irina, teachers say, is a waste of time.

If this deterministic point of view is shared by the majority of teachers, some express the contrary opinion that such weaknesses may resolve over time. After experiencing more of life, some teachers believe, students may modify their personalities. Such a view was expressed in an informal conversation between two male teachers: "So, this one, she plays as if she is sleeping—The Sleeping Beauty. She is cold. I'm dying to see her fall in love and get into some craziness. When she will stop being so well behaved? You will see her 'Carmen,'[33] how she will play with fire under her fingers!!! For now, she lacks balls, but when she finally gets into bed with someone, she will play with a wild temper."[34]

The relationship between teacher and student can become conflicted when the disciple exhibits "too much personality." The teacher may consider this an obstacle to education, as in the case of this teacher, speaking with the parents of a seventeen-year-old student: "Your child is extremely gifted but I won't work with him because he has too much personality. He doesn't hear me, and that's not good, because he still has a lot of position correction to do. It's a pity, but he probably needs another teacher who will have much more authority over him. If he achieves the stage where he has corrected his defects, your son will play very well, but I cannot work with him anymore. Besides, he doesn't even show up for lessons."

The student must try to conform to the teacher's expectations and be careful not to commit the sins of weakness or excess "personality."

Asymmetrical Relationships

The example of the three lessons shows the variety of situations encountered in this field. The students seem to conform to the behavioral expectations of the soloist world, yet their relationships with the teacher differ. During these three lessons, the teacher was the active agent and the students demonstrated his authority over them. The students' reactions, such as very tactful facial expressions, show that their communication of emotion with the master are limited to very subtle nonverbal expressions. The master's role, following Erving Goffman's term of "performance" (Goffman 1973: 26–27) may be defined as all the activity of a given participant on a given occasion that serves to influence in any way any of the other participants. Taking a particular participant and his performance as a basic point of reference, we may refer to those who contribute the other performances as the audience, observers, participants.

The lesson is the teacher's performance: theatrical as are the public master class lessons. The students play their roles by adopting appropriate behaviors. This is clear in the question-response exchange: the teacher's role is to question and to speak, the student's to respond; to say nothing but to play following the master's indications. During our three lessons, only one student dared ask a question; another responded a few times, but most frequently the three just played. The behavior of these students was so similar that it is only through the behavior of the teacher that we can perceive the character of each relationship (Andriej–Irina, Andriej–Fabiola, and Andriej–Jane).

The student tries to meet, as closely as possible, the master's expectations. The reaction of the teacher, whether satisfied or discontent, causes a series of directives. Thus, the student's actions influence the relationship although it is directed by the teacher. Consequently, we can consider these interactions as asymmetrical relationships—the teacher imposes certain norms to which the students either conform or not. Out of the three lessons, the last student, Jane, best met the different expectations of her teacher.

The analysis of the relationship between the teacher and student is the subject of numerous studies, but the analysis of H. S. Becker (1951), concerning pedagogical relationships between school teachers and their students, seems applicable here. According to Becker, the variations in the relations are the result of a shift between the idyllic image teachers have of their students (clients) and the variations observed by the teachers at work. This shift is the source of conflict between two categories of actors (teachers and students). Becker states that in public schools, the difference between the teachers' representations of the students and the workplace reality, is related to the social origin of students. This conflict appears in three areas: teaching, discipline, and moral acceptability.

The question of social origin does not figure in the relationship between teacher and soloist student in a similar way such as in Becker's work, while social diversity of the students is poor. Most students originate from families closely related to the teacher's social origin. The rare student from a different social milieu assimilates through deep immersion in the first stage of soloist education. The acquisition of this culture is necessary to pursue a soloist education. This issue appears clearly in the case of Eastern European teachers' classes.

Consequently, variations in pedagogical relationships in soloist classes depend on the interplay between the image of a future soloist that each teacher possesses, and the behavior of a given student. What is the dynamic of the distance between the teacher's expectations and the student's behavior during each of the three observed lessons?

The first student, Irina, did not know how to meet the teacher's expectations. In Andriej's eyes, she lacked the "soloist temperament." The teacher viewed her slow reactions as incorrect. With his expectations unmet, Andriej responded impatiently. He was inconsiderate and even unkind and disrespectful toward Irina, and didn't care how she felt about it. He was angry that Irina did not understand his directions sufficiently and thus deprived him of the opportunity to display his teaching art and his brilliance in public. Irina's attitude showed a distance from the ideal soloist student. Importantly, however, she continued to take lessons with

Andriej. Each soloist class student knows that "bad lessons" and "bad periods" can happen, and that they must put up with them at least for several lessons before abandoning one teacher for another.

Young virtuosos are accustomed to rude treatment; the lesson I describe with Irina and Andriej is not at all exceptional. The teacher dominates the relationship and puts pressure on students—this is one of the tools of education for excellence. However, their interaction did reflect how a teacher's self-control can affect the relationship. Unable to play the role of elite master guiding his student, Andriej lost control of the relationship and lost his self-control. He screamed and spoke in an unpleasant manner, grimaced and gestured to display his disdain for Irina. Andriej's loss of control made him nervous: he bit his fingernails, unhappy at his inability to influence Irina's playing. This behavior does not correspond to the ideal of the soloist master in the violinist's world. Gaidamovitch, also a soloist teacher, quoted his own teacher to explain how authority is to be worn by the violin master:

> Yuri Yankelevich's authority and power of persuasion were nearly absolute, but the use of pressure was totally excluded from his method. "We, the teachers [Yankelevich remarked], need to be extremely vigilant in the relationships with our students. Despotism has no place in it. The student should not be as obedient as a dog. On the contrary, he needs to be sure of the validity of the teacher's advice. . . . A method could help in playing, but it never transforms the student into an artist. It is the human qualities of a student, his greatness of intellectual horizon and his capacity to see and enjoy life, that will always have the last word." (Gaïdamovitch in Brussilovsky 1999: 249)

Through her appropriate behavior, Fabiola, the second student, was closer to the model of soloist than Irina. Andriej was most involved in his teaching work. He showed himself more relaxed and very attentive to Fabiola's reactions to his instructions. Though Fabiola did not say a word, she was clearly an active participant in the lesson because she had a very involved and enthusiastic attitude. Fabiola expressed huge energy and with a beautiful smile, she showed how much she wished to follow her teacher. He was sensitive to this message, without being particularly attracted by her young feminine charm. I could observe Andriej working with young boys and being as well involved and passionate in his teaching of male students. As for other students, who followed as much as possible advice of their teacher, Fabiola's capacities and her "potential" motivated Andriej. He knew how to show Fabiola that she was capable of making huge progress. His actions enabled her to perceive her own skills and possibilities, and to be aware of his role in this process. The student needs to feel and know that this teacher, and no other, is indispensable to his or her development. The disciples of our model soloist teacher, Yuri Yankelevich, explain the logic of this behavior, which is similar to Andriej's logic: "When we attain a very difficult goal that seemed unattainable at the outset, we stimulate and accelerate the progress of the student, who becomes self-assured, conscious of his or her own value, and while placing all trust in the teacher starts to believe in his or her own capacities" (in Brussilovsky 1999: 67).

The development of the third lesson suggests that the last student, Jane, is closest to Andriej's expectations. He was totally involved in the transmission of his knowledge: Jane was the quickest—almost instant—in the application of his instructions. The master's involvement was visible through the tone of his voice, the quality of his explanations, and the size of the program worked on during this one lesson. Jane was the only student who played nearly without a break. Because she applied the teacher's advice without any difficulties, she gave her teacher professional satisfaction. Their collaboration was profitable because the persons assisting the lessons could notice immediate results—for example, in the quickly perfected execution of very difficult passages. In spite of the personal closeness between them, which showed through gestures, tickling, and bursts of laugher, the lesson's ambiance did not have a relaxed character. The teacher and his student worked together fruitfully thanks to very stimulating reciprocal exchanges and intense focus.

Here, during this last lesson, Andriej conformed to the image of elite teacher, and played the master's role according to the norms of the soloist world. This was possible because his collaborator excelled in the role of the soloist student. We observe here the dependence of teacher's work effects on student's behavior: when his collaborator (student) was unable to play her role in an ideal way, the teacher failed to maintain his "professional attitude" and could not live up to the image of the elite teacher. The public exhibition of work with a soloist is a specific feature of the soloist education. The teacher tries to convince the public about the quality of his work, which is revealed in the performances of his or her best students.

The Soloist Student's Expectations of the Teacher

While the teacher has a model of behavior for soloist students, the students have their own model of the relationship and expectations of their teacher. But there is a dissonance between the ideal model of the soloist teacher and real teacher behavior types. Entering the stage of soloist education, students already have had various relationships with teachers, and each student carries his or her own model of the ideal collaboration. For example, two former students of Ivan Galamian contrasted their experience with him. As a teenager, Itzhak Perlman spent eight summers at Meadowmount and remembered, "I loved every minute. The atmosphere was such that you are totally moved into achieving. Everybody around you was practicing and showing off." Arnold Steinhardt (now first violinist of the Guarneri Quartet) has a more negative recollection: "It was slave labor. It was terrible. You had to get up and practice all day long, and he demanded an almost monk-like existence. We all moaned and groaned and vowed we'd never go back, but somehow we all loved it" (in Schwarz 1983: 549).

The question, "In your opinion, how should a soloist teacher be?" provoked a swift reaction among violinists, who described their model teacher. The lack of hesitation in their responses showed that this was a subject of frequent reflection. In fact, this question is one of the main topics of discussions among soloist students. The length of collaboration between teacher and student at the second stage of soloist education strongly depends on the evolution of their relationship and the needs the student develops. These individual needs develop as a result of several factors. The student's expectations are based on the tradition of soloist education, as practiced in Eastern Europe and in the West,[35] on his or her earlier educational trajectory, and on the successes and failures experienced with former teachers. How, in the second stage of their education, do students decide what relationship model to follow, and how do they find the teacher who meets the model?[36] What type of relationship do the students expect from their teachers?

The Distance between Master and Disciple in Two Different Traditions

Interviews with students suggest that they perceive a difference in the relationship between the master and his or her disciples based on two main categories of teachers. These categorizations correlate to the geographic area of soloist education. Teachers behave differently based on whether they teach in conformity with "traditions practiced in Eastern Europe" or according to the "Western tradition." The testimony of the following student, who experienced both systems, is an excellent starting point in analyzing this comparison. This student was educated first in the Soviet system, the prolongation of the famous Russian school of playing (Schwarz 1983), and afterward in the French system. Asked about the different approaches to the student-teacher relationship in the two schools, the student responded:

> In Armenia, we were always guided by our teachers. We had more than two lessons per week. In France, it is always once a week, then it is the work with an assistant [of the master]; however, it is different. Here [in France] we are left more to our own devices. I think those who are more successful here are those who have trusted only in themselves, whereas there [in Armenia], all the responsibility is in the hands of our teachers.

Asked which relationship was preferred, the student responded:

> In between. And above all, not the relationship of "father-son." It is the worst thing, I think. . . . I know only one exception—David Oistrakh. I think that he was . . . someone who . . . was a genius, because to be successful in his profession as a father and as a teacher. . . . it is necessary to be a shrink. He was the teacher of his son, and his son did not become just anybody![37]

A fundamental problem appears in this extract concerning the teacher-student relationships at this second stage of education. What is the ideal distance between the parties? In the "Slavonic" tradition, the teacher's first responsibility is to look after the welfare of the student. Said one teacher from this tradition: "This is the first and obligatory question to ask each student before the lesson. You need to be sure that your student isn't going hungry or thirsty . . . that the student is happy. The problems that worry the students prevent them from doing good musical work. The teacher needs to know all that before starting his work with students."

The first (Slavonic) approach, characterized by taking care of the students, contributes to the creation of a strong bond, which extends beyond the framework of musical education. Here, I will cite some former students of the soloist teacher model, Yankelevich:

> He was, for all of us, a teacher in the widest sense of the term. He worried not only about our violin education, but he was also interested in our problems and helped us in solving them. He provided us with love and with truly paternal attention. (Brussilovsky 1999: 29).

> He was not only an excellent teacher for his students, but also a human being who was interested in their lives and who, in difficult situations, helped them with his advice and even helped them financially. (Fouter in Brussilovsky 1999: 331)

The distance between master and student is greater in the Western tradition, where teacher and student spend less time together and the time is devoted only to music. For the teachers of this tradition, the students' private lives are outside of the relationship, as the following example illustrates.

A sixteen-year-old student from Russia studying in France was visibly disappointed by the attitude of her master. She had huge financial problems and was unable to pay the rent on her flat. She even had problems paying for food. I suggested that she could perhaps speak about this problem with her teacher. Her response illustrated how large the distance between the teacher and student is, and how the student respected this distance. "He doesn't give a damn about my problems with money. What he is interested in is '*piano*' here and '*forte*' there. This is an artist, and when you come into his lesson, it is for music and not for speaking about my problems." I pointed out that she was the teacher's best student. Doesn't he know that her parents are musicians in Russia who are entirely unable to provide financial support? "Yes, of course! He isn't an idiot. He plays in Russia each year and knows the situation there very well, but he thinks that there are a lot of scholarships, and I need to get along on my own. Sadly, each year there are fewer and fewer scholarships and not everyone gets one, but he doesn't give a damn if I eat or not before coming into his lesson." This student was accustomed to her Russian teacher, who before each lesson asked her if everything in her life was fine. She was raised in an environment where there was a strong bond between teacher and student. The new relationship was difficult.

That said, some Western violin masters act more in line with the Eastern European tradition in this regard. Dorothy DeLay, an American professor at the Juilliard School of Music (see Lourie-Sand 2000), spent twenty years as an assistant to Ivan Galamian, a Russian teacher, who transmitted some elements of this Russian relationship tradition. As a teacher, DeLay maintained very close master-disciple relationships.

While students are familiar with the master-disciple relationships in each tradition, each student has his or her own ideal of collaboration and distance. Bond with the master is frequently the first, and sometimes the only quality mentioned by students: "My ideal teacher? For me he should be a good father with whom we live and with whom we are like family. He makes us work at any hour. Even spiritually there is unity. Yes, the ideal teacher for me is he who does everything. A spiritual father. Someone we admire. It doesn't matter if he is well known or not—he teaches us to do what he does." This point of view is widely shared by other students. A former French student—one who in fact had never had a long collaboration with a teacher from the Eastern European tradition—suggested that a closer and more "human" relationship of master and disciple was more likely outside of the conservatory: "I think that it is important to be free of institutions. I'm for more of a Rousseauean style of education, in which we learn with a master at home. We don't need to enroll in the conservatory; there is something sick about these institutions. We need to be liberated from all that. With a teacher, we need to have a very human relationship and a lot of respect—human and musical. To become a musician, you need a master."

In referring to their model teacher, rarely do the students speak about the technical and musical side of their expectations, as if this point were completely secondary.[38] For the following student, however, it was the main question: "Ideal teacher? It's a teacher who takes care of their students, who thinks a lot about violin technique: how it sounds, each movement of the bow, each position of the left hand, and at the same time, gives me a lot from the musical side. This is what is lacking in the teachings of Madame Z. Her teaching is interesting, but she doesn't push us to our limits."

Students' expectations of their relationships with teachers progressively crystallize during the second stage of the soloist education. The young violinists remark on the distance between their expectations and the relationship they have with their master. For some, being a student in a soloist class is not enough. They seek a very close and personal relationship with their teacher: "Good question! A good master? It's someone who can adapt himself to the student, and not the contrary. Oistrakh, for example."[39]

THE MISSING GENDER ISSUE

Earlier I describe how the bonds between teacher and student depend on the teacher's geographical origin and on the tradition of socialization within the virtuoso world. For a sociologist working on the relationship between teachers and students, especially when those relationships are maintained for several years and includes individual lessons, the question of gender influence is important. Data from gender studies conducted in other settings show that sexual exploitation is a common outcome when young women are in a position of dependence upon older men.[40] During more than ten years of observation I never directly witnessed such phenomena in the virtuoso world. However, gossip frequently circulated among teen violinists to the effect that certain teachers provided favored treatment to students of a chosen gender. This was a common theme animating the milieu of young virtuosos. I heard several stories about male professors who preferentially supported female violinists, as well as female professors who preferred boys. Infrequently there were also allegations that homosexual male professors supported only male violinists.

Gender issues often seemed to arise at the moment of choice of a new teacher. As in the academic world (in which women are viewed as generally less supportive of younger female colleagues, while men are seen as gender-neutral in their mentoring choices). I heard about several female professors who "hated" girl violinists and always gave more attention to their male students. That treatment was perceived by the violinists as "natural," and one of the informal discussion points regarding gender among students who work or worked with a given professor. I have only one example of a lasting relationship between a master and her student; this couple married and are parents of a violinist. Teacher-student relationships with more than a twenty-year difference seem exceptional, however.

Many teachers have unstable relationships. Most are married (to other musicians), some divorced, and a great number live in a partnership of some kind. In the opinion of my respondents, geographic mobility and intense commitment to work were elements that made couples fragile.

The gender aspect of the teacher-student relationship had many passionate aspects and was often compared to the complexity of familial ties. Many professors work with students from the time they are small children to budding adulthood. Observing growing girls and witnessing their first loves (frequently with other violin virtuosos) implicated teachers in their students' lives in a strong way. Sometimes the teacher would attempt to control his or her feelings in order to not damage the virtuoso's development.

This probably explains why I did not observe much in the way of sexual attraction or interaction between teachers and students. I witnessed a lot of relationships among students (during master classes and competitions, as well as in long-term classes), and some flirting between male teachers and the mothers of young virtuosos. Such affairs could play a role in the relationship between teacher and student.

When observation is a method, the investigative tool is the researcher. He or she observes the world according to his or her background and life experiences. Going into this study I was probably not sufficiently focused on a number of gender issues. In my Eastern European culture (before the political changes of 1989) gender problems were different than in the West. Women and men had relatively equal positions, especially in the artistic world. Public discourse and scholarly reflection on gender differences was not as developed as in, for example, the United States—nor was gender discrimination. Before 1989, Polish women earned the same salaries as their male colleagues in similar positions.

Second, I did not pay special attention to extramarital sexual affairs because I had not reflected on the extent that love relationships, sexual attraction, and forbidden affairs are part of the life and experience of many people. Today I would probably notice more of these effects. Thinking back on my research, I suspect there were probably teachers who had hidden sexual affairs with younger students.

CRITERIA FOR CHOOSING A TEACHER

Each student dreams of the ideal relationship with the teacher. But of the soloist students interviewed here,[41] few were enthusiastic and happy about theirs. Their responses are mostly reserved, such as the following: "He's a professor who gives a lot of lessons. He's rarely absent, when compared to other teachers here who have their soloist classes and are never around. The teacher freaks out with some of his students, but not me. With me he's free, although sometimes he imposes certain things. But he's exclusive and he hates you if you go to see another teacher, even for a master class." (This student changed teachers six months later.)

This relationship provided certain benefits for the student's education and career, and though he was not enthusiastic about his teacher, he stayed with him for some months. Other students consistently remained in relationships with a single master. Most have difficulty describing this relationship:

> Sometimes I find that she [the teacher] is invasive. The lessons take place quite frequently during the week. Each lesson lasts no more than two hours, but they are usually four or five times per week. She never announces the times beforehand. She tells me only after my lesson when I will have my next one. One time, I had a lesson each day for fifteen days because a competition approached. After my lesson, I went home and worked on what she had advised me during the lesson. The next day I presented her with what I did the previous day at home.
>
> Sometimes I want her to let me work alone. I have the feeling that she's choking me. On the other hand, I don't have the right to waste my time. I am obliged to work like this.

Asked whether the "choking" feeling bothered him, the student replied: "Yes and no. Yes, a little, but on the other hand, this [the discipline] is why I came to work with her. So, I grumble, but despite that I can see the good side. Here I am now, still working with her."

I was able to find students happy with their master-disciple relationship, such as this twenty-year-old violinist: "He teaches me everything. He's a great master, the best in the world, and almost all the soloists who are on stage, and winning the first places in the big competitions, are his students. I didn't know how to play before joining his class, and he taught me everything. I owe him everything."

The relational expectations and experiences help create a repertoire of desirable traits described for the soloist teacher, traits that weigh on a student's decision whether to stay with a teacher or choose a new one. What is interesting is that at the last stage of their education, the students' criteria for making this choice have changed. In the third stage, the teacher's reputation plays the most important role. A twenty-four-year-old violinist, born and educated in Poland and Germany, said: "When you are twenty-four, you play on your own! It is not for learning that you go to a teacher, because at twenty-four, you already know how to play. You go to have the universal key to the stages—the big ones, not the small ones! You have to make your name in this small world." Another violinist of the same age, educated in the European Union and the United States, said, "I chose this teacher because he is well known all over the world. Okay, I have very few lessons with her, and she does not teach me anything new as far as playing is concerned. However, on my CV, it is very important."

In terms of criteria for choosing a teacher, the technical, musical, and human factors are principal for the second stage, whereas at the last stage, the students speak only about the teacher's reputation and networks of support.[42]

In the matching process, reputation plays an important role (Faulkner 1983; Zuckerman et al. 2003). A candidate who has studied in a famous soloist class and under a famous virtuoso master has a better chance of finding a match than a candidate whose pedigree is unknown. To optimize their relationship, the skills and reputations of the collaborators must be similar. A participant with a good position in the field cannot work with a participant unknown in their social world. Yet teachers may have a different sense of a candidate's potential, as demonstrated by the comments of two teachers of Gino, a Romanian-born violinist from a family of Gypsy musicians. The first teacher, a fifty-six-year-old, educated in Moscow and living in France, says:

> You know, Gino is a Gypsy,[43] and he will become a great musician, but he lacks a brain—he doesn't have a great culture; he does not read enough, and he plays only instinctively. It is good for playing Sarasate,[44] but this is all! . . . In addition, he has a very troublesome custom. He forgets to pay me. I am forced to ask, "Listen, Gino, did your father give you money for the lesson?" And he responds, "Oh, yes, I forgot!" And he pays me one part; "Father will pay the rest next time," he says. However, I am sure that his father gives him all the money, but Gino takes a part for himself. OK . . . You know, this is the personality!

A second teacher, working with Gino at the same time, says: "Gino is an extremely gifted student—a wonderful talent, and he plays the virtuoso pieces like nobody else! He will learn Mozart, too. He will make it, because he makes very good progress."

Hence, matching is a decisive factor in the process of career coupling in which the reputations and the expectations of the participants must correspond. Irina, the first student we saw in Andriej's master class, will never collaborate with this teacher. She has never won a competition, never enrolled in other famous soloist classes. And, by the insiders' rule of thumb, she was too old (eighteen) to attain a high place in the soloist world. Irina did not bring any value to Andriej.

On the other hand, the second student, Fabiola, was much younger (fourteen) and had better potential—some TV recordings on popular programs, some finalist places in children's competitions, and she was starting to become a celebrity in her country. She had the possibility of obtaining a soloist position after years of hard work. This master lesson was a perfect example of the matching and trial period in Fabiola's career coupling with Andriej. Nothing was sure yet. Fabiola was not yet in Andriej's soloist class, and Andriej was not yet "a signatory" of her performances. He was her master class teacher, but not a year-round teacher. The following school year, though, Fabiola entered his class as a regular student. The trial stage was over and she started the next stage of career coupling—the stage of active collaboration.

ACTIVE COLLABORATION IN CAREER COUPLING

After a master and disciple have found each other, they start the second stage of the career coupling process—a time of intensive collaboration. The teacher devotes additional time and works far more intensively with these exceptional students, and becomes involved in the disciple's career trajectory.

Bridge-building between master and disciple also involves reciprocal investment in the student's development and what students call a "specific dynamic of work." The teacher makes him or herself available to the student, knowing that only this availability insures the quality of work indispensable to a soloist's developing.

Yuri Yankelevich is an exceptional example of teacher dedication, because once he had chosen a disciple, he remained involved even when the student's hope of becoming a soloist was lost, as Yankelevich's assistant, Inna Gaukhman, recalled:

[Valery] Zvonov's accident perfectly illustrates the relationships Yankelevich maintained with his students. Zvonov was accepted into the Institute of Music attached to the Conservatory (of Tchaikovsky in Moscow), but during the summer his left hand was badly injured. The tendons of his hand did not heal and he saw himself abandoning the violin. Zvonov originated from a working-class family living in the Moscow suburbs. When I received his desperate letter, I told Yankelevich about it. . . . Professor Yankelevich invited Valery to Moscow, and despite many obstacles, he got a year of treatment at the Institute of Balneotherapy and Physiotherapy in Moscow. [Yankelevich] felt that Zvonov could become a good violinist, and he did all he could in order to support him so he could return to music. (in Brussilovsky 1999: 312)

The intimacy of the master and the disciple is a sign of distinction that shows others in the soloist world which students might benefit from preferential treatment. For example, one teacher gave private lessons at his home for his star students only. The other students perceived this as a sign of the teacher's preference for the "chosen." The privilege of proximity is granted to students placed atop the teacher's hierarchy. Thanks to them, the teacher achieves or confirms his or her reputation as an excellent soloist teacher. While almost all students try to reach this privileged place, few will make it.

THE INTENSIVE RHYTHM OF WORK: TEACHER-STUDENT RELATIONSHIPS

In the soloist class, I observed different rhythms of work that veer between times of crisis and periods of ordinary work.[45] During the "quiet" period, when there are no approaching deadlines and the teacher has time, he may help the student prepare a new repertoire, and lessons are set less frequently.[46] When a test, concert, or competition approaches, the soloist teacher always sets aside extra time for new and prolonged lessons. The teacher increases the pressure to push the student to more effort during the lesson and during practice. The student pushes on and does not think about relaxing.

During crisis times, the current program is worked to perfection, while technical problems and new pieces are put on the back burner. During the quiet time, some students get the feeling that their progress has stopped. Sometimes the teacher, finding the quiet period has gone on too long, will fix new deadlines in order to get the student into a higher gear. To complete these projects the student must work harder; quiet time changes into crisis time. This transformation of work rhythms is a typical phenomenon of intensive collaboration, the main activity of the career couple and highly specific to this second stage of soloist education, which I call "active cooperation."

This intensive collaboration has certain consequences for the relationships of the teacher and his or her students. Often, the fee is waived for some of the supplemental lessons. The reduction of distance is palpable in the ambiance of reciprocal confidence and trust, which is indispensable for the building the career coupling. This reduction of distance sometimes extends into the private realm. There are instances in which the student moves into the teacher's home.

Teachers of the Eastern European tradition are most likely to host a student; such pupils become part of the entourage that indicates the greatness of the teacher, as this soloist student recounts:

> Because of the hodgepodge of accommodations that was so widespread in the Soviet Union, it was very hard for the teachers to live with their students, but some did. This kind of teacher was constantly surrounded by people. It was like a royal court that moved with them: they never walked alone. Two or more students were always around, as well as the accompanist and one of the parents, or an assistant. It was a veritable royal court! My teacher's apartment was too small to house students, but from early in the morning, the whole court was there in the corridor of the conservatory. One student looked at the teacher's plane ticket, another looked for the keys of the concert-hall before the rehearsal, and another spoke to her about the scores, or whatever. There were always people around her.

Some teachers from the Eastern European tradition continue to host students while living in the West. Ivan Galamian housed several of his students simultaneously in his apartment in Manhattan. David Nadien[47] was among a handful of students who lived with the Galamians.[48] His recollections of Galamian are much warmer than Steinhardt's, perhaps because he came to know Galamian on a more intimate basis:[49] "The Galamians' apartment had great long hallways and a lot of rooms. Galamian had his studio in the front, and we—Helen Kwallwasser, Yura Osmolovsky, and I—had rooms in the back where we practiced three or four hours a day. It was a very relaxed atmosphere, and all of us had fun" (Lourie-Sand 2000: 50).

Teachers' private lives are intertwined with their professional lives, a state of affairs that is strongly characteristic of elite education. As teachers grow closer to certain students, they want to be always at their disposal. Yuri Yankelevich never taught at his home, but he organized gatherings for listening and analyzing classical records. In the Iron Curtain era, when Soviet Union citizens were isolated, Yankelevich could travel around the world and often returned with records. His library was unique in Moscow and became legendary, his apartment a place of privileged contacts with students who learned about musical culture there: "These evenings weren't ordinary evenings. There he taught his students to listen and to hear, to respect and to love the heritage of several generations of performers. He also taught how to elaborate one's own approach to music, knowing that the style of interpretation changes periodically" (Broussilovsky 1999: 266).

The practice of hosting students is rare among teachers not originating from an Eastern European tradition. I found only one example of student hosting by a French teacher, and this happened in the particular context of World War II. Devy Erlih, in a letter addressed to the Israeli commission that awards those who risked their lives to prevent crimes against humanity during the Nazi occupation, described how he was taken in by his violin teacher, Jules Boucherit:

> For that I will always grateful. And I will never forget that he oversaw my studies during all those war years, whatever the circumstances, and he never asked me about remuneration. He never spared an effort to help me. To the contrary! He took me with his other students on vacation to the island of Marlotte, and in June 1944, knowing that my parents didn't have any resources, he offered to have me live at Chansonnière despite the danger for him posed by my presence at his home. I lived there until the end of the summer, even after the liberation of Paris. (Soriano 1993: 126)

In normal circumstances, the hosting of students is an example of the extreme closeness of the master and his or her disciple. This intimacy is not only a custom, maintained out of respect for tradition, but also the result of work organization.

The Organization of Work

Frequent shared travel for master classes and competitions bring student and teachers closer. The close spaces (the abbeys, the castles, empty schools) where these events are often organized favor isolation that helps deepen the relationships. Time spent together on musical activities like concerts, festivals, and competitions strengthens the bonds. Teacher and students frequently stay in the same hotels; during trips, too, some teachers give supplemental lessons. These lessons rarely adhere to the schedule. Meetings are fixed at the last minute, frequently late at night or early in the morning; the student must be completely at the teacher's disposal. This environment has an impact on the private lives of both parties. Even the meals and rare moments of free time are frequently shared by collaborators. They work in close proximity (the students' practice rooms are in the same building as the teacher's class), and they meet constantly. Downtime activities are also shared. I observed a chess game between a Russian teacher and his disciple. Chess is popular among the masters, who believe that it promotes a type of focus beneficial to young performers. Not every joint activity is cerebral—some teachers and students occasionally enjoy a game of soccer together. An eighteen-year-old student recalled: "I've never been interested in football [soccer]. But one day I was at my new teacher Adam's house for a lesson, and when we stopped working at one point he said: 'OK, now we need some down time. Let's watch a match.' Then, he plugged in the TV and we watched a game together. It wasn't so bad; I'd never seen a game before. And my teacher suggested that after the lessons we watch football, just to let off steam. . . . He loves that game, my teacher."

One day I observed a nonreligious student accompanying his teacher to church. His master was religious, the student said, and he wanted to please him. Participating in such activities, the student shows he is at the master's beck and call. At the same time, spending time together outside music hours enables the student to get help from a mentor for personal problems. Some teachers find this proximity indispensable for good instrumental work with the student. "The teacher," said Yankelevich, "needs to know how to live the life of each of his students, pierce their nature and their psychology, to follow them in their evolution" (Brussilovsky 1999: 260). Yankelevich spent each summer working with his students for competitions. Walking in the forest with his charges, Yankelevich taught them the history of music and shared his other passions, such as botany.

Teachers often help their favorite students with administrative problems, such as immigration, housing, scholarships, or obtaining a prestigious borrowed violin.[50] I know teachers who have lent money to their students to purchase a violin, or even to pay rent during periods in which students were waiting for scholarships or contracts and having a hard time financially. The biographies of famous violinists give many examples of such support.[51] One of Yankelevich's students, Victor Trietiakov, reported that

> Gorodine [his first teacher] wrote several letters asking the famous violin teachers of Moscow to hear this "gifted child," but everybody refused. Y. Yankelevich was the only one who had accepted this request. It was after that, in 1954, at the age of seven, that I came to the capital with my parents. Y. Yankelevich tested me and enrolled me in his class. And so I began my life as a student who was the object of great care by Yankelevich. . . . He started the efforts to get permission to move and the order to transfer my father to Moscow. My father's status in the military [he was a soldier-musician] made moving tough. However, this didn't stop Yankelevich. He spoke to General Petrov, the conductor of the Orchestra of the Red Army, and obtained permission for moving my father through the intermediary of the Joint Chief of Staff. Today, I can imagine all these efforts very well, which Yankelevich needed to use at that time. (Brussilovsky 1999: 315)

Teachers who are very close to their students and who are confident, helpful, and understanding, clearly optimize their students' efforts to learn the violin. Intense and personal coaching makes it possible not only to engender a passion for the instrument, but strengthens the student's singular attachment to the teacher.

The following section is devoted to this type of coaching, which is similar to other elite coaching in sports and other arts or sciences.

Strict Supervision of a Young Violinist's Trajectory

During the second stage of soloist education, the teacher takes over the parent's job of motivating the student to practice and progress. The teacher is rushing to speed the student's accomplishment, and liberally compares him or her to other careers as a prod to get the young violinist to blaze a soloist trail. The idea is to inspire the student to overcome obstacles with the pleasure of success and the knowledge that the student is passing the milestones of a successful career. The comparison with model trajectories of the past is not enough; the teacher must guide the student through more intermediate goals. This helps the future soloist feel that he or she occupies a well-defined space, moving along a clearly marked pathway in good time.

The teacher constantly points out new goals, using a variety of techniques. For example, during the intermission of a concert, the teacher of three violinists who have just performed enters their room with scores in hand and tells them, "Not bad. We will work out the details in our next lesson, but I brought you new scores. I already put in the fingering. For Zaria, it is 'Spanish Fantasy,' for Caroline, the Beethoven concerto, and for Yann, 'Tzigane.' This is a beautiful program. Work on it for Monday."

Using intermediate goals as a tool for student supervision is, of course, not the sole domain of the soloist musician. In his book, *The State Nobility: Elite Schools in the Field of Power* (1996) Pierre Bourdieu reports that the students at a preparatory college (where they are groomed for the "grandes écoles") suffer from overwork. In a certain sense, the school has taken them under its strict tutelage; they have no time for anything other than scholarly activity. The sole difference between the soloist students and the preparatory class students is that the latter know before enrollment that they will work very intensively for a specific period of time. These French students make a strategic choice: they can choose preparatory classes and undergo a monkish lifestyle for two years, or enroll in the university system and have some free time for other activities besides study.

The situation of a soloist student is different. From their childhood, for as long as they can remember, soloists work hard. This norm is not questioned. The student does not say to himself, "In the next few years, will I work with Mr. S, who will ask me to practice seven hours a day?" The parents worked to implant the rigorous practice regime in their child, and this gives the expected results. The young violinists say they "feel the need to practice" and most feel guilty if they do not practice several hours each day.

The busy schedule helps the teacher maintain the student's dependence on them. The teacher imposes a trajectory, and valorizes the student's work with specific gratifications. The successful students I observed did not question the weight of work; only those who perceive their soloist student trajectory as a failure doubt the validity of their education. Without a strong belief in soloist education, nobody makes the monumental effort that is required. Therefore, the teacher needs to maintain in the students (and their parents) the conviction that their education is legitimate—and succeeding.

Competition prizes, performances in prestigious places, and media coverage are all considered promising indicators of a successful path and confirmation of a future soloist's status. The main goal is to accumulate successes, and to do that the young soloist must multiply his or her opportunities. The spouse of the accompanist of several of the biggest violin competitions, a very clever observer of the world of the musician, told me: "It is not enough to participate only in one competition per year, as some people do. You have to do five, six. In the first two, you don't win; the following two, you reach the third stage [of competition], and in the last competition, maybe you get into the final. And one day you win. This is how it works. You don't win every time. You need to work hard to have a chance."

COLLABORATION IN CAREER COUPLING

After the matching period, when teacher and student are satisfied with each other, the second stage of coupling, which I call "active cooperation," begins. To create favorable conditions for collaboration, the two actors spend a lot of time together. Playing chess, sharing meals, etc., gives them time to develop their relationships. Sometimes, a professor can provide accommodation for his student. Proximity allows the mixing of private and professional relationships and influences the work dynamics required for the stimulation of results. Because teachers typically have many students, and career coupling relationships take a lot of time, this kind of strong attachment is possible only with a few students at a time. The young virtuosos realize this, and therefore seek as close a relationship as possible with the master. Intimate access means more free lessons and other supporting actions (concert organizations, participation in competitions, recordings, etc.)

This strong relationship not only fosters intensive and passionate work, but also constant negotiations between the actors, who may not perceive the relationship exactly the same way, as a nineteen-year-old violin student suggests:

> She [the teacher] rather wants to be my mother. I think that it embarrasses me—I do not want her to know where I am at midnight. Of course, her reaction is natural because she wants me to work very hard, so I can only be grateful to her. This is why I say that she is a tyrant—and that is normal. She also works with me a lot, and I do not pay for all this time, because she says I am her means of showing her knowledge. We are tied together; we have a common interest, and that is all.

During the stage of active collaboration, each actor constructs his or her career using the partner's knowledge or abilities. Knowledge from the initiator enriches the novice, and the initiator profits from the performances of his or her young follower. The teachers show their artistry through the performance of their students, principally through participation in competitions.

CONSTRUCTION OF REPUTATION

By participating in competitions and other public performances, master and disciple build their careers together, and their world quickly learns about the partnership because the "hand of a master" is visible (or audible). When the violinist plays, other violinists recognize aspects of interpretation and style that result from the teacher's work. These include not only coaching and psychological preparation, but also the professional "touch"—the master's brilliant fingering, masterful bow strokes, and profound sound. The violinist plays, and the professional public judges both student and teacher. Because the violin soloists' world is so small, people know one another personally or through their production: CDs, news from competitions, and/or TV programs.

In this world, information about actors, their work level, and their improvement spreads rapidly and becomes the basis of reputation. In the worlds where the process of career coupling builds careers, and only the best musicians work with the best, Robert Merton's "Matthew Effect" (1968: 56–63) applies to both partners. Certainly at this stage of the collaboration between master and disciple their situation is not equal. The professor is in a dominant position, not only because of previous achievement of former students but because in one class each professor has more than one student, whereas the student usually has only one professor at time. Because the artists build their reputation in reciprocity, the extension of the Matthew Effect is a consequence of career coupling; reputations are linked and each builds on the other. The world comes to recognize an unknown actor through a well-known career partner. That is why the first question to an unknown virtuoso is: "Who is your master?"

The extension of reputation is a consequence of coupling, but it can be risky. For example, the conductor of a German orchestra gave the following advice to a young twenty-year-old virtuoso who was weighing an intensive collaboration with one teacher: "You must be careful, because it is dangerous to join his class. He does not have a very good reputation in Germany, and you will have difficulty playing in concerts after being in his class. You might not win any competitions unless he is on the jury. Think about this before you join his class."

Reputations are not fixed, and there is always a risk of losing one's standing. This happened to a famous teacher whose students stopped winning competitions, sinking below the level the teacher's students had achieved at the beginning of his career. When one collaborator loses his or her good reputation, the partner must save face by cutting off the coupling process, and communicating this breach to others in the soloist world. Such a case occurred with an English violinist who had studied, between the ages of eleven and fifteen, in the class of a famous teacher in Germany. When the teacher began to lose his good reputation, she changed teachers and worked with a new teacher, herself a famous soloist. Although the new teacher worked with her for only about a year, the young soloist sought to erase her association with the old teacher, whose reputation had soured, though he had taught her much of what she knew. She cut the process of career coupling and made a new start. The soloist world quickly recognized that she had changed her career-coupling partner.

To be sure, such conflicts are rarely the cause of the end of an active career coupling. More often, the student makes the move to seek more distance, wanting the professional world to evaluate him or her independently from the master. When the world of soloists has recognized the link between the actors of career coupling, and the student has acquired professional skill and knowledge, the activities of both actors are less dependent on each other than in the period of active collaboration. The actors enter the third stage of career coupling, which I call "passive collaboration." This stage of career coupling corresponds frequently to the third stage of a soloist's education.

Rupture of the Teacher-Student Relationship

The evolution of the disciple's relationship with his or her master determines the soloist's education. The teacher must respond to the student's ideals and needs within a flexible and dynamic relationship. As the young students grow, their behavior changes, as do their expectations. If in the first stage of a soloist education, the teacher imposes his knowledge on the student and expects certain results, in the second stage the student gains the confidence to assert what he or she wants to learn. The instances in which a teacher and student can cross through both stages together are few and far between. A young eighteen-year-old violinist describes the more common transition in the following words:

> I joined Gregor's class at the age of twelve, and I spent one whole year learning how to understand his teaching. He was a violinist, a musician. And me, I was too young to see that. But, during those three years together, it was very good. He took care of me and I admired him for his playing. Then, I realized that I wanted to move at a faster pace than what he wanted; also, he promised many things but fulfilled very few. He was not a good technical teacher. His lessons became second-rate, and even his concerts lost their high quality. So, naturally, I was very disappointed. In addition to that, I entered into my adolescent period, which didn't make things easier, and I left his class. Today, I think he could have taught me some things, some visions of interpretation, some specific approaches; but, pedagogically, he wasn't good. He himself was a former student of the best soloist class in the world, but he couldn't communicate what he had learned. It's a pity, because he reacted poorly to my departure. He is still angry with me and I haven't had any contact with him since.

When a relationship between teacher and student sours, the student most often changes classes. A teacher tries to keep the student inside of his circle of influence—if there is no hope for a good result, the student will be sent to an assistant or collaborator. It is rare that a professor directly fires a student. It is usually the student who decides to end the relationship. Anselm Strauss, in his analysis of relationships between master and disciples, remarks that

The student has the final responsibility of judging when the coaching relation-ship is genuinely harmful to himself or to his "potential." . . . The coach may have poor judgment. It is not impossible that he evinces faulty judgment because he loves or hates his pupil too much, although he may be actually malevolent or merely indifferent. The learner always has an obligation to himself of assessing when he is being harmed and when he is being helped, even in those very tradi-tional situations where the coach is supposed to be supremely knowledgeable. The reverse side of great risk and danger is trust and faith. (Strauss 1959: 115)

Students who decide to abandon a teacher usually proceed in one of two ways. He or she may make a gradual departure, starting classes with a new teacher while continuing with the old over a period of a month or more. Usually the first teacher is not informed of the situation, because most teachers refuse to teach a student who has another, unless the other teacher is the first teacher's assistant. The fol-lowing testimony illustrates a gradual shift:

I had been in Laszlo's class for ten years when I was sixteen. Adam, my friend and a student in his class, left about two years earlier. Laszlo was hard on his students in the sense that he could hurt them very deeply and emotionally in the soul, although unintentionally, and not always over their musicianship. He had a big and strong personality, though not very strong. He pressured his students and some couldn't bear that style of teaching . . . Adam, he couldn't. Well, he took it for several years and then had enough. Lazlo's students . . . broke free from him . . . one by one. [Eva sighs] Laszlo was a very famous violinist, an excel-lent musician . . . that was his biggest contribution to my education—this desire to become great—because when you have a teacher of this caliber, you have the desire to become . . . like him. But he was not present enough with his students. I did not have enough lessons with him, and he wasn't following my course of education. . . . In retrospect, he wasn't a good teacher. He didn't have any direc-tion in his pedagogical work, not enough rigor, wasn't well organized. He had perfect technique, but he didn't know how to teach. . . . So when I realized that he was not giving me proper instruction anymore, I went to see Madame Kalina. With Laszlo, I felt that I had uncorrected mistakes and that I wasn't making any more progress.

Also, at that time, I was in contact with Adam, and he advised me to join Madame Kalina's class. He had been enrolled in this class for more than two years by then.

Leaving Laszlo's class was very difficult, Eva said.

Adam had left his class two years before, and it ended badly. As for me, I never told him that I was going to leave, I just left. He was someone who never ran after his students, and wasn't about to start now. He was tired and old, and had many other problems to address. I decided not to tell him that I was changing teachers. Later on, I told him that I had sacrificed the violin in order to do better in school. But I think he now knows where I actually am and what I am doing.

Asked whether she thought the break could create turmoil in her career, Eva responded, "No, because he doesn't have the power anymore. It is true, however, that I can't compete in X [the contest created and presided by Laszlo]." She laughed.

The second way a teacher change occurs is when the student leaves and only afterward looks for a new teacher. Such situations are less frequent. Enrollment in a soloist class is typically organized according to a certain routine—contacting the teacher through a previous teacher, auditioning, taking private lessons and master classes. But there are no ground rules for leaving a soloist class, especially in the case of a conflictive relationship.

No official rules exist because the student is simply not supposed to leave his or her teacher. Eva managed a well-organized transition by using her friend Adam to help her move to Madame Kalina. Other violinists do not organize their departure in advance, and their actions are less well coordinated. They simply desert one teacher and begin trying to arrange lessons with another.

The friend-violinist, or sometimes another person from the musician's circle, can help make the switch happen. We observed the father of a brilliant, successful violinist advising a young soloist student who was in the process of changing his teacher:

> If you want, I can give you two addresses. You can sample both teachers, but I recommend my friend. Call him, say that you got his number from me. Take one lesson with him, then a second, and a third. Afterward, you can decide for yourself. He's my friend and he works with my son—we don't say anything to my son's main teacher, but my friend helps my son elaborate interpretations. He's a wonderful teacher. He's not frustrating. He's a very good violinist, and I am sure you will understand each other. Take some classes with other teachers as well and compare them; you alone will know what's best for you.

The student tries, takes a few lessons, and decides whether to stay with this teacher. The students believe they can evaluate teachers' work enough to make their decision. This type of teacher change most often takes place after a master class, but at times it is the old teacher who takes the initiative. The teacher may believe the move will benefit the violinist's development skills. Sometimes, the teacher does not want to prolong the collaboration with one of his students. In the first case, the teacher contacts another teacher belonging to his network in order to prepare the reception of the student. After some private lessons, the new teacher usually points the student to the music school at which he or she teaches. After an entrance exam (or even without one), the student enrolls in the new class, and by doing so, integrates into a new professional network.[52]

CHANGING MASTERS AND ENTERING A NEW NETWORK

Students enrolling in a soloist class are aware that they are a part of an enterprise, and that their actions are enmeshed in a network of collaboration and support created by their teacher and others around them. In a given soloist class, the student benefits from the collective efforts of all members of the complex organization that gravitates around the master. The workings of this organism are specific to the virtuoso's world, but similar to other artistic milieus. The student must act docilely toward his or her master, who is the one actually making the "collective decisions" as to which competitions to take part in, concerts to play, and how to interpret pieces. When the break with the teacher arrives, the student's whole world collapses, and very often it is at that precise moment that the student measures the role played by this network of support. In his analysis of the relationship between a master and disciple, A. Strauss noted that in the case of the rupture "a special danger is that the relationship may be broken off midstream, before 'the treatment' is completed, with potential danger to both but particularly to the learner" (Strauss 1959: 114).

This feeling of lost opportunity is one of the many factors that push the student to accept his or her teacher's expectations. Without the teacher's help and the help of the entire entourage, the students would be unable to pursue a soloist education. Yet for some young violinists, the master's network is a kind of golden cage. In it, they find that despite conforming to the internal rules, they are unable to gain the reputation necessary for a good career debut. Conflicts arise with the support network; the network sanctions students who challenge it. One student explained such a way in the following manner:

> You enter the camp as if it is a religious order. You belong to your teacher and you must adhere to his technique and interpretation. You play a violin loaned to you by his violin maker, and you perform concerts organized by his friends. You partake in the competitions chosen by him, which he judges in your favor. You spend your holidays with him (because you have the master class, festivals, and concerts). Your dates (planning, schedule) are all fixed by him and his machine. You spend time with him, you play with his pianist, you meet the people who are in his entourage, you record in the studio of "his friends," and you are introduced by him everywhere, as well as to people of the press—obviously his friends. And the day you leave him—you are alone.

To escape the isolation of the bubble created by the network, and in the case of conflict, the possibility to stay without their teacher, students frequently prepare their change of class in advance, so they can quickly be supported by a new network of collaboration. They know very well that staying without the teacher and his network of support is dangerous for continuity of training and can damage their career. This explains why students look for a new teacher before definitively leaving the former. Teachers are not always interested in a new candidate, but will almost always not lose the opportunity to welcome a new student into their circle of influence by directing them to a friend. The teachers can declare unavailability at any moment using exceptional concert tours or other projects as an excuse. In order to hold onto a new student, some teachers may give a few lessons, but only occasionally, at which point they tell you to contact their friend, who "was in the same school as me and who works exactly like me, in whom I have complete confidence."

This procedure is indispensable in order to hang onto a student as a backup, to keep him or her within the teacher's network of influence. This kind of situation presents several possibilities. In the first case, the student agrees to work with the recommended assistant, and is satisfied with this collaboration, which prepares the student for entrance into the master's class.[53] The second possibility consists of a teacher change inside one of the friend-networks (the network, which collaborates at that moment with a former teacher's network).

Sometimes, when students change their teachers, they upset the balance of the soloist's environment, which provokes an intervention by the teachers, who attempt to return to the previous state of collaboration—coexistence between teacher networks, as we can observe in the following story, which I heard first from a Russian emigrant teacher in a formal interview, and later confirmed with other participants.

> For a whole year, I worked with Pablo in response to a request from Serge, who wanted me to prepare him for Serge's classes at the Flowertown conservatory for the eliminatory exam the following September. You know, . . . he does not have much culture. He does not read enough and he plays only instinctively. . . . So, Serge sent me this boy and I started to work on him. It was hard work, but even Serge was surprised with the results. After the summer, I had no news from Pablo. Two months ago I saw him play somewhere, and Aza [another teacher who emigrated from Russia] told me that Pablo just attended her class in the conservatory of Y. She also knows Serge very well, and I told her that Pablo was supposed to be in the conservatory of X working with Serge, and not in her class. She immediately called Serge to apologize, saying she knew nothing about his arrangement with Pablo. Realizing what kind of person Pablo is, he will not be missed in Serge's class.

This story illustrated the perturbation of the soloist's world's functioning. Pablo transgressed three basic rules obvious in this milieu. First and foremost, the loyalty to the teacher—Serge, who introduced him to his collaborator—in order that the former prepare Pablo for the entrance exam for Serge's class. Pablo failed to inform Serge about his change of plans and switched to another teacher, Aza, while Serge waited for him. He broke another rule by failing to inform Aza that he had been prepared for Serge's class. Thirdly, in switching classes from Serge to Aza, Pablo had ignored the rule of hierarchy, which states that when he drops a teacher this places the dropped teacher in a lower status position compared to the new one.[54] In their country of origin, Serge was a well-known performer in the capital, a former prodigy at the top of the instrumentalist hierarchy. Aza, meanwhile, was only an assistant teacher in a soloist class in a provincial city.

After their emigration, Serge continued his career as a soloist with much less success. To assure a regular salary (with social benefits and a pension),[55] he teaches in a conservatory located in the suburbs of a European capital. Aza, meanwhile, works in a well-known conservatory based in this capital. The professional status of the two teachers had changed but not in a definitive way because of their earlier, pre-emigration reputations. Pablo, through his ignorance, transgressed the rule that implies that a change of teacher means a step up. Also, it is customary and polite for the new teacher to contact the former teacher before others learn that the student has switched.

Although Serge was betrayed by Pablo, it was Aza who apologized, showing that she wished to conserve a good relationship with Serge, although she was not directly dependent upon him. Neither Serge nor the assistant showed any wish to reclaim Pablo. Even before the episode, teachers badmouthed and scolded him for lack of culture and being a "difficult student." These qualities certainly contributed to the fact that this story did not cause much of an uproar or trouble among the teachers. The discussions that followed the "misunderstanding" were provoked by a concern for the reestablishment of the insider soloist milieu's equilibrium. Little concern was shown for the ungrateful student.

Aza's conciliatory call to Serge was not unfruitful. Two years after this event, both teachers were members of a jury in an international competition, and their collaboration made it possible for them to attain their respective goals—both selected their own students as winners. They had conformed to the rule of their professional milieu that stipulates that musicians from the same teaching tradition should stay on good terms, since a cordial relationship may serve, at any time, as the basis for joint action.

At the second stage of their education, students look for a teacher—a master—who will find in them "the gift," which will lead them to success, helping in the development of their self-confidence and giving hope for their future soloist career. By the end of this second stage of education, the interaction has become a collaboration, rather than the unilateral transmission of knowledge from all-knowing teacher to obedient student. The evolution of a conflictive situation depends on the student's ability to evaluate the benefits of collaboration with the master in balance with vigilance over their own progress. For example, students who have a problem with "sonority" (the quality of achieving a beautiful sound) will want to see a teacher known for his or her work on the right hand; afterward they work with another who is gifted in teaching the "interpretation" of pieces.

During these changes, and as an effect of these changes, students realize that the future is in their hands. Their previous dreams of a master who gives them everything and requires only that they do what he expects, no longer hold up in reality. Still, though their belief in an all-powerful teacher is diminished, the students need a teacher for their work. Progressively, the voids in soloist education are filled and the young virtuosos acquire the experience to cross into the realm of independence. They do not need a teacher in the matter of instrumental work anymore. As the need for independence grows, relationships with other young violinists become very important.

RIVAL OR CONFIDANTE? RELATIONSHIPS BETWEEN PEERS

In the earliest stages of the soloist career, fellow students typically meet each other in the context of contests. Gradually, students learn how to maintain peer relationships that enable the exchange of professional experiences and knowledge.

Relations among students who are in the same soloist class and work with the same master are different from those between students in different classes. In the first case, the exchanges are of a practical nature. Students exchange scores in order to copy fingering notation and bow details, and frequently swap lesson times. Students from different classes, meanwhile, have questions for each other: How does your teacher work? Does he or she work a long time on the same piece, or change the repertoire quickly? Is he available to the students? Interested in students outside of violin playing? What are her hobbies, how does she live, what is her reputation? And, sometimes, how do students enter the class? Other topics are also discussed, for example, how to find a good violin maker, or where to borrow an old and prestigious instrument. Tips about violin care (done mainly by violin makers) are shared easily, but instrument lending information is a preciously kept secret, because the number of old violins is limited, and the candidates who wish to play on them are numerous.

Violin students frequently exchange the "dope" about master classes. They look for master classes that are "cheap and proper." The perfect master lessons are done by the teacher and not his or her assistant; the lessons are individual, not collective; they are frequent and inexpensive and done in a good site with practice rooms and a spacious lesson hall with good acoustics, a good accompanist, and a good piano, tuned for violinists (about 442 Hertz for A). The possibility of playing the competition's program before a public audience is also highly desirable.

Information that is less frequently shared concerns financial support, scholarships, and the names of potential sponsors, who are limited. Usually, students reveal information about a potential source only if they are not applying for it, for example because they are too old, the wrong nationality, or have already received the award and cannot apply again.

These exchanges of information take place not only inside the same soloist class, but at competitions, the master classes, or even at concerts. The milieu of soloist students is limited, and they frequently meet each other several times a year. Alice met Frank during his master-class in August in Zurich, Switzerland, then in September during a violin competition in Italy, and afterward at the Parisian Conservatory in November. Traveling a lot and taking part in soloist-student activities, the young violinists build and maintain relationships with those who will become a part of the soloist world in the future. It is through these peer ties that students become progressively independent, indispensable for the final part of their soloist education.

This independence is actually not complete. After years of very strong dependence on others, the emancipation from parents and teachers is only partial. They continue to care for a young violinist's career: parents, through financial and or psychological support, teachers through their own actions and the support work done by their networks.

Inside the Soloist Class

It is impossible to overlook the issue of hierarchy when discussing relationships between students from the same soloist class. In-class relationships occur somewhere on the spectrum between strong and devoted mutual aid and a complete lack of communication. The following excerpt from an interview with Sarah, nineteen, offers insights into the complexity of student relationships. "In Stiepan's class, we knew each other very well and there was a nice ambiance," Sarah says, but this was not the case in Madame Zora's class, where the students do not even exchange scores or fingerings:

> I am the oldest one in the class; there are a lot of young students, and this makes it that much more difficult. They are not my friends, while in Zurich [where Stiepan taught] I . . . befriended practically all of them. . . . We had concerts with our orchestra ensemble. This created ties. . . . We lived together, ate together, while here, every one is alone. Here, I only have one student in my class with whom I hit it off, because he's of my age and also because we know each other very well and have known each other for a long time. He was also in the same class before, in Zurich! But now other students . . . Mireille[56] and others . . . but especially, Mireille. She is younger than I . . . but it is not only that . . . her mother pushes the competitions very hard and it creates a feeling of jealousy. . . . They [Mireille and her mother] don't like me, that's all there is to it!

This student's comparison embodies many of the determinants of sociability within a soloist class. These include the proximity of residence, common activities (in fact, it is rare for soloist students to participate in the same orchestra in Europe), shared hobbies, and similar age (a large disparity, ten years or more, is frequent inside a soloist class). Parents play a role when they isolate their young children, seeking to shelter them from all peer relationships. Such parents often see every other violinist as simply a competitor. Such parental attitude, which is related to the student hierarchy inside the class (student-stars and their competitors), can constitute a huge obstacle to friendships.

Examples of isolation and conviviality can occur at the same time in a single class. Sometimes the students isolate themselves, as Eva, a thirty-year-old violinist, did as a student. "With feedback, now, I realize that I did not have a normal teenage experience. I never went out with my friends. I was always alone at home because I worked. So, I experienced a little of my 'adolescence' only last year. In order to have more of a social life, I had my 'teenage crisis'; because beforehand, I didn't have a social life at all!"

International Competitions

Competition between soloists is fierce, and presumably limits friendships between musicians involved in a given event.[57] Yet even at these events, relationships develop in a very interesting and varied fashion. They start with individual conversations, which lead to the possibility of creating groups. Discussions usually begin among musicians who either live near one another or come from the same place.

At a competition organized in Germany a few years ago, most of the sixty-five competitors lived in an old castle, isolated and surrounded by a huge park, with a dining hall downstairs and a coffee shop nearby. I observed violinists making initial contact in two ways: moving with a group of existing friends (from the same class, or met at previous competitions or master classes), or an individual, spontaneous approach. The first type of contact usually means enlarging small groups with the addition of students from related violin schools. Students under two teachers who once were soloist classmates can constitute a "large family" that grows spontaneously, especially if language is not an obstacle and if some members of this circle knew each other before the event. Interestingly, these groups consist not only of students, but also their parents, who form close and lasting groups until the end of the competition.

On the second day of the competition, I observed that the groupings were organized on the rapport built between students who had similar origins and languages, whether or not they lived in the same country. During the following days, the groups expanded beyond these limits. These relationships took more time and occurred toward the end of the competition, when successive passages before the jury (playing three sets of selections) made it possible to make new acquaintances. We should keep in mind that passages before the jury are public and other competitors listen to their colleagues and frequently after they start the conversation about the performance, program played, and other professional topics.

A smaller group of students sought out colleagues on their own, independent of spheres of origin or common artistic heritage. Persons who acted in such a manner began to speak with several peers from the outset of the competition. They were principally bilingual or multilingual and bicultural, and had already had the experience of competition. Because of their facility with creating new contacts and their attitudes toward creating new relationships, these students distinguished themselves from other participants who always circulated in groups.

This was the case with an eighteen-year-old Dutch girl, living in Germany, and a fourteen-year-old Russian boy, living in Austria: both spoke three languages and communicated with all participants. Between the musicians ranging in age from fourteen years old to nineteen,[58] the English language was more popular, and sometimes, Russian; German, and other languages (Romanian, Polish, Italian) were less used.

Formed into groups, the young musicians spent their free time together outside the competition hall and practice rooms. Some students walked in the park, while others played ping-pong. In the evening, participants sat on the benches in front of the castle, laughing and joking and telling stories. Some of the older musicians smoked cigarettes and drank beer. These activities helped release some of their anxiety, which grew daily; common activities allowed them to demystify their adversaries, the other participants. Hanging out together with their peers was unusual, because each student was a soloist, and even within their soloist classes they did not always have close friends with whom they could share their experiences.

Belonging to a given group is crucial at the age of adolescence (Lepoutre 1997), and it is also important for the young soloist, which partly explains why many like these competitions. Frequently, students said they weren't competing to win, but rather to meet people. I sometimes heard that two participants were planning to take part in another event, although they didn't think highly of it, simply to see each other again. Some students rated competitions based on their ambiance. For example, the International Competition of Paganini in Genoa was said to be a "nice competition . . . where it is easy to find nice people."

Not all participants experienced the competition this way. Some participants did not feel free all; they had strict schedules, prepared most often by their teachers. Violin work was broken up with a few moments of chess or playing with a small smooth ball, which is supposed to improve manual technique. The team from Moscow was very isolated from other participants, the students moving in a group with the two parents in attendance (many of the other participants were accompanied by one or even both parents), or an accompanist or violin teacher. The students from Moscow were also unique because they did not need the official accompanist of the competition. One of their mothers played with all the class's participants. The behavior of the group was reminiscent of the Cold War days, when Soviet participants were discouraged from contact with people from outside the USSR. Mingling with other participants was considered in bad taste, and would have created problems after their return home.

The participants spoke most often about the competition itself: the program, the instruments (from which period? made by whom?), the soloist classes they were from, their teachers, the concerts they had played, earlier competitions. They discussed the information contained in the competition "booklets," which had the name, photograph, age, and nationality of most of the candidates, with place of birth, schools attended, musical program, and a short CV. All this information made it possible for participants to place themselves in relation to others. Then they made prognostications about the outcome of the competition, encouraging each other, meaning that they believed in the possibility of their future success.

Some participants listen to other candidates, but not all do. Most listen to the young virtuosos, who are unknown but generally supposed to be strong candidates. Some musicians never listen to each other, or listen only after they have finished their own performances.[59] As the competition goes on, players critique the participants from different groups, but they rarely give a negative critique about a particular player. Strong support is expressed for any given soloist, particularly when speaking to the player's relatives. Almost all participants respect the competition's informal rule, which demand moral support for other candidates. "Good luck," said in English, is an obligatory remark to those who are about to face the jury.

Participation in international competitions from a very early age makes it possible to build a dynamic international social network.[60] From the second stage of soloist education, competitions make it possible for young virtuosos to establish an address book of musicians around the world. Those contacts are their professional capital and are invoked on multiple occasions when the young musicians meet and gauge each other in the soloist hierarchy. The following extracts are typical of the discussions between participants in competitions: "Look, Ivan won the Bach competition," a sixteen-year-old student says to a seventeen-year-old. "But two years ago, in the Mozart competition, he was behind me." Or "Oliver is now in

Zwonow's class. He will come to Cologne [a competition]. I am curious to know how he will be evaluated."

Some participants in these competitions will probably make international careers and meet someone famous down the line, and their acquaintances will be able to boost their status and reputation from the fact of knowing them. On a TV music program, one of the spectator-violinist musicians exclaimed: "See! Sacha on TV again. . . . I remember ten years ago, when he only thought about eating cookies! We played chess matches all the time! He played chess as well as the violin!"[61]

During the second stage of education, relationships between young soloists are usually sporadic, but can be renewed according to the circumstances. Young musicians learn how to maintain ties based on musical activity, independent of national borders and linguistic barriers. For example, a Polish student living in Germany contacts a Ukrainian living in Austria through the Internet, asking for a place to stay for three days to attend private violin lessons given by a famous teacher. The violinists had met a year earlier in Switzerland for a master class, and saw each other again a few months later during a competition in Italy.

Competitions, master classes, and festivals are the spaces in which the musicians create links that become social networks. They learn how to maintain courteous relationships with their musical rivals, an important adjustment to life in a competitive field. These events also allow students educated in solitude, apart from their peers, a chance to create a social environment and a reference group for sharing their singular experiences.[62] The young virtuosos know they are different from other young people; some of them suffer with that. One exceptional student, who had attended a normal school until she was seventeen, told me about this aspect of a young soloist's life:

> I rarely go to parties, I don't have a million friends; I have a few, and that's enough. I don't take holidays. When I was in school I had a kind of "jet lag." For the last two or three years now, I have only been with the people who do the same thing as me. I am not complaining, but when I was younger . . . in middle school, going out with friends and all this stuff, it was very limited. On the other hand, I don't miss anything. I was very isolated from my other classmates, because of violin, but also because of my personality. I had one year in advance; I practiced my violin intensively, so I wasn't available. I was in another world, because I went to Cologne almost every week, because I had friends who were older, and not in regular middle school anymore.

In spite of language differences, young soloists have similar preoccupations, similar interests and values.[63] Although most contacts between soloists recede at the end of a competition or master class, sometimes their importance grows. Couples sometimes form during these meeting, and while they frequently break up because of distance, those between members of the same violin class may last longer. One day, a teacher, very surprised and a little shocked, told me that two of her old students had fallen in love. "They are not even embarrassed to kiss each other in front of me between lessons!" The two violinists had agreed to pursue their soloist education together in the United States. Couples originating from the same violin class are not unusual in the musical world. Two of the most famous examples are Itzhak Perlman and his spouse, Toby, and in the younger generation, Gil Shaham and Adele Anthony; all four were students of Dorothy DeLay at the Juilliard School of Music in New York City.

FEAR OF NOT FLYING ALONE: FINISHING THE SECOND STAGE

The second stage of soloist education is a time of changes with consequences, and the modification of relationships between the young virtuosos and their environment. Parents lose their positions as assistants, and their children become more independent, even if they remain financially dependent. The students increasingly make their own professional decisions concerning the path that was chosen and blazed by parents, as well as their relationships with the teacher.

This stage of education is one of social and professional maturation. Relationships with peers take precedence, because the exchange of professional information is vital to their future entrance into a saturated market. Relationships with teachers frequently turn confrontational. The teachers, who have accompanied them since childhood, often have trouble adapting to their students' independence. These crises are eventually resolved by some modifications in the teacher-student arrangement.

An excellent example for the conclusion of this second stage of education is provided by Boris Schwarz and deals specifically with the celebrated twentieth-century violinist Ida Haendel. Haendel, the youngest of Flesch's "Polish prodigies," was born in 1923 in Chelm.

> Her precocious talent was developed by a number of teachers; the most influential was Flesch, with whom she had a somewhat troubled relationship. She came to him as a child and played with childlike instinct; Flesch wanted her to play with an intellect she did not possess at that time. Ida was dominated by an ambitious father (a painter and amateur cellist), who pushed her career aggressively and made many enemies along the way. When he took her to Paris to consult Enesco, Flesch became very angry and dismissed Haendel from his class, and though they were later reconciled, there was never much warmth between them. Despite her adolescent problems, Haendel won a special prize for Polish contestants at the 1935 Wieniawski Contest—quite an accomplishment for a twelve-year-old girl. (Schwarz 1983: 349)

SPECIFIC PROFESSIONAL CULTURE

Howard Becker in his book *Art Worlds* remarks that

> knowledge of professional culture, then, defines a group of practicing professionals who use certain conventions to go about their artistic business. Most of

what they know they learn in the course of their daily practice, and, as a general rule, none of the art world's other participants need to know such things to play their parts. . . . The group defined by knowledge of these working conventions can reasonably be thought of as the inner circle of the art world. (Becker 1982: 63)

Following Becker's analysis, because of specific socialization and particular culture we can consider the soloist class already as the example of the circles of the art world. The professional violinist's culture contains a particular savoir-faire, not only in regard to playing technique and interpretation, but also in terms of knowledge of their social world. In the following section, I focus on these particularities of soloist culture, which like musical knowledge are transmitted during the student's education. The first aspect concerns the anticipated socialization of young students, which gives them a feeling of belonging to the elite music world.

Like students in French preparatory classes (whom we can compare to students of very selective American or English universities), young virtuoso students in a soloist class express a common feeling of cohesion. The specific organization of these classes influences such feelings, bringing all the students of the same class closer together, despite their varied ages. During their study, the students learn to perceive, play and interpret music, and gain a similar sense of how to maintain relationships in their professional world. Despite some animosities and relationships strained by competition, students who finish their education usually keep the feeling of belonging to their former class.

This feeling is comparable to what is called "esprit de corps," which various group trainings generate. By "esprit de corps," Pierre Bourdieu means that the "feeling of group solidarity in fact lies in the community of schemata of perception, appreciation, thought, and action, that grounds the reflex complicity of well-orchestrated unconsciousness" (1996: 84).

Two different aspects of this perception of belonging can be distinguished. The first concerns the affiliations of students through three successive generations: the master of the teacher, the teacher, who is at the origin of a class, and the students. This adherence is frequently demonstrated in the soloist world. The first information given by a violinist is, "I studied in the class of Skripov, who was himself a student of Rajalov."

The second aspect of adherence relates to other students of the same class. Usually, students educated in the same class support each other in the musical market, following the teacher's model of a system of mutual aid. For example, a teacher indicates to his twenty-year-old student, making his first steps in the soloist market, how to benefit from the help of a former student of this class.[64] This aid system is widespread in the musicians' world: during competitions, in financial support, CD record selections, juries, and elsewhere. Very often, support is directed to a person who comes from the same class, or school, indicating a similar tradition of education.

Former students play an important role in maintaining this feeling of membership. Official and unofficial support practices by former students constitute a common practice outside the musician world, such as in elite general schools in

France (Le Wita 1988) or the Science-Po or Polytechnic (Bourdieu 1996). In his analysis of the students of *grandes écoles,* Bourdieu states that former students "play the determinant role in the mechanism of circular reinforcement of the belief in the superiority of elite members. In fact, they justify the finalities and the tools of pedagogical actions with which their excellence is related (following the logic of type: we are excellent because the education of which we are a product is excellent because we are excellent)" (1996: 111–115). Such practices also exist in the soloist world. For example, I learned of a support foundation created by former students of Yuri Yankelevich. This organization, offering scholarships, helps only young musicians who study under one of Yankelevich's former students. In other words, this foundation helps the musical grandchildren (and the next generation) of a single violin master. Whether this support is official or unofficial does not matter. The size of this world is limited, and musicians can detect the origin of a given performer; his or her soloist class.

Future soloists know whom they need to ask for support, and whom to avoid. In practice, the teacher first contacts the former student. The following excerpt illustrates the explicit knowledge of this support procedure among the former students of the same class. Six months before an international competition, the teacher from a well-known soloist class informs his sixteen-year-old students: "Don't worry. The president of the jury, the creator of this competition, is my friend. For many years we were in the same class. So I will give him a call, and when he is passing through Paris, I will present you to him. He will hear you and he will certainly give you some advice." This insider savoir-faire is a component of the soloists' social background, which they acquire during their education. The soloist class students quickly learn which school they belong to and that they are the elite of the musician world. A young violinist with a similar technical level, but without the experience of a soloist class, would have many difficulties entering into this elite milieu. Becoming a violin soloist is impossible, as we will see later, without social references.

The lifestyle of the soloist aspirant, ingrained by coaching from the start of their education, is very different from that of other teenagers and from other music students. Soloists are not obliged to take courses judged inessential that could encumber their schedules. This attitude, frequently supported by violin teachers, results in missed orchestra, chamber music, and other collective music lessons and courses. The soloist class may be taught in an institution where regular instrumental classes take place, but the soloist students form a separate group.

This "apart from the crowd" attitude is also visible at public performances by other violinists. Soloist students frequently take for granted that they are virtuosos. After a concert of a well-known musician, I heard young violinists remark that with similar conditions (the same concert-hall and violin), their performances would have been much better. An eighteen-year-old student criticized the work of a famous soloist in the following manner: "I liked his interpretation of the Sonata, but in the Capriccios, he cheated, as the majority of people do. Anyone can do that. I thought he would strictly play the text. And no, it's a pity. He didn't slog, that's it! I can do that better. I only need a violin like his and you'll see. I have been deceived."

I frequently observed soloist students speak poorly of the performances of violin students not educated in soloist classes. Although there is plenty of animosity among soloist students, all soloists distinguish strongly between themselves and lower-status students. During a concert performed by regular music class students, I observed soloists joking and sniggering about the quality of the performance. These elite students refused to participate in concerts with violinists who were not soloists or had lower technical skills. This refusal illustrates their feeling of difference, and to show how they rank in respect to the regular music-teaching world. Rejection is a tool of distinction, an element in the construction of professional soloist identity.[65]

Soloists express the spirit of belonging to an elite not only in their relations with other musicians, but also with nonmusicians. The soloist students work harder than most children and teenagers. Those who play in concerts have lives similar to those of working adults, while their peers only have school problems. Soloist students play in prestigious concert halls, sometimes before a large audience. They consider their activities to be responsible and significant.

The affiliation with an adult, elite world is significant. The young musicians rub elbows with the celebrities of the musician world. In discussions among soloist students I frequently heard name-dropping that revealed their proximity to the personages of the elite musical world. "We had dinner with Vitkov after his concert at his festival," one student said. "He was cool and he invited us to participate in his new project."

These components of the construction of a feeling of elite membership are not peculiar to the soloist student. Bourdieu, in his study of French elite students, wrote,

Thus the inevitable practices imposed upon preparatory class and *grande école* students by their sense of difference tend to objectively reinforce their difference. It is undoubtedly through their efforts to dress themselves in the trappings of nobility and intellectual grandeur, especially in the presence of their peers, that they acquire not only the assured manners and style that are among the surest signs of nobility, but also the high opinion of themselves that will lead them, both in their lives and in their work, toward the most lofty ambitions and the most prestigious enterprises (Bourdieu 1996: 112)

THE INTERNATIONAL CULTURE

While violin soloists are not the only young French students to have a sense of themselves as belonging to elite, the international aspect of their existence provides a particular distinction. The acquisition of "international culture" is a necessary precondition to enter the soloist occupation. In this sense, soloist students can be compared to the foreign managers families living in France studied by Anne-Catherine Wagner. "International culture," Wagner writes, "can be considered as a form of capital." She adds,

What is unique to this culture is that it rests on the concurrent utilization of resources that come from different spheres. The knowledge of foreign languages, cultures, and foreign lifestyles, the management of the geographic scattering of family and relationships, and the possibility of organizing a professional career in several countries produce a kind of mixture of linguistic, cultural, social, professional, economic, and symbolic capital (A.-C. Wagner 1995: 12)

The varieties of geographical mobility, training background, and languages spoken give soloist education its international character. Since about 1980, many European students—and not just elite music soloists—have participated in international education programs.[66] However, the travel and professional mobility of violin soloist students remains higher than others.

While most university students complete their education in one country, young musicians stay on the move throughout childhood. The universe of a soloist is not bound by geographic frontiers, and the mobility of a soloist is not a recent phenomenon—quite the opposite. This mobility is a tradition and a sign of success, though the political changes pursuant to the fall of the Berlin Wall have intensified it. Young virtuosos followed their teachers, emigrating from former Soviet and other Eastern European republics toward Western Europe, the United States, and Israel.[67] For soloist students, mobility does not mean only short-term travel. Many young musicians change their country of residence, either alone or with their parents, to join teachers that they have chosen (or who have chosen them).

From a young age, soloist students learn to speak several languages and are ready to move abroad to pursue their education. Language facility is important since the young students often travel alone, without their parents; also, the teacher may not speak the student's native language. In addition to English, the knowledge of those languages that are commonly considered in the EU as "rare" languages such as Russian can be useful in the soloist milieu. Such linguistic skills allow students to obtain closer relationships with teachers from the former Soviet republics. Russian can also be useful during competitions, for example during informal discussions among juries, rehearsals, and communicating with other students. Many students I met during my research work have a basic facility in Russian, an established part of the tradition of solo violin education.

Owing to this strong mobility, almost every soloist class has musicians from various countries. For example, in one Parisian class, six of the thirteen students were French, three Russian, two Polish, one Italian-Japanese, and one Armenian. This diversity is typical for European classes, except that the percentage of Asian students is increasingly higher. In most classes in the European Union, the majority of students come from countries other than where the class is held. European classes are composed in large part of students that are immigrants or have one or more parent from an immigrant family. The international culture is also visible in the networks: the universe of soloists and soloist students is woven from numerous networks that are free of geographical borders. The soloists state that this kind of organization is traditional to musicians' culture.[68] However, the collaborations between musicians of different origins do not guarantee equality among the participants. The musicians take different hierarchical positions, and in this ranking, the place of education is important. Violinists originating from

Eastern Europe and Jewish culture,[69] mostly from the "Russian School," dominate the soloist milieu, which contains powerful networks of teachers, violinists, and other professional musicians. Some perceive a domination of the soloist market by what many informants call the "Russian mafia"—Eastern European networks of teachers, soloist musicians, and other professionals.

The following anecdote illustrates this strong perception of domination: during a master class which took place in France, I heard, while taking part in an informal conversation, one student's mother (French) cite a common saying about violinists, "The Japanese play in tune, the French with great musicality, and the Russians do both."

The reputation of violinists originating from a Russian tradition of violin playing is, according to Schwarz (1983), the consequence of the imposition of norms concerning virtuoso performance.[70] There are large numbers of young soloists on European stages who originate from Eastern Europe or who were educated by Eastern European teachers. However, Russians were not alone in imposing these norms. Asian violinists, with their strong involvement in technique preparation and extremely high level of playing, also progressively modify performance norms. As large numbers of Asian students began to participate in violin competitions, the technical rigor of playing has increased.[71]

In conclusion, international culture is neither homogeneous nor unique. As Anne- Catherine Wagner stated, international culture "does not appear as a culture in the anthropological sense of the word, which could be in a competition with national cultures. International culture is more of a situation, which puts in the relationship the different nationalities, and as a consequence, returns a possibility of the particular approach of the 'national'" (A.-C. Wagner 1995: 545).

Analyzing the international aspect of soloist education, it is worth noting the peculiar relationship that soloist students have with their "national" violin education, that is, their institutions of national reputation, as for example, the Academy of Music in Warsaw or the Superior Conservatory of Paris (CNSMDP). Soloist students and their teachers residing in France judged that entering the CNSMDP was neither a worthy goal nor a sign of success.[72] Said one soloist teacher: "The CNSMDP is not a place where international soloists are educated. It is a very good school if you want to get a job in France in an orchestra or in the conservatory. But for the violinist-soloists, the preparation is not good enough. It is very important for French people, but they actually don't prepare soloists there anymore."

French violinist soloists (born after 1945), who graduated from CNSMDP, before definitively taking their place in the soloist market, needed to complete their education outside of France.[73] This is not the case for soloist class graduates from Juilliard, the Curtis Institute, or Indiana University,[74] or the Moscow and St. Petersburg conservatories, all of them of international quality. When young French musicians speak to the media, pointing out their education with famous foreign musicians, they show that the most important aspect of their education is collaboration with a master of international reputation. In the French monthly magazine for music lovers and musicians, *Diapason*, the journalist Y. Petit de Voize, in an article entitled "Young, Gifted, Hardworking, They Are the Elite of French Instrumental Music," wrote: "To the question of generation or of the strategy of the escape in the future, many cite their first French teachers and their education in the Conservatory of Paris. However, they insist a lot on their meetings and their master classes with international musical top brass" (1997: 32. 214). Though soloist class students attribute a negative reputation to the Parisian Conservatory, some of them join this institution. For them, the education in this conservatory constitutes a strategic solution; it can provide support such as scholarships, violin loans, and easier access to the French concert stage. And by joining the Conservatory, foreign students may also benefit from staying and working in France.[75]

Soloist students, in general, do not adhere to the French vision of excellence concerning instrumental education. Their relationship to the French success path is different from French students in professional institutions of musical education. This difference is similar to the split between the point of view of international managers' families and French families concerning the "grandes écoles" of French elites.[76]

The mixing of various national cultures does not perturb the soloist class' functioning because the students who originate from similar social classes possess a common cultural background: that of the soloist world.[77] For young soloists, their culture, which includes this international dimension, is acquired through their precocious immersion in the professional universe.

CHAPTER 5

Entrance into Adult Careers

THE THIRD STAGE OF SOLOIST EDUCATION

Passage through the third stage of education enables the student to obtain independence from the master and partial independence from the early support network. This process takes place progressively, rather than being marked by abrupt events. However, it is possible to identify some indications that the student is in the third stage of education.

The first signs of this transformation are the rise in self-confidence and a gain in independence with regard to their teachers. Soloists seek sponsors, or "godfathers," and professional collaborators—anyone who can help them support their careers by themselves. The soloists generate new relationships that they initiate during competitions, master-classes, and festivals, which often include social events such as cocktail parties and prize ceremonies. At such events they meet other elite musicians but also members of the artistic, political, and financial elite.

How do young people earn their place into this world? What kind of relationships do they maintain with professionals who play high-ranking roles at this third stage of education? This last period of education constitutes the decisive passage into soloist status. The duration of this stage varies from a few to ten years; it gives some young violinists the opportunity to install themselves in the soloist market, and others the chance to discover alternative ways of life.

PROGRESSIVE DETACHMENT FROM THE MASTER

At this last stage of education, the soloist's focus, rather than mastery of violin, is social insertion into the adult soloist world. Here again the soloist relies on his or her teacher, but the student's self-assured performances strengthen his or her emerging independence from the latter's violin lessons. The regular lessons they received in the past are less necessary for the soloists' progress. Soon, they realize they will be on their own, working without lessons. But this too must be taught. A nineteen-year-old student noted: "The teacher needs to teach me how to be disciplined, so that I may be able to work without his support. Because when I'm thirty, obviously, I will no longer take lessons from him and I will work alone. We can't have our teachers for eternity."

In the previous stage, a change of teachers frequently ruptures the support network. In the final stage of their education, students may distance themselves from their master, yet they do not cut their ties. In most cases, after realizing that lessons no longer have a similar effect as in the past, they ask their concert partners (accompanists and conductors) for help in completing their musical education.

The work with the master is transformed into exchanges that occur during informal meetings (never remunerated). After sharing a meal (during a visit in the teacher's apartment) or following a discussion, a student may take out his violin and play a piece for his teacher that he is preparing for a concert or record, which they then discuss. This is not like a lesson where the teacher speaks and the student corrects. A new type of relationship, which may last for many years, is born. Even decades after finishing their lessons, many soloists seek the advice of their former teachers before important events. Says a forty-year-old soloist: "Each time I prepare a record or a new repertoire—a truly new one with modern music creation and the original stuff—I see Joana [his last teacher] and ask her to listen to me. She gives me some advice and it is always beneficial. She is more than seventy years old, but in spite of that she can hear new things and make truly pertinent remarks."

The accompanist in a famous soloist class, T. Gaïdamovitch, relates:

> Each person received similar attention from Professor Y. Yankelevich, who didn't limit his interest in his students only to the years when they were in his class. He closely followed the successes of his young musicians—always entranced by their achievement and touched by their failures. This is why his notes contain so many names [of those] who became famous long after. His former students visited him from time to time in order to recharge batteries, to receive professional and protective advice, or even to get a less than positive critique. (Gaïdamovitch in Brussilovsky 1999: 256)

In this third stage, the relationship of teacher and student consists of sporadic meetings and informal exchanges. The teacher is a privileged interlocutor of discussion about the interpretation of pieces and the professional strategy to adopt. The teacher's role changes from a professor of violin to an initiator and guide in the soloist world. This transformation sometimes surprises parents, who have difficulty seeing the value of this new relationship, as illustrated by the following extract of an interview in which parents (both violinists) speak about the violin lessons of their twenty-two-year-old son, Vassily:

> His violin lessons are completely useless. Moreover, they are not even once a week, but once a month. He comes to the lesson, plays his program, Mazar [the teacher] gives him some advice about the interpretation, and Vassily chooses whether to take the advice. Also, some lessons take place in the restaurant with the teacher, other students, and sometimes other musicians. I cannot understand that, but visibly it is normal. They speak, they discuss, but not about how

to play. Instead, the conversation is about who plays with whom and when and where it is possible to hear concerts, etc. . . . Only chatter and gossip take place. . . . Although . . . OK, in this way, he makes contacts, and thanks to these meetings he got to play a replacement concert, or participate in a new and interesting project, a new festival . . . perhaps not all of his time is wasted.

While parents of the young soloist are sometimes reticent at the advent of this transformed relationship, the young musicians are very enthusiastic. The information transferred during these exchanges may be precious, making it possible to adopt the proper behavior while embarking on the conquest of the soloist music market. When the students attain a level of performance judged as sufficient by teachers, the teachers transform the topic of their teaching and initiate students to the "art de vivre" in the soloist world.

Advice about this topic is rarely given in an explicit form, except in the exceptional case of a former soloist student and soloist, who had the idea of creating the first consulting firm for violinists in Europe. This person argued that playing well is not sufficient. According to him, "It is necessary to know how to make with the 'tribe.'" The use of the term "tribe" is not accidental here. This teacher imported the term from anthropology because he felt it aptly described a close-knit world that imposes its own rules.

Technical questions now come second, as students have acquired this knowledge and no longer need external help. In the domain of interpretation, however—which is frequently called the "musical side"—the need for further education continues. The soloists rely on stage partners to work on interpreting pieces played in ensembles. The teacher steps down in favor of other music specialists, such as pianists and conductors, because the work of a violinist in the preparation of a sonata, for example, demands collaboration with a pianist—a role the violin teacher cannot assume, except in rare cases. The student's master is progressively replaced by other musicians.

It is also necessary to solicit other active professionals in the soloist world; for example, violin makers, who can provide the tools (prestigious violins) for market conquest. The master can also put former and current students to work supporting their younger colleagues.

In contrast to prior stages, the teachers no longer demand exclusivity of their student. They allow them to "go out," "to be seen" in the company of people in whose company it is "good to be seen" in order to expand their circle of relationships. All teachers know that one single network of support (the teacher's network) is not sufficient to implant the young virtuoso in the market. There are a few exceptions, such as the big U.S. agents like Sol Hurok in the first half of the twentieth century, or the powerful "godfathers" who specialized in the introduction of young "talents" to the classical music market, such as Isaac Stern (from 1960). The creation of new ties with different networks increases the chances of launching a young violinist's career. The teachers are no longer afraid of "betrayal" by their students,[1] because they have already finished their education, so the names of the students will be permanently associated with their teacher.

Consequently, changing a teacher at the third stage of education is not the same as changing a master earlier in training, when it signified dissatisfaction. At the third stage of education, students can, or even must consult with other teachers. These consultations, while including advice on the details of interpretation, are aimed mainly at widening the student's circles of support and collaboration.

Career Coupling—Passive Collaboration

To sum up the relationship between the master and his student, it is important for both parties to maintain a professional relationship. After a period of intense collaboration ("career coupling—active collaboration") teachers and students take their distance in order to devote their time to building other ties. Students intensify their work with other music professionals; teachers concentrate on other students who are still developing their musicianship. I call this third stage of the career coupling process "passive collaboration."

Both teacher and student take care to assure that their connection is preserved, and observed by their milieu. Students make sure to mention their teachers in the personal biographies printed on concert programs or in the media. Teachers include the names of their former students in publications as well. Dorothy DeLay's eightieth birthday party—which all of her star alumni attended—exemplifies the extent to which ties bind a master to her former students.

In addition to the public acknowledgments, if a former student has a successful recording or performance, and the press mentions this event, the teacher publicly comments on the event, providing more information about the successful soloist by describing his or her relationship with the former student.

As in other artistic worlds, peer recognition determines careers in music, and the coupling of actors constantly builds reputation. In the passive collaboration stage, each person is evaluated independently, but the development of the ex-collaborator's career continues to influence the reputation of his or her former partner in career coupling.

Some soloist teachers are one-time or temporary teachers, and do not develop a career coupling relationship with a particular student. As a former student from the Tchaikovsky Conservatory told me, "Yankelevich had hundreds of students when he was well known, but his esteemed soloists were only those who took lessons every day for years." I heard a similar statement from a student about Dorothy DeLay and her privileged students. To achieve recognition of the career coupling relationship, the actors must go through the three stages of coupling. The most successful careers that I observed were those that were based on a long-term career coupling relationship. However, not all coupling processes are optimal. For the success of both actors, the stages of both of these categories of careers must be synchronized.

Synchronization of Career Trajectories—an Element of the Success

We should remember that teachers of virtuosos also have a career track and go through different stages. The quality of the work and foremost the disposability of a teacher are not similar when the chosen instructor is a debutant or at the peak of the professional activity. The following extract illustrates bad synchronization of the stages of a young virtuoso and her teachers' careers:

> At six, I came to M.T.'s class and I stayed with him until I was sixteen. He was hard . . . he had personality, big presence, very strong . . . and he was over-whelming, and some people could not stand him. Then, I moved to Mrs. B. She is excellent for technical teaching, she is always available, and she spares me a lot of her time, unlike M.T., who is a great violinist, a great musician. I think that his main contribution to my violin education . . . was a desire to play . . . because if you have a teacher of this kind, of this greatness . . . However, in the day-to-day work, he did not spend enough time with his students; he very often missed lessons. . . . I lost my time. . . . I could have come to Mrs. B. sooner. All I am learning here, I should have acquired before. I do not regret studying with M.T., as I learned a lot. He gave me things Mrs. B. will never be able to give me. . . . However, it is true that I should have studied with her earlier. The best solution would have been to have had them in the opposite order.

As this extract suggests, synchronization in career coupling is of the utmost importance. The students in the first stage of their occupational life do not need a great master, who is in the last stage of his career, and who is really too busy to teach at least twice a week. In addition, the young virtuoso in the final stage of the socialization process cannot enjoy all opportunities if his or her career is coupled with a master in the first stage of his career. In the absence of a high reputation, and because of a low position in the milieu, and the haphazardness of powerful networks, the teacher does not introduce the student into the labor market.

Hence, the optimal solution is that a student and a teacher go through the stages of their careers at the same time (they should pass through three stages of their respective pathway in parallel). This rarely happens and is difficult to achieve for many reasons. Only for rare cases, this would work with a young teacher who is working with a young child and when his or her student starts to participate in the competition for young virtuosos, the teacher passes to the second stage of her or his career. As we saw it is extremely difficult to find at the beginning of virtuoso education an available professor who will possess necessary knowledge to handle the education of the young virtuoso. Also, it is rare that a teacher would accept the modifications of the relationship that occur with the time (especially during the crisis period).

When a student after several years needs the support of the network of profes-sionals and the prestige of a teacher, the teacher should be at the last stage of his or her career—well known internationally (that could happen if the teacher was previously well-known virtuoso and then started to teach). In fact this matching of two different careers is possible for a few of a given teacher's students. And this career coupling requires long-term collaboration, which is also rare in the virtuoso universe (however, it was the case for Zahar Bron and his two students: Maxim Vengerov and Vadim Riepin). This is an almost impossible challenge: the position of such a teacher should grow sufficiently enough for creating good conditions for the young soloist's development. Not all teachers like to work with children, and a lot of professors are working only with students who are at the last stage of their education process. Rarely, but I noticed some examples, students at the third stage of their education will take courses with a young professor, but in almost all cases, those last are well-known virtuosos enjoying a soloist career.

This is why young musicians need a powerful person who can help them acquire a strong position in the circle of their elite group. The professor should have a large and efficient network of support in order to prepare the students for their future.

The Power of Informal Networks of Support

Numerous sociological studies have been devoted to support networks. For an examination of ties specific to the soloist world, I cite the approach of Mark Granovetter (1973), who places attention on the impact of weak ties in job research. Contrary to his work on young people looking for a job and the conclusion that the weak ties are more important than strong ties (kinship), in the case of the violinist the most important for a virtuoso career are strong ties (teacher/student). However, other types of supports and relationships constitute additional important elements of the young virtuoso's trajectory. In most cases, people employ these networks in an informal manner. I use the term "informal network of support" to indicate the mode of informal grouping prevalent in the soloist world. In the previous chapters, I included several examples of how teachers use the networks they have created, and how the activity of these networks is indispensable for the soloist's education.

How do teachers create and animate their networks? How are these networks built? How do collaborative members of the same network collaborate? What kind of connections mobilize the members of networks in order to make a soloist class work, and how are these resources mobilized?'

The Construction of a Network of Support:
The Continual Process of Mobilizing Various Resources

The occupation of violinist requires specific competencies acquired over many years of education; their value is based on peer evaluation and a market controlled by cliques.[2]

The informal relationships between individuals determine the functioning of their professional universe. The people involved in soloist world activity have the knowledge about how it works, whereas outinsiders need to acquire it. Soloist class teachers utilize their environment to find various sources of support, and they coordinate all such actions. They solicit their professional partners, who react according to the informal rules of the soloist world. However, the contribution of each network participant to the activity of these networks varies with the place of a given person in the given network. The music professionals (accompanists, violin makers, conductors) simultaneously fit into several networks of similar types. As a consequence, their involvement in a given network is of a different nature than the involvement of parents.

The parents possess the knowledge in the domain of creating and maintaining social relations. They maintain relationships that are helpful for the pursuit of their child's education.[3] It is among the parents (musicians and nonmusicians) that the teachers get exclusive involvement in the activity of their network. This involvement is constantly solicited. For example, during the preparatory meeting before a student's concert, a teacher asked the mother of her student: "Could your sister-in-law, who works in the Ministry of Culture, perhaps do something for us?" Speaking with a father of another student who always has a high-quality copy of the score, "Your friend has a printing office. Could you ask him if he would support our activity by making beautiful invitations and programs for our concert?"

This kind of resourcefulness is appreciated in the soloist world. The individuals take all opportunities and mobilize each contact at their disposal to advance the process of realizing their common goal: developing the career of a young soloist. No wonder that persons originated from the upper classes are much more efficient and active in such activities; those who have modest resources are less successful in mobilizing support for virtuoso activity. However, it is not an individual game (parents mobilize the resources only for their child), but it is a group activity (parents help all students from their child's class in their activity). Many diverse resources might be mobilized by one single family:

> Madame Weber is a homemaker with three children; the youngest is a student in a soloist class. Although Madame Weber is not a musician, she spends much of her time organizing events for the students in her daughter's soloist class. She constantly mobilizes all her relationships: family, neighbors, and her husband's professional ties. Her sister is an employee in the regional administration [department of culture], and she organizes annual concerts for the soloist students in prestigious places throughout her region. Thanks to her position, the venues are secured without fee. The soloist students also play once a year in the luxury retirement home where Madame Weber's mother resides. The Weber family cottage, three hours outside Paris, is where the soloist class members meet when they organize an annual concert in the church of a village close by. Most of Madame Weber's network contacts are the acquaintances of her husband, a public figure. As Madame Weber explained, their name "opens doors," and she has access to important information about scholarships, financial support, state support, and other financing for cultural projects. Her husband's political activities allow Madame Weber to meet the spouses of powerful men and some attend concerts she organizes. She constantly solicits these people for support, and they often introduce Madame Weber to high-level cultural administrators who control projects of support for young musicians. Thanks to all these activities, Madame Weber is well known in Parisian "society" and in the musician world; she is solicited to select child-musicians for "prodigy children" concerts and TV programs.

To analyze such networks, it is helpful to categorize the exchanges that build it. These may be commercial: that is, the teacher sells his or her knowledge, or barter arrangements; in exchange for lessons, the parents perform services (e.g., dressmaking, babysitting, loaning out their apartment for violin lessons, etc.) for the teacher. The relationships between two professionals in music could also constitute an exchange of services: the sound engineer records one student of his child's teacher, who, in exchange for this service, gives free violin lessons to the sound engineer's son. Or an organizer prepares a master class for the teacher and the teacher comes with his own "clientele." Even if these kinds of exchanges are mostly dyadic, we can find cases of more complex relations, such as when a parent helps a teacher who collaborates with a violin maker who lends the violin to their child. Such services are not always simultaneous (as immediate exchange) but may be conducted over a longer time span.

Musicians who offer their support receive the reinforcement of their position in the universe of soloists. The long-term investment of teachers, through time spent transmitting knowledge, yields positive results on their reputation because of the disciple's career. I present a perfect example of these complex exchanges in my section on violin makers, in the story of the thirteen-year-old student who received a prestigious violin from a violin maker who was an acquaintance of the teacher. In exchange, the teacher sent the violin maker his students, who then became new clients. Parents and students are grateful to the teacher for this help and they have run up a sort of a debt to both the teacher and the violin maker, which ties them more strongly to their current network. The teacher gambles a favor on the student's loyalty, but also hopes that playing with a better violin will make his student more competitive.

These kinds of exchanges go on continually in the soloist universe. They are rarely equitable simultaneously, and it is necessary to take this into account in the analysis of soloist network functioning. This is certainly the case with "multiple networks" functioning, wherein the control and the acquisition of resources is obtained as a result of various networks' activity, with different types of ties (Padgett and Powell 2012). The virtuoso field provides an example of a networking system in which we see the interpenetration of musical networks, kinship networks, media and political networks, as in the classical example of the Medici court analyzed by John F. Padgett and Christopher K. Ansell (1993). In the following section I will show how different actors, through activities assigned by the network, contribute to virtuoso socialization.

THE PRINCIPAL ROLE OF SECONDARY ACTORS

Professionals who play an important role in the education of a soloist, but who step in only at the last stage of this process, can be called "secondary actors." These specialists may be involved in the activities of a given teacher's network, but their support is not indispensable in the earlier stages of soloist education. When solicited in the earlier stages by the soloist entourage (most often parents), these specialists generally demur, saying that they are busy and that the request is pre-mature. Conductors, for example, almost never respond to requests to play with "prodigy children," and pianists rarely work with young violinists who are without a teacher (if the teacher is absent, his or her advice regulates the rehearsal). During the first two stages, the ties between the students and secondary actors are indirect (in the case of accompanists, violin makers, and other specialists, the relationship is maintained by the teacher) or nonexistent (for conductors).

At the end of soloist education, the teacher solicits other professionals, announc-ing that the young soloist is ready to complete his or her education. This is a moment for young musicians to meet sound engineers, composers, conductors, and agents. Even if the last category constitutes part of the world of the virtuoso, at the final stage of their education rare are those young violinists who already have "their agent"—most often, they have relationship with concert organizers (amateurs, associations, people organizing festivals, and events and not directly driving a chosen musician's career). This is the reason for the relatively small part of this study devoted to agents, who are key professionals in the period after virtuoso education.

The role played by specialists in soloist education depends on the domain and the position of the soloist in the market. The piano accompanist, in general, remains in the violinist's shadow, while the conductor is considered an important person in the soloist world. Each person plays a different role during the third stage of soloist education.

Accompanists in the Shadows of Violin Soloists

Yehudi Menuhin once compared the violinist's accompanist to a Don Quixote traveling with Sancho Panza: "Your accompanist can be many things: companion, likable scoundrel, a real musician; a great support, and sympathetic character—or he can make touring a most weary business indeed!" (Menuhin 1986: 35–36). During the first two stages of soloist education, the student plays with a pianist chosen by the teacher, except in the case where the pianist is a parent or member of the violinist's family. (Such cases are not rare.)[4]

For students in the first and second stages of soloist education, the accompa-nist (a musician over thirty, most often)[5] is frequently the fall guy. The failures of young violinists are attributed to poor work on the part of pianist-accompanists. The following example given by a soloist student's mother illustrates this attitude: "Everything was going well. Françoise (her daughter) was so well prepared for this competition, but everything was ruined by this idiot pianist. She played so poorly that Françoise's mind suddenly went blank, and then her pianist was not even able to find her. And stopping in the middle of a sonata was a fault the jury didn't forgive."

Young violinists often complain about their accompanists. In the early part of soloist education, violinists often fail to value the pianists who accompany them, considering them mere backdrops for their virtuosity. An illustration of this kind of attitude can be seen during concerts, when violinists forget to thank or acknowledge the pianist while soaking up applause from an audience. This kind of behavior leads to reproach. A violin teacher was heard correcting her fifteen-year-old student: "You walked past your pianist as if she didn't exist! Not even giving her a discreet nod to say 'Thank you,' not even a wave during the applause! The public didn't like that! And your pianist? How does she feel now? You don't deserve to play on stage!"

Young virtuosos slowly learn that the pianist is a very important partner in their career. Sometimes the violinists meet an accompanist with whom they "click," and have an instant connection. The violinist realizes that the pianist supports and assists his or her playing. Said a nineteen-year-old violinist: "It was fantastic. I had never played with a pianist like him before. We were in complete symbiosis, in spite of the fact that we had never played before, or even spoken to each other. He's a great [musician], and it was a great moment when I was playing with him. I would like to meet him again."

Then too, not all young virtuosos are as ill-mannered as the girl in the first example. Many realize the importance of the pianist, especially when they have a parent who is one. These violinists search for the opportunity to play with pianists that they consider good accompanists. Whenever they can (if their teacher accepts their initiative), they choose their own pianists, noting the names of competition and master-class accompanists to seek them out again. Students who are concluding their soloist education said that a good accompanist listens closely to the violinist; the biggest mistake a pianist can make is to play as if the pianist is alone on stage. On the other hand, having an impeccable technique and knowledge of violin repertoire is not enough—it's also crucial that they prepare with the virtuoso.

During the last stage of education, the seeking of one's "own pianist" is common among young violinists. Cases in which both musicians are in a comparable stage of instrumental education are rare, because the pianist does not envisage an accompanist's career as the final stage of socialization. Pianists do not desire to devote their time to preparing and training as accompanists, viewing this as a waste of their time. Thus, long associations between these two categories of musicians are usually the consequence of private relationships. Another possibility is the creation of an ensemble for short projects: a concert, an exam, a concert tour, or a year-long "course of chamber music."[6] Duos that play over a period of several seasons can improve their reputations.[7] Yet violinists may find it expensive to train with a pianist over a long period, contrary to the professional accompanist who is paid for their work (which may be expensive for violinists). These costs are difficult to cover for young violinists, as the following excerpt from an interview with a twenty-year-old violinist illustrates: "The accompanist is a big problem, because we need to work a lot with the piano, and we need to put together sonatas. We need to learn how to listen to each other, to feel one another. And we have to pay for each hour of this work, and it is very expensive. The concerts are not sufficiently numerous to cover the pianists' fees, to pay for the luxury of numerous rehearsals; yet these are necessary to reach a high level of performance."

At times, the high costs can hurt a young virtuoso's performance. An international competition participant told me that her accompanist, who was very good, was not playing with her because she [the violinist] was unable to host [the accompanist] and pay for each rehearsal and passage before the jury. In the case of success, the pianist receives a certain percentage of the winnings. All this is too expensive for many young violinists, who instead play with the official pianist of the competition (who, according to my respondent, was not as good as her pianist).

The Russian mother of a twenty-year-old male violinist told me: "What my son needs now is to fall in love with a good pianist, preferably of Russian origin (they are considered the musically best-educated), who can play concerts with him. Because every time there's a public performance, he has trouble finding a good accompanist."

The Double Role of Conductors

Symphonic orchestra conductors play a double role in the education of a soloist: they participate in the market launch of a young soloist's career, and they also instill in young players the indispensable knowledge of good collaboration with a symphonic orchestra. The conductors have the power to invite young artists to play, to spread word about their abilities, and to present them to other well-known musicians. They help decide who will achieve soloist status.

This is an elite role in the classical music tradition; in the twentieth century there were many conductor-driven violinist careers. A recent case is that of Anne Sophie Mutter, a German violinist who was "discovered" by the conductor Herbert von Karajan. Another, more recent example is provided by the Russian soloist and conductor Vladimir Spivakov, who has promoted several young violinists, among them a young Chinese soloist, living in Canada, Yi-Jia S. Hou (educated at the Juilliard School of Music in the class of Dorothy DeLay). Hou won the 1999 competition organized and presided over by Spivakov himself. Then, in a postcompetition contract, she played with several orchestras, some of them conducted by Spivakov himself. Two years later, she won the Grand Prize of the Jacques Thibaud competition in Paris (where Spivakov was a jury member) and again played concert tours in which some were accompanied by an orchestra conducted by Spivakov.

Some conductors have the power to make a soloist's career, and are solicited by teachers and other persons belonging to the narrow soloist environment. However, the opportunity of working as a soloist with an orchestra is rare: the number of young soloists who are at the final stage of their education is much greater than the number of opportunities to perform with a symphony ensemble. The only conductors with whom it is easy to get an audition are conductors of little repute.[8] The father of a twelve-year-old soloist, who, despite of her young age, was at the last stage of her virtuoso education said,[9]

I sent many records, cassettes, video-cassettes, letters, and I succeeded in getting the phone numbers, and, everywhere I heard: "Again a Wunderkind from

Russia. We have no need for another one. They are plentiful. . . ." Some of them were more sympathetic: they congratulated me for her performance, encouraged her to pursue her education, gave me some advice, though nothing concrete [imitating conductor's voice]: "Perhaps in the future, let the time pass. The teen years are difficult." If the occasion occurs, they will think about her, but she has to continue in the soloist class of someone well known, and all that. . . . Only wind and beautiful words; no concerts, nothing. However, they all said that they liked her performance.

Even for students originating from a soloist class conducted by famous teachers, an audition with a reputed conductor is hard to obtain. Some teachers organize meetings between conductors and young soloists, as did Dorothy DeLay, soliciting chiefs with whom she had collaborated to hire her students as soloists.[10] Some music schools, Juilliard for example, hold competitions in which thirty or more students play a concerto before a jury, with the winner playing the same piece with a symphonic orchestra. This opens a window of opportunity to play with an orchestra, which is generally reserved for the finalists of international competitions. Yet most violinists who win international competitions have played with an orchestra before. This experience is vital for providing the savoir-faire for the final stages of the competition.

Particular skills are required when the accompaniment involves dozens of musicians. The opportunity to play with an orchestra is so rare that some young soloists choose their school based on whether it may offer this chance. Joining a class whose teacher is also a conductor offers the possibility of being selected as soloist. A twenty-four-year-old violinist related: "I plan to go to Z. [a conservatory in a European capital] because I know that H. [the teacher] makes his students play with the orchestra of Z. He's the second conductor there. For me, anyway, it is what I need—regular work as a soloist with a symphonic orchestra. I know that during lessons with him, I will learn nothing, but I will work with his orchestra and this is very important for me now, and it is very difficult to find today." To some extent we can say that this student is not really taking lessons in the sense of classical transfer of musical knowledge from professor to a student; however, at that level, the informal knowledge concerning the work with an orchestra certainly constitutes an indispensable part of a virtuoso education. The students are learning how to communicate and collaborate with orchestral members and with the conductor—this tacit knowledge as well as the connections they get throughout those experiences are part of the professional capital of students (Pierre Bourdieu would say, social capital).

Young virtuosos need conductors to initiate them into the mastery of orchestral work. The father and agent of a violinist said of his daughter:

She knows all the basics, she has mastered the violin. She develops interpretation by herself. She doesn't need lessons anymore. What she does need is a good pianist to play sonatas with her, and not just as an accompanist. And she needs a chief—a conductor who teaches her how to play with an orchestra. If you think that it is Vengerov who plays the Prokofiev concerto so well by himself, you are wrong! He worked on it with [Daniel] Barenboim, he listened to him. He followed what Barenboim wanted, and then it was wonderful! It is like that; it is necessary to have a great conductor in order to progress. When we analyze the big violinists' careers, we always find a big chief backing them.

Playing a violin solo with an orchestra is indispensable today; this was not the case before the twentieth century, when violinists played with a pianist alone. In those earlier periods, orchestral repertoires were transcribed for piano. Today, this practice is gone, perhaps among other reasons, because the musicians play original final versions of pieces and not "modest versions"—a concerto for violin with 100 orchestral musicians is not the same piece as its transcription for violin and piano (the violin-solo part is the same but 100 musicians from orchestra are played by only one pianist on one single instrument); musical, emotional, and artistic expression of both versions is really different.

Another form of performance of for the solo violinist is chamber music; however, the preparation for that type of performance is not really provided in soloist classes. The virtuoso teachers that I followed focus on the virtuoso repertoire, which, in majority, was composed for violin and orchestra or violin and piano. Performance that is highly valued in those classes are solo violin with symphonic orchestra.

Nowadays violinists need to be prepared to play in huge concert halls, where specific difficulties must be confronted, such as acoustics, conductors' directions, and the sound proportions among as many as one hundred instruments. Conductors also teach soloists how to behave while playing repertoire during rehearsals or concerts with their orchestra members.[11] The conductor may say to a young violinist, "When you leave the stage, don't forgot to salute the concertmaster."[12] The conductor shows when the soloist needs to look at the first violin, and when to look at the cello players; the conductor teaches what role each of his hands plays, and how to read his facial expressions.[13]

Training with Other Specialists

Other specialists involved in the soloist's training include sound engineers, musicologists, and composers. The quality of their work weighs heavily on the future of young candidates vying for soloist status.

Sound engineers record live and studio performance, and their work can modify a violinist's sound. They initiate soloists into the technical possibilities that are important for the final stage of the recording process. A sound engineer, a former pianist educated in Russia, gave a sense of the importance of this role in his description of his work with two young musicians—a fifteen-year-old violinist and a nineteen-year-old pianist, that he recorded in a church:

> It was not so bad yesterday. It was clear that the live recording was good, but I needed to do remakes, and I could only use my machinery in the church [where the concert was held] at night. So, after the concert we went to dinner with the mayor and other city notables,[14] and then at one A.M. we went back to the church

and recorded until five A.M. I did several retakes. I explained to them what I wanted and how the sound circulated in this church, and how this affected the soundtrack. After two hours of work, I started to get good results. But at about four A.M., they began to complain that they didn't want to do it anymore, that they were tired, so I couldn't continue. OK, they are not professionals, they tire quickly. It is their right . . . they are still young. . . . However, I got good material for doing a passage on the radio, even perhaps for part of a CD.

The young musicians clearly were unaware of the technical difficulties of recording, but over time they learn the importance of recording and the choice of a sound engineer. Recordings are obligatory almost everywhere in the pre-selection of international competitions;[15] badly recorded performances can become just another obstacle in the way of soloist qualifications.

In Yuri's class, all the records were made by Jasha, a friend and partner of the teacher who was also a part time soloist. Jasha recorded and produced almost all of Yuri's CDs, and he recorded Yuri's students' performances for nothing more than the cost of cassettes. This unpaid engineer's service helped several students participate in competitions and other musical events. At the same time, Jasha explained to the young musicians how to collaborate with a sound engineer. Jasha later contacted the former students, offering them work in his series of recordings of forgotten composers and pieces.

CDs are an indispensable tool for a young virtuoso who wishes to conquer the soloist market. They have become a kind of "business card" to increase awareness of the soloist among music professionals (agents, conductors, event organizers). To make this an effective tool, the young soloists need to have a well-attuned sound engineer. This relationship could become the part of professional ties (maintained during years), while a "good" sound engineer working on string recording is, according to the opinion of my participants, the "rare pearl."

Doing fieldwork I met two sound engineers who were also CD producers. In EU, some classical music is recorded and distributed by modest labels; producers who are at the head of those houses are frequently musicians or other music professionals; I observed work on several musical projects usually focused on music by Eastern European nineteenth- and twentieth-century composers rarely played in Western Europe.

Musicologists also can influence the development of a soloist. These professionals have intricate knowledge of the history of the creation of certain works and the lives of the composers. Contact with a musicologist can provide the soloist with forgotten or unpublished pieces whose public performance can be an excellent strategy for entering the soloist market, as suggested by a former performer during an informal interview:

How many times will the public hear Beethoven's concerto? Everyone plays the same thing. Because we are not pianists, we do not have such a large repertoire. So, why record Paganini's concerto number two for the 101st time? There are many interesting pieces, but it is useful to find some new ones, create new CDs. Once the violinist becomes known and has their own CD producer, many people want to see that artist. And then this violinist, after becoming famous, can play Beethoven one more time. But in order to be famous, it is necessary to find something rare to play.

Young soloists devote their time and training to the mastery of pieces for international competitions, which generally are limited to established works. Research into an old or rare violin piece requires a huge investment in time, as well as specific knowledge that soloists do not possess.[16] This is why collaboration with a musicologist is helpful. Older musicians are more likely to take it upon themselves to search for rare pieces.

Young virtuosos can also benefit from the help of composers.[17] Examples of this kind of collaboration are few, but violinists value the privilege of being the first to play a piece, especially one written especially for them. This first performance is a tool that displays their instrumental gifts but also inscribes them in music history. Numerous performers of the twentieth century appear in music encyclopedias as the first interpreter of a given composition.[18] At times, the relationship between composers and soloists can be deep and fruitful. The rich correspondence between Pawel Kochanski (1887–1934), a well-known Polish violinist, and a professor at the Juilliard School and Polish composer Karol Szymanowski (1882–1937)[19] testifies to a long friendship marked by periodic, yet very intensive collaborations that resulted in several masterpieces for violin and piano and for violin and orchestra.

Szymanowski benefited systematically from the advice of Kochanski for the violin part in all of his compositions. In their letters, they spoke about "our concerto" so much that it is clear how crucial Kochanski's contribution was. Both concertos for violin and "Les Mythes" were played for the first time by Kochanski, and the fact that he included these pieces in his repertoire allowed Szymanowski to become known by the American and Western European public. Kochanski immigrated to the United States, where he led the life of a virtuoso for many years (with the help of some sponsors), financially supporting his friend, who stayed in Poland in a very difficult financial situation (Chylinska 1967).

While Szymanowski lived in the shadow of the worshiped violinist, after Kochanski died in 1934, he dropped into oblivion, sharing the path of nearly all performers. Today, Kochanski is mostly known to musical historians as the violinist who made the first recordings of Szymanowski, and to whom important composers such as Szymanowski, Serge Prokofiev, and Igor Stravinsky dedicated their works (Pâris 1995: 569–570). By contrast, Szymanowski became famous, and is considered one of the major composers of the twentieth century.[20]

SUPPORT OF VIOLIN MAKERS AND POSSESSION OF THE VIOLIN

There are two major elements to success in a young violinist's career: the instrument and the audience. Access to the public through recordings and the concert stage is, as can be imagined, a complex issue. One might think that violin acquisition, on the other hand, is a simple undertaking—that the artist must simply find and buy a good violin. In fact, the price of a prestigious violin is so far beyond the wildest dreams of almost all musicians that networks and reputations also come into play in this transaction.

Upon finishing their studies, violinists hope to benefit from the protection of a sponsor, or to be discovered and supported by a personality within the music world. They also hope to meet an agent who will manage their career.[21] These elements, which determine entrance into the soloist market, are the main focus of attention for young violinists. The obtaining of a "work tool," that is, a superior violin, is part of this pursuit.

The following excerpt from an interview with a Parisian instrument maker gives some insight into the relationship between violinists and those who make their instruments. Asked how young violinists can obtain a "good" violin,[22] he answered:

Starting from the beginning: when a child decides [laughing]. . . . Is it possible for such a young child to decide? OK, after the decision that the child is on the path of becoming a musician. Nowadays, the choice is made earlier and earlier, a collective project built upon parents, teachers, etc. They [parents] give him supplementary lessons; they have him play in concerts, participate in master classes, and the time arrives, one day, that they need an instrument. If the parents have the money, it is less of a problem. If they don't, they need to borrow one. This is how things work. In rare cases, the sponsor says, "This child is very talented," he listens to him in a concert and decides to help him. Although this is very rare, it exists, nonetheless. If not, the child must [borrow the instrument], but that it is complicated. The child usually must be eighteen years old to get such a loan. . . . If not, the violin maker may lend a violin from time to time, especially for the period of a competition. Also, there is an instrument fund that loans violins to musicians.

Prestigious violins, such as those made by famous Italian craftsmen, are extremely expensive (Antonio Stradivarius's violins can sell for several million dollars).[23] The need for a prestigious violin that allows the full expression of virtuosity is a crucial problem in the career of a violinist.[24] To explain to nonmusicians the impact a violin has on a performance, a violin maker used the following comparison:

It is as if you wanted to participate in a Formula 1 race with an old *deux chevaux* instead of a Ferrari. You have virtually no possibility of winning. Even Schumacher cannot win with an old, small car. Violins are similar. An old "Italian" does not have the same sound as a modern violin. You play and afterward people say: "Wow, this violinist has such a beautiful sound!" We [violin makers] know which sound is produced by the violin and which by the violinist.

Playing a good violin can reduce the amount of time spent for concert preparation. As a twenty-year-old violinist remarked, some sound effects are more difficult to produce than others. As a result, it may take two to three times longer to get the desired sound if a violin is not of the highest quality. Prestigious old violins are difficult to play at the outset, but after time become "easy to play," he said.

Old instruments, in particular those of Italian origin, possess several qualities that many violinists look for to play at a superior level. In fact, soloists who cannot obtain a prestigious violin often abandon even the idea of participating in certain international competitions. A nineteen-year-old violinist said,

> Without an old "Italian," it is not even worth it to go there. It is a waste of time. They [the jury members] will say: "He does not have a beautiful sound." When I was in X, there was one Guarneri, two Strads [Stradivarius], and two Guadagnini, along with other prestigious violins I don't even know of. So, with my new violin, which is only two years old, playing a Romance of Beethoven, I can't compete. [My violin] lacks timbre, sonority, volume, colors. It was the weakest of them all.

Teachers express a similar concern, as observed in the following remarks by a teacher to his student: "OK, we will start the preparations for the big competitions. You are skilled enough to be a winner, but it is useless to go there without a true violin. With yours you can forget your ambitions of becoming a soloist and go directly to playing in an orchestra. . . . It is not even worth practicing the program for the competition." This opinion is shared by the majority of students, who take great pains to obtain a prestigious violin. An excellent illustration of the young soloist's situation is the documentary movie, *Stradivarius, la magie du son,* whose plot summary was published in *Le Monde*:

> London, New York, Moscow, Cremona . . . the Impossible Pursuit of a Chimeric Violin. The story told by Sven Hartung, director of this documentary, is sympathetic: an eighteen-year-old violinist, a student of the Conservatory of Vienna, seeks a violin that will allow him to conquer the world. But he has no money to buy a Stradivarius, and besides, none of those which he has played on have satisfied him 100 percent. He needs to test two to three hundred more violins and then convince an investor to buy one of these "rare birds." . . . "I try to teach him to express his emotions and feelings," says his teacher, while Dalibor Karvay—the Slovak Paganini—unwinds the sterilized arpeggios of Bach. . . . It is said that "it is almost impossible to start an international career without a Stradivarius."

But when Karvay played behind a curtain, 476 of the 553 listeners thought that they were listening to a Stradivarius rather than a modern violin. Besides, when an artist of similar stature, Joshua Bell, affirms that the smallest modification affects a Stradivarius, a sign of absolute perfection, he has forgotten to specify that not one Stradivarius that is played on stage today is in its original condition (Gé. C. in *Le Monde Télévision*, June 5, 2004, 29).

The majority of violinists and violin makers claim that a modern instrument never sounds as good as an old violin; I only heard one contrary opinion, provided by a young violin maker who stated that the quality of old instruments is overstated to maintain financial speculation in them. According to this violin maker, more and more soloists play with modern instruments.[25]

The Owners of Prestigious Violins

Lacking sufficient funds for buying an old violin, musicians are forced to request the help of people who possess or distribute them.[26] It is difficult to know how many violinists own the instruments they play, but certainly a large percentage play on instruments borrowed from groups like the Stradivarius Foundation, which is frequently an intermediary between the owners (a person, a company, or bank) and the musician.

I heard the following anecdote from a soloist close to a person who administered one of these prestigious instruments. This story illustrates the risk inherent to the practice of playing a loaned violin:

> After September 11 in New York and the crisis that followed this event, an owner of some Strads and one Guarneri decided to sell his violins. He informed the soloists who played on his violins of his decision, and in the space of two months, half the soloist world was without violins for their concerts. . . . There was a lot of panic even among the biggest [soloists]. One of them, knowing what would happen, ignored the owner and wouldn't even respond to phone calls and letters. He continued his world concert tours without giving any sign of returning the violin. Then one day, when he was back home [in an American city] but out of the house, private detectives who had put him under surveillance entered his empty house and simply took the violin, leaving a letter from the owner.

Violin Makers: Artistic Craftsmen or Artistic Salesmen?

One would imagine that violin makers are primarily craftspeople who produce new violins and take care of old ones. Soloist students share this perception of the violin maker until the moment they begin searching for a prestigious violin to play. Then, they discover that the violin craftsman is also a violin lender. A nineteen-year-old soloist described her relationship with violin makers thus:

> When I was younger, [a violin maker in Lyon] always loaned us violins.[27] Now that I am living in Paris, I go to see Julien. He made very good adjustments; I am satisfied. . . . I hope that he will loan me something. I can't pay the insurance, so I hope that he will pay it, or if not Julien, then the person who is actually lending me the violin—because the violins that Julien lends are not necessarily his property. In any case, it is not I who will pay for the violin insurance—it is much too expensive for me.

The role of a lender is presented by violin makers as something of secondary importance. They prefer to emphasize their role as craftsmen. To underline this activity, they display photos in their violin shops with dedications from well-known clients, with inscriptions such as, "Thank you for your knowledge and all your heart, which you put into taking care of my violin" (these shops are visible in the Rue de Rome in Paris). Their work apparel, which is usually a white blouse, or beige apron, suggests that their occupation is to restore the life of old instruments.

Violin makers in three-piece suits are not a common sight, because that kind of costume suggests they are clerks and not craftsmen.

Most of the violin makers I met think of trading as an ignoble task in comparison to the complex restoration of old instruments, or the fabrication (very rare) of new violins. This distinction between "bad" or "dirty" work and "good" work is shared by other participants in the soloist world. A thirty-year-old soloist described three violin makers she works with thus: "In New York I have MR, whom I like a lot; in Paris, CD, who is young, but I appreciate his adjustments. However, in V (South America), I have a friend who is extraordinary: this is a violin maker 'from the good old days.' He has an atelier; he doesn't seem to be a violin trader at all. Everything is very 'handcrafted.'"

In the soloist world, violin makers like to be considered "physicians of old instruments," a catch phrase much used by them and by the virtuosi performers who patronize them. Several factors uphold the parallel to the medical profession. First, the nature of the operations which violin makers need to perform on old instruments are technically complex—risky interventions, because certain restorations can harm the sound quality, even to the point where the violin could become unusable and lose most of its value.[28] Such operations are risky and complex tasks, but considered noble.[29] Once I observed a twenty-nine-year-old woman enter an atelier, embrace the violin maker and say with sadness in her voice, "I am desperate, Jean; help me please. I am scared that my violin is very sick."

Like doctors, violin makers have regular clients over many years, punctuated by requests for service that may be urgent or routine. I heard of one "urgent" case in which a violinist broke her violin (loaned from a rich family) on the eve of a concert and urgently needed a replacement. The relationship between the violin maker and a violinist is based on reciprocal trust; it is important that the craftsman know the instrument to perform proper restorations and maintenance, and the possessor of the prestigious violin must know enough about the violin maker to entrust their instrument to him or her.[30] The violinist describes "my violin maker"[31] in much the same possessive terms as they would describe a trusted family physician.

The proximity of young violinists and their violin makers allows them to link their reputations and promote personal relationships.[32] (The loan of the violin, and its maintenance, require many meetings, giving rise to long talks).[33] How do violin makers perceive soloist education? The following exchange with a forty-five-year-old violin maker provides some insights:

> We don't think about profit, publicity or anything like that [when we loan a violin]. But I will tell you. I saw, in international competitions, children who have fabulous instruments—from Cremona, eighteenth century, while other competitors have nothing. So, from the outset it is clear that this is a huge disproportion!
>
> Q: How does the judge deal with that?
>
> A: This is unjust and I am not sure that the jury members realize it. I think that it would be better to introduce the competitors by saying, "Mister So-and-So plays a such-and-such violin from year . . ." When I am close to the musician,

I can see the instrument and I can see the difference, and I say to myself, "This one is a jewel. Let's see what it will sound like." Because there are many competitors from poor countries, and their violins are crap.

Q: How much would you estimate, would be the range of prices for a typical violin used by a competitor of an international competition, such as Thibaud, in Paris?[34]

A: [Interviewee initially makes a face signifying that he does not want to give a response.] Listen, it is not really the problem of the price, but it is true that it is necessary to choose one's instrument. It may not be hugely expensive, but the instrument must be built for a big hall, it must have a sound that fills the auditorium. . . . Perhaps it will not have the same quality as a violin from Tyrol, which can be very nice, but which is good for chamber music. . . . For chamber music it would be wrong to use a powerful instrument; a modern violin would do. A violinist who plays at big competitions needs to test the instrument in a big concert hall, because the acoustics of a hall are important.

Violin choice is a highly strategic decision in regards to the type of career expected by a given violinist (chamber music or concertos with a symphonic orchestra). As a sociologist, I could never get information about the price of violins. My violin maker interviewees refused to speak with me about money. The situation was different when I was a potential client (as the mother of a soloist-student). My financial situation, however, was inadequate to discussion of acquiring a prestigious violin.

Because of the high price of such violins, transactions usually have to do with loans rather than purchases. The procedure is long and complex for young soloists whose value in the market has yet to be established. Violin makers who collaborate with a soloist class are members of the elite in their occupation. They are in charge of maintaining famous instruments and also the middlemen of their sale. Some of the prestigious producers have their own instrument collection; in a 2001 auction, Parisian violin maker Y. Ullern bought a Stradivarius for more than one million euros.[35]

Locked in a safe, the violin loses its value, because stringed instruments must be played to conserve their sound quality. "If a violin does not work," goes the expression, "it dies." A violin that loses its sound proprieties falls in value, however prestigious its name.[36] Thus nonmusician owners of expensive violins seek players to keep them in shape, and they go through violin makers to find young musicians who are responsible enough to fill the role. Hours of daily practice can even improve the instrument's sound and keep its price high enough eventually to attract a buyer. Instrument owners, like owners of thoroughbred horses in need of a good ride, require their violins be played.

Likewise, the violinist needs the violin maker to provide the loan instrument or make the connection with an owner. When this request is not fruitful, the violinist begins a tour of the illustrious violin shops, talking with owners and testing instruments proposed by craftsmen. To complete a transaction, the violinist's performance needs to satisfy the violin maker, as well as the owner of the violin.

This loan procedure could be compared to the sponsorship of an athlete, or the support of scientific researchers.[37]

Most often, the loan occurs without financial compensation.[38] However, the beneficiary can be solicited by the violin maker or owner of the instrument to play in a concert. The violinist also needs to inform the public what instrument he is playing and who loaned it (except in cases where the owner desires to remain anonymous). Usually, the programs of concerts (and competition booklets) bear such an inscription, "S. M. plays on Stradivari 1987, loaned graciously by Z."

Vera is a violinist who was educated in an Eastern European country to the age of sixteen; now she is continuing her studies in a well-known soloist class in Switzerland. As is customary in this city, Vera lives for free in the home of a rich family that hosts poor foreign students. She often participates in dinners that end in spontaneous concerts with her as a soloist. The family, well-known supporters of the local music scene, frequently invite a friend to their musical events—an old violin collector and former soloist who was forced to stop playing because of a skiing accident. Three weeks after their first meeting, the former soloist invited Vera to see his collection. Immediately, without requiring any documentation, the violin collector loaned Vera a 150-year-old Italian violin for several months. In exchange, he asked Vera to play at a charity concert that he organizes once a year. In addition, Vera is invited to play in the violin collector's house for his guests a couple times a year. "He wants to see how I take care of his violin," she says.

Two years into their relationship, the violin collector invited Vera to test another violin, one more than two hundred years old, which he had bought recently. After this test, he committed the violin to Vera, and writes into his will that the violin would become her property after his death. Vera's violin maker believed that this violin could be a less-known Stradivarius, or an old and perfect copy of it.

The story above illustrates the fondest dream of every violinist. The idea of a donation or extended instrument loan is a frequent theme in conversations among young violinists. They search for this kind of opportunity in private evenings or concerts that attract a prosperous audience. They search for rich people amenable to helping them obtain the extended loan of a prestigious violin, because the reliability and duration of loans vary, and the possibility of a situation in which the violinist does not have a proper instrument on which to perform is very worrisome.

The loan of a prestigious instrument is based on trust. The beneficiaries are the acquaintances of violin makers or young musicians advised by a teacher who is close to the violin maker or owner. There are networks of acquaintances utilized to help young violinists equip themselves well and thus, to participate in competitions. The power of trust is strong through these networks. A young thirteen-year-old student needed a good violin for his participation in a competition. His teacher (a Russian residing in France) called a violin maker, "his friend"—an old acquaintance from the time of his study in Moscow, and asked him for support. After three weeks, the student went to the friend's violin shop to pick up the loaned violin. This instrument, priced at around 35,000 euros, had been reserved for a

British client who would take it in two months. The violin maker paid the insurance and did not ask the student or his parents for a deposit. An official document concerning this loan was not even signed. The violin maker loaned the instrument to the parents based solely on the relationship he had maintained with the teacher.

Such behavior is common in the soloist world. Violins are loaned among parties bound by relationships. In exceptional cases, a violin maker helps someone outside his or her network, illustrated in the following situation I observed in my house. A violin maker provided two instruments, valued at a total of more than 300,000 euros, to a violinist for ten days. The violinist was young—eighteen years old—and had come from Poland for an international competition in France. In this case, the violin maker was so enthusiastic about the violinist's abilities that without ever having met him or his teacher, without signing a contract or even knowing where the participant lived, he authorized the loan. When, some days after, the violin maker wanted the violins back, he called the musician's host family (our family), which directed him to an address where, however, he did not find the musician. Eventually, the violin maker found the violinist, who was terrified about his delay in returning the instrument (this was before cell phones were in use). When the violin maker realized that the misunderstanding was an innocent one (confusion over "rue" versus "avenue"), he confided that some years before, he had lent his violin to a young Romanian finalist for the same competition. It took him two years to recover the prestigious instrument, because the violinist had returned home with it and the Iron Curtain made it difficult to get it back.

Loan conditions are usually arranged by word of mouth, and all participants seem confident that the young violinists will not sell instruments that do not belong to them. However, violin makers do not always agree to lend their instruments, and sometimes a bit of dishonesty is required to get a loan of a good violin, as demonstrated in the following extract from an interview in which a former soloist class student described how she and her friends obtained a prestigious violin for a competition:

It is simple, you just have to be very well dressed and know exactly what to say.

First, you make an appointment with a violin maker. Then you test several instruments, explaining that you have inherited money or found a sponsor who will buy a violin for you. To get to know a violin, you need time, to test it in a big concert hall, with an orchestra, in different places and with various repertoires. So you borrow the violin and then after three, perhaps five months, after he's constantly called you, you tell him that you don't want to buy the violin. Perhaps you have another that you like better. OK, this only works sometimes, and it is not a good idea to do it with violin makers on the same street. But if it works, you get to participate in a competition using the proper instrument.

Obviously, violin makers know the risk of putting a violin into the hands of a false buyer, but it is difficult to avoid. It is quite normal for a violinist to take an instrument home and play it over a period of several days before an acquisition. The violin maker hopes that after becoming familiar with, and perhaps attached to, the instrument, the musician will endeavor to acquire the necessary resources for buying it.

Certain musicians may find themselves in a troublesome situation when they accept an initial loan from their violin maker, as exemplified in the comments of this thirty-three-year-old violinist (in the following excerpt the "new violin" means another—certainly old one but "new" because not bought yet):

> We're always searching for a new instrument. We always want a better instrument, with the best sound! And the violin makers know that very well. So, they loan the instrument "just to test it," they say. So we borrow this violin, and yes, it is much better than our current one, so we quickly become used to it. Then, after several days, he calls you while you have been practicing for your next, very important concert, which is just three days away, and he asks you to return the violin. This is a tragedy! You are addicted to it, used to it, the violin is "yours" and you can't live without it anymore. The only problem? You didn't pay for it. So, you begin to search: a bank-loan, family, sponsor, godfather. . . . Many violinists become trapped like this and stuck in very difficult situations. When it is necessary to resell the violin, it's never as good as it was when you bought it, and it is very difficult to sell. So I've stopped buying violins. For ten years I was in debt, because during that time I changed violins four times. Now, it's finished. But I spent a lot of time trying to understand how it all works . . . I was naïve.

Violin makers and young soloists need each other, and their collaboration is realized in an insecure universe. A future soloist could become successful and famous, and might then give credibility and a good reputation to the violin maker, who, "recognizing his talent" helped him by loaning a prestigious instrument. But the number of future soloists is greater than the number of violins that can be loaned.

Violin makers are not the only violin lenders. Several governmental or private institutions manage the stock of old instruments. In Europe the Instrumental Foundation and the National Collection lends violins, as does the Stradivari Society (based in Chicago), which manages instruments owned by patrons or companies; banks and other enterprises also invest in prestigious instruments and support young performers. The Foundation of LVMH in France loans instruments owned by the LVMH company. Some cities or regional governments (such as the German *Länder*) maintain a collection of violins for loan. Most of these institutions organize competitions, in which the winner gets a violin on loan for one or more years.

Other prestigious violins are distributed through networks, on the basis of complex negotiations among teachers, collectors, and others. While speaking to a noted soloist in my home one day, my interlocutor, who represented a famous society that supports soloists, received a call on his cell phone. The call, from a member of an American foundation, concerned a violinist who was overdue in returning a prestigious violin. He explained to the caller that the beneficiary needed to play an important concert the following day, and subsequently had a recording project, which made it impossible for him to return the violin. The animated conversation suggested that this violinist had failed to meet the owner's expectations, and the foundation was requesting the return of the violin so it could be loaned to another player that the foundation had promised to support. The discussion lasted several minutes and was stormy; secret information was disclosed concerning the estimated value of various instruments and the certification of their authenticity.

The loan of a violin can be tied to power struggles in the soloist market, where a prestigious violin constitutes an important asset. The informal negotiations that I witnessed revealed something of the relationships that exist between people from the financial world and the soloists upon whom they bestow their beneficence. According to young soloists, there are always negotiations involved in the loan of a prestigious violin, even if the loan was won in an open competition. By the term "open" violinists define a competition in which they can win only a violin loan for usually one year, and the information about this conquest is largely spread in their milieu. Participants in the soloist world also complain that certain networks abuse the privilege of the loan of an expensive violin. A violin maker told me:

> The instruments that are not yet loaned in the national collection sound like an old saucepan. They are old, it's true, but they are not good, because the good ones are in the hands of distinguished teachers and their students. For example, this Montana [a violin named after its creator] has been on loan now for three years to Skripov. After the competition it was loaned for a year, because the rule states that the violin must be returned to start the competition again, and loan it to another violinist. But Skripov took it and played in the entrance exam for the Academy of B. [a European capital]. Then, as a student of that academy, he played in their philharmonic orchestra, earning more than one thousand euros per week! And he always played this violin, although it belongs to a national collection for students residing in our country, and is intended for those who are preparing and participating in international competitions. This is a scandal but not exceptional. The violin maker responsible for the technical condition of the country's violins, who signs the documents for their export,[39] says he doesn't even know the color of the good violins, because the teachers dispose of them as they wish! It is a mafia, which keeps everything in their grasp! So, if you are in a class of a teacher who is used to that procedure, he makes a call, you wait a few months, and you have your violin. It is really not worth it to play at their competitions and to waste money for the train.

Competition prizes, which often include money and or concert tours, may include the loan of a prestigious violin for the period between competitions. The most famous competition of this type is the International Violin Competition in Indianapolis. The winner received $30,000 in 2002, along with the joy of playing four years on a 1683 Stradivarius that belonged to Russian-born Josef Gingold, who founded the competition and taught at Indiana University after his career as a soloist.

Occasionally, young violinists decide to engage as soloists in ensembles that offer a prestigious violin for the duration of the contract.[40] The negative side of this arrangement is the loss of freedom, because the young violinist's foremost commitment is to the ensemble rather than a soloist career. For a young violinist to accept the position of concertmaster means to abandon the goal of becoming a soloist.[41] Soloists do not view concertmasters as equal peers. The number of violinists who played as concertmasters and went on to become soloists is small. Most young violinists first try to conquer the soloist market before deciding to compete and accept a position in an ensemble.

Another possibility is to borrow a prestigious violin from a person who possesses several instruments. Some soloists and soloist teachers are collectors. Henryk Szeryng (1918–1988), a celebrated soloist of the twentieth century, owned a "surprising collection of instruments," according to Pâris. Toward the end of his life, he played on a Guarnerious del Gesù from 1743, a Le Duc, and a Stradivarius. He owned the Stradivarius of Charles Munch, rebaptized Kinor David, which he donated to the State of Israel in 1972. He also offered a 1685 Guarnerius, the Sanctae Theresiae, to the State of Mexico in 1974, for the concertmaster of the National Orchestra of Mexico, and provided the Guadagnini to Shlomo Mintz (Pâris 1995: 913). Other soloists, such as Stern, Menuhin, Kremer, and Mutter, have possessed, or do possess, several prestigious instruments. Yuri Yankelevich was also known as a collector of violins.

It is part of the soloist class tradition for teachers to loan or donate their own violins to their most promising students (which may occur even if the teacher has only one violin, if the teacher is at the end of his or her instrumental career). This is neither a simple act of kindness under difficult circumstances nor a question of creating competition among students. The violin donation sometimes constitutes an act of filiation: the teacher recognizes this student (and not another) as his or her direct successor or most important success.

The following narrative illustrates multiple paths that must be envisaged for playing a prestigious violin. The mother of a young violinist told me in detail how her daughter, Julie, had successfully obtained loans of old violins.

She presented her first competition in W. with a small Mericourt,[42] yet she won first place with it! And then her talent made things happen, because you know, when the kids are very talented, people [help them]. First was the Instrumental Fund. M.Z., the president of the association, tried to help those who earned it, and who truly needed support; it was not Madame Gribov [Julie's teacher], but Michel—the director of the conservatory—who organized everything. He saw the level [of Julie's performance] and he knew we did not have millions of francs to buy [a violin]. The director is the one who organized everything, and then she had financial support from the city of Paris for a whole year—it was a check for 2,500 francs reserved for the conservatory students who are brilliant and who deserve it. Our financial situation was not easy, and she had this support once.

Then she borrowed a violin of C., "seven-eighths," from Mr. Dubois[43] It is a remarkable violin, Italian. Because he [Mr. Dubois] found that she played very well during the Musicora,[44] he loaned this violin to her. And after she played with this violin in L., she grew, and Mr. Michel proposed, through the national instrumental fund that she play 'the C,' a full-size violin, with which she participated in the Varna competition. It is true there was a difference, when compared to Sarah P.'s violin [her facial expression and voice indicate that the "C" was not good enough]. I don't know exactly what violin she [Sarah P.] has, but perhaps a Guarnerius or another extraordinary one; almost all of the students in this competition have extraordinary violins—here I am speaking about those students who made it to the finals, where they have all received prizes.

. . . The American girls and little Siergiej, the Russian Grilov, or I don't know who, the Australian girl, Wong, the Israeli boy, Jacob—they all had great violins. But Julie and Michal [Polish violinists] had only good violins; they do not have similar sounds and scale as other prestigious ones. . . . So it was something extraordinary that happened to us. We were in Paris, and a couple of a certain age and wealth—who don't want us to mention them—they heard Julie playing. . . . They came to each of her auditions.[45] They are music lovers, who follow all of the competitions, whether it be cello or violin. . . . They swim in music, they love it. . . . And when Julie played here, she played the same program as her competition in Varna the year before and the concert in which Madame Gribov presented all her students (because she started working for this conservatory). . . . And then Julie played a recital; and from that time forward, they have always been present when Julie plays. For Christmas, the one before last, they had spoken with Mademoiselle Elisabeth [their cousin, who worked in the conservatory] and she told me, "My cousins have been listening to Julie for months now, and they want to do something for her—but what kind of [support], you need to decide." So, we thought: "Should we ask for a regular scholarship, to support payment for private lessons or master classes? A lesson with Losov costs one thousand francs[46] for forty-five minutes. What should we do with the violin on loan, which she plays knowing that she won't have it forever; perhaps it will be possible to request that these people acquire a beautiful violin, not to give it to us [as a donation], but to loan it so that it will be in our house; or perhaps we can ask for a very good bow?" So, we made an appointment and ate together. Then . . . I mentioned all of the possibilities and explained to them that it was their decision to make. And they made a decision. As it is with people who are infatuated with beauty, who have a manor that is restored and all that . . . they bought a very beautiful violin, a G., for a "beautiful price," even for them. They loaned the violin to Julie until she turns eighteen in order for her to play on it. Julie's violin is estimated at just less than one million francs,[47] yet it is a beautiful instrument. For us it is exorbitant; it is the price of a flat. We could never afford that. . . . She will compete with this violin until the age of eighteen, longer if she wants. It is worth noting that the beautiful violins are very difficult to play, and she has had several difficulties; she initially preferred her former violin because she felt that she would not reach a high level . . . but after a while she got used to it, and now she will compete with this violin.

The family is paying part of the insurance on the violin—5,000 francs.[48]

This long interview extract shows the involvement and interaction of numerous persons: the patrons, the conservatory directors, the violin maker, the parents, the teacher, the director of the national instrumental fund, as well as secondary actors—the employee of the conservatory who is the patrons' cousin and perhaps was the most important link in this chain of collaboration (Becker 1988). All of these people contributed to the young girl's ability to play a prestigious old violin. As shown here, parental involvement is crucial in the search for a virtuoso child's work tool, and for clearing the obstacles that a poor instrument can create for a soloist's education. In some cases we can even trace a career's dynamic to successive loans of prestigious violins. After being loaned a fine violin, the virtuoso can gain access to an even better one. But the act of returning a prestigious instrument before the deadline could be seen as a breach of trust and a kind of insult. Thus there are strategic career decisions involved in the loan of a prestigious violin: from whom to borrow and under what kind of agreement. The time when soloists simply bought a prestigious violin for themselves, with rare exceptions, is in the past.

Yet the acquisition of rare violins is not always the result of simple commercial transactions. For example, Pawel Kochanski (1887–1934) received a violin as a wedding gift from his stepfather, a rich international attorney; Mischa Elman (1891–1967) received a Stradivarius as a wedding gift from his wife. Occasionally, a prestigious violin is part of the familial legacy, as in the case of Gidon Kremer (born in 1947 in Riga) who started his career with a Guadagnini that was owned by his grandfather. Several violinists received their prestigious instruments as expressions of gratitude from crowned heads or rich music lovers. Others bought their violins, and in earlier years many famous virtuosos had more than one. But after World War II, violin prices skyrocketed, and the acquisition of violins of major value became rare.

Young soloists today sometimes have instruments purchased by their family,[49] but these are not violins that would be considered "prestigious." It is frankly rare for a young soloist to own a prestigious violin—the following example, from American soloist Gil Shaham, who owned a 1699 Stradivarius, is an exception:

> The history [of the violin] is effectively extraordinary, because after being the property of this grand lady of Louis XIV's court, hearsay has it that it belonged to the mistress of Benjamin Franklin, when he was ambassador of the United States in France. . . . Whatever the case, to play on a grand violin is inestimable luck for a violinist. In Chicago, I met a former owner of this Stradivarius, who had intended to sell it and who was kind enough to loan it to me for a while. I really fell in love with it, but it was not at all within my means. For American banks, I was hardly credible. At the age of nineteen, I had neither diploma nor employer. When I told the amount I needed, nobody took me seriously. Finally, I found a bank in Switzerland. (*Diapason*, March 1997, 26–27)

The great expense of violins has forced some musicians to buy instruments whose origins are untraced. Old violins are the object of financial speculations, like old art. Certifications of authenticity and appraisals are required for transactions, because a "true" Stradivarius is not the same as a copy or a violin rebuilt from several others. The number of "patchwork" violins on the market is sizable. A restored violin with unoriginal pieces is frequently called by violin-masters a "harlequin," and does not reach a price similar to an authentic one.

The fall of the Berlin Wall led to the appearance of a significant number of old violins without verified pedigrees in Western European and American markets. There are violins sold on the black market, and are described as "without papers." The environment of the prestigious violin business is salted with suspicions of abuse concerning the certification of the violin's origin. Numerous anecdotes concerning violin makers who produce false documents circulate among violinists and violin makers. Like other realms of the antiquities business, in which transactions reach several hundred thousand euros and the value of a piece is based on documentation and expert appraisal, the universe of the violin business is rich in tall tales of falsification.[50]

The question of ownership in countries in economic and political transition can be confusing at times, especially when the state is bankrupt and undergoing privatization. Some rare instruments from the East arrived on Western European markets with unusually low prices. How did this happen? According to an Eastern European violin maker, "The cooperative that owned some Italian instruments from the eighteenth century decided to sell their collection. They asked for the expertise of the violin maker responsible for the instrument museum in this city. The expert set the prices no higher than 5 percent of their value in the European Union. These instruments were immediately sold by three of the most respected teachers at this place, obviously at much higher prices."

Other violinists were attracted by low-cost instruments lacking reliable certificates, but such purchases are fraught with risk. Crossing borders or during competitions—where violin makers frequently examine instruments—they risked being suspected of an illegal transaction.[51] If the suspected violin were declared stolen, the musician could lose the instrument and also face prosecution. It is nearly impossible to establish just how many violinists have had to resort to this practice, but I witnessed negotiations over instruments "without papers." The violin was often presented with explanations such as, "I found it in my grandfather's attic," or "I bought it while bargain hunting."

A prestigious violin, in general, is an instrument around two hundred years old that has been played without interruption. The value of a violin depends on the market, but it also has a symbolic dimension. Several of these prestigious old instruments have a famous past—bonds with historical personalities such as royal families, aristocrats, politicians, or famous artists. Their symbolic value is endowed by the violinists who played them.

The loan or donation of a "great violin" to a soloist student constitutes a sign of recognition and a mark of admission to an elite world. The violin maker, patron, or group loaning such a violin exercises strict selection criteria. As in a competition, in which the prizes constitute stepping stones for soloist careers, the loan of a prestigious violin sets the student above others. One loans an exceptional violin only to an exceptional person. The soloist class teacher offers his violin to the best student. Some young soloists receive their violin as a sign of recognition and attachment to the teacher, as in the cases of some of Yankelevich's students.[52]

Sponsoring a Musical Career

When a musician possesses a good reputation in the soloist milieu, his or her support is key to the career of a young virtuoso. The participants of the soloist world call this kind of support "sponsoring" or "patronage." It is a very old and deeply anchored musical practice that also exists in other professions.[53] Canadian sociologist Oswald Hall (1949) describes the phenomenon in relation to the support accorded to young physicists by colleagues who are more advanced in their careers. The criteria that Hall shows are employed to choose a young scientist to support are comparable to those seen in the violin soloist world. These choices are independent from the professional criteria that have been used during the stage of preselection.

Musicians as Patrons and Their Support

In the last stage of soloist education, potential is not enough. The aspiring soloist needs to play with perfect technique, interpreting the pieces according to the norms imposed by competition jury members. And the young candidates for the soloist occupation must be accepted and backed by established soloists. Musicians in the final stage of their careers frequently take young virtuosos under their wings, helping them enter the soloist market—one generation is leaving the stage for the younger generation. The middle generation, to which the majority of teachers belong, no longer benefits from the support of the older generation, which has no interest in a violinist of forty. A musician of forty already has his or her vision, style of playing and future in mind. A patron could have only a partial influence on such a protégé. If a violinist does not belong to the elite by age thirty, he or she has little hope for an international career. The availability of seniors is much greater than the number of soloists at the peak of their activity, who lack time to support the debutants. The elders, though, have as much time as they wish. Isaac Stern discussed his sponsoring activity thus:

> There came to my attention in the early eighties, an eleven-year-old girl named Midori, who had been born in Osaka, Japan, and was studying in New York at the Juilliard School of Music. Accompanied by her mother and her teacher, she arrived at my home one day to play for me, and I found myself listening to one of the most extraordinary talents I'd heard in the last forty years. She was a tiny figure of a girl, with enormous control and thoughtfulness, and an astonishing repertoire already committed to memory. I was determined to take a personal interest in her development. (Stern and Potok 2001: 265)

In the soloist world, the search for a patron is the object of much research done by teachers, students' parents, and students themselves at the final stage of their education. All participants are convinced of the power of the elder patrons, though these same typically minimize their role in the music market. Stern continues:

> Now, I was a loyal, severe, and compassionate friend to a new generation of violinists. In the year 1991, when some were lamenting the crisis in conducting

and the dearth of great tenors and the meager presence of supreme artists at the keyboard, there was astonishing virtuosity on the violin, the most difficult instrument of all: Itzhak Perlman, Anne-Sophie Mutter, Gidon Kremer, Maxim Vengerov, Gil Shaham, Midori, Joshua Bell. Some saw me behind much of this flourishing of string players: a sort of Svengali[54] known in violin circles as "the godfather," snapping up gifted ten year olds, funding their education at Juilliard with Dorothy DeLay, who, when they were ready for the world, picked up the phone, called Lee Lamont at ICM, and urged her to listen to them play. Completely untrue, but what they thought. Well, a youngster with great talent merited the loyalty and the learning of the older generation that he or she would one day replace. I was simply giving back what friends in the past had once given me. (Stern and Potok 2001: 283)

Through patronage, senior members of the soloist world exert a form of social control. To support one musician is to refuse others. Facilitating concert engagements, the patrons keep control of the "protégé." The beneficiary henceforth feels a loss of independence and an obligation to follow the advice of the patron, as suggested by the following excerpt from an interview:

Our daughter participated in a competition in order to have a violin. In the jury of this competition was Sabine [the famous soloist]. When she heard our daughter, immediately, she offered a scholarship in the US, hoping that we would never come back here [European city], where she is well installed. Evidently, we don't have the violin (she was not a winner), which we will have to obtain [elsewhere]. [Young violinist] was not directly in the competition with Sabine, but she certainly did not belong to her network, and being a "stranger" designated to be competing with Sabine's protégés.

The possibilities for exploitation of patronage can be illustrated by the following example. A twenty-two-year-old violinist had recorded a demo CD for concert organizers. Just before the first piece, we hear the easily recognizable voice of a famous soloist encouraging listeners to appreciate the music of this "great talent." Evidently the introduction was given nine years before the recording was made, but this fact is not explicitly communicated to listeners. For the senior musician, patronage offers the hope of inscribing a younger musician into one's "school of interpretation." Ideally, the senior musician must be departing the scene, leaving a place for his or her successor. And the successor must be young enough to accept the patron's advice.

There are exceptions, though rare, and this relationship concerned two different specialty performers. One concerns the sponsorship of Henryk Szeryng by Arthur Rubinstein, the famous pianist. Rubinstein heard Szeryng while visiting Mexico City in the 1950s and asked his manager, Sol Hurok, to hire the violinist for a concert tour. Szeryng's New York appearance in 1959 was a major success, sparking an international career. As in this example, the musical patron may sometimes play a different instrument. Daniel Barenboim—pianist and conductor—not only supported the musical career of trumpet player Sergei Nakariakov but also helped on the administrative side, negotiating with the Israeli authorities to excuse him from military obligations. The singer Montserrat Caballé, through her TV program, helped various instrumentalists; and the pianist Martha Argerich used her CD label to favor the debuts of young violinists, cellists, and pianists.

Various nonmusical criteria can inspire support a protégé: nationality, ethnicity, religion, similarity of taste, hobbies, or life experience, or even sexual attraction can be involved in this decision. The support for persons originating from similar cultures or countries is especially common. Isaac Stern's support of numerous Israeli violinists is one example (though Stern also supported violinists from other origins). This activity was institutionalized through the America-Israel Cultural Foundation, created to help violinists like I. Perlmann, S. Mintz, and Pinchas Zukermann come to the United States during adolescence to study at the Juilliard School of Music, Indiana University, or the Curtis Institute. Conductor Herbert von Karajan (an Austrian citizen working in Germany) was a famous patron of the German violinist Anne-Sophie Mutter.

Nonmusician Patrons

Various nonmusical criteria motivate nonmusical patrons such as politicians, religious groups, clubs, or political parties.[55] The example of Jean-Pierre is a typical illustration of political support. His family is well known and powerful in one of the French regions. Jean-Pierre's father is a physician and deputy for the governmental majority, and several family members belong to the local elite. In his third year of violin education, Jean-Pierre's conservatory teacher declared him a "child prodigy," and the young violinist played on several occasions for municipal and regional events as a soloist, often in the repertoire with the city's symphony orchestra. The young violinist was the star student in the regional conservatory and got a lot of assistance in pursuing his education: the loan of an old violin, funding for masterclasses, costs of his first CD production by departmental authorities and support in the local media for its distribution, and public fund for study and travel costs. Jean-Pierre is a frequent soloist in the numerous festivals in his region of France. Without the support of local politicians and public institutions, he would have many more difficulties.

I frequently observed circles of support for immigrant musicians in which the movers and shakers of a community lobbied to propel their protégé. The pianist father of a violinist originating from Armenia remarked, "It is crazy, our situation: we are living in X [the name of a Western European country] and my son almost never plays there; even for the events in our city, he was never invited even though all the organizers know him. On the other hand, he plays all the time in Z [neighboring country] because the community, the Armenian conductors, and agents support us—luckily for my boy."

Another form of support is similar to one largely practiced in sports—the support in exchange for publicity. For example, the producers of cosmetics, fashion, or luxury items sponsor young musicians through their companies. Aisha, a fourteen-year-old violinist born in a former Soviet Republic but residing in Vienna, was supported by a cosmetics firm that covered all her costs in the United States and obtained for her the loan of a prestigious violin in exchange for some concerts. This young violinist was able to live with all of her family in Vienna because of this financial support. In return, she provided the symbolic values of beauty, talent, and romantic origin—her modest family comes from a war-torn country—to the company. Aisha's example shows how important these ancillary features connected to the soloist can be; we will see that in detail later; sometimes, these characteristics can be crucial for the development of a soloist career.

Rarely, issues such as common taste, rather than strict musical criteria, influence a sponsor/client relationship. A fifty-year-old soloist and organizer mentored a virtuoso of nineteen, providing accommodation and career support for more than two years; they spend a large part of their time sharing common passions such as chess, parties, and concerts in their European city.

Frequently, participants say that support is accorded for reasons of sexual attraction, but I was never able to get information other than third-person accounts. According to the common conviction, young female violinists are favored in some competitions; the male violinists must play perfectly, it is said, because male members of a jury tend to be stricter with males than with physically attractive females. Following similar logic, gay male participants could benefit from special support. All this information is part of the discourse in the soloist universe, but nearly impossible to verify.

Proving that support for a particular musician was accorded for a single reason is difficult; all patrons use musical arguments to explain their decisions. As in other professions and social universes, decisions of this type are complex, and the decisive factors are many—some easily detectable, some not, some very concrete and specific, others more vague, some conscious, others the result of long analysis and reflection.

Then too, not all patronage is the same. A single patron might help a young musician over the course of many years, but a single episode of support might be crucial. As in all areas of life, each situation is different, and thus the analysis of these practices tends to be difficult and somewhat subjective.

INTERNATIONAL COMPETITION AND SELECTION FOR SOLOIST CAREER

Patronage and support networks facilitate access to the soloist market, as do competitions. One could say there are two career paths: one leading through competitions and other without these kind of events. Some soloists seek to win an important conquest or more than one. Others never participate in the competitions.[56] Yehudi Menuhin (1916–1999), Isaac Stern (1920–2001), S. Mintz (born in 1957), Anne-Sophie Mutter (1963), Gil Shaham (1971), and Midori (1971) never took part in a competition for violinists. Certain well-known soloists have benefited from the support of important and powerful patrons; with their support these soloists directly accessed the important performing stages. Other soloists, such as

David Oïstrakh (1908–1974), I. Haendel (1924), J.-J. Kantorov (1945), G. Kremer (1947), L. Korcia (1964), and M. Vengerov (1974) were winners of international competitions. During the young soloist's lengthy education, he or she may partic- ipate in competitions of various levels of importance.[57] For those who are at the third stage of their education, success in a competition can be the means of access to the soloist market.

Until 1970, there were several dozen international competitions, and most of the winners had easy access to the prestigious concert halls. By becoming finalists they became well known and could expect to perform on the most prestigious music stages.[58] The number of competitions is rising,[59] a fact that preoccupies the violinists, their parents, and their teachers. Noting that there were more than eighty-five contests listed in the *Guide of Competitions*, one former competitor stated, "So many! . . . Do you know all these eighty-five first- place winners? I don't know them. So what is all that for?"

A violin maker had this to say about the proliferation of competitions:

> So, the debut of the career for the young person who is gifted . . . we see that in Thibaud [famous French competition] every four years . . . and then, suddenly, we no longer hear about the one who took first place. Take the list of winners from the first edition of a competition and look at those who made careers for themselves. . . . Certainly they all continued to play, but going from that to making a career where they step onto the stage and into the spotlight is all hearsay. Take the list from one international competition and look. What's the secret to success? Because after all, [success in a competition] is related to one encounter. . . . It is necessary to do it perfectly, without any errors! . . . After- ward, [success] boils down to the personal talent of knowing how to manage one's own career or meeting an agent. The secret of that? I don't know. . . . Some are well known, and others, not at all. . . .

Around the same time, another important issue came up, the decrease in the age of the participants. Even if it seems unfair for this stage of a career, some important adult competitions are won by teenagers, who already are at the last stage of their violin education:

> Q: Have you observed that the age of candidates has decreased?
> A: Yes. Certainly yes. It means that it is the tendency to . . . it is not a tendency supported by all participants. In fact, it is the tendency that was made almost naturally. They put children on the violin at an earlier and earlier age. They have a time-lag. Those who play violin best of all do the common circuit— the competition for the conservatory, and after their arrival to the level "best- of"—the international competitions. It is a little like in sports. Young people, and it is an approach to fashion, yes, fashion—it is very charming to make a child not yet pubescent play the repertoire of a man of thirty.
> Q: Did they play exactly like the violinist of thirty?
> A: Yes, because the program played is carefully chosen in relation to that: these are pieces of pure virtuosity, rapidity, played louder and louder and faster

and faster.

Q: It is the technique?

A: Yes, the technique, but with music finding its place in these performances, I don't know, because it is close to sports, sport-shows, the gym where, you know, they enter kids of twelve and thirteen years old. Then after they damage their foot, they fire them—after, they wash their hands of them. It is foolish to think that children competing younger and younger like that is good. It is good, but I find it surprising that the kids I know now—fifteen-, sixteen-year-olds have nothing to learn anymore. They know everything already. But this is . . . is confusing, a little confusing because the maturity is certainly not yet there. It is clear in certain masterpieces. For Paganini, I don't think that this is the problem, but for Bach it is more complex.

Young prodigies were not unknown in the past. In 1935, when the first violin competition in history took place—the Wieniawski competition—the youngest candidates, Ginette Neveux and Ida Haendel, were sixteen and eleven years old, respectively. (Neveux won first prize.) What has decreased is the *average* age of all competitors. The race for precociousness is most frequent among violinists, because of the features of the instrument. A child pianist or flute player does not have the option of playing an instrument of reduced size, so most children must grow a bit before playing the adult repertoire on these instruments.

If everyone agrees that competitions do not necessarily indicate future success, why do soloists participate? According to a survey carried out in 1994 by the World Federation for International Competitions, 75 percent of candidates had their performance at the competitions as a concert, 51 percent saw it as a chance to extend their repertoire, 50 percent hoped to attract the media's attention, 41 percent profited from practicing the particular pieces, 38 percent hoped to meet other young musicians, 31 percent were interested in confronting other schools of interpretation, and 22 percent enjoyed the competitions as tourism (*Guide de concours* 1999/2000: 25).

At one international competition, the following snatch of conversation between two young violinists, a twenty-four-year-old Korean woman and a thirty-year-old Italian man, gives a sense of what young soloists expect from participation in competitions:

Hello, what are you doing here?
And you?! What you are you doing here?
You have already taken third place in the Verdi Competition!
And you? You have a job already!

The Italian musician was surprised that someone who had done so well at a prestigious competition would want to come to another. The Korean woman was surprised to see her former co-contestant, because he was by now concertmaster in a well-respected Italian ensemble. He had a comfortable job, and she assumed he would no longer aspire to a soloist career, rendering it pointless to participate in the competition. As this conversation illustrates, young soloists have different objectives. The Korean violinist continues to participate with dreams of starting her soloist career; even if she took a place in an ensemble, or a teaching position, the number of prizes she receives seems to her an asset for her résumé. The Italian participant claimed to like the ambiance and the competition itself. He told me he had come to meet people and found that preparing a new program for competitions was very useful. His current job did not provide enough "distractions," he said, and the competitions motivated further hours on his violin.

One former participant said that the competitions were "aberrant." "It becomes almost an obsession. . . . When you are young, it is truly motivating and this is the goal in itself . . . but this is not the goal itself." Young soloists rarely told me they come to a competition to earn money or a good reputation. They often hoped to play the program in its entirety, meaning that they would pass all selections and become finalists. Some hoped to win because it would enable them to play a prestigious violin for a period of time. Others, especially those who lived in Eastern Europe before the political changes, were interested in traveling to the West. Some hoped to win first place because this automatically endowed the winner with citizenship in the country that organized the competition.[60]

Jury members, however, see their role as vital in selecting individuals for the stage. Although the relevance of competition is less important than it was before 1970, these events are still a tool for selection and an important element in a soloist career. First place allows a player to "make a career." Gaining a place on the finalist list may also be taken into account by concert agents and CD producers. This opinion is true; however exceptionally, it is possible, once benefitting from support of patron and reputable teacher, to have a long-lasting international career without participating in a competition. Winning a competition is not sufficient for making an important career. Other variables, such as an excellent and powerful teacher and his network of support, a patron, and other features presented in this book, are also indispensable to pursue a soloist career.

The competitions open a door to the soloist market and form a point of contact between the circles of education and those of music production—the agents, concert organizers, and record producers. A violin maker explained,

> The record companies . . . see what they need for their repertoire; for their stable they choose artists who are likely to play this given piece. . . . These are the competition's finalists. . . . It is a kind of . . . a kind of preselection. It is not always very nice to observe that eliminatory stage . . . the ambiance is cold, all these kids are extremely tense, an ambiance of pure competition. For some of them, it is very expensive to come here, very expensive in the time of preparation, stress, and so on. What is interesting to see is the result . . . the difference between the first and the second place is so minimal after all that happened. . . . I think that the competitions and the eliminations for competitions are too hard. In the hall, everyone knows the pieces. Some have played them. One small error and it's finished. It happened in the frozen ambiance this morning. It was cold. . . . The ambiance is heavy, each one thinks that others play better than him, yet they are all good.

The competitions are important not only because of the prize list. They are also a place where people active in the soloist world meet. For the young soloists, it's a place to be seen and heard by critics, agents, and the public. The "scandals" that occur there could also be useful in winning notice. The scandals almost always concern failure—negative selection—but sometimes result in positive selections. Failure is not always related to the musical aspects but sometimes to heterodox interpretations of pieces in the classical repertoire. The lack of success in selection sometimes seems to arise from the divergence between public perception, the candidate's performance, and the jury verdict.[61]

Access to public visibility is not only related to musical performance. The behavior of an artist is very important in the conquest of visibility. Some attract attention with atypical dress and uncommon behavior, as in the case of a British violinist Nigel Kennedy who chewed gum when he entered the stage. The Yugoslav pianist Ivo Pogorelich passes into history of competitions as a man of scandals who "paid a price for his sartorial eccentricities" (Cresta and Breton in A. Pâris 1995: 123).

Jury Negotiations and the Perception of Equity among Soloists

The president of the jury chooses collaborators from various places around the world to show its international commitment. To secure a good reputation as a jury member, members must know how to negotiate and accept compromise. It is necessary, one former jury member said, to "avoid posing too many problems." Cordiality is important, as the following interview suggests: "I was invited to M [city] for the competition. I like this place because we have already worked together several times and I know that with this team, it will be good. We will understand each other . . . no problems. None of us is stubborn, and that is important."

The backstage negotiations of the jury are rarely published. The remarks of a former jury member in numerous competitions, Nathan Milstein, published in his autobiography, are a rare window on this subject, but his testimony reflects the perspective of most soloist world participants concerning the selection criteria during competitions. During a cocktail reception in the Embassy of Japan, Milstein, a soloist of Russian origins residing in the United States, reported giving this advice to the ambassador who was profoundly sad that his candidate had failed in the Thibaud competition in Paris: "'Listen,' I said. 'You see how the Soviets treat these competitions. If you want the Japanese to win prizes, you have to approach this business just as seriously. Your cultural attaché has to work on it, since he has the contacts. He knows important people. And the Japanese government must provide your young violinists with good instruments and comfortable lodgings when they come to Paris, and so forth.' Just what the Japanese are doing now. . . . Music, unfortunately, has turned into a big political game" (Milstein and Volkov 1991: 225).

In nine formal interviews with jury members, and several informal ones, I posed the following question, "How do you select your candidate?" In the majority of responses, the jury members pointed out that they look for excellent technique joined with great musicality. They also expect a soloist candidate to show his or her artistic personality. To go through all stages of competitions, the violinist needs to meet the jury members' expectations.[62] Some creativity is allowed, but soloists do not stray far from the conventional interpretations. If they do, they could hurt their chances. One juror said,

> It is necessary to play "for the competition," that is, to conform to the jury's norms, go gently to the final. Only at the gala concert [played by the winner following the competition] can they show their true personality, as Martha Argerich did. Once, a student passed well through all stages . . . [but] at the concert of laureates, all the jury members of the jury asked themselves, "Who did we give the prize to?" Because his playing had nothing to do with what he did previously!

Most of the interviewed jury members conformed to the official discourse, which can be heard during the opening or closing of a competition ceremony. This discourse corresponds to what Howard Becker stated about the judgment of artists and their works: "It is as though making art works as a competition, like a school test, and we have to render a fair judgment based on all the facts" (1988: 22).

Jury members' comments about selection criteria suggest that many choices are subjective.[63] They all stated that the interpretation of pieces must to correspond to the canons in vigor, but these canons are not always shared. The diversity of criteria is a major factor in conflicts among jury members. In the matter of the arts and music, a sole model of interpretation (even in the same epoch) does not exist. Almost all candidates possess a technical level good enough for performing the program. Jury members often remark that "all competitors play very well," or "the level of competition is very high."

They state that the selection of the finalists is based on the quality of interpretation. To match the jury's expectations, young violinists seek to conform. "I had to think a lot about the choice of program for competition. OK, for example, Bach. If we can avoid him, it's better, because each member of the jury has their own vision for the interpretations of Sonatas and Partitas of Bach. Three of them recorded Bach, and it is always a risk [when you play him] that the judges will not like your version. You can play very well, but if it is not suitable for them, then your results are damned."[64] Some of the jury members said that a "voting by points" system protects the candidates from preferential treatment that some judges could apply to a protégé. One juror, who had been invited to numerous competitions, shouted, "What scheming? It's mathematics! That's all!"

Other jury members emphasized the ban on grading their own student as a measure that guaranteed impartiality. Only one respondent admitted another discourse. This former soloist is the father of a violinist who had participated in international competitions. Perhaps this explains why his point of view was so different from that of his colleagues: "False notes of one's own are less false when played by others. They [jury members] know very well how to make an arrangement among them. They are obligated to understand each other. If not, they will be burned in the circle of competition [not invited to be a member of jury]—very fruitful, by the way."

While negotiations among jury members remain in the shadow, I witnessed some behind-the-scenes action around an international competition of medium importance in a European capital. The jury was international: six members variously from France, Russia, Hungary, England, and the United States, but every one was a graduate of the same Eastern European institution. Two weeks before the competition, Anton (a teacher and friend of one participant family) called a participant mother, asking in which group her daughter—Olga—would compete. When he learned that she would participate in the last group, he blew up. "This is bad! You must change her category immediately!" The mother justified the choice by the fact that Olga had the level to play in the last group. But Anton, a jury member, warned, "It is not a question of level. If you want your child to win something, she needs to change the group!" Despite these cautions, the young violinist stayed in the highest-level category, finished in the middle of the pack, and was not selected for the 800 euro prize. That evening, after the last jury meeting, Anton called the mother: "Listen to me. . . . When I heard that Zoltan, son of M. [a famous female soloist] had entered our competition . . . I knew that your daughter had no possibility of winning! She could play like Heifetz with the same result! That's why I wanted you to change the group. I couldn't explain that to you before, because I was, after all, a member of the jury . . . you understand me, I hope."

In fact, Anton was not only a jury member. He had been a student in the same class as the mother of the winner, and his son was a young violinist who was trying to enter into a soloist career. The support of a famous soloist (the mother of the winner of this competition) could certainly be helpful in the struggle for this competitive position. Thus, it was not entirely clear that Anton himself had not bartered his jury position to further his own family.

The Perception of Selection by the Candidates and Others in the Soloist Milieu

Observers of these competitions like to make a game of predicting the results. Though I never heard about actual money being wagered over the predicted winners, in other aspects these practices are reminiscent of the racetrack. These observers told me that the following information is required to make the right prediction: the list of the judges and the list of previous competition winners (to predict which judge has the most power to push his or her protégés).

According to these skeptics, jury members select "their" candidate based on criteria that stray far from actual musical performance. Because this is so, competitors try to meet the jury members beforehand—often taking master classes from them—in order to get a sense of their criteria. This statement, from a twenty-one-year-old student, reflects the consensus of soloist candidates:

If you go into the competition without preparation, you must be crazy. Even if you play like Heifetz,[65] you need to make the master classes and not with one but with several jury members, and with those who are powerful. This is how you prepare for the competitions. Then you play what they suggest and not what you prepared before, which you had practiced for a long time. They want

[a different interpretation], so you show how quickly you've learned your lesson. If you come unknown [to the competition] and you play very well, you are
dangerous for their "horses" [the musicians they support], so they reject you in
the first round. . . . It's harder to do this in later rounds, because the public has
time to know a little, but the first rounds are less visited by the public. . . . In
order to pass the stages before the final, it is necessary that the jury know you. If
not all of them, then some of them. They listen to the same program fifty times
over two or three days, so they are not even able to hear the notes anymore. But
during the master class, they have worked with you several times and they have
tested you already. They know what you can do and where your limits are. It is
less risky to vote for someone who they know can play than for someone who,
maybe, has had an excellent [competition] but would die of jitters and fail in
the concert of award winners. They [jury members] are much more at ease with
their own "horses." So the competition starts long before the opening ceremony,
with the master classes or even the new class several months before.

Among the ten laureates of competitions included in my study, nine were the
disciples of at least one jury member. Except in rare cases, all candidates had
personal contact (master class or individual lessons) with the jury members. The
conviction that the results are rigged and that the "game is over before the first
stage" is shared by young violinists who are at the final stage of their education. A
young soloist told me:

The play is done before the first note plays. They [jury members] prepare the
dish and you play the best you can, but the violinists present here all have an
excellent level. OK, a few came here for nothing, but almost all play well. The
competitions—well, almost all, from what I know—are rigged: everyone knows
everyone; the teachers are the judges and came here with their students. But we
still participate, and we prepare for that. We take the master class with whom
it's necessary, and we work every day for months before . . . and we hope to be
in the final. Everyone takes their chances.

Similar criticisms are formulated by other people close to competitions for other
instruments. A very suggestive book about the biggest U.S. piano competition, the
Van Cliburn International Piano Competition, written by a musicologist and music
critic, Joseph Horowitz, provides similar testimony. Horowitz concludes: "These
inflamed personal relations illustrate a common circumstance at international
music competitions: jurors and contestants know one another and harbor strong
opinions before a note is played" (Horowitz 1990: 95).

And there is nothing new about this phenomenon, as illustrated in this letter
from the mother of French violinist Ginette Neveu, who wrote to her daughter's
teacher at the time of the 1935 Wieniawski Competition:[66]

Shortly before the results of the first examination were communicated, we knew
that Ginette had been admitted to the second round with very good grades. The
level of competition is high. There are remarkable technicians, but they lack

musicality. . . . I beg you, Dear Master, to come here. In the second examination, the power of the contestants will be very hard. It is to be presumed that
the members of the jury will steadily support their compatriots. If no French
member is present, we worry that Ginette, despite her talent, will win a place
lower than her value, as was the case in Austria. . . . Certainly, this is worth your
while because not only does Ginette represent a French school of violin playing,
but she is also the top of your class. France is wrong not to be interested in these
international artistic events, from several points of view. Ginette played the
entirety of her program without any breaks. And she was the single contestant
for whom the jury proposed after Chaconne, the Polonaise, and the Tarentelle,
to play Tzigane the next day.[67] . . . Dear Master, we wait for you impatiently. We
do not believe that a French member will be part of the jury for the second exam;
after the execution that Ginette achieved yesterday, this would be a travesty. . . .
N. Neveu (Soriano 1993: 120–121)

Critique of the Competition Principle

Many members of the music world (conductors, recorders, violin makers, and
agents) strongly criticize the participation of young musicians in these competitions. Even jurors, such as the famous cellist Gregor Piatigorski, have described
the competitions as "absurd." Said Piatigorski, "I suffer agony to see young artists
go through the humiliation of a competition. . . . The joy of those who succeed
is spoiled by the sorrow of those who have been hurt. . . . It cannot be useful to
discourage a hundred merely to encourage one" (Horowitz 1990: 16).

Clearly, even some jurors find the competitions painful and emotionally damaging. Yet as one analysis of the competitions states,

The competition is a fundamental element of musical life. . . . People criticize
competitions. They scoff at them. Certain members of the jury resign noisily, but
nobody dares to truly insist on the suppression of this mode of talent recruitment. To the contrary! It seems that the horrors of the competition enforce
the feeling of their necessity, if we are to judge by the multiplication of these
events. . . . We have the institutions that we deserve. Competitions are not a
foreign body in musical life, or an aberration against nature. To the contrary,
we have to examine what kind of spirit, what advantages they develop in the
young instrumentalists who are submitted by force to their discipline. (Cresta
and Breton in A. Pâris 1995: 118)

For participants, the competitions are sports events rather than musical ones,
which confront technique against art. Most young virtuosos and some teachers I
interviewed find that judgments in the competitions are strictly subjective. Said
a teacher who sometimes judges in the competitions: "How does one compare
competitors when each one has an irreproachable technique and each one has
a different interpretation? It is impossible to judge and rank! They are different:
one will please one type of public, another a different public, but attributing first

place and then second and so on is certainly unjust and partial! It is not the best who arrive first. It is not a race. Between Oïstrakh, Kogan, and Stern, who takes the grand prize?" A thirty-year-old soloist, who has competed around the world, shares this opinion:

> It is difficult in a competition. It is not always the art that will be compensated, because taste varies. Someone who plays perfectly—whom we can't distinguish from the others—is perfect. He gets first place. What about the person who plays artistically? Some will like it because he played with personal investment, but others won't.
>
> Q: So, perfectly is not artistically?
> A: It could be, but not necessarily. Perfection is foremost technical perfection. When you are not invested emotionally, it is "easy." It is much more difficult to be perfect technically and to be involved emotionally at the same time, because you take risks. It is as if you are driving on the turnpike ninety miles per hour. You feel a kind of exhilaration; others times, you won't take the risk.
> Q: So, when it is not risky, it is easier to have control?
> A: Exactly! Maybe the car metaphor doesn't work so well [he laughs].

Another student, nineteen, told me about his experience:

> When I failed my first round, I asked four jurors about their opinion of my performance. The first said to me that my Paganini was not good, but in contrast, Bach was fantastic; the second said that my Bach was poor, but Beethoven . . . exceptional; the third that in Wieniawski, I had problems with intonation, but the interpretation was excellent; and the last juror said that Wieniawski was very in tune, but badly interpreted. None of them had the same opinion about my performance, but they were all in perfect agreement that I was "very talented, but poorly taught," and I needed to change my teacher. See! [he shows me four business cards] They all invited me to join their class. So, what are the competitions for? It's rigged.

Despite those kinds of opinions, the soloist students take their chances and participate in two or three competitions each season. Armed with an excellent violin supported by the patron, and after several passages in the competitions in which they won some recognition of jury members, virtuoso teachers, and students, the young musicians achieve their education, play in concerts, and enter a market parallel to that of a reputed soloist. Thanks to different organizers, they perform while waiting to be accepted by a professional agency specializing in soloist productions.

A professional agency is a business that organizes the concert tours of several artists, groups, and orchestras, also taking on CD production. The artists playing in important concert halls have their agency and in Europe and in the United States. (The International Artists Managers' Association provides 307 members directories—agencies of different sizes and all working in the field of classical music.) Almost all soloists performing in the United States and Western Europe are working with this kind of institution. However, only exceptionally young virtuoso students from soloists class have had an agent. Most often they are playing thanks to the efforts of an amateur organizer.

Contributions of Concert Organizers

The soloist students at this stage of education, and sometimes earlier, meet amateur and professional concert organizers. Samuel Gilmore distinguishes three categories of classical concert markets in New York City: Midtown (repertory), Uptown (academic), and Downtown (avant-garde) (Gilmore 1987: 213).

The first category encompasses concerts with soloists and conductors of ensembles with a widespread international reputation at important concert halls. The second concerns concerts organized in various places (the majority on university campuses) with well-known performers. The last category refers to avant-garde music events in which the performers are frequently composers themselves. This categorization describes the case in New York City; however, in other places important for classical music (Berlin, Paris, Zurich, London, and others), we can admit that the division between the categories of the classical concert market could be similar (repertory/academic/avant-garde).

Soloist students aspire to enter Gilmore's first category. While waiting for this entrance, young musicians accept all opportunities, in order to be visible and optimize their chances of success. They play everywhere: in churches, modest halls, in provinces and suburbs, but also in the more important concert halls in small cities and towns, where classical concerts are organized by professionals. Access to the better-known halls is conditionally based on the artist's reputation and the work of the agent, while other locales are accessible for amateur organizers, and constitute the "parallel market" for soloist students. I use this term to distinguish this market from the one organized by professional agencies. The parallel market constitutes places like churches, culture community centers, or private spaces adapted for one event into concert hall. In addition, soloist students often play for charity events, homage concerts, and, as lucky finalists of competitions, at gala concerts.

During the last stage of soloist education, young musicians profit from each opportunity to implant themselves in the soloist world. Their characteristic activity at this time is participation in numerous concerts belonging to different categories. The desire of market expansion guides their strategy, as seen in the following example. The father (and agent) of a seventeen-year-old violinist, residing in Germany and well known in the musical milieu of this country, explained why he had accepted a concert engagement in a French manor in a small community: "What's the point of Miriam's playing there? I ask myself that. Here in our country, for a long time now we've been refusing offers like this one. Playing for 800 euros is ridiculous, and they pay the travel by train—we've been traveling by plane for a long time now. But we had to accept the offer, because it was in France. In Germany, she plays only the big halls, with a serious orchestra, and on important festivals."

Unlike Miriam's father, most young musicians do not find that playing in less well-known locales is "degrading" to their career or image. Without small halls and modest

concerts, professional work would be impossible, they say. It is exactly in these amateur organized contexts that the musicians learn how to collaborate with organizers
and accumulate experiences that can be useful in their future work with agents. Their
activity in the amateur organizer market constitutes an introduction and preparation
for the next stage in their career—that of adult soloist.

AMATEUR ORGANIZERS OF YOUNG VIRTUOSO CONCERTS

In most of France and Eastern Europe there are few professional agents and hence,
few offers accessible to young musicians. In these circumstances, they most often
play concerts organized by their entourages. Among the amateur organizers, I
distinguish two types of individuals: the principal organizers, for whom show
organization is a principal activity, and "occasional" organizers, who work in
a given support network. Concert preparation is a team activity, and principal
organizers are assisted by other participants belonging to the soloist universe.
Relationships—private and professional—are mobilized for this activity.[68] In each
community or city, and even within political, artistic, or spiritual communities,
specific individuals are identified as key to organizing a performance. In the mid-
1990s, Cecilia, a housewife and former saleswoman, started organizing concerts
and master classes in prestigious locations in her European city, in association
with the teacher of her twelve-year-old daughter. As a result of these activities,
she was frequently solicited by young violinists and their associates who sought
her support in arranging events.

   In the last several decades, a new form of collaboration has sprung up involving
professional and volunteer organizers. Instrumentalists solicit voluntary associations to help them organize festivals.[69] These instrumentalists, calling themselves
"artistic directors," often play at these events and invite other artists from their
milieu. The principle of reciprocal services (as French musicians say, "kick-back")
is widely followed among soloists and strongly respected by them. The model of
these festivals was created by the Spanish cellist Pablo Casals, who wanted to reunify
his collaborators in order to hang out with them and play concerts. For political
reasons, he organized this "European holiday" at the Spanish-French border, in
Prades. Building upon the success of this event, numerous violinists and teachers
created festivals or took over an existing event: I. Stern and S. Mintz in Keiset
Eilon, Israel; Dorothy DeLay in Aspen, Colorado; V. Spivakov in Colmar, France,
and other places.

   The program of these festivals frequently includes an evening devoted to young
musicians. Participation in these events constitutes a supplementary selection,
which may have as much punch as participation in the final of a competition.
Soloist students solicit the attention of these soloist violinist-artistic directors
(who may be their teachers) to be included in the festival program. For example,
a student may participate in the master class of Jasha in Barcelonnette in order to
play the next season in the festival of Perpignan, where Jasha is "artistic director."
This type of organization is not specific to the soloist students' world. In the case

of baroque music, studied by François (2000), the festivals debuted in associative and amateur circles, and progressively were professionalized.

PROFESSIONAL AGENTS

The young violinists play in concerts organized by amateurs, but dream about working for a professional agency. The narratives of famous soloists of the twentieth century, for example, those who were in the Sol Hurok agency in the United States, impress young soloists. In France, there are few big agents; the majority of the top category of concerts are organized by important international agencies (Productions Internationals Albert Sarfati, Valmalète).[70]

To understand what young soloists' expectations are in regard to agents and to know how the agents go about their business, I obtained information from some thirty soloists living in France and Poland.[71] The violinists describe these relationships as conflictive. The majority of interviewees, after being asked the question, "Were you satisfied with the work of your agent?" responded that they were disappointed by unfulfilled expectations and failed promises. Agents are expensive and organize too many concerts, they said, and as a consequence, some musicians decided to do their own booking. A thirty-year-old soloist told me she has "a lot of concerts" (forty to fifty), but only one year out of two. During one year, she spends her time preparing a concert tour, and the next year she plays. She books herself concerts in Europe, Asia, and South America; she has kept her North American agent (for concerts in the United States), because she finds him serious and efficient. Another violinist, a forty-year-old, confided in me that she thought she had an agent, but seeing the results, he will probably stop working for her. According to her, her experience is typical for French violinists who need to shift for themselves when finding concerts.

Lastly, a new type of agency has emerged: Internet agencies. The development of this communication tool contributed to the proliferation of the virtual sites that include the names of violinists along with their photo, repertoire, and sometimes, excerpts of recordings.[72]

Few professionals "produce" young soloists. They are young by age but their performance is similar level to an "old" virtuoso. However, their collaboration with agents is rare because of the difficulties stemming from child labor laws.[73] Among young violinists I interviewed, only two declared that they had signed a contract with a professional agency. In the case of an important concert, most musicians participated only in a "young, special musician" concert or concert-homage.

YOUNG VIRTUOSOS MOVE CLOSER TO ORGANIZERS

The soloist students need to see and be seen by agents in order to create relationships that will allow them to be heard, so they find the right receptions and parties the agents frequent. Many professional artists rely upon relationships of this sort,[74] but soloists are different in that their projects cover short periods. The soloist can play only one or at most two concerts with a given orchestra, each season in the same city. Sometimes, the soloists present a cycle of concerts, but they are always short projects in comparison to other artistic occupations, such as with painters, who may prepare and present a show over a period of a year, or actors who prepare a movie over several months, or a theater piece that they will act in over several seasons.

Soloist participation in these kinds of mundane social activities seems to be a part of their professional life. Almost all of the interviewees know that during these parties, new projects arrive. Young virtuosos distinguish two major kinds of situations: the parties organized after their own concerts, and those arranged for other musicians or for a celebration of another occasion, such as a political meetings, a birthday party, and so on. Parties that take place after young musician concerts constitute a kind of "natural" prolongation of the performance; rare are those who refuse to participate in such events. The guests—a part of the audience (sometimes the whole public) also have the occasion to converse with musicians. With a drink in their hand, the musicians may share some information about their life, about their familial origin, their teachers, experiences, and sometimes, the organization of their practice.

My interviewees were generally less positive about other types of parties and social events. The strategy of hunting for concerts during parties ("playing the relationships technique") is proof of professional insufficiency, many said. During a party after a concert, the security service of the concert hall let a violinist enter who had failed to show his invitation letter, and who arrived just before the last note was played. Just after the applause, the violinist started to talk first with a woman leaving the concert hall. This scene attracted the attention of a young female violinist,[75] who was speaking to her colleague: "This one is present at all parties, at all cocktails. I am sure that tonight he wasn't invited either. He books his concerts around glasses of champagne! It's crazy! He doesn't play any better than the others, but he knows how to speak with beau-monde! Besides, he's a good-looking guy, the girls are crazy about him, and they organize the concerts for him. It is that easy." Following several concerts in these places, I saw this man with his old-fashioned "à la Gipsy" violin case and "artist's look," always coming in late and never paying for his tickets. His presence didn't surprise the gatekeepers either—they were accustomed to seeing him at the postconcert parties.[76]

The majority of soloist class students did not find this manner of concert research to be legitimate. They refused to admit that the auxiliary characteristics could also be important in their career (Hughes 1971). Nearing the end of their musical education, they found it hard to accept that part of their work involved the maintenance of relationships—networking. The model of soloist behavior that these students construct during their socialization is not compatible with what they learn when they enter the soloist market. The constraints of a highly competitive market, where a musician needs to use the door-to-door strategy in order to find concerts, is worlds from the image the soloist developed on the basis of the stories of famous soloists like Oïstrakh or Stern. This gap between an educational model and experience perturbs young soloists. An eighteen-year-old student said, "I don't know how to sell myself, how to make eye contact, how to say 'Yes' all the time. And worse, preparing to talk to all these people. It is not my job. I have no time to waste. I prepare myself seriously for the concerts, and I play as best I can. On stage, I give my all, but they have no problem asking me to spruce up." Instead of currying favor with people who might provide commercial opportunities, another student told me, when at parties he talked to anyone whose conversation he found pleasing.

Q: How about using these relationships to find opportunities to play?

A: Evidently there are people like that: they do nothing, are worth nothing, and are successful.

Q: So, are you saying it is possible to perform without being a good musician, with only the relational skills?

A: I don't know if these are talents or perhaps nontalents? [laughs] These are people who are pushed by powerful people, those who are successful—it is not difficult.

Q: It is necessary, however, to know how to enter into a good network, isn't it?

A: It is sufficient to have no character and to change with each shift of the wind, with the change of the time.

Q: What personal advantages do you use in your professional life?

A: I try to stay true to myself. I don't think that I will start to use my relationships. Those who refuse to behave like that are truly good, those who deserve to be well known. It should not be possible to make an important career through relationships, as a big violinist or in another domain of activity.

This ambivalence about self-promotion is very characteristic of soloists nearing the end of their professional education and the beginning of an adult career. It reflects a lack of clarity about the tasks required of the soloist profession. Some activities, such as commercial prospecting by a musician himself, may be accepted by one and rejected by another. Location plays an important role in this regard. Soloists educated in the United States consider commercial prospecting part of their occupation; in Europe (especially among those educated in an Eastern European tradition), the soloist shirks "business," which is viewed as negative, or in any case unworthy of the attention of "the artist."

TIES IN THE SOLOIST STUDENT'S WORLD

In the last stage of soloist education, the young virtuosos meet numerous people who play various roles in their professional path. Examining relationships that are fruitful in job research, Marc S. Granovetter (1973) distinguished three types (strong, weak, and eventually, no-ties), focusing on the "weak ties" that he described as particularly important. Another study of the networks of collaboration, conducted by Brian Uzzi in the garment industry, showed that actors maintain a portfolio of weak and strong ties, each useful for different types of exchanges. Uzzi distinguished arm's-length and embedded ties and showed that networks of collaborations are stronger when they comport an important proportion of embedded ties. By this term, the author defines long-term, based on trust, and mixed personal and professional relationships. Uzzi observed that each social environment due to the specific features (economical context, specificity of work performed by actors, history of sittings, and culture of participants) produces particular types of relationships, which animates their networks (Uzzi 1997).

In the young virtuoso world, in concordance with Uzzi's findings, both—strong and weak ties—are important. Those last are especially useful in establishing young virtuosos in the soloist market. The particularity of those ties consists in their long-term specific relationship maintenance. To ensure the development of their careers, international soloists need to perform in several national markets,[77] involving themselves in geographically distant projects, some cyclical, but most one-offs such as CDs, promotional concerts, or concert tours.[78] Such actions are not durable; as a consequence of a competition prize, the soloist may play several concerts in one country, but have nothing there in subsequent seasons. Yet the networks need to be maintained. "You never know if a contact will be useful one day," is a commonly heard statement in the milieu. Each new relationship may be a potential stepping-stone for the soloist career.

The small size of the soloist world, with a very high level of inter-acquaintance, makes it possible to collect a portfolio of addresses that may be used in the future. The bond between two people belonging to the soloist world is almost immediate. Musicians who meet each other on concert tours or in competitions often spend intense periods together in which they share their opinions about music, projects, their careers, and so on. But these contacts are sporadic because the soloists are constantly on the road, and the connection may become a "cold, deep tie." While most people maintain contact through phone and e-mail, this is typically not the case among soloists, even if two of them have developed a strong understanding.

The silence that follows the deep initial connection can surprise outsiders; it may last several years until, at a given moment, someone decides to reactivate the relationship. The other party may or may not respond. This manner of regulating one's relationships allows soloists to maintain a large stable of contacts while eliminating the cost in time and effort of maintaining regular relationships. This mechanism is similar to the freezing and thawing process. Ties are created and then almost immediately frozen and stocked away until the day the necessity of thawing appears. For example, a former student, belonging to his teacher's network, after finishing his study, may not contact his former colleague anymore. Several years later, he may call this colleague in order to prepare a project together that necessitates intensive day-to-day work over a period of months. The ties between the former soloist class students can be reactivated because the maintenance of relationships in their world does not require intensive (or even periodic) connections. The initial contacts are a part of the professional capital of a soloist.

CHAPTER 6

The Soloist Class
Students' Careers

After finishing their soloist education and passing through several selections (the continual elimination of weaker candidates according to various criteria, not only musical), the young soloists enter the soloist market. The classical music market offers few opportunities to achieve the highest goal, that of becoming a soloist. My examination of the paths of several former students suggests that most fail to become international soloists. In the years after soloist education, the careers of former students are of three types. Most become violin teachers or musicians in symphony orchestras with various chamber music activities and occasional soloist performances. Some players abandon their careers and change to different occupations. Even more exceptional is the accomplishment of the main goal—becoming an international soloist.

In order to assess the career orientations of former students, I focused on the aspirations that have accompanied them throughout their education, and analyzed the phenomenon of "comparative failure" (Glazer 1964). This means that when comparing their careers to the model that has guided their education, the young soloists perceive themselves as failures. Comparative failure is one of the particular aspects of artistic education (also in intellectual careers).[1]

HIGH ASPIRATIONS AND THE ACCOMPLISHMENT OF GOALS

It is not easy to trace the graduates of a soloist class, especially if they have "comparatively failed." Only a few of the students whose education I followed have kept in touch with me. Their teachers and other soloist class participants also have trouble tracking these wonderful violinists. Some of the students included in this research are still struggling for a place in the market, still hoping for the best. My assessment of outcomes is based more on personal accounts than on direct observation. This method provokes an important bias. Oral transmission informs us more about perceptions than facts, and certain topics are more frequently and openly discussed than others. Most participants spoke easily for hours about the successes of soloist education, but they rarely remembered those who had faltered during the stages of soloist education. In the soloist world (and in other highly competitive universes, probably), those who are successful are the objects of constant interest, and those who fail are quickly forgotten.

Teachers carefully hide the fact that success is rare, even nearly impossible. Professors believe that the parents and their children do not need this information. Without faith in a glorious future as a globetrotting soloist playing packed halls such as the Albert, Carnegie, and Pleyel, how can the teacher motivate young students and their parents? The shadow of failure could dull the enthusiasm and provoke the demobilization of the teacher's entourage. It is absolutely contrary to the teachers' interest to speak about the relative proportion of successful students. And so, the teachers continue to support the notion that students' aspirations are realistic. David Westby, in the study of orchestral musicians, has said "the highest aspiration a string musician can have is to someday become a self-employed soloist. This ambition was expressed by many young violinists particularly" (Westby 1960: 7).

The ambition produces faith in a glorious future. Without this faith, soloist education, which includes so many constraints, is impossible. Faith must be shared by all in the entourage of a young violinist. If not, the weakened involvement of the many actors required to propel the student forward would lead to abandonment of the soloist path. Without this faith, not one student would play eight hours per day; without it, no parent would change country of residence and spend a fortune for his or her child's education; no patron would loan an expensive and prestigious violin. The world of the soloist class operates on faith.

When they were soloist students, the teachers also believed they would be international soloists someday. As adults, the teachers, in their turn, make their own students believe a future as a soloist is accessible; this form of education could not exist without these unrealistic projections. The majority of teachers declare that they know the secrets of success better than their colleagues. Cultivating hope for accessibility to the desired status, these teachers do not disclose information about the path of other students, especially those who slipped from the career path along the way. Rarely, it is true, they speak of the "deserters" who are visible to everyone, but viewed as simple failures. When such students leave the class, the commentary of the teacher is as follows: "He was not good enough . . . she didn't have the talent."

In the soloist classes, abandonment takes place in stages. We can compare this process with Goffman's "Cooling the Mark Out" phenomenon (Goffman 1952), which consists of readjusting of the student's expectations and redefinition of failure. Professors participate in this important multistep process. First, the student joins another soloist class, sometimes in another country, with another support network. In the class he or she left behind, the milieu shows little interest in the fate of this "unstable" student. His or her failure does not discourage those deeply engaged in soloist education; there is silence around such people that makes it possible to avoid blaming the organization or doubting the quality of the teacher's work. Failures are so rarely evoked by soloist world participants that the following excerpt from an interview of a former soloist (he actually teaches at university and is also the son of a composer) is exceptional. This violinist speaks about his colleague, Ivan, who has a reputation as one of the best teachers in the world. "The problem with Ivan, and with others who work with children as he does [in the soloist class], is that for every ten students, one will attempt suicide, one will become mentally ill, two will become alcoholics, two will slam doors and jettison the violin out the window, three will work as violinists, and perhaps one will become a soloist." Although this may be exaggerated, the ratio of success is certainly accurate, and the risks of failure are not unrealistic.

FAILURE AND SUCCESS IN THE CAREER OF SOLOIST STUDENTS: AN EXAMPLE OF THE TYPICAL SOLOIST STUDENT PATH

The most surprising fact for an exterior observer of the virtuoso world would probably be that young students, who during years persevering in their education, do not have knowledge about the statistical chances of achieving their goal, which are very small. In fact the probability of becoming a soloist is very modest. The following example concerns the career of a student who, after finishing her education successfully, was unable to exercise the occupation for which she had trained. Nothing had prepared her for this situation, and she perceived herself as a failure.

Svieta was born in Eastern Europe in the 1970s into a nonmusician family. Her mother was of Russian origin and trained as an engineer, but after emigrating was forced to take a secretarial job, which she left to devote her time to the education of her two daughters. Svieta's father was a technician in the army. Svieta's sister debuted on the violin at the age of six, and Svieta, followed her, starting at four. Less than two years later, unsatisfied with their violin education, the mother decided to consult a famous teacher and traveled more than six hours with both daughters to the lesson. The teacher wished to work only with Svieta, but after long negotiations with the mother ("You take two or nobody!") the teacher took both girls, and for several years, they traveled twice a week for their violin lessons. These lessons were free, as the professor had a position but gave more lessons than were imposed by the contract with institution—this practice is reserved for best students.

Svieta's mother had made arrangements with the school director in order to organize the girls' general education at home. Both girls were required only to pass exams to verify that this education was continuing. The majority of their time was devoted to practicing the violin, which was always done in the mother's presence. Svieta remembers her mother's role at that time: "She was much more strict than any of my teachers, and it was she who taught us most things. She didn't know how to play the violin, but she knew very well how to work, which was the most important. She never let anything slide, and frequently, she was screaming. OK, more at my sister than at me, but it was hard. We had worked like that every day until I left to live in the boarding house. I was twelve or thirteen years old." The mother sent Svieta and her sister to a music school with a boarding house in another city, miles away from their house. She did not tell the original teacher, who said she thought both girls had suddenly died (a manner of speaking in order to underline how unexpected the situation was).

After divorcing her husband, the mother noticed that her daughter was working less than before. She bought an apartment in the city where the girls were studying in order to coach them. Her efforts seemed to work because Svieta, at the age of sixteen, became a finalist in an important international competition; she became famous, and thanks to the media, was well known even outside the soloist world.[2] Despite her success in the competition, a conflict developed with her principal teacher—the most powerful teacher in the country—and she became a student of his assistant. Her mother considered that Svieta's soloist career had been compromised, and sent her to another famous teacher in Western Europe.

This teacher was a jury member in one of the competitions in which Svieta had participated. The assistant of her former teacher loaned her the money for the scholarship that she needed to reside in the new country, and her former teacher, in spite of their conflict, loaned Svieta a violin (one of the best in the country). Even if that seems to be strange, the former teacher helped her because he wished that all his efforts and years of work would be fruitful, even if the last stage of education would be conducted by another teacher. Also, the change of the country (going to Western Europe from Eastern Europe) seems like fate in this story, but at that time a massive migration movement touched not only the musicians' world but the whole area. This is perhaps why the former teacher (very experienced and almost retired) understood that young women, after some years of education in her class, should go abroad for additional training and better conditions of education. Also, the girls would gain perspective in a new and powerful network of support, which would open to Svieta the doors of the virtuoso market. The new teacher organized the network of support, and Svieta spent five years living on scholarships and her patron's support. She was presented to this patron by the new teacher after the charity concert.

During this period, Svieta participated in several international competitions, but without success. She took part again in the competition she had been a finalist in at sixteen, but failed utterly. After Svieta's teacher retired, she left her class and moved to another city to join the class of a respected teacher known for his efficiency at pushing his students into the finals of competitions. She stayed in his class for three years, living in the house of rich music lovers. Thanks to her hosts, she created relationships with several of the most famous international musicians who played in this city and were often invited to dinner parties at the house. The dinners frequently ended with her performance. She obtained several scholarships for master classes, had a bow and violin on loan and the support of private collectors, and had received promises of future projects.

Despite her "wired" position in the musical world, Svieta was unable to enter the soloist world. Her participation in the competitions was a complete failure, and concerts and recitals became increasingly rare. At the age of twenty-four she again decided to seek her education in another country, but unlike in past instances, was required to pass the entrance examinations and go through all the stages of selection again.

During her first lesson, her new teacher said she was not yet ready for a career as an international soloist, but promised to prepare her. But he rarely gave her lessons, while she benefited from only the institutional amount of time (one hour per week) and was not treated like the privileged students to whom teachers give free additional lessons. During the two years in this class, Svieta played only twice as a soloist. She carefully maintained her relationships with important people and had little free time for instrumental practice. Svieta noted that her enthusiasm had dimmed. In her new country, without a rich patron or scholarships, she had money problems. Svieta became scared about her future. Her expectations were those of a former young soloist, used to a worldly life and the glitter of the stage, but her reality had become empty days without the prospect of any concerts.

At twenty-five, she was in conflict with her sister (who got a job in an orchestra in Western Europe), far from her mother, expatriated, without attachments, and having problems accepting that her dreams of a soloist life were over. She continued to believe she had a chance, convinced, she told me, that she was "an excellent violinist who knows how the 'milieu' functions, with good relationships with all the important people." Violin, the passion for playing, the day-to-day work, took up less and less space in her life. She gave herself a year before making a decision: perhaps she would study psychology or become a housekeeper.

Two years later, Svieta wrote me an e-mail: "Everything is better for me. I am the concertmaster in a symphonic orchestra in MS. I live in the most beautiful town in the world (somewhere on the Mediterranean Sea). I am in love, and I am happy." Not untypically for a soloist student, Svieta had become concertmaster in a middle-rank orchestra.

Insurmountable Failure and Insurmountable Success

For some students with elaborate pedigrees who entered consciousness as "child prodigies," it is impossible to create a new life project after failure to achieve international soloist status. On some occasions, professional deadlock results in personal tragedy.

Mark, twenty-two, returned to his country after seven years and closed himself into his parents' flat for more than two months. The conductor who played with him at a time when everyone applauded this "prodigy child," was worried: "I am scared for him. He stays in his room and does nothing. He hasn't touched his violin for several months. It's horrible. Nobody is in touch with him, not one young person. I don't know how this situation will end."

Mark had played as a soloist with an orchestra at age ten and was chosen to represent his country in a soloist school in England. He dropped out of school and left his parents to live in a boarding school for musicians. Famous virtuosos, private patrons, and the cultural authorities of his native land supported him, and the media sang his praises. When Mark became an adult, all this help stopped. Other "prodigy children" needed support. His protector was dead, and Mark found himself in a hard place—no financial support, no work, without a diploma or any knowledge other than how to play violin, a skill that disappeared a little each day due to lack of practice. Was it any wonder that his psychological health had crumbled?

Four years later, nobody in his town and in the virtuoso world remember him. I was not able to learn what finally happened to Mark. Mark's story is a cautionary tale of "failure" in the soloist world, but even some success stories succumb to the peculiar pressures of the milieu. Depression, alcoholism, and other troubles have accompanied some of the most famous musicians. The most famous soloist tragedy was Michel Rabin, whose exemplary and successful career could not protect him.[3]

> In January 1972, the musical world was stunned and saddened by the unexpected death, at the age of thirty-five, of Michael Rabin, a violinist of immense talent. The glowing obituaries spoke of his years of success—he had made his Carnegie Hall debut at thirteen, had covered 700,000 miles on six continents, had been applauded by millions of enraptured listeners. But no one mentioned the tragic crises that befell young Rabin during his growing-up years, when he was trying to make the transformation from child prodigy to grown artist, and nearly faltered in the process. There were times when Rabin cancelled engagements simply because he felt unable to perform, struck by feelings of inadequacy or insecurity he could not overcome.
>
> Rabin was born in New York City on May 2, 1936. His father was a violinist and long-time member of the New York Philharmonic who had once studied with Kneisel; his mother was a pianist. Michael gave evidence of a perfect ear when he was three, and at the age of five his lessons began. He came to the attention of Ivan Galamian—recently arrived from Europe—who accepted the nine-year-old boy as a pupil. He played his first engagement in 1947, at the age of eleven, and in 1949 he won a contest of the National Federation of Music Clubs. His debut at Carnegie Hall took place early in 1950 with the National Orchestra Association, followed by a reengagement a few months later. The choice of concertos stressed virtuosity. . . . Rodzinski was impressed that young Rabin was different from the "usual musical prodigy story. . . . He was not overprotected and shut off from the world, but managed to enjoy a perfectly normal American childhood."[4] Michael's "normalcy" extended to the Professional Children's School in New York, where he received his general education while studying with Galamian. Of all the gifted students he taught over the years, Galamian considered Rabin the greatest: an "almost extraordinary talent—no weaknesses, never!"
>
> In May of 1951, the fifteen-year-old Rabin made his first appearance with the New York Philharmonic, . . . Around 1960 there was a noticeable decline in Rabin's performances. . . . There were rumors that he was under the influence of drugs and that there was some mental instability. His death was attributed to an accident. In Galamian's words, "He did not die of drugs, but that time he had the drugs and was playing better than ever. He slipped on a rug and hit his head on a table."[5]

This was the official version of his accidental death. Some speculated that there was too much pressure, too much responsibility thrown at him during his adolescence. Be that as it may, young Rabin seems to have been a victim of his early fame, and the world of music suffered a grievous loss. (Schwarz 1983: 567–568)

In other cases, perhaps involving less famous musicians, the somber parts of a career are usually not known to the public. Most often, violinists stop playing and abandon the soloist world without press fanfare. The case of Eugene Fodor is an exception.

Eugene Fodor was born in 1950 in Colorado to violin-playing parents. Like his older brother John (now a violinist with the Denver Symphony), Eugene started the violin early, at the age of seven. At nine he was heard publicly for the first time, and made his debut at eleven with the Denver Symphony. . . . After Juilliard, Fodor spent two semesters as a student of Heifetz at the University of Southern California. Heifetz is his idol—"That's whom I owe everything to. . . . From him I learned a lifestyle, a way of living with music . . . I practiced my tail off." (Schwarz 1983: 585)

The results of this tremendous work would come—first place in the Paganini Competition in Genova, second in Tchaikovsky in Moscow. After playing for President Gerald Ford at the White House, he received from one of his fans a Guarnerius des Gesù made in 1736.

He appeared on talk shows, endorsed a brand of whiskey, and became a matinee idol with his handsome face, his flashing smile, and his "normal" hobbies. It was an American success story; all that was needed was the approval of the New York critics. . . . but it was his New York debut festival (in November 1974) that damaged his career. . . . [The] review was devastating: Fodor had failed, not as a violinist but as a thinking musician. He responded like a pouting child, saying that he would continue to play the virtuoso selection he liked. "I'm not going to cater to anybody . . . I'm just there to make music." And a reporter added, "He believes in giving his audience the programs that they want."[6] . . . Fodor's second recital program, in December 1975, was more substantial . . . but the damage was done: there was again criticism of his musicianship. The "establishment" was distrustful of his qualifications as an interpreter of great music. The New York Philharmonic failed to invite him as a soloist. A January 1980 recital was canceled because of family complications. (Schwarz 1983: 586–587)

In 1989, Fodor was arrested on drug trafficking and burglary charges in Massachusetts (Parîs 1995: 410).

Comparative Failure and the Abandonment of the Dream

The majority of students are compelled to abandon their initial objectives and modify their professional project. While only a few virtuosos leave the musician world, most must revise their aspirations downward. This process of disillusionment is similar in other instrumental fields. Studying studio musicians, Robert Faulkner remarked: "Almost all of the violin and cello players, and to a lesser extent, viola players, emphasized that they aspired to be a soloist. Their adjustments to perceived comparative failure involve several related lines of adaptation" (1971: 58). The analysis of their career's perception by these instrumentalists allowed Faulkner to employ the concept of "comparative failure":

> The concept of comparative failure has been used to describe the fact that people engaged in consistent lines of activity (1) designate a certain group to serve as a point of reference, (2) which they use to make judgments about the attributes or values which they themselves possess (status, success, the self), and that (3) when they compare themselves to these reference points, they perceive themselves as having failed. It is an evaluation resulting from social comparison; estimates of attributes or values vary according to the reference group. (Faulkner 1971: 52–53)

The perception of failure is relative, related to the original aspirations of each instrumentalist and comparison with other persons who, in parallel, followed the soloist education. After having internalized their high aspirations (which is part of socialization in early soloist education) the soloist students revise their projects, orienting them toward new options in a musical career. These options are considered less prestigious.

This mechanism is not specific to soloists; people are constrained to adapt their aspirations in other fields, of course. Joseph Hermanowicz analyzed the aspirations of young physicists who graduated from prestigious universities concerning the Nobel Prize, world reputations in the hard sciences, and later deceptions (Hermanowicz, 1998: chap. 3). In Faulkner's study, "a persistent career problem for some of the studio musicians is their feeling of comparative failure as solo artists. They failed as concert performers" (Faulkner 1971: 53). Starting from Barney Glazer's (1964) explication of the feeling of comparative failure, in which ambition and the models of a professional path play an important role, and taking into account the development of this concept by Faulkner, who showed the importance of group reference, one can use this concept for analysis of feelings among soloist students. Hermanowicz's work on physicists makes this phenomenon clearer (Hermanowicz 1998). However, I observed that among soloists, even those who had attained their initial objectives experienced feelings of comparative failure. How this is possible? As Hermanowicz showed, communitarians (as the author defines scientists who were not trained in famous institutions) were not frequently touched by this feeling. It is foremost the elite members who suffer from this disillusionment. This conclusion seems paradoxical, because communitarian scientists are much less successful than elite scientists. Two factors are responsible—socialization and ambition. Elite members were socialized to achieve high goals, and difficulties accomplishing them resulted in feelings of failure. Elite scientists' ambitions are greater than those of communitarians.

In the soloist universe, the situation is similar. The violinists who are perceived by others as extremely successful see themselves as failed soloists. Even if they play in prestigious places with famous musicians, they do not feel very happy with their careers. I believe that socialization is responsible for such feelings. For years, the young soloists heard about famous violin careers, hundreds of success stories from which all failures were excised. The rule of avoiding speaking about failure has, as a consequence, the perception of failure as something exceptional and proof of professional weakness. The young soloist rarely learns how to deal with failure. Failures in competitions, of course, are externalized through the mechanism of dismissing the competition as corrupt. Other failures are new to the young virtuoso, who does not know how to react to them and is unaware of their frequency. This explains why even very successful violinists can feel comparative failure. Consequently, the phenomenon of comparative failure concerns not only those who failed to achieve the objective of a soloist career, but also those who were not socialized for failure at all.

Despite failure in pursuit of the soloist path, the position of ex-soloist class students on the music market is much better than the position of an average violinist. While most former soloist class students work as "ordinary" musicians, their soloist student past offers them certain advantages. It is comparable with the situation of the former students of the elite Ecole Normale Superieur. Even if they will not get the highest positions in their specialties, they still enjoy a privileged position in the labor market and benefit from social recognition because of their educational past. Pierre Bourdieu (1996) remarked about those: "In fact, alumni disillusionment is never as complete or as painful as the difference between anticipated and materialized futures might lead one to expect. . . . The mere fact of belonging to a group that is generically offered the possibility of greatness (symbolized by all its famous alumni) entitles one to a share (at once subjective and objective) in this success or, more precisely, in the symbolic capital guaranteed to the group as a whole by all the exceptional proprieties accumulated by all of its members, and particularly by the most prestigious among them" (Bourdieu 1996: 160).

Alternative Careers

For nonmusicians, it is surprising to consider that soloist students view a concertmaster position, or a university professorship in music, as a case of changing professions. In the soloist world, however, these moves are viewed as failures. Young musicians trained in soloist classes consider an orchestra position as existing in a different universe from soloist playing. They spend their entire lives preparing through intensive practice to be soloists on the stage and not parts of an orchestra (not even as a concertmaster). Without such individualistic and solo-career-oriented education, the achievement of virtuoso-level musicianship would be difficult. Professors rarely speak with their pupils about an orchestral career.

Moreover, if your soloist career is only maintained in one country (here one European country), this is not a dreamed pathway for a student virtuoso. If the adult career of the violinist is not international (big concert halls, important agents, and major CD producers), such career development will be seen as another career path. Even being highly evaluated by adult musicians, such as playing in a chamber ensemble, is not interesting in the opinion of the young virtuoso. This is why I describe the alternative choices these musicians must take as "professional conversions."

While it is very difficult for most violinists to earn a place in an excellent orchestra, former soloist class students attain these sought-after positions with ease. In comparison with other musicians, they are in a very comfortable professional position.[7] The professional insertion of soloist students into orchestras is similar to that of graduates of prestigious universities. These former elite students who occupy high positions in firms and institutions of an average size hope to get key positions in multinational companies or other important institutions. The chances of getting a good job increase with the number of years spent in a soloist class. The greater the technical level and progress in the stages of soloist education, the more numerous the possible alternatives to a soloist path. Soloist students' assets include not only the musical knowledge they have acquired, but their relationships. What Bourdieu called the "portfolio of connections" ("portefeuille de liaison"; Bourdieu 1979: 516) are the soloist student's main assets for the future.

Parent-musicians can again play an important role in these professional conversions. In all professional worlds the "inheritors," not only in Bourdieu and Passeron's sense of the social class membership (Bourdieu and Passeron 1979), but also in the professional narrow sense of being a part of the professional universe of its parents. The social and professional positions of musician parents provide ways of helping their young soloist escape work as an orchestra musician. Parents seek to find their child a place in a chamber music orchestra, or in a teaching position, or even temporary solo projects in regional or national markets. The difference between international and national markets is crucial here—this is why the following example, despite describing the situation of an active violinist, should be considered as a case of conversion.

Jurek is a twenty-four-year-old violinist, the only child of parent violinists. His father is a soloist, plays about thirty concerts per year, and teaches in the Superior Conservatory—the best teaching institution in their country. Jurek's mother also teaches in this institution. Both parents are jury members of several violin competitions. Jurek was a soloist class student and also frequently took lessons from his parents.

Family connections have greased Jurek's path. Since the age of sixteen, he has played with his father in a repertoire for two violins throughout the entire country. Jurek competed in only one international competition, of average reputation, in Japan, and won second place (his father was the chief jury member). W., a well-regarded composer and friend of Jurek's parents, has been working with Jurek to record W.'s pieces; Jurek played first soloist in W.'s new composition. Thanks to some of his parents' other relationships, Jurek has created music ensembles that play concerts and recorded a CD for the general public. His father's record producer also manages Jurek's recording projects. He plays many concerts without having to take part in any important competitions.

This kind of parental support for professional work is not peculiar to the soloist world.[8] And not all former soloist students can benefit from their parents' support, for not all have musician parents, or their place of residence is not conducive to it. For immigrant students, the parents' relationships are rarely useful, because they reside in another country. This kind of support is frequently insufficient to start a soloist career.

Professional conversions into a career of a concertmaster or violin teacher are not always the result of failure down the soloist path. Sometimes, situations from private life constrain young soloists to urgently seek stable employment (in France, for example, some orchestral musicians have the status of a national employee, which includes a lot of benefits and job security). This decision is equivalent to the abandonment of the majority of activities related to starting a soloist career. Such was the case with Wlad. After winning several prizes in numerous international competitions, he stopped competing because at age nineteen, he became a father and needed to earn a steady salary in order to provide for his wife and child. A twenty-three-year-old violinist who had won international prizes abandoned his project of becoming a soloist and became an orchestra concertmaster because his young daughter suffered from a rare illness and needed constant hospital care. The violinist needed good health insurance and wanted to avoid frequent absences on concert tours. Health problems of the violinist or his or her family are the most frequently cited explanations for voluntary professional conversion, in these cases, the feeling of comparative failure is absent from discussions. These violinists do not consider their actual position as frustrating, unlike those who tried for many years to make it onto the stage as a soloist, then were forced to surrender this dream.

Changing the Professional Path—Leaving the Music World

Few soloists leave the musical world entirely. David Westby (1960) remarked that among orchestral musicians, the best players, and violinists especially, have a strong professional identity, which is the consequence of their soloist-oriented education. "The fact that intense training begins so early means two things: (1) that other experiences, particularly work experiences, are considerably circumscribed, and (2) such an early investment of time, money, and effort typically creates a firm basis for a strong occupational commitment while the subject is still a child. Consequently, other identities have little chance to develop" (Westby 1960: 227). A recent study of seventy-eight professional symphony orchestras undertaken by Richard Hackman and Jutta Allmendinger confirmed those results: "Orchestra players are, indeed, fueled by their own pride and professionalism" (interview with Richard Hackman by Paul R. Judy, 2012). A twenty-two-year-old violinist gave the illustration of this analysis:

> In school, I was very good in math, biology, and physics. To be sure, I rarely attended school, but I never had problems with sciences or any other disciplines either. I completed school by correspondence, and I got my bac S spe bio[9] because I was interested in genetics. I read a lot about that topic, but after that, music studies took over my time. Sometimes I ask myself if I should pursue biology, but beginning all of it again, while I am close to the end—in one year I will write my MA thesis [in violin performance]—I don't know. . . . On the other hand, I was very interested in bio, and if I were not in my violin class, I

would like to study biology. Now, I have no time for that . . . I forgot a lot . . . I only know how to play.

The distance from general education and a deep insertion into the professional milieu contribute to the feeling of incapacity to pursue another occupation. This phenomenon is similar in competitive fields where children are socialized from a young age, such as figure skating or chess.[10] The following testimony, in several aspects, is identical to those of young virtuosos, but is provided by a chess champion: "Like most professional players, I started around five or six with my father and brother. Later, my brother stopped playing chess, and his mission was to teach me how to move the pieces. He's basically more intelligent than me—he became a doctor. He could have been a lot of things, but as for me, I know only one: how to play chess."[11]

Going step by step into the soloist career, young musicians are cut off from other centers of interest. While following the path it is extremely difficult to change one's day-to-day activities and above all, to adhere to values other than those in which one is socialized. Also, it is not easy to jump into another complex profession; state exams for finishing secondary school—especially those in the sciences—are very difficult. Intensive practice and the difficulties of emigration, which is so common among soloist class students, make it almost impossible to gain a good background in any other field. While it is not difficult to find former pianists among various professional groups (engineers, physician),[12] former violinist virtuosos are rare among this population.

However, history provides us a few examples. The violinist and composer Giovanni Battista Viotti (1755–1824) "dropped music for several years in order sell wine" (Soriano 1993: 150). During World War II, Henryk Szeryng was an official translator for General W. Sikorski in London (Szeryng spoke eight languages).[13] In 1930, a violinist had a skiing accident and was forced to reorganize his life; after several years, he became an architect and a successful developer, who collected prestigious violins and supported young soloists. And a soloist class teacher said her student, who had performed in important U.S. concert halls, chose to become a physician: "She had had double interests in medicine and music throughout high school. When it came to college, she decided on medicine and went to Yale" (Lourie-Sand 2000: 160).

Gerda was born in a musician family in a European country; her father was the director of a music school, and her mother was a violinist. At the age of three, Gerda took her first violin lesson, and at age four she joined a famous class with an emigré teacher, who worked previously in the Tchaikovsky Conservatory in Moscow. The next year she also started taking piano lessons. Gerda's first important concert on violin took place before an audience of 2,000 when she was seven years old. She played as a soloist with orchestras conducted by two famous conductors. At the age of twelve, she recorded her first CD for DORE, one of the most famous producers in the world, and it received critical acclaim.

Gerda's career began very well. When she was fourteen, she decided to devote her time to violin, halting her intensive piano practice. As a violinist, she often played on TV and radio in her country and even abroad. Gerda also received prizes for the popularization of classical music. By the age of sixteen, she had already played with the world's leading musicians and many orchestras: the NDR Hannover Orchestra, the London Philharmonic, and the Dallas Symphony Orchestra. Very young, she was at the last stage of virtuoso education. However, at the age of eighteen, she announced to her teacher that she had decided to abandon her violin career to study medicine. Her master, who had taught her for fourteen years, stated that she was wasting her talent. Two years later, as a student of medicine, Gerda said that she regretted nothing. When she played, she said, it was only her teacher playing through her. Studying medicine was her choice, she said, and it would let her help people.

When students are asked, "Why have you chosen to became a musician?" the response is generally, "I don't know," or "It was always that way," or "I only know how to play." The lack of knowledge in any other field seems to pose an impassable obstacle. At the end of their education, after abandoning hope of becoming a soloist, the easiest solution is to find a job in the larger world of music.

AN ADDITIONAL FEATURE TO THE SOCIAL PROCESS OF SOCIALIZATION—AUXILIARY CHARACTERISTICS

In his article, "Dilemmas and Contradictions of Status," Everett C. Hughes (1945) calls our attention to the importance of auxiliary characteristics that may be indispensable to the acquisition of status or social position.[14] The analysis of the three stages of soloist education allowed me to show the multiplicity of expectations that young musicians need to satisfy. The young soloist's complex trajectory is interwoven with criteria to which the musician needs to conform. Making the list of these characteristics, as a kind of supplement, I will limit this inventory to the nonmusical criteria, allowing other authors (instrumentalists, musical critics, musicologists, and specialists of aesthetics of music) the possibility of compiling the list of musical criteria.

Nonmusical characteristics, I believe, are as important as musical criteria. The nonmusical characteristics determine the soloist's career; their absence or insufficiency can block or end soloist education. Depending on the stage of education, the student needs to respond to various expectations that are, to some degree, contradictory.

Some of these nonmusical characteristics are specific to violinists, while others are seen in many other occupations. Among the generally desirable aptitudes, some seem to be indispensable during the entire educational process and others only during one stage of formation or over a short period. Sometimes, the virtuoso needs to develop opposing characteristics. For example, during the first three stages of education, students must relate docilely with their teacher in the domains of technique and musical interpretation. In the final point of their education, however, the future soloist must show independence and prove his or her ability to interpret pieces creatively.

In most occupations that require public performance, whether artistic or political, a particular set of characteristics are required: the ability to adapt to the expectations of the entourage appropriate to one's role, adaption to the desires of the professional world, adaptation to changing work conditions, work discipline, physical and psychological resistance, sociability, and physical appearance that conforms to public expectations.

All of these components could be decisive in the public performer's career. Among the characteristics specific for soloists are ease in learning foreign languages and the particular attitude of the "good soloist student," which unifies obedience with what the soloist world calls "artistic personality." Following, I present several examples of situations that reveal the role these auxiliary characteristics play in the pursuit of a soloist career.[15]

Adaptability to the Unstable Conditions of Public Performance

One of the most important characteristics is the ability to adapt to the changing conditions of performances and to the irregular rhythms of work. There are large disequilibria between the routine of instrumental practice and the unpredictability of public performances, where the artist must know how to react instantaneously—in some cases, on stage—to new situations. This requires excellent self-control and the "acceptance" of unexpected situations. This quality is particularly appreciated in the young soloist world. Immediately after a concert, an accompanist gave his opinion about the eleven-year-old violinist:

> Little Misha can hope to became a soloist. He's born for this. When we played during the competition, in the middle of Tchaikovsky, there was a power outage—the government was saving electricity. I told myself, OK, we have finished our performance—but he continued, so I did the same and we finished our piece in utter darkness, but without any errors or wrong notes. Well, congratulations! Even the big performers sometimes have problems in reacting like that.

During another competition, a candidate stopped playing in the middle of the piece. Her accompanist continued (following the common rule, which is to never to stop the music on stage), hoping the violinist would "find her," but without success; the violinist was not able to join her pianist. Eventually, the accompanist stopped playing and there was silence in the hall. The violinist approached the pianist's scores (exactly as during rehearsal) and started to play again. The commentary of her teacher was poignant, "She's shit! We never do that! We never stop on stage!" Others said the violinist would never become a soloist, because she "lacks stage instinct." Said another, "she is a very good student, but not at all 'the artist.'"

This quality of instant adaptation can be taught, however. Some teachers do not hesitate to trick their students into learning to adapt to unexpected situations. One teacher has the habit of modifying the "bow sense"[16] previously established for his student—exactly the day before a public performance. Another teacher prepared three pieces with his students for monthly class concerts, although the students were to play only one of them. When the concert was about to begin, the teacher informed the student and audience simultaneously which piece would be executed.

The Stage Reflex

Another specific characteristic is known as "stage reflex," and refers to the extent to which the artist behaves according to the expectations of stage behavior. These actions include greetings addressed to conductors and orchestra musicians after the performance, or gestures of acknowledgment to the accompanist. It is regarded as important to be "natural" and "very easy and cool on the stage" (some state that such "stage animals" are like fish in water, "Ils ont de la bouteille," say the French). But this can be overdone, especially by very young performers, who are discouraged from "playing the star," as one frequently hears. Some teachers teach these expected behaviors, while others do not, and are shocked when a young student does not intuitively understand them. During a charity concert, a twelve-year-old musician went across the stage between two performances without waiting for the intermission. Her teacher, in the audience, muttered, "The stage is not a sidewalk! You can't stroll along like that! She walked as if she were alone here, in private! How can that be?"

Mundane Sociability and Self-Promotion

We already saw that musicians do not finish their performance with the last note. Their work continues over cocktails and at parties with musicians, organizers, and sometimes with audience members. Savoir-faire in the milieus of business, art, politics, and diplomacy are appreciated; similar sociability is required of the musician.[17] In such situations social origin and family background are very important. Certainly those who are used to such mundanities are generally of the upper class. The young virtuoso students are mostly from musician families. Their familial education is not exactly such as the children from upper class, however, and as a part of their professional socialization, they become familiar with such events as parties after concerts and charity receptions. They know how to behave and how to be dressed.

At such festivities, it is necessary to "have elegance," as the young musicians say, and to "play the game." Musicians must learn to use these events to make new contacts, to "sell themselves." Personal relationships initiated at these events may lead to support from powerful sponsors or others in the musical world.

Selling oneself is not limited to milieus in which the evaluation of work quality is based on subjective criteria. It also exists in areas where the selection of newcomers is based only on objective criteria, such as sports.[18] Even here, as Pascal Duret remarked, "the reputation, the celebrity are directly related to sale value. The knowledge of how to sell oneself is a part of the champion's qualities" (Duret 1993: 49). But if such qualities are appreciated in the sports domain, the capacity to sell oneself is deemed indispensable in the young violinist milieu.

A nineteen-year-old violinist spoke with me about the use of relationships in her career.

Q: What is necessary to "make a career"?
A: To know how to do business.

Q: Do you think you know how to do business?

A: No, not really.

Q: Do you think that someone will know how to do that for you?

A: I don't know yet, but I will ask myself about that when the moment arrives. What is important now is knowing how to maintain relationships and knowing how to present myself to people when it is appropriate. And after knowing, how to . . . as they say . . . build relationships, diplomacy is important. Because I know that there are a lot of violinists who play well, who play very well and who even won competitions, but nobody knows them, and they stay in their place. And on the other hand, there are violinists who are average, and who play everywhere. For example, B. C., he's a genius of diplomacy. He knows how to deal with people. I've seen how he does it! People remember him and he's visible everywhere. It works like that, dinners, parties, and relationships. And I also think that it is necessary to have luck. There is a moment when you need to take things, because if not, you pass it up . . .

Q: You are anxious about passing up certain opportunities?

A: I am not sure how to avoid missing them, but I am not worried about it. I'm not worried about my professional future because I know my level. Maybe my job won't be pure ecstasy, but I will have work, that's for sure.

Q: Do you have a personal advantage that you want to use in your professional trajectory?

A: I would like to try to play as well as I can, and I will try to mail my records to people who need to get them—this is one half of success. I don't think I need to take lessons to know how to drive my career, but knowing how to present on stage is important. . . . But I know how to do that. After that, I think practice is the most important issue, with regularity in the work.

In the years after this interview, this former child prodigy, who had played a Vivaldi concerto as a soloist at the age of eight, joined a radio orchestra in a European city after failing to score success in several international competitions. Later she played in a quartet.

Appropriate Physical Appearance

It would be pointless to inventory the physical particularities that could be advantageous to a violinist. At the least, a soloist's looks need to meet the audience's expectations. As with other performance fields, these expectations are molded by the media,[19] and appearance has grown in importance in recent decades. On CD covers and posters, musicians are depicted like actors or rock stars. Classical soloists of beauty have an important asset for their careers.[20] The "star quality" of classical musicians varies from country to country. In France, most musicians are not recognized beyond the rather small audience for classical music. In Germany, however, classical musicians are in the public spotlight like show business stars, and their lives are followed like other stars (violinist Anne Sophie Mutter is a good example).[21] Looks can determine whether a CD gets made, a CD producer told me, and I heard similar remarks many times. During an informal talk, this producer, and a sound engineer shared their opinions about the career of Charles, a violinist "in fashion" at the time:

> Charles was lucky because he was ripe and ready to be used at good time. MMA [an important record label] had changed owners and they needed new heads to draw attention to their products. They changed their logo and their artists. Charles was attractive, and they liked him. He was young, brown-haired, typically a guy from the South, a little Gypsy-looking, whereas their previous stars were blond-haired Russians. . . . Sometimes, things like this can be decisive.

It is difficult to imagine an ugly soloist. Looks are part of the spectacle. The use of Internet publicity tools like YouTube encourages artists to stress their appearance. These characteristics are only rarely the principal source of support for the soloist, but they exist, and good looks definitely benefit an artist.

Students and their teachers say that juries show indulgence to contestants who are "nicer to look at." I observed a former teacher, who serves on juries at competitions around the world, examining a CD cover featuring a young blond woman with big blue eyes and a nice smile. "I don't know how she plays," he said, "but I immediately give her supplementary points for her beauty." During fieldwork I was frequently told that an authority figure "doesn't like boys and adores female violinists," that during master classes a particular teacher was much more patient with female violinists. I observed many master classes and noticed that female violinists frequently got extensions of up to thirty minutes. I never saw a male violinist get a longer lesson.

Could soloist milieu professionals believe that male violinists are less talented? Perhaps, but performance organizers are also quite open in their belief that the musician's physical appearance must correspond to public tastes and expectations. The term usually employed by musicians is "stage appearance," and a lacking one can be a difficult obstacle to overcome. Strong compensatory advantages are required to satisfy concert organizers.

The clearest example, historically, may be that of Itzhak (Isaac) Perlman. Recognized as one of the greatest performers of the twentieth century, Perlman has been handicapped since a childhood bout with polio, which forces him to use crutches to walk. Although he played (better than his colleagues) at the Juilliard School, he had serious difficulties finding work. His wife, a violinist in the same soloist class, described their moment of finally breaking through this barrier in an interview with Lourie-Sand:

> It was unbelievable. We lived in a dream. I found myself at dinner with Jascha Heifetz, and I had to pinch myself. We would be invited to Arthur Rubinstein's house. Unbelievable things. You went from having no work to being in tremendous demand. Nobody would engage Isaac before the Leventritt[22]—the only concerts he got were the ones Miss DeLay [Perlman's teacher] got for him. Nobody would engage him, nobody was interested. Because of his disability? I asked. Well, sure. What else would it have been! (Lourie-Sand 2000: 200)

Availability and Flexibility

Another particular quality required of soloist musicians is flexibility, because they must adjust to their teachers' complex schedules. The absence of this quality could cause a student's expulsion or departure from a soloist class, as was the case with the following student, who left a well-known class despite receiving a good scholarship.

> It was not at all a question of person. Gunter [the teacher] is very nice, but the lessons with him! I was sick of constantly having to wait for the lessons, to wait for him to say to me: "Come this evening, I will be free for you about 2 A.M." It was like that two or three times a month. I was young at that time, and I couldn't work like that. I needed more lessons and to be better organized. This same year, three of us abandoned this class. Lessons in the middle of the night—his schedules were crazy.

For performers in this and similar milieus,[23] teaching is often regarded as a supplementary job, and students bear the brunt of this by being obliged to deal with fluid schedules and odd hours. With conditions like these, students must be willing to sacrifice their private lives, as exemplified by the young soloist that I accompanied to a lesson in a Parisian suburb one night at 10 P.M.

> I am furious, but not surprised! I knew that it would be like that! As usual! If the cell phone didn't exist, it would be fine! I've only been in Europe for a few days—I had a long tour in Asia. Yesterday, I played in London and my professor said to me, "You come to Paris, and I will give you a lesson." And I came. The lesson was planned for 6 p.m., before dinner. So I called my friends who are in Paris, and they prepared a party for me, or to go out—it has been more than a year since we last saw each other. Now I need to cancel everything and go for my lesson. And it will finish at about 1 or 2 a.m. . . . too late. And . . . anyway, I will be exhausted after my lesson.

Rolling with the Punches and Physical Resistance

Young musicians must adapt and perform despite weird hours, changes in diet, jet lag, and unexpected changes. Being adaptable while performing at a high level is difficult. A soloist described the conditions during a competition:

> The worst one took place in Taiwan. Not only the length of the flight and jet lag, but also the lethargy and the stomach trouble, probably due to the change in diet. For more than twenty-four hours I didn't sleep, and it was more than three days before I played violin again, and I needed to play my first tour. OK, I am used to that, but not my violin: it came unstuck and the air humidity caused the strings to keep loosening. So, somebody immediately lent me a violin. It was horrible to play in conditions like that.

Jet lag and a changing diet are familiar issues for businessmen who travel the world, but the age of the young soloists must be taken into account as well as their lack of experience. Sometimes travel and playing conditions are good, and sometimes they are very poor. Young soloists must prove their courage and flexibility.

On the eve of an international competition in a tourist city in Western Europe, I went walking in the evening in the old town center. I saw two men dressed in black with luggage and two violin cases sitting on a bench. One ate a sandwich and the other slept. The next morning, I found them at the same place, and two hours later we met in the castle during the opening ceremony of the competition. The aged man—the father of the participant—told me, "We have no money, so we took a train and spent two days traveling. We couldn't afford a hotel, but the competition has refunded our travel funds, so we can rent a room in a modest hotel. Tomorrow my son will play; he has to prepare himself beforehand." This competitor traveled over 3,000 kilometers to reach the competition. He needed a strong physical constitution to play for a jury after spending two nights in a train and a third sleeping outside on a bench. On another occasion I spoke with the father of a Russian violinist living in Germany:

> We were in France for a competition which turned out badly for us because Ala failed to win a prize. The return trip was hard: no money. Luckily, we had return tickets. Ala was very young; she was eight years old, and we had never seen Paris before. We took a break in our travels because we wanted to visit the city, but how to do it without money? So, the three of us [Ala's mother was also a violinist] played in the street of Montmartre. Playing every day, we earned what we needed to stay in Paris for five days.

Physical endurance is required for travel and also for each workday; the instrumental practice imposed on children is physically demanding. To attain a high level of virtuosity, violinists must devote a vast amount of time to practice. A single idle day can endanger the quality of performance. As a consequence, Itzak Perlman is a rare exception to the rule that a child of fragile health may not successfully pursue a soloist career. I heard of soloist aspirants who abandoned their plans because of physical problems, but I never met a weak child in a soloist class. Very early in childhood, the teachers push instrumental practice, and problems quickly appear—tendon, back, or spine pain. A violinist with these problems will never make it as a soloist, so there's no point investing in such a future. The extreme treatment of children eliminates those who would have problems in the future.

Psychological Resistance

Psychological resistance is another key trait of the successful soloist, and some teachers believe it is necessary to develop emotional toughness in children from an early age. Some will intentionally raise the tension levels during lessons, explaining that their rudeness develops calluses that harden against the stresses of public performance. The child must learn to deal with pressure, with yelling and screaming. "The world of violinists is not a fairy tale," a teacher said, "it's a world of hard competition. The young must be strong. If they can't maintain self-control because they are hurt that I screamed at them, they have no place here. This is not a world for little children who need their mum." Students are well aware that this testing is going on, and they admire colleagues who withstand it well. "He plays it very cool, he has no problems with his performance or himself," one student said of another. "After lessons with his teacher, who is like, crazy, and pushes you to death, the competition is child's play!"

Jitters and self-control issues appear frequently at certain ages (around twelve to fourteen); children who played calmly in the past start to lose their edge because of stress. European psychologists have studied this problem, and some institutions of higher musical education have staff psychologists who assist with performance problems. Some teachers encourage use of these resources, while others coach their students through encouragement and by reinforcing self-confidence. Other teachers prescribe yoga or swimming. I once observed a teacher suggest that her student take psychiatric medications. Students who are older than fifteen years share certain stress-relieving tricks. I heard about methods such as sleeping just before a performance (one student was late for an appearance because she was so deeply asleep), staying alone in a room, doing relaxation exercises, speaking with someone, taking a drink (one small glass of vodka), smoking a cigarette. Among older musicians (twenties and above), beta-blocker drugs are sometimes taken.

Many musicians are convinced there is a contradiction between musical sensibility and stress insensibility. In this view, these stress-resistant "beasts," as they are known, cannot be true artists. Their skill at "cold playing" and "over-control" diminishes artistic sensibility, musicality, and expression. This kind of ice-cold performer, colleagues may say, is an excellent technician, but lacks an artist's sensitivity.

Obedience and the "Artistic Personality"

In the first stages of soloist education, teachers expect exemplary obedience from their students. This is partially related to the specificity of the violin—deep rigor is necessary to play this instrument correctly at a high level. Docility permits the student to achieve good results quickly. The following excerpt illustrates the typical teacher's ideal of discipline: "The best students are Asian ones, because they know how to work. They do not open their mouth: no tantrums or perversity. They are not in the revolutionary mood. They work and that's it. And how they progress!" Yet this virtuoso model-student, so obedient at the start of his or her education, must be transformed in the final stage into a "true artistic personality," according to participants in the soloist milieu. Concert organizers appreciate artistic personality on stage—coupled with docility in business negotiations. Some musicians from Asian backgrounds are said to have difficulty transitioning from submissive students into strong, independent musicians.[24] In fact, few violinists of any ethnicity achieve this difficult transformation.

Several soloists living in the twentieth century have the reputation of being rebellious, of having what the musicians call "a strong personality." The career of Boris Belkin is an excellent example of this type.

> He was rebellious even as a child. He studied the violin from the age of six to eleven, but then gave it up because he "hated the violin." At seventeen he started again, working very seriously and long hours—seven to eight hours a day. "I practiced like mad." Professor Yankelevich helped him enter the Moscow

Conservatory. Here he found the spirit of competition all-consuming; every-thing seemed to be geared "to win," as he said, "a very bad system—it kills all individuality." Nevertheless, Belkin submitted to the system—he trained for the Paganini Competition in Genoa in 1971, but at the last moment was forbidden to go. The shock was such that he developed a numbness in his hand. After six months in a psychiatric clinic, he was cured and began preparing for the 1973 Paganini Competition—again in vain: no visa. That year he won a national Soviet contest. He decided to apply for emigration to Israel. By that time he was known as a troublemaker, and in May 1974, he left for the West. Belkin quickly adjusted. "In my playing, everything changed because I was free. It's a com-pletely new feeling about life." (Schwarz 1983: 480)

Most soloists must be able to demonstrate their "artistic temperament" within the milieu without hurting members of their entourage or seeming "dangerous" for the equilibrium of the classical music world. Youth rebellions are generally put down with varying levels of brutality.

During a competition, the father of Sasha showed concern about his son: "We met [jury president] Victor two weeks ago and he gave us some advice concerning the Tchaikovsky concerto. My [fourteen-year-old] son said he didn't like Victor's version; during the lesson he followed his advice, showing he could play like that. But this evening he told me he will play it the way he wants. The jury will fail him, I am sure!" Two days later, after the announcement of the results, the famous Victor said to Sasha: "You didn't listen to me. It's a pity. You only reached second place even though you were the best. Next time you will do as I wish." Sasha's father concluded: "It is a pity he didn't place first, but it's good. My son has this goddamn character! It is necessary in this world of wolves."

Although Sasha was sanctioned for his independence, his trajectory continued; his suppression was gentle. In spite of his young age, Sasha was already in a strong position in the soloist students' milieu thanks to earlier successes and the support of powerful people. Losing out, barely, was a slap on the wrist for a soloist who showed too much independence of soloist world hierarchy.

Linguistic Capacities

Since the fall of the Berlin Wall, university students across Europe (through pro-grams such as Erasmus—EU program of university students exchange) have been encouraged to complete their education in foreign countries.

But young musicians have long been accustomed to this large geographical mobility. The opportunities for such mobility are numerous: concerts, competi-tions, and master classes, across Europe and elsewhere. To regularly take lessons with certain teachers, students must follow them around the world. In the soloist world, the command of languages is useful, including languages not generally stud-ied in Western Europe and North America, especially Russian. Knowing Russian can help forge relationships with certain teachers.

Sophie is a French violinist, aged sixteen. Her teacher, Vera, is from Russia, but resides in France. The lessons are in French. In order to prepare for an important competition, Vera decided that Sophie should participate in a master class with Anton—a well-known Russian teacher who would come to France. Vera explains her decision. "I am sending my students to him, because he works very well and foremost, because he's a jury member in the majority of major competitions. This way he will meet my students before the competitions."

The master class lessons are public and take place in a French Mediterranean town. Anton speaks well in German, properly in English, knows many words in several languages, but teaches in German and especially Russian. Because Sophie speaks French and no German, Vera is in charge of translation. The student plays and Anton listens to her, and at the end of the first part of the piece he asks Vera in Russian, "Why is she interpreting the piece in this manner? It needs to be played in another way! This kind of interpretation is incorrect and illogical. No one has ever played Bach like that!" Vera responds in Russian to Anton, "I don't know what happened to her. I said the same thing as you yesterday; we worked on it for two hours and it was much better. But now she's playing it the way she did before." Then Vera turns to her student and says in French: "He [Anton] said that it is not bad, that you need to practice more, but you're on the right track." They start to work on the details of interpretations: Anton shows how to play certain excerpts, and Sophie's mother notes each of Anton's remarks (translated by Vera) in the scores. Sometimes Sophie plays, trying to apply the advice and corrections.

After the lesson, during a discussion with Sophie, I learned that her original interpretation of the Bach had been imposed by Vera. It was clear to me that Sophie did not realize that Vera had been mistranslating, was convinced that the lesson was good and that the modifications were not accompanied by strong criticism. In my discussion with Anton, some hours later, he stated that Sophie had the wrong conception of the interpretation of the piece; he described this as proof of serious problems in her musical education in terms of her theoretical analysis of musical works. Clearly, the lack of linguistic knowledge constituted an obstacle in Sophie's communication with Anton, and thanks to this linguistic barrier, Vera's work suffered no loss of credibility with her student.

I can provide several similar examples of advantages due to the use of Russian in professional communications. One famous Russian teacher sometimes sleeps during lessons. In the discussions with several of his students, I learned that only two things will wake him up: playing very well, or speaking—especially jokingly—in Russian, the only language he knows fluently.

To summarize—the chances of success increase for those who enter the soloist class very early in their life, when a likely change in the country of residence (for some period of time) is not quite as difficult linguistically. At an early age, the students learn new languages easily. Many soloists speak several languages fluently. This faculty is not related to political changes, globalization, or progress in communications; many nineteenth- and twentieth-century soloists were multilingual.[25] Some of them had residences in several countries during their lifetimes, and some even had a few different passports. Twentieth-century music history is rich in such examples. The Romanian virtuoso and composer George Enesco never settled anywhere, spending his life as a nomad (Pâris 1995: 383).

The Career of a Virtuoso:
The Example of the Official Discourse

Over two hundred pages were necessary to explain the process of virtuoso production. Yet all this complexity of human interaction—the activity of multiple networks, the years of socialization within this artistic professional world—are invisible to the world as it sees the virtuoso, who has achieved his or her education among the best at the top of the music universe and now performs as a soloist. What follows is a typical account of one such exceptional trajectory. Superficially it stands as a model pathway for actors involved in the virtuoso production process. Yet behind this picture of the individual achievement of a gifted person are all the restless years and processes we have described—the hidden practices and complex phenomena related to the social organization of this world. We could think of this chapter as a complementary one that brings up individual characteristics that are necessary and helpful for a soloist career. However, the process described in the proceeding four chapters tells the deeper story, the one that tells how various categories of actors help build the pragmatic and passionate platform from which the virtuoso, finally, can take off. And that departure also plays its sociological role. For these circles and informal networks need the virtuoso's success in order to survive. He is their product, their showcase.

In exceptional cases, when a soloist student accomplishes his objective, he attracts the attention of all soloist world participants. A career with a slow debut, such as in David Oistrakh's case, seems to be less used as an example in comparison with careers characterized by a sudden rise, like those of Yehudi Menuhin or Jascha Heifetz in the past, or Maxim Vengerov's current career. Among the young virtuosos observed in this study, only one achieved the status of international soloist.[26] His biography sums up the trajectory of a successful young contemporary soloist.

David (a pseudonym, not related to Oistrakh) was born in M. (capital of a former Soviet republic) in the early 1980s to a family of musician-graduates from the prestigious Tchaikovsky Conservatory in Moscow. Both parents and an older brother were pianists, and someone was practicing piano all day long. At the age of the five, David began violin lessons, and two years later the family moved to a Western European country. Thanks to numerous parental relationships created in the Moscow Conservatory, and with the help of powerful countrymen in the diaspora, his parents quickly found work—his mother as an accompanist and father as a teacher. The main activity of the father, however, was the musical education of his children. He traveled around their new country seeking the best possible teacher for his violinist son (the pianist parents mostly took care of the education of the older son).

David progressed very quickly and seemed to be particularly adapted to becoming a soloist. With his "happy-go-lucky" nature, he adapted himself to various conditions. At the age of ten, he spoke four languages fluently and practiced violin with remarkable application. While searching for an ideal teacher, the father presented David in competitions for young violinists. He chose competitions without regard to jury members, unless one of them had already worked with David in one of numerous master classes. Practically from the beginning, David was a successful student, and always finished as a finalist. His lack of jitters was legendary.

When he was fourteen, David's father said,

> He loves competitions; for him it is a game. One year ago, we were in the second stage of the competition and it was his turn to play. I was in the audience listening to other participants, knowing that he was practicing in the practice room near the concert hall. Five minutes before he got on stage, I started looking for him and I couldn't find him. The violin was in its case in the practice room and my son was not there. I searched for him everywhere, and someone said to me that he was outside. I thought maybe he started to get the jitters and went outside to get some air and relax. I went outside and saw my son playing football with other boys his age, dressed in the stage costume completely crumpled, speaking with his companions in their language, which he never learned at school or anywhere else. I took him away from this wolf pack, combed him, put on his trousers and shirt and he played immediately. Despite this football séance, he played wonderfully and won second place in the older group. And it is always like that with him.

Around this time David began taking lessons in the class of a teacher with whom he would stay until the end of his education at age twenty-three. Before this teacher, he had several others, each one recognized for their work with young soloists. Each time, after a few months, David's father took him away because he was not satisfied with their methods.

> He needed a teacher, a true one. Nobody stayed behind in Moscow. All those who were excellent emigrated. . . . They stay [in Russia] half the school year; the other half, they are in foreign [EU] countries, working on master classes and earning money, each one looking in their wallet. And me, I still had to think that one lesson is not only one hour but 100 euros! He needs at least two lessons per week. . . . [Finally] I found a teacher who gives him two lessons per week. We come for this hour and take the lesson, and we never knew how long it will: two hours, three, and sometimes four. . . . And I pay nothing—this is the conservatory. . . . In order to have some good and new ideas, I also take David twice a month to my friend. He's a very good violinist who could have a great solo career, but because of the war, and after, because of his family, he's not famous. He's a very good concertmaster with a lot of fresh ideas, and it is for that reason that David plays a little differently from the others. Now, after so many years of sweat and blood, we have finally found it!

David was "in the hands" of an excellent and involved teacher who entered him in many competitions that David often won.

According to his father, David needed more support in their country of residence. He was perceived as a "foreigner," "again a Wunderkind from Russia! We've had enough of that phenomenon!" It was with these words that he was often turned down for new concerts, but David was supported by members of his community, who saw him as a symbol of success in immigration and a continuation of an artistic tradition. Thanks to their support, he obtained a loan of a prestigious violin, worth over $1 million, at the age of thirteen. Three years later, he recorded his first CD. His numerous concerts outside his adopted country result from a support network of musicians and important persons from the Russian diaspora. His agent, also of former Soviet origin, solicits affluent people to organize concerts and records.

The typical teenage crisis did not seem to touch this young violinist, who followed his soloist career and, at the same time, was able to attend general school. With a huge smile, he moved some obstacles aside (such as lacking support in his country) and advanced with self-confidence. At eighteen, David had already won several prestigious prizes, made CDs, and met with an important record producer. His reputation now extended beyond the milieu. David passed through the three stages of soloist education in a short time, and by the age of twenty, he was already a part of the elite.

Conclusion

CAREER COUPLING AND NOTHING
NEW IN THE SOLOIST WORLD

During the three stages of education, young soloists pass through several selections. Their education is among the longest and most complex of all professions—eighteen years at a minimum—and filled with intensity, with a variety of relationships that must be maintained and assets that must be obtained. The acquisition of these characteristics begins at an early age. For several years, the child who possesses this potential (musical capacity and the soloist "personality") will be shaped and improved in various technical and social competencies. Market conditions and the personal circumstances of the musician and his or her family are decisive in determining the path of the young soloist.

The most important factor is the career coupling process, which optimizes the probability of success. No important careers are built without that mechanism—the mutual dependency of teacher and student. This process is typically hidden from the general public, and we only see the soloist, the genius, climbing higher and higher on the career ladder. The people close to this "wonderful person," however, are aware of the multiple actors working behind the scenes to make such success possible. As Pierre Bourdieu once said, Sociologists discover the evident truth, which was so obvious, that it was part of us.

Career coupling is not only a phenomenon present in this relationship between teacher and student. Other professional worlds are built on similarly narrow expertise, the specific skills in which reputation plays a principal role and constitutes the perfect context for the career coupling process.[1] The failures of a career are, in large part, the failure of the career coupling process, which must be a close collaboration between teacher and student. In addition to that complex process, several other factors play an important role.

Soloists achieve their elite status after a long trajectory. For those who believe that all social phenomena described in this book—geographical mobility, emigration, networking, the struggle for fame, the education of gifted children, parental ambition, master-disciple relationships, career coupling, and elite membership—are recent, I produce the following example, from another epoch.

N. P. was born in a big European city in 1782. His father, a passionate music lover, played the mandolin. The family was not rich but was well-off enough to afford music lessons for their children. N. P. first took mandolin lessons with his father, and then, at the age of seven, took up the violin. His father was strict and obliged N. P. to practice the violin. . . . N. P. had several teachers: first, the musicians from the local orchestra, and then the best-known teacher in their city. When N. P. was eleven, this teacher decided to present the boy to the public. In his first concert he won "universal admiration" (Schwarz 1983: 176). N. P's teacher presented him to a well-known violin virtuoso in their country, and the young violinist received encouragement and compliments. This, N. P. stated several years later, gave him the enthusiasm necessary to continue his training. N. P. progressed and went to another big city to pursue his education with another well-known teacher. This travel was paid for with proceeds from concerts N. P. played in his native city. N. P. and his father settled in another city in order to further N. P.'s soloist education.

N. P. actively participated in the musical life of this new city, and there he met other violin virtuosos who played in the area. Only a few months after their move, N. P. and his father, who played the impresario role, went on their first concert tour, which lasted about a year. At the end of 1799, when N. P. was seventeen, he broke free from his father and took control over his professional career. In 1801, he began his own concert tours, and after a concert in Livorno, a rich patron offered him a Guarneri del Gesù violin. Then, for four years, from the ages of nineteen to twenty-three, he disappeared from the stage.[2] Nobody knew of his activities during that time; it was speculated that he was in some sort of crisis and low in spirits during this period. The crisis ended just before his international career began.

The young violinist, whose life exactly matches that of the soloist students described in this book, was named Niccolò Paganini.[3] It is perhaps surprising that this musician, whose name is synonymous with virtuosity and genius, followed exactly the same path as thousands of violin students who came after him. This violinist—divine or devilish, as some believed[4]—went through exactly the same stages of soloist education described in this book, marked by days of rigorous practice, a change of teachers, a crisis period and the emancipation from parental tutelage, as well as the support of patrons and important musicians in the country of residence and beyond. In the space of two centuries, technical innovations (recording, innovations in transport) have only slightly modified the process.

It is possible to play on three continents in the same week, now, and recording effects may have provoked some changes in soloist training, but the core elements of the work are the same. The number of soloists and prodigy children has risen, but if we consider the increase in the human population, this effect is commensurate. Interestingly, the people who play a role in the soloist's life are little different from those of two centuries ago. Then as now, interactions between the student and the professionals in the soloist world are crucial to the student's career.

THE POWER OF THE FAITH

These interactions rely heavily upon a strong belief in the future among a chain of collaborators, something similar to religious faith. Without faith, the entire project risks collapse. For this reason, the power of the milieu is important, and the main activity of the group is to maintain its strong belief. As in the situation described by Leo Festinger, Henry Riecken, and Stanley Schachter (1956) in a study of a religious sect's maintenance of belief in an impending doomsday, the entourage of the soloist must maintain faith in ultimate success.

Faith is contagious but must be constantly maintained, as Festinger and his colleagues demonstrated. The first dimension of this faith is the conviction that this small person—a child—has the extraordinary potential required to become a solo violinist. Parents and teachers must believe equally, while the teacher spreads the word among his or her network that will transform the young musician's belief in himself, and as the potential of success grows, the more people share that faith.

The second dimension of this faith is the conviction that success depends on a chain of actions directed by the primary violin teacher. Each network chief—the soloist teacher—pretends to know the secret to a successful path. Without faith in the teacher's knowledge, power, and sphere of influence, the student will not sacrifice these precious years of his or life in blindly practicing under the teacher's management.

The third component of this faith relates to the role of classical music in one's life. This faith can be lost if the musician comes to believe that classical music is a "dead art" for "old people" that has no future. "What are we necessary for?" the musician may ask him or herself. "Why should I play? How am I useful to society?" When these kinds of doubts arise, it signals a waning in the imperturbable faith in the necessity of virtuoso activity. The hope for a brilliant future, the soloist's faith in his or her own destiny, must always be present, or it will be nearly impossible to follow the path to becoming a soloist.

This book is not for everyone; in particular, one sort of person should not read this book: someone who still believes.

THE SCANDAL OF ANASTASIA, DECONSTRUCTED

This book opened with the story of Anastasia and her scandalous concert performance. Having examined the soloist world in the pages since then, it is now time to return to Anastasia to explain why she ignored all conventions and dared to play a violin solo instead of an accompanied piece in her concert gala performance. I met Anastasia through the father of another soloist that I was interviewing in Italy. Learning that I lived near a European capital where a major competition was to take place soon, he asked if I could host one of the participants and her parents. I immediately agreed, considering the excellent opportunity for my research.

A month later I received a call from Anastasia's father, a Russian violinist who had immigrated to Western Europe with his wife and Anastasia eight years earlier. We ended up hosting them for about three weeks. I informed them about my research project on the socialization of soloists, and they were enthusiastic about assisting me with my research. My husband, children, and I experienced the competition as Anastasia's extended family. We hoped for her success and got a thrill each time the phone rang and the competition organizer spoke with the formulaic notification language: "Anastasia has been chosen for the next round. We congratulate her and ask her to contact the pianist in order to organize a rehearsal."

These phone calls were in a language that Anastasia didn't understand, so I frequently translated. Anastasia performed brilliantly, and despite her young age (sixteen), she was identified as a potential winner from the first round. She spent her time practicing, walking outside, relaxing, and engaging in conversation with all the people living under our roof. Her parents coached her and spent many hours in the kitchen speaking with us as we prepared organic meals for the whole "competition team."

Although we were ostensibly just hosts, our lives were also perturbed by the rigor of the competition. In my car, on the way to the venue, I was afraid of being late because of a traffic jam, or of arriving too early, which provoked a lot of jitters. I felt stress because the pianist, who normally accompanied singers, was playing with violinists for the first time. Rehearsals took place in the pianist's tiny sixth-floor apartment, with scarcely enough room for the violinist to play. I was stressed because Anastasia's family, who were used to the competition lifestyle, found that this one was poorly organized and unprofessional. I worried about the unfriendly-seeming jury members, and the competitive nature of the performances.

The final part of the competition concluded this stressful phase as we waited for the results. As usual, the discussions at home were warm. We played the typical competition game of predicting of the results. Anastasia ignored us; she spent the time with a friend—another teenager and violinist. Her father was sure that without support from the jury, his daughter would obtain only sixth place. We (his wife, my husband, and I) hoped for more, judging by her brilliant performance. In our opinion, she was much better than the other finalists, but we realized that our opinions were colored by the fact that we knew and loved her. As longtime observers of the milieu, we of course knew that prizes were awarded not only according to the violinists' performances, but through the support of jury members.

The finalists played their last round on a Saturday, and later that evening, the places were announced. As her father predicted, Anastasia took last place. This confirmed that his knowledge of the inner workings of this world were very keen. During our return to the car, our discussions turned immediately onto the choice of the piece that each finalist would perform for the gala concert two days afterward. In such competitions, the winner plays a concerto with an orchestra, the second plays a shorter orchestral form, and the remaining four finalists play pieces with piano or solos. The performers chose which pieces to play, deciding in order of their ranking. Consequently, Anastasia (as sixth place finisher) had to wait for the other finalists' decisions before she could select her piece.

She wanted to play a violin sonata by a twentieth-century composer—a very expressive and touching piece of music. She had spoken with the other participants and knew that none had chosen this particular piece. The organizers were expected to contact each performer to get their choice, in order to print them correctly in the program.

The day after the finals, we were eating lunch with Anastasia and her family when the phone rang. The women from the organizational staff called to announce that Anastasia would play a Schubert piece with piano. I was surprised and told her that Anastasia had made another choice. "Impossible," said the organizer, "the jury decided that she would play Schubert in the gala." I told Anastasia what had happened. "But I have chosen another piece!" she exclaimed. "The jury has no right to impose the piece!" declared Anastasia's father. I translated both of these comments for the organizer, who was distressed and told me that someone else would call us to better explain the situation.

An hour later, the phone rang again. The lead organizer of the competition told me that it was the jury's decision that Anastasia play Schubert: "She does not have a say in the matter. Anastasia needs to be happy and grateful for winning this prestigious prize at sixteen. She needs to respect the jury's decision." I translated this to Anastasia and her father. Anastasia's father responded by saying that it is in the competition rules that the finalists can choose their piece, and his daughter did so according to this rule. The organizer responded, "No, she needs to obey the jury's decision. All these famous people, who is she to be against them?" Anastasia's father, hoping that this proposed compromise would be accepted, said: "She can play another piece for violin with piano, for example, 'Tzigane' of Ravel." "No," said the organizer, it was "Schubert or nothing!"

While I translated, Anastasia's father explained to my husband (the only non-classical musician present): "With this Schubert piece, they [the jury] can hide the fact that Anastasia is the best of their all laureates. [The Schubert piece must be played with a gentle, moderate style that does not show the temper, fugue, and romantic personality of other pieces.] Only with Schubert can they justify their decision. This is why they impose this decision and refuse to accept another choice. Their authority and credibility are at stake."

To the organizer, he said: "I thought we were in Western Europe—here in the heart of democracy, you violate the law! We are not in China here! Even in the Soviet Union we had more liberty!"[5] Anastasia's father demanded to speak with the president of the contest, a fellow Russian violinist of the same generation. The organizer said that the president was gone and that Anastasia must abide by the jury's decision. She was yelling so loud and fast that I was having trouble translating: "He will ruin Anastasia's career," she said. "She is completely under his domination! I must speak directly with her! She will listen to me!" No problem, Anastasia's father said, smiling. "My daughter is free, and you can speak with her." Anastasia picked up the phone and, with a determined voice, spoke in English.

The organizer said again that Schubert was the jury's decision, and she needed to obey. If not, she could not play the gala at all. "This is blackmail," responded

Anastasia. "It's against the law!" "No," shouted the organizer, "The law is the jury's decision. They have every right to impose the law, and they have decided! You have no choice! You obey!"

Anastasia was nervous and angry. At sixteen, after an exhausting competition, after so many tensions, she was tired and disappointed. At this moment, my husband said in a soft voice: "Say yes. If not, they will block your entrance onto the stage. Say yes! Once you're on stage, you play what you want." Anastasia smiled. "OK," she told the organizer. "I will play the Schubert."

When she hung up the phone, all eyes turned to my husband, who said: "I do not know how it is in this world, but once Anastasia is on stage, she can play what she wants, no?" And then the discussions started again—what could be the consequences of this act? Everyone agreed that the Schubert piece would not give Anastasia a chance to show her playing skills or the character of her interpretation. We all agreed she should not succumb to the pressure of the jury. Anastasia's father found the idea of going on stage and playing a piece of her choice was the most appropriate response: "Show them [the jury and organizers] that you are not scared, that you are not a slave to their preferences. We are not in a dictatorial system. This is Europe and this is democracy" (Anastasia's father knew plenty about totalitarian regimes.)

Anastasia's mother was against it: "Why do you always want to make war with these people? They will ruin our daughter! Her career will be finished! Why all this struggle? Why doesn't she just change her program, and we stop talking about it? So much stress, fear, and trouble for five minutes of music." Personally, I wanted Anastasia to play the piece she chose and show people that blackmail did not work at the end of the twentieth century in a European democracy. But I felt it was not my decision and refrained from giving my point of view.

Finally, Anastasia's father said, "Anastasia, it is your life, your career, your decision. Whatever you do it will be right, and we support you."

Anastasia responded, already relaxed: "I will ask the others winners tomorrow: if they got to choose their pieces by themselves, I play what I choose. If everyone else got this kind of imposition, I will play Schubert."

The day, during a rehearsal of the Schubert piece, she spoke with the other participants and learned they had all been free to choose the pieces they played. In the afternoon before the gala, she said to me, exhausted: "I don't know what to do. . . . I will decide at the last moment, if I have enough energy."

Her parents and host family sat in the first rows, where it was easy to see the faces of the artists on stage. Anastasia played first. As I described in the introduction, she began playing the sonata for solo violin while the pianist was still adjusting her chair. And thus, Anastasia showed her courage before two thousand people, by not playing the piece that the jury members had imposed with such a heavy hand the day before. For Anastasia, it was the only way she could preserve her pride and the feeling of being a free and independent person.

All of this pressure for just six minutes of music—six minutes that showed everybody that this girl could play the violin in a way that those who played after her could not match. Knowing the story behind this situation, this music seemed to be written especially for this "revolutionary" moment. Someone in the audience said, "Why did she get only sixth place? She is much better than the others!"

After the last note was played, Anastasia looked at her parents: her mother was scared and proud, her father smiled happily. He looked around, noting the reactions of others. Backstage, the storm was waiting: the organizers were protesting, speaking to each other with disgust about what had happened. One of them yelled at Anastasia: "How dare you!" The most famous jury member, a man of more than sixty, ran behind Anastasia screaming: "I will do everything I can so that you will never play again! Your career is ruined! You are finished!"

Anastasia ran, following her close friend, a violinist who was familiar with the layout of the theater. He led her to her dressing room where she put her violin in the case, grabbed her coat and went outside, running through the hallways, out an exit door and down the street, followed by a yelling jury member.

Anastasia's friend knew a café near the concert hall, and they found refuge there. They spent two hours drinking tea and waiting for Anastasia's parents and hosts. Anastasia cried through the entire ride home. In the house, she told me: "I felt . . . I can understand now what the Jews felt like during the Second World War. I have never been scared like that before."

The next day, previously booked venues began calling Anastasia to cancel her performances. The cancellation of concerts started always with the same explanation: "What she did to her pianist and what her behavior suggested; we can't accept that . . ." A week later, after Anastasia's family returned home, her father prepared a letter for the press, explaining what had happened at the concert and how the rules of the competition had been violated by the jury. Not a single journal was interested in publishing this story. In that Western European country, classical music matters to only a small part of an elite audience—an older audience. Anastasia's family was unable to tell the world why she had insisted on playing the sonata for solo violin.

What happened to the other winners of this event? The first-place finisher, after some concerts with various orchestras, stopped performing and now teaches at a superior school of music in Europe. The second-place winner is concertmaster in his country's radio orchestra; the third finisher might have developed a soloist career, but for family reasons had to take a concertmaster position in a provincial orchestra, from which he graduated to concertmaster of an important European orchestra. The fourth-place finisher recorded many CDs and plays a lot on stage, but as a jazz musician instead of a classical soloist. He is a member of a famous jazz band, but plays contemporary classical music and ethnic music from time to time. The fifth-place finalist, who had won other competitions, played as a soloist a few times but failed to make a career of it.

Anastasia appears to have been the true winner of the competition. With her behavior, she proved she had temper, character, and a strong personality, and a strong belief in her power and future, the most important factors in soloist success. Anastasia's father recognized that no jury would have treated his daughter this way if we were the client of a powerful person, so he enrolled her in a famous soloist class. Six years after the scandal, she won first place in one of the biggest competitions in the world. Her relationship with her teacher allowed her to build a strong soloist career.

Today, Anastasia is the only one of the six finalists to have become a successful violin soloist. She has played more than seventy times with prominent European, Japanese, Russian, and American orchestras, and played with smaller ensembles as well. Her career was reassuring to those who were touched by her performance at the gala. It took several years before she was able to play in the country where the competition took place, due to the power of the organizers and the jury member who had threatened to destroy her career. In the end, her punishment will weigh less than her fame, and she is young enough to be able to change network connections and open new doors. Despite all obstacles, having enormous faith, she maintained her path of excellence. She is an international and successful soloist today, happy to play music.

Difficulties and Limits

SOME METHODOLOGICAL ASPECTS ABOUT ATTACHMENT AND DISTANCE WITHIN ETHNOGRAPHIC WORK

Daniel Bizeul writes about the work of the ethnographer:

> The progress of a researcher depends first upon the work routines, preconceptions, and intimate preoccupations of the ethnographer, and on the other hand, on the results of encounters with people, favorable or non-favorable by coincidence, and only to a lesser degree is the consequence of well-ordered and perceptive work. The social processes being spotlighted in an ethnographer's work are inseparable from the studied milieu and the relation of inquiry. Inevitably we must admit that the work relies less on certain tested methods and more on our own personality, the movements of others, and circumstances that enable us to take full advantage of different sorts of data and situations. At various moments, the ethnographer could be "off the mark," take the wrong road, become isolated or rejected from a given group, be hoodwinked by someone, like in ordinary life, and this happens not because the work is bad. (1999: 112)

During my research I was confronted with various difficulties. The sociologist's main bias arises from the more or less representational quality of the sample. In this study, much as in other studies based on observations (Howard Becker studied musician culture based on his own involvement in his jazz group; Davis was a taxi driver), I started with a familiar field: a class conducted by a Russian teacher. This was familiar territory for me because I was educated in Polish musical institutions, which were more like Soviet than Western European educational traditions. In Eastern Europe, before the transformation of the 1990s, musicians enjoyed a much greater social position than in Western societies. In the early days of my research, I feared that my sample was "Russian-slanted," but when I extended my research into other soloist classes, I realized that almost half of my participants originated from Eastern Europe anyway. Although my study began in Paris, only a small percentage of my participants were of French origin.

Still, as my research developed, I had doubts about its bias because of the high number of Eastern European participants. I started to observe two "French" classes, but they were not the same as the soloist milieu I had determined to study. The students did not participate in international competitions, for example. These classes lacked strong involvement of teachers in the education of certain students, the specific role of parent involvement, and the wide age range of students. For these reasons, I did not include those "French" classes in my sample, though my observations there provided interesting elements of comparison.

My research primarily concerns classes whose origins lie, at varying levels of remove, from Eastern Europe. Nationality does not determine everything about teaching and violin-playing style, but the culture of a given tradition is the basis of the socialization that young musicians undergo. A German student educated by a Russian teacher, for example, will convey the characteristic Russian work culture, regardless of where the education occurred. The visibility of the careers of Russian violinists during the twentieth century resulted mainly from the fact that they took a strategic position in the distribution of resources necessary to the soloist career. For example, they were jury members in international competitions; they led associations that loaned students prestigious violins, and, most importantly, they knew how to create and animate successful soloist classes.

Most famous violinists of the twentieth century were educated in classes led by teachers of an Eastern European tradition (Schwarz 1983). Of the violinists listed in *Baker's Biographical Dictionary* (Slonimsky 1997) and *Dictionnaire des interprètes* (Parîs 1995), 59 out of 125 were of Eastern European origin. Thus, it is not surprising that violin students follow this tradition as the most promising one for a soloist career. The sample of students on which I focused represents a larger sample of Eastern European musicians who were representative of European classes in the 1990s and the early 2000s.

An exploration study of this type has a fleeting context; we can imagine that if conducted around 2050, such classes would have an Asian majority. At present, this tendency is clear in the Americas, though not in European classes. This study focuses mainly on Europe; I did not have the opportunity to make a comparison with American violin classes, and my sources on the United States were secondhand. Although I conducted four interviews with American violinists, I was unable to observe American soloist classes. However, these appear to have much in common with European soloist classes.

One difficulty that arose in my study resulted from the fact that in some settings I had a dual role as the mother of a violin soloist student. At times this could limit my access to information about scholarships or sponsorships, because other parents were competing with me. When other parents knew me only as a sociologist, I obtained much more detailed information. However, my relationships as a soloist mother also allowed me to obtain precious and hidden information. My friendships with two teachers whom I've known for more than twenty years, and friendships with a sound engineer and violin maker (both parents of soloist students) were crucial. Thanks to the trust and reciprocity of these relationships I could obtain intimate information that would never have been accessible through standard interviews. Those rare relationships were built over many years.[1] The duration of this study was particularly long, and thanks to them, I knew the underground conditions of transactions of very precious instruments. I knew the "tricks of the trade" for placing someone in the final stage of a competition. But, as Phillippe Masson states (1996: 9), "There exists a certain resistance to long-lasting observation." This obstacle was partially overcome by privileged informants who could awaken my attention at key moments. As numerous ethnographers before me have reported, observations allowed me to detect how the behavior of people differs at times from their declarations. Nathalie Heinich, in her study concerning writers, says that it is not right to apply systemic suspicions to all cases, that the interviewed person may lie, but it is important to take into account that the interviewed person "builds a partial narrative because it is congruent with their value system; this narrative also does not have to be read as a reflection of the past, but as a public construction of an acceptable version of this past" (Heinich 1999: 29).

Jean-Michel Chapoulie suggests that witnesses "accept . . . voluntarily, without verification, their own memories or the testimonies of their colleagues when it is related to their own activities or their area of activities, meaning their familiar universe" (Chapoulie 2001: 431). The verification of information provided from interviews can sometimes be accomplished with archival materials, but this work is time-consuming. In my study, I was able to check certain information by cross-referencing the data provided from interviews with my other observations. However, the reconstruction of certain facts is not always possible, especially those which concern the activity of my participants. Sometimes I was forced to accept data from interviews without checking its validity.

Ethnographic research often uses a mixture of first- and second-hand sources. When I conducted observations on my own (for example, when I accompanied my children to a violin lesson), I observed the lessons of other students and eaves-dropped on conversations in the corridors of concert halls or in my home. In such cases I was collecting data first-hand; information provided from the interviewee who relayed a story about an event or a certain situation was second-hand, and I sought to verify such accounts to use them as an illustration of observations made in similar circumstances. Sometimes, these testimonies are irreplaceable, especially in situations where certain activities are unobservable, such as negotiations between members of a competition jury.

I also employ indirect or reported speech ("they told me that . . ."), and sometimes I do not mention the source in order to protect anonymity. Although I observed soloist activity in numerous countries, this elite milieu has a very high level of inter-acquaintance (Wagner 2004). The actors know each other, or can quickly locate one another. Consequently, the examples cited in this book omit the information that is regularly mentioned in an ethnographic account, about the circumstances and places accompanying the collection of data. By doing so, I again preserve the anonymity of the actors.

Translation was an additional challenge I encountered. More than half of my interviews were conducted in Russian and Polish, the rest were in French and English. Several field notes contain the citations in these four languages. I also used sources published in these languages and carried out all translations independently (the most recent version was proofread by a native English speaker). While understanding was not a problem while collecting data, the translation of interviews and discussions imposed barriers. How could I translate without losing the specificity of expressions? How could I preserve the character of familiar exclamations, muddled sentences, idioms, colloquial phases, or expressions specific to the culture? How would I preserve the diversity of the spoken language of people, and how would I preserve this specific attitude, in order not to seem ridiculous or unbelievable? How could I escape having a flat translation? How could I uphold the individual voices of each respondent?

This is an issue for my writing that is particularly sensitive and creates a specific difficulty with research done in international contexts. However, the major difficulty mentioned by numerous sociologists or anthropologists who use participant observation (Adler and Adler 1998; Bizeul 1999; Powdermaker 1966) concerns the strong involvement of the researcher in his or her "field." The strong involvement is an obstacle in the description and analysis of the observed actions, because sociologists have difficulty remaining impartial. Because I was familiar with the musician world, I was aware of this potential pitfall. However, I could not escape the consequences of the strong attachment to my field.

Specific Problems Linked to Fieldwork Attachment

Research workers doing fieldwork often tell us about the first experience in which they received the recognition for their fieldwork that made them a true sociologist.[2] They disclose the hidden parts of their work so that young researchers can avoid the pitfalls typical to the undertaking. Most of the difficulties that arise during the work of participant observers are linked to the integration process and their apprenticeship as performers of a given role: the scientist must change from sociologist to participant, and therefore play a dual role.

My testimony illustrates the opposite situation: the change from participant to sociologist and the difficulties linked to keeping up with this dual role. Below I list the steps that were required as a "novice sociologist," so as to "acquire a sound knowledge of, and abiding love for [my] discipline," as Davis stated in his *Urbane Life and Culture* (1974). During classes, and while I was preparing for my fieldwork, my teachers warned me of the difficulties that I would have related to this type of data collection. I also read accounts written by anthropologists, in particular Nigel Barley (1992; 1994), and learned about the setbacks he had endured with the Dowayos tribe. I thought that being born to the world of musicians would spare me this kind of mishap. Now I realize that all fieldwork teaches us how ignorant we truly are and how rich and constantly changing human behavior is.

Some sociologists devote themselves to studying their family environment, either because of their social origin (Donald Roy, who studied workers; or Lee Braude, who studied rabbis), or because of life events (Julius A. Roth, who had to stay in a hospital for some time). I combine all these factors into my fieldwork: my family background, my professional life, and my private life.

In 1997 I started investigating a closed world of activity to which I thought I belonged. As the mother of a violinist, for some years I had attended classes for children who had the potential to develop as soloists. Compared to other sociologists, I thought I had a leg up by way of identification with my subjects—I was a Pole from a family of musicians, residing in France and married to a Frenchman—which put me squarely in the category of the typical "young virtuoso parent." I thought my musical background would serve as an advantage and figured that I knew the language and rules of the field. But this was not exactly the case.

After a year of investigation, I came to be a participant observer in a virtuoso competition. On the morning of the first day of competition, I prepared to conduct my first informal interview. I arrived early at the building where all events were to take place and met the father of one of the competitors. I was glad we shared the same language and thought I could carry out my first interview quite easily. We started talking, and after a few minutes, I realized that "my subject" had managed to extract information from me about my child, while I had discovered nearly nothing about his child. Our short interview was interrupted by members of the jury, who started to come up and greet my interviewee. He shook their hands and said a few words to all of them, showing he belonged to their world. Later on, I learned that he and some jury members had been friends at university.

From that moment, I became aware that the field I was studying was different from the one I knew—that of music teachers—and that the world of musicians is not homogeneous. Soloists are part of an elite that has its own operating mode. The person I was speaking to knew this group perfectly well and was a very clever amateur sociologist, who was strategically working for his own child's success. I was of some interest to him, and he spared me some time—not because he was, as Rosalie Wax suggests "lonely and bored" (Wax 1971) but because my son could, in the future, become his son's competitor. My son was still unknown to the competition circle, and he could have potentially jeopardized his own son's victory.

Valuable information, such as the names of the people who taught or are teaching this violinist, the instrument he played with and who lent it, as well as the program he was to perform, enabled participants within that world to assess the position of the instrumentalist within the restricted group of virtuoso violinists. A totally unknown candidate can affect the order of the prize list. Once my informant had collected the information he wanted from me, he kindly provided me advice and indications about the steps I should take in this world—steps that in fact were provided to ensure that nothing would compromise his son's future. I was being trapped by the man I thought I was interviewing without his knowledge.

My field is overflowing with these types of amateur sociologists, and data collection is the main activity for parents of virtuosos. However, such a deep immersion and strong attachment to the field studied also presents many drawbacks. One of them is to be overwhelmed by information and to not be able to set up proper and comprehensive sociological work, which means regularly noting down everything seen or heard. My position sometimes resembled Festinger's (1956), when he recalled investigating a sect and the difficulty that he and his team had in taking notes. They worked undercover and the researchers sometimes felt as if they were under certain external pressures.

I often listened, for hours, to enthralling stories told by the members of this world, but the informal aspect of my fieldwork prevented me from recording or taking notes on the spot. When living "within" the field studied, we sometimes take part in very intense events for weeks, and sometimes, in spite of ourselves, we become just like Festinger's team when they experimented with the preparation and waited for a deluge (according to beliefs that unified the observed sect).

During such heavy periods when there is a continuous flow of information and when events and peoples' reactions to them start to move faster, it is highly frustrating not to be able to note all of these interesting discussions accurately. For six years now,[3] I've been regularly confronted with such situations, and I keep blaming myself for being too tired to take notes, but it is really impossible when, for instance, you share your house for three weeks in a row with the family of another competitor, accompanying them to many competition selections, staying up late at night discussing the way tests are going to turn out, and speculating about what is going to happen to the candidates. It is even more difficult when, in the morning, as all your guests and informants are still asleep, you have to manage such mundane logistics as food catering, cooking, and planning for a specific activity.

Indeed, competitions for virtuosos not only require the competitor's total commitment, but also the commitment of their family for several weeks. People within the close family circle can have no other activity than that of attending the tests and supporting their candidates during rehearsals and performances. After three weeks of such a life, exhaustion made me less receptive, and I found myself waiting for it to end. In other aspects this was process so exciting, I found myself swearing that I would write down everything just after "the deluge" was over. Often, collapsing from exhaustion and trying to make up for lost sleep, I failed to do so. I still wonder how Whyte (1955) managed to note down his daily observations every night.

In an account of his work, Roth wrote that "without the fieldwork schedule to maintain, my work hours became more regular, with portions of time set aside each morning, afternoon, and evening, when not interrupted by other tasks and activities" (Roth 1974). For me, this was simply impossible because I was always immersed in my fieldwork. When I sat in front of my personal computer, there was often a violinist training in the room next door (at least seven hours a day). During breaks, the violinist would come tell the little stories that were so precious for my study. Occasionally, the telephone would ring and a concert organizer, a stringed-instrument maker, one of the dozen violinists, a teacher, or a parent would be on the other end of the line. He or she would request invaluable information that would allow him or her to get to a foreign country, take part in a competition, perform at a concert, take lessons, or spare the cost of accommodation by organizing help. And I was trying to concentrate and ponder over the use of specific tricks Becker describes, so I could distance myself from my field and develop proper sociological and analytical thought. One can be swamped with fieldwork and get humiliated by it, too, especially when it is conducted through secret investigations in which you play the part of an ordinary participant. Here, I was not commissioned to investigate, and therefore I cannot claim my status as an excuse.

I went through a sociological baptism by fire (so to speak) and took on a stance that I would never have taken otherwise, because of my social and educational background. My sociological side was stronger, and curiosity took over my sense of pride and upbringing. This occurred during the discussion I had with a famous soloist teacher. I was playing the desperate and naive mother, someone ignorant of all the subtleties in the soloist world. I was forced to reveal that I was in financial straits and begged for help, so that my son could continue training. Faced with the lofty air the teacher put on, I would certainly have left had it not been for my sociological work and the hunch I had that I was getting close to one of the crucial elements of my study. Such detachment toward my personal "self" was of great help. Thanks to our discussion, I became convinced that the main activity of a certain category of people (some music teachers) is neither that which is expected (training soloists) nor one the people around them ascribe to them (earning fame and money by giving music lessons), but a very different one (selling expensive instruments).

However, the sociological side does not always take over the ordinary individual one, and sometimes fieldwork can be very painful. Once I was giving a ride to a young virtuoso who was crying throughout the drive because of the pressure she had from the people who play major roles in her world. She was experiencing harassment although she was only sixteen years old and had feelings of disillusionment that a person with many years of professional life might go through. Sometimes I thought that the soloist world was a cruel place for young people. I sometimes found it difficult to keep my distance and forbid myself to take a stance.

Many sociologists choose the world of relatives as fieldwork, but I do not think many study their own children. When my position as a research worker opened the possibility for me of seeing my world from a different point of view, I developed profoundly mixed emotions. It was frightening to be more fully aware of a world where competition is strong and the market is saturated. I came to realize the stakes that participants of that world—including my son—were up against. I hadn't seen how high those stakes were before, because I had embraced the ideology of the world. The sociologist in me was overjoyed—the mother in me panic-stricken. I tried to retreat and find ways for my son to leave this milieu and find another field of study and work. But I failed, for the bonds between him and the soloist elite were too tightly wound for his escape.

I found myself in somewhat of a predicament with my dual role as a sociologist and virtuoso parent. I couldn't just break with my fieldwork and devote myself to writing a distanced account. I felt that I knew everything and had seen all that was to be seen; then I found myself in a new world—that of a laboratory of life-science researchers. I am still involved in this research and I am testing the accuracy of my theoretical propositions in the world of life-science researchers. I try to see how the careers of researchers are working and if the relationships between participants are of similar nature to those in the virtuoso violinist's world. I took a new interest in my study. It had become a field that I couldn't seem to escape. I think I'm far from being through with my investigations; then again, can anybody be through with learning about relationships that keep evolving? Taking the wrong way is endemic to researchers who study their own world. The following anecdote can stand as an illustration.

As the mother of a soloist-to-be, at the moment that I thought I know almost all from my first fieldwork—the world of the soloist—I had gotten in touch with a professor who specialized in teaching soloists. After the initial audition, he had failed to offer to accept my son into his class (at university), because it was full. He congratulated him on the performance and wished the young musician a successful career. I had the feeling this encounter was a failure but thought it strange that he had not advised me to get in touch with another professor, as they usually do in such cases. I did get in touch with another teacher, who now happens to be my favorite informant. She had attended a soloist class ten years ago as a student. When I told her what had happened, she claimed that it meant the professor was interested in the student, but wanted to give him some private lessons before committing more seriously and accepting him into his class. This explained why he hadn't suggested another teacher. I then got in touch with the professor again for private lessons, and he indeed accepted. It took the explanation of this other teacher for me to be able to understand this situation fully. This is, in fact, the main drawback of acquiring deep knowledge of a world by seeing things from the point of view of one category of participant, and not the different points of view of several categories of people. Despite everything, one tends to partially adopt the point of view of the category one belongs to and to lack the necessary distance to encompass the whole world. This situation requires watchfulness; one must make sure not to be lulled into assuming a familiarity with the fieldwork. If one cannot break from it, one must go on observing. I continue to do so, for I'm a prisoner in my field, just as Bronislaw Malinowski was stuck on the Trobriand Islands (during his internment at the start of World War I).

Postscript

One year after I wrote this book, we left France. I could now partially distance myself from the elite violin field. I changed my realm of investigation, and began working on the elite careers of biology scientists, whose international environment is in some aspects similar to the artistic world. I still correspond with some of the violinists I met, and from time to time, I take the opportunity to interview one of them. We no longer live in a Parisian home with a slew of guests, but sometimes we take in a violinist or pianist who is traveling through our city. In these instances, we talk until the early morning about all these people that we know, their careers, and lives—reminiscing over past memories.

I hope that this book has successfully conveyed their experiences, hopes, emotions, and desires. I sincerely hope that the former virtuoso students are happy with their music and that their tremendously hard work provides them wonderful moments of success. They deserve appreciation for their tremendous activity and impressive talent, which grows as they overcome many difficulties and obstacles. I am grateful for their trust and candor, and I thank all participants for their knowledge. I learned with them and from them. This research constitutes ten years of strong emotional involvement in their world, which I hope I have come (at least partially) to understand. I aimed to present what was hidden behind these "genius performers." I believe the musicians will agree with me when I state that their level of playing is dependent on hard work, and that the soloist education is not only a musical education, but also, and perhaps foremost, a social process.

Notes

INTRODUCTION

1. I use the word soloist as defined by D. L. Westby (1960: 225): "A soloist status—this term means here a self-employed entrepreneur, a free agent, not to the first men of the wind section, who are also referred to as soloists. Instead, such names as Menuhin, Heifetz, Serkin, and Rubinstein come immediately to mind."

2. My book concerns people perceived by professionals in their field as people who, by virtue of their occupation, are members of an international elite.

3. Soloists are considered young up to the age of twenty-five.

4. My role is comparable to Adlers' "parent-as-researcher" role (Adler and Adler 1991). The couple studied adolescent culture, from the world of their children and their peers (Adler and Adler 1998).

5. In the soloist world, a long period without any contact from someone does not mean that the ties are broken (see Wagner 2004 about the special ties in the artistic elite world).

6. The name is changed for reasons of confidentiality, as are all names in this book.

7. The master class is a particular form of musical education devoted to the "best" and most highly motivated students. Soloist class students are enrolled regularly in those classes, which are organized during short periods and includes daily lessons, frequent concerts of teachers and students—all those events taking place in attractive places: sea or countryside towns, manors, and other prestigious sites.

CHAPTER 1 A SHORT HISTORY OF THE VIOLIN VIRTUOSO PROFESSION

1. This classification is also practiced in other worlds of vocational training, such as in sociology. J. M. Chapoulie, in his historical book about Chicago sociologists, provides a detailed account of such transfer of knowledge dependences (Chapoulie 2001).

2. Mozart was not the first "enfant prodige" but one of the most famous. About genius kids see Hausfater 1993: 73–85.

3. See A. Penesco, L'estro Paganiniano et son empreinte jusqu'à nos jours (1997).

4. See Joachim and Moser 1905; Waldemar 1969.

5. The twentieth century and the first part of the nineteenth were for the virtuoso violinists what the twentieth and twenty-first centuries are for actors and other show-business activities.

6. We can find similar examples of centers of virtuoso training today; the same beneficial factors present in Berlin before 1933 are significant today in these chosen cities listed at the end of this chapter.

7. "The sun-browned skin of this beautiful man—Kubelik made his public really crazy, especially women. When he performed one extremely difficult piece after other, women threw their diamonds on the stage; I saw it on my own eyes! Then the curtain went down and . . . probably their servants picked up the jewels. Then the curtain opened and Kubelik appeared again, and the spectacle continued." This anecdote was given by Milstein in Milstein and Volkov (1990: 14, French edition).

8. After World War II the Conservatory of Paris progressively lost its dominant position and reputation as the best place for violin virtuoso training.

9. Edicts of the czar prohibited Jews from residence in the city center.

10. Their trajectories were typical for the virtuoso of the first part of the twentieth century. This wave of musical emigration inspired George Gershwin (himself the child of Russian-Jewish immigrants) to compose a song that became a hit (in 1932, with lyrics by Arthur Francis):

When we were three years old or so
We all began to play the fiddle,
In darkest Russia.
When we began, our notes were sour,
Until a man, Professor Auer,
Set out to show us, one and all,
How we shall pack them in—in Carnegie Hall.
Names like Sammy, Max, or Moe,
Never bring the heavy dough—Just
Mischa, Jascha, Toscha, Sascha,
Fiddle, fiddle dee.

Qtd. in Schwarz (1983: 447)

11. Numerous artists came to Sverdlovsk, a town in Siberia, during World War II, because Stalin decided that artists should be protected from German occupation and the dangers of war in order to protect Soviet culture.

12. It is important to mention that musicians emigrated not only from Russia but from other Eastern European countries. However, for example, the eastern part of current-day Poland was officially part of the Russian Empire until November 1918.

13. The Palestine Symphonic Orchestra was created in 1936 by Bronislaw Huberman, a Polish-trained musician. In 1948, this orchestra became the Israel Symphonic Orchestra; in *Baker's Biographical Dictionary of 20th-Century Classical Musicians*, 597.

14. As one Israeli professor I interviewed noted, when compared with the Soviet Union or the United States, for example, Israel has a high number of soloists proportionate to its population.

15. Ashkenazi Jews—a population that emerged around the second millennium—settled in Central and Eastern Europe. They created the Yiddish language.

16. For more information see http://internationalsuzuki.org/. It is worth noting that an international meeting of Suzuki method practitioners in Japan in 2013 had 5,400 participants. The method has become the most popular way to teach classical music.

17. In the sciences, this phenomenon of massive emigration by scientists is commonly called "brain drain."

CHAPTER 2   BEFORE ENTERING THE SOLOIST CLASS

1. Violin practice requires specific behaviors (static body position, concentration on specific movements of the arms and fingers), which is contrary to a child's natural, spontaneous, restless behavior.

2. Vibrato—specific technique that requires left-hand skills.

3. Positions—placing the left hand on the fingerboard.

4. Though it is difficult to give the age limit of entrance into a soloist class, the majority of violinists join these classes at the age of ten (the youngest student I saw was a six-year-old

Korean girl). Most of these very young performers are Asian. When they enter into a soloist class, the students had already taken violin classes for at least two to three years.

5. These results were obtained from the study of biographies contained in B. Schwarz's book (1983).

6. Bustabo was an American violinist (1917–2002), and well known in the United States as a child prodigy; she played her first concert at the age of four (Baker's Biographical Dictionary of 20th Century Classical Musicians, 1997: 194).

7. The soloist classes in Europe do not have any specific appellation. Their students find each other by the teacher's name. Some teachers use the term "soloist student," and sometimes they add the adjective "international." I also heard the expression: "the stable of [teacher's name]" in the informal discussion between parents and between teachers.

8. Solfeggio (do, re, mi, etc.) contains the basic information in theory and musical practice that allow the students to play an instrument (in classical music education).

9. In order to enlarge this analysis, you can find in the literature the description of a musical audition by Nancy Huston (1999: 55).

10. Some parents, in a race for this qualification, show their child to many violinists, waiting for the verdict. They find a teacher who declares their child "very gifted" and then choose that teacher.

11. In the soloist-student world, two categories of agents are active: professional and amateur. The first is frequently not involved in the production of young soloists in Europe, due to legislation prohibiting work by children under the age of sixteen. For amateur agents, meanwhile, the performances of young musicians constitute their a principal volunteer occupation (officially, the musicians do not earn money from these concerts, but benefactor pay for master classes, scores, lessons, travel, etc.)

12. Soloist classes thus differ from the general school system, when children in the same class are of the same age.

CHAPTER 3   TRIAD COLLABORATION—TEACHER, PARENTS, AND CHILD

1. Violinists use rosin for their bow to obtain friction necessary to produce sound.

2. Open strings means the right hand plays without the left (which usually places fingers on the strings). With this exercise, violinists develop their bowing sound and technique.

3. The musical scale is an arrangement of notes in ascending or descending order of pitch: the scale of C major.

4. Détaché is a bowing technique in which each movement is played separately.

5. A mordent is an ornament consisting of one rapid alternation of a written note with the note immediately above or below it on the scale.

6. C is the note here.

7. In music, *becare* means to neutralize the sharp and flat.

8. Forte: loud.

9. *Rallentando:* slowing down.

10. Trill: rapid alternation of notes.

11. Crescendo: a gradual increase in loudness.

12. Anselm Strauss (1992) illustrates this relationship between teacher and student as a game of pressures in the interaction between master and disciple.

13. Maxim Vengerov, born in 1974 in Novosibirsk, Russia, is a famous European violin soloist.

14. American violin master Dorothy DeLay illustrates the teacher's exemplary power: "DeLay is hardly just a nice lady who teaches the fiddle. For more than half a century, she has been a power-behind-the-throne, unknown outside the classical music world but a legend within it. It is a world in which all the standard emotions—ambition, greed, hunger for power, desire for self-expression, approval, recognition, friendship, love, and so on—are present in greater or lesser degree, as they are when it comes to striving for a major career in any field" (Lourie-Sand 2000: 16).

15. Ruggierro Ricci, American violinist born in 1918. He is providing his opinion about ambitious parents—the opinion is based on his own experience; Ricci's father was very ambitious and Ricci is said to have had a sad childhood.

16. Fingering: the technical indication supplemental to the notes.

17. Perestroika—the word refers to the reconstruction of the Soviet economy, but also signifies the end of the communist period. Political and economic changes in postcommunist Eastern European nations modified teacher behavior in ways that affected the world of soloists. Before perestroika, it was frequently said that the best students benefitted from free lessons. Now this is rare, especially with teachers who have emigrated, who feel no requirement to give free lessons and say they need money for retirement. Most of these teachers are over forty-five years old, and feel a need to make up for lost time. Throughout Europe, parents now pay for lessons.

18. In Europe, it is rare for parents to be required to make major investments in a child's education. Some examples of prices: one sixty-minute lesson: 30 to 200 euros; strings (changed every two to four months)—40 to 150 euros or more; change of bow hair (four times a year): 30 to 100 euros; music school, in France, per year: up to 1,700 euros; master class (at least two per year): 400 to 1,500 euros; accompanist fee, per hour: 30 euros.

19. Excerpt from *Diapason*, February 2001 interview with V. Repin (27). Repin is an international violin soloist, born in the Soviet Union in 1971. For the violinist, it is important to have an excellent violin and a good bow. A good bow can cost thousands of euros. Kittel is a renowned bow-maker.

20. I have observed families who organize the student's life: participation in the master's class and competitions, study in soloist summer classes and at music school. The parent and student meets with the teacher several times a week—or each day; during summer they plan their holidays including regular lessons or participation in competitions.

21. A sentence heard several times during my study.

22. In France, Italy, and Spain, children stay at school until 4:30 P.M. The homework and a long commute to school are incompatible with intensive and lengthy instrumental practice.

23. Exercises developing the technical basis of violin playing.

24. Sight-reading is the first playing of an unfamiliar musical piece.

25. In other countries, where the school day finishes at about 2 P.M., going to school becomes very difficult for those older than twelve, who begin to practice more intensively. They frequently miss most of their school day for their violin education.

26. Journalist Dorota Szwarcman wrote about the parent-musicians of young soloists: "They know how to get a scholarship, how to get into the master classes, how to organize the concerts. These parents become the impresarios of their own children, supporting them [in the musician world] with their own authority." In *Wprost*, no. 32 [Warsaw] (August 2000).

27. Maxim Vengerov: from a biography broadcast on Muzzik channel.

28. Enesco was a famous twentieth-century violin soloist.

29. This is the story originated from the Russian novel by Vinogradov Anatoli, *The Condemnation of Paganini*, published originally in 1936.

30. Grade on the metronome scale.

31. See chapter 4 for an example of this observation concerning the master class.

32. About the preparation of American students in sixth grade and parental behavior, see the very thought-provoking paper of Chin (2000).

33. These concerts were organized by different associations and took place in churches, small concert halls, and private homes.

34. The majority of professors who teach Asian-culture students state that they are exemplary students who like work, obey their teacher, and apply all advice. "They are the best students in the world. They follow their teacher blindly, but in the arms of a bad teacher, it is very dangerous; it is a catastrophe," a French violin teacher said. "With a good teacher, they have excellent results, especially when they are kids. Then one day the problems with interpretation start, because for becoming an artist, you need to impose your own interpretation of the music. They do not have this capacity; but in work, they are the best. It is fascinating, terrific, and scary at the same time."

35. In regard to the analysis of work (see, e.g., Donald Roy 2001), I examine the problem of resistance to work in the instrumental practice of soloist students. I believe that this intensive instrumental practice constitutes work, and therefore, the concept of work resistance is appropriate for this activity.

36. Kreutzer was active at the time when violin performance was not under similar conditions as today—the difference is in the technical expectations and education of a public listening to CD recordings. The standards of performance (especially in tuning) before high fidelity systems were different. For more information concerning virtuoso practice, see Schwarz 1983.

37. Hall (1949) shows this for physicians; F. Reif and A. Strauss (1965) and S. Cole and J. R. Cole (1967) for physicists; C. Paradeise (1998) for actors; and N. Heinich (2000) for writers.

38. See, for example, H. Becker (1963) or Ph. Coulangeon (1998, 1999) concerning jazz musicians. For the specific process of construction of reputation in the case of the soloist and the teacher—the coupling career process—see Wagner (2006b).

39. The previous year Monique had spent two weeks with her family at the campus grounds in the south of France.

40. My research (Wagner 2006a) suggests that many students are expatriates or possess dual nationality status. This is a relatively recent phenomenon, most pronounced in the classes of teachers who originate from Eastern Europe. To maintain the high level of their teaching, they move with their best students (Wagner 2010).

41. This formulation was used in the letter of recommendation of the president of a musical association included in the family's housing case file.

42. These examples—French students educated in Switzerland, Swiss students educated in France—illustrate the complexity of virtuoso education.

43. This aspect concerns principally children between the age of seven and fifteen.

44. For details of this study, see Wagner 2006a.

45. See, for example, the finalists of one important competition, the Queen Elisabeth in Brussels. Between 1937 and 1980, out of fifteen violinists who were winners of first and second places, thirteen originated from the USSR. Between 1980 and 1997, out of ten finalists, only two were Russian, three from Eastern European countries but educated by Russian teachers, and five from Asia. The rise of Asian-origin winners is a clear tendency.

46. Soviet musicians' careers depended on the Soviet state agency for concerts, which could refuse even famous artists permission to play outside Eastern Europe. Some musicians immigrated to Israel or to the United States through Israel, using their Jewish origin as a motive for departure. Some waited for permission from emigration services for more than a year; during this time, they were blacklisted: no concerts, funding, travel, or assistance so that they would receive a passport.

47. The information books are printed at almost every competition.

48. Dorothy DeLay (1917–2002) was a violin instructor at the Juilliard School, generally regarded as the most influential American violin teacher of the late twentieth century.

49. These are the soloist classes not belonging institutionally to the Juilliard School of Music—the students are generally younger than seventeen.

50. This section concerns classes and private lessons in Paris, Moscow, Vienna, Polish cities, New York, and Philadelphia.

51. This excellent piano in a violin soloist class indicates the reputation of the teaching. Usually, the best pianos are not in a class in which only accompanists play.

52. An exception is Dorothy DeLay's class, still merely no. 530 in the Juilliard School of Music (Lourie-Sand 2000: 79).

53. Their role is interesting. Often, students need a place for practicing; for acoustic reasons, the teacher's class is better than practice rooms, and the caretaker is important, controlling key distribution (sometimes a commercial arrangement is made between students and the caretaker).

54. Good acoustics, a piano that works well, enough space for practicing, a place for public lessons, and the possibility of public performances for each student.

55. Ivan Galamian was Auer's student, and may have wanted to imitate Auer's Old World class setting.

56. We can find several examples of these descriptions in the autobiographies of violinists such as Jacques Thibaud (1947); and in the biography of David Oistrakh in J. Jouzefowitch (1978).

57. I speak of the dynasty, not in the genealogical sense, but the personal relationship between master and disciple, extended down the generations of soloist classes.

58. Similar phenomena exist in noble and bourgeois families; see Béatrix La Wita (1988).

59. Proximity with the elite world can be beneficial remarks one physics student, cited by Hermanowicz (1998: 48), who said, "You swim with Olympic swimmers, you behave like one."

60. Created in 1912 in Odessa, Ukraine, by violinist Pyotr Solomonovitch Stoliarsky, this school became a "talent factory." After 1917, it became the state school of music in the USRR.

61. Sviatoslav Richter was a pianist. The violin class conducted by the creator of the school, Pyotr Stoliarsky, was the most famous class. David Oistrakh and Elizaveta Gilels were famous Soviet violin performers.

62. Becker (2002) showed that the nature of jazz locales impacted musicians' performances.

63. The student does not play for the teacher but observes lessons of others students.

64. About the development of musical capacities and instrumental practice, see, for example, the works of Wronski (1979).

65. According to *Guide de concours* (1999/2000: 21), "Among competitions organized in Europe are some created for very young musicians. The majority of competitions are inscribed in l'Union Européenne des concours de musique pour la jeunesse (UECM/EMCY European Union of Music Competitions for Youth)."

66. See ethnographical study conducted by Hilary Levey Friedman (2013) about the competitions as a particular contemporary culture—a part of the education of primary school kids (in a field of dance, chess, and youth travel soccer). Also, for the system of competition in Canadian ice hockey, see the article by J. Poupart (1999: 163–179).

67. Here I develop those aspects that are important during the first stage of education.

68. This is why I will discuss the question of competitions at each stage.

69. In order to define the art school concept, I use Florian Znaniecki's definition: "Art school is the community bound by the personal relationships between the [artists] contemporary and their successors, also tied to the similar canons of beauty and the instruction of method" (1937: 510).

70. This prohibition is the subject of numerous anecdotes. At an important competition, one jurist asked the other—a woman over seventy—what relationship tied her to a twenty-two-year-old competitor, whom she was said to favor. "Perhaps the next question will be if I slept with him?" she responded angrily.

71. I discuss the relativity of these criteria later.

72. Except figure skating, gymnastics, etc.

73. In the third part of the book, I describe goals of competition participants.

74. The majority of competitors use an official accompanist who works with competitors. This is a paid service.

75. This kind of mechanism, in which the access to the information is crucial, occurs in other social organizations of similar features (such as competitions based on problematic selection related to the quality ambiguity: beauty contests, fashion contests, or dance competitions).

76. Among numerous examples of support, I can provide a crucial one: lending a prestigious violin for competition. In the case of young students in competitions, the majority play an instrument made in the twentieth century, which is considered moderately good. Three candidates in this competition had "exceptional" violins made in the eighteenth century by Italian violin makers (the price of each was over $1 million). The first was played by a Russian candidate, who borrowed the instrument from a Russian national collection. The second, played by a German candidate, was borrowed from a private sponsor. The third was played by an Italian participant and belonged to the player's family, which was a rare exception in several competitions I had observed.

77. By doing so, jury members make sure that they will teach students of a high level.

78. Here we will observe the phenomenon called by Erving Goffman "cooling the mark out": in the case of competition failure, the teacher will perform cooling the mark out by the readaptation of the goal and the redefinition of failure (Goffman 1952).

CHAPTER 4   CRISIS AND CAREER COUPLING

1. We should keep in mind that the age limitation is not strict. We can find in this group students younger than ten years old as well as late adolescence students; this is why the examples given in this chapter concern not only teenagers.

2. This is the age of youth in crisis—see more in the classical psychological literature (Erikson 1968, 1980; Stephen, Fraser, and Marcia 1992).

3. For several examples, see Schwarz (1983).

4. Most will take the baccalaureate exam at age eighteen or nineteen.

5. In the past, the majority of boy prodigies played in shorts.

6. I followed a cohort of young violinists over ten years; based on that work I can estimate which trajectory is less or more frequent.

7. Philippe Coulangeon (1998) remarked on this phenomenon in his study of jazz musicians.

8. The study by Dominique Defoort-Lafourcade, concerning the Conservatory of Paris students, indicates that the choice of these special classes is infrequently adopted by the young people who hope to become professional instrumentalists (Defoort-Lafourcade 1996).

9. The French science baccalaureate, required for entrance to many good graduate schools, is considered very difficult.

10. In the French, Italian, and Spanish school systems, students are kept until 5 P.M. This way, parents are ensured that their children are supervised.

11. Students under sixteen need official permission to study this way; a letter from the violin teacher, prizes from competitions, and good grades in general school are required. Today, this course operates through the Internet.

12. Also see the biographies of Oïstrakh, Thibaud, Menuhin, Stern, Wilkomirska, Bacewicz, Yankelevich, and others. A contrasting presentation is provided in the book of N. Milstein and S. Volkov (1988). Milstein strongly criticizes soloist education.

13. This type of class is described in chapter 5 on the master class. I observed eight teachers who work in a similar manner.

14. As well as benefiting from my previous occupation, I was able to present myself as a specialist in musical pedagogy.

15. An Arabic market, because of its crowding, is used to describe a crowded, seemingly disorganized place.

16. While aware that I am a sociologist, Andriej knows me more as a music teacher.

17. The difficulties of the organizer probably contributed to the lack of publicity.

18. Teachers commonly allow students to make lesson recordings, which they can use to support practice at home.

19. Waxmann's "Carmen," based on variations upon the theme of the Bizet opera, is a classic virtuoso piece. In the observations notes I did not change the repertoire.

20. *Ruhe* means silent.

21. *Nicht so laut* means not so loud.

22. "Tune" refers to intonation, one of the major problems of violinists and other musicians whose instruments are not "tempered" like pianos and guitars, on which notes are broken into distinct halftones. In violin, viola, cello, and bass, the musician can produce several sounds between two notes, but it requires great mastery to play the right ones. A false note can result from a one-millimeter movement of the left hand.

23. *Cantilena* means a smooth melodic line.

24. In this case *stretto* is a passage in a faster tempo.

25. *Rubato*—temporary disregard for strict tempo to allow an expressive quickening or slackening, usually without altering the overall pace.

26. *Accelerando* is quickening the tempo.

27. *Leggiero*–lightly.

28. Quite frequently, teachers would tap their student on the back, arm, or neck, in order to check for excess tension.

29. For an example, see Hughes 1996: 72.

30. Such teachers often have an unusual technique themselves and are convinced that it is superior, so they systematically correct almost all their students. Such corrections are a source of professional satisfaction every bit as important as the work of interpretation. This approach is rare. I met only two teachers who work like this.

31. The corrections here concerned certain aspects of her playing position and no radical changes. Changing the position of the bow or left hand (of the violin) is called "playing position change."

32. They are not the parents of the student being discussed.

33. This violinist speaks about a virtuoso piece for violin and piano "Fantasy on the theme of Carmen by G. Bizet" written by Pablo Sarasate.

34. I do not address here the sexist character of these remarks.

35. Since the collapse of the USSR, the system of free virtuoso education is weaker, and parents must support professional training by themselves. While the state saw to the education of "gifted children" in the past, today the family bears more of the burden. When in a given country the official system of virtuoso education is working well (which means that advanced students can obtain supplementary violin lessons within the music school system) a family's financial situation is less important. In the case of master classes (paid, short-term events) the situation is more dependent on familial investment. The importance of the family's financial status is complex; family spending may be unnecessary at the higher levels thanks to public support for such education.

36. Some students have a strong conviction that they need a particular master and not another for this education. This conviction could be the result of the teacher's goal, which is to secure their students' certitude, not only in order to gain their confidence, but also to validate their choice of teacher, and in doing so, fortify their own position.

37. The son of David Oistrakh, Igor Oistrakh, was a famous violinist and presently is a soloist teacher in Belgium.

38. All my interviewees knew that I had graduated from a music school and that I understood the musical (especially the violin) side of their education process.

39. David Oistrakh had a reputation of being a teacher with great heart. His students always underlined the exceptional "human" character of the relationships that he developed with his disciples.

40. I am grateful to Paul DiMaggio for his remark about the absence of the gender issue in my book.

41. Sociologists need to be attentive to distortions implicit when people are asked about a situation years earlier. The informant's opinion can change. In my interviews, soloist class students tended to be more positive about their earlier relationships but negative about their current teachers.

42. We will examine this question in chapter 5.

43. Here the teacher's expression about the Gypsy origin of Gino is discriminating in a double way: positive and negative. Positive because he is recognizing that Gino, thanks to his Gypsy origin, has musical talent (in the discussion before citation), and negative, because he is saying that Gino has no brain. In fact this is a very stereotypical and foolish example of injurious prejudices—typical for people educated in Eastern Europe. Unfortunately in the world of music we could also meet the worse human attitude: racism is also present among violin teachers.

44. Sarasate was a Spanish composer and violin virtuoso.

45. "Newhouse gives an amiable smile and says . . . 'When the kids are taking their exams, the phone sometimes rings non-stop. It is reminiscent of Secretary of State Kissinger, saying, 'This isn't governing—this is crisis management.'" Newhouse, husband of violin teacher Dorothy DeLay, cited in Lourie-Sand (2000: 38).

46. Margot's lesson was a typical "quiet period" lesson, while Jane's could be considered a "crisis time" lesson, although it was not prolonged.

47. David Nadien is a concertmaster of the New York Philharmonic Orchestra.

48. See, in this chapter, the section about the student's perception of teachers and the example concerning Galamian's students—as well as Steinhardt's.

49. The transformation of a teacher's apartment into a workplace is very common. One student told me that his teacher, a single woman without children, had transformed her four-room apartment so that a student could practice in each room while awaiting a lesson.

50. This closeness is very convenient for both parties; if the student lives with the teacher, he or she is always available for a lesson. On the other hand, if the teacher is preparing a student for a competition, he or she cannot leave on a family vacation; time must be organized around continual violin lessons.

51. This was reported by former students of Auer and Galamian during their first months in the United States after fleeing the October Revolution in the Soviet Union.

52. In Europe, most professors teach in several schools. If this is the case, the teacher chooses one of the schools for the new student, based on convenience, reputation, cost, or other issues such as the new student's requirement to participate in other classes.

53. The more senior teacher helps his assistant this way, providing him short- or longer-term students.

54. One of the important indicators of the place in the hierarchy of teachers is participation as a judge in international competitions.

55. Social benefits in some European countries make up the 20 percent of the salary devoted to health insurance and retirement pension. These are important factors of state employment in Europe.

56. Mireille was the class's star student before Sarah joined it.

57. I analyze international competition and master classes together, because for my purposes they are similar.

58. The youngest and oldest participants are less involved in social activities during competitions; the youngest are with their parents, and some of the oldest come in pairs or stay with the people they already knew.

59. In most competitions there are three stages, and each candidate prepares three different performances. Typically, competitors in the first part of the program listen to other participants only after finishing their own performance. They do this to protect themselves from being influenced—or discouraged—by the earlier performance. Violinists often play the same piece of music in each stage.

60. International dimensions aside, the relationships among young violinists are comparable to relationships among the young basketball players studied by Adler and Adler (1991).

61. This manner of referring to soloists who reach celebrity status is a common motif among students of a soloist class, who are aware that at a given moment, they belong to the same world as those who will lead the soloist milieu.

62. Singular compared to the experiences of other young people, but nonprofessional musicians.

63. We can find a similar mechanism of mutual recognition and the shared pleasures of common culture, for example, in the phenomenon of fans (see Segré 2001).

64. The following excerpt, cited earlier, illustrates this well. "Now I will introduce you to Frank. He is only four years older than you, but he plays everywhere. It will be good for you to meet him. It is good to be seen in his company. He doesn't play better than you, far from it. But he copes very well in order to play a lot."

65. The distinction practices are frequently present in the construction of a new identity, as in the case of religious conversion studied, among others, by Arnold Rose (1971)

66. For examples, European university exchange programs (Socrates, Erasmus) and the practice of business schools to host a semester or year abroad.

67. The immigration of Eastern European teachers to Israel was very significant in the 1960s and 1970s.

68. The international organization of the soloist milieu is similar to the professional internationalism described by Emil Durkheim: "In our day an internationalism of an entirely new type has appeared—professional internationalism. The rapprochement did not operate exclusively from people to people, but from professional group to professional group of the same order. One saw similar workers of different countries join directly in associations more or less durable, more or less organized—in spite of national hostilities—and the drawing together of

peoples resulted from this instead of being its initial cause. In succession, there were established international societies of scholars, artists, industrials, workers, financiers, etc., which went on specializing further as they multiplied, and which, because of the increasing regularity of their functioning, soon become an important factor of European civilization. . . . Professional sentiments and interests are endowed with a far greater universality. They are much less variable from country to country among like categories of workers, whereas they are different from one profession to another, within the same country. The result is that the corporative spirit sometimes tends to bind similar corporations of different European societies more tightly than different corporations in the same society. Thus, national spirit encounters a formidable antagonist which it did not recognize until then, and as a result, conditions are exceptionally favorable for the development of internationalism" (1958: 173–174).

69. In the early twentieth century among the Jewish bourgeoisie of Europe, playing violin was part of regular education. The traditions of professional musical education were also widespread among Jewish families before World War II. Within my sample, several students who originated from Eastern Europe emphasized their Jewish roots. This aspect was rarely pointed out despite its clear origin. The large presence of Jewish musicians in Eastern Europe started under tsarist jurisdiction. The members of Jewish communities were not allowed to live in the center of towns, except in rare cases. One of the exceptions was the enrollment of a child from a Jewish family in music conservatories. Immediately the whole family received the privilege of residing in the center of the city. That derogation was (in parallel with the great value placed on education) an important factor (for social and economical position, as well as physical safety as Jewish districts were under the constant danger of pogroms). This explains why so many bourgeois Jewish families offered their children the highest level of musical education (Milstein and Volkov 1990). For more than one hundred years, the success of numerous children originating from Jewish families is, in part, due to the factor of extended hosting, such as having a network of relatives living in several places throughout the world. One of the most famous examples is the pianist Arthur Rubinstein, who, as a child, lived in Berlin in his aunt's house. This familial hosting network is efficient not only for Jewish students but also for those originating from other cultures, which constitute ethnic diasporas (Armenian and post-1917 Russians). This crucial factor contributes to the high mobility of young children, which may lead to their later success in soloist careers.

70. In his book, *Great Masters of Violin,* Schwarz (1983) describes how the Russians came to impose their playing norms in the early twentieth century.

71. It is worthy to notice that traditional Asian music is based on scales that have smaller units than conventional European scales. In Western music the unit is a half tone, whereas throughtout Asia we can find so-called quarter-tones. Perhaps, this difference influences the capacity of Asians to listen to smaller variations in music tuning. This is why the expectations of playing "in tune" were higher with the massive participation of Asian violinists. In parallel with these modifications, technical innovations in recording and distribution—the digital and CD revolutions—also contributed to the change of quality performance norms.

72. For teachers and their students in an ordinary music class, on the other hand, acceptance at the CNSMP in Paris or Lyon is synonymous with success and constitutes the outcome of lengthy study in music school.

73. For example, Laurent Korcia went to the Royal College of Music in London to study with Felix Andrievski; Virginie Robillard studied at Juilliard in Dorothy DeLay's class; Marie-Annick Nicolas completed her study in Moscow with Boris Bielinski and David Oistrakh; Pierre Amoyal worked with Jascha Heifetz in Los Angeles, and Renaud Capucon worked in Berlin with Thomas Brandys.

74. It is very difficult to provide an exact number of violin students trained in U.S. virtuoso classes. However, in 2013/14 at Juilliard (21), Indiana University (8), and Curtis Institute (7) it was thirty-three teachers (three worked in two mentioned places in parallel); each of them work with about ten to fifteen students at different ages and levels. All of these students, because they have enrolled in those prestigious institutions, are enrolled in intensive training and virtuoso education. This is probably a group of over three hundred young musicians intensively studying the violin.

75. For foreign students, a long-stay visa covers social benefits—health insurance included.

76. According to A.-C. Wagner, "scholar strategies and international models of excellence are distinct from those of French scholar elites and the 'nobles of the state'" (1995: 550).

77. Among foreigner violin students we find increasing numbers of Asian students coming from Eastern Europe, but a few of those came from the United States. Even if virtuoso culture (dominated by Russian teachers' traditions) influences the style of teaching and shape the relationship between teacher and student, both European and American virtuoso markets are separate, and the structures of music education are not the same. In the United States the majority of virtuoso classes are within the university or in a specific school of music; mostly these are private institutions; in the EU, the places of excellence for violin training are mostly state institutions. This diversity of nationalities, accompanied by social homogeneity, is often discernible in other milieus. A.-C. Wagner remarks that, in the case of international managers' families, "the mixing of the nationalities is parallel to the social homogeneity of the circles of sociability" (1995: 544).

CHAPTER 5   ENTRANCE INTO ADULT CAREERS

1. Switching from one teacher to another is commonly considered treason in the elite musical world.

2. This phenomenon was examined by H. Becker (1963: chap. 6).

3. This kind of networking is not peculiar to the soloist world. It exists among parents who want to help their children obtain jobs in different worlds of work, independent of social origin: see, for example, Newman (1999: 77–82).

4. In some performances, both musicians have important roles to play (for example, in the Brahms sonata repertoire).

5. Pianists' education is usually longer than that of violinists; they rarely seek a soloist position before the age of twenty-five. At that time they may decide on (or be obliged to accept) a career accompanying violinists or other instrumentalists. Violin accompaniment is a highly valued position because of the quality and range of the repertoire.

6. The repertoire of chamber music for violin and piano is most often sonatas in which the musicians share the spotlight, rather than a violin virtuoso repertoire.

7. If musicians are of the opposite sex, they correspond to the myth of a perfect couple, which the audience appreciates. Some teachers and concert organizers feel it is easier to market musicians who are a young couple.

8. The teachers, young virtuosos, and sometimes their parents solicit conductors who have a good reputation in the market, because those who do not have that reputation do not have the power of launching a musical career. The collaboration with someone who does not have a reputation could be perceived negatively by participants, who can conclude that the violinist plays with a "bad" conductor because he is not able to play with a reputed one. Conclusion: the violinist will be judged as "not good enough."

9. The girl had won international competitions and performed in important concert halls; however, she did not belong to a famous soloist class, which is crucial to furthering one's career.

10. See several examples in Lourie-Sand (2000).

11. In the earlier period of the relationship between a conductor and a violinist, the latter follows the conductor's lead, while a more seasoned soloist can impose her or his own interpretation of a piece. The soloist who debuts has scant likelihood of negotiating with a seasoned conductor.

12. The concertmaster is a member of the orchestra and of the violinists, and makes decisions about all technical questions concerning the violin part (for example, bow movement).

13. This relationship is described in Faulkner (1983), Lehman (2002), and François (2000).

14. The concert was organized in conjunction with a festival in the city.

15. More and more frequently for international competitions, violinists must apply by sending a video recording.

16. Baroque musicians, meanwhile, are more likely to play rare pieces. See Pierre François (2000).

17. See Gilmore (1987).

18. See Pâris (1995) *Dictionaire des Interprêtes*, 570.

19. Szymanowski originated from a noble Polish family and possessed property in the Ukraine. After the revolution of 1917, he lost his property and went to live with his mother and sister in Warsaw, where he was obliged to take a job as a teacher in the conservatory. He performed several concert tours as a pianist, but suffered from tuberculosis that often confined him to his house in the Tatra Mountains. The help of Kochanski and other Western supporters allowed Szymanowski to make several professional tours (Paris, Spain, United States).

20. For most performers, the career ends with death, while a composer's fame may grow long after he or she has passed away. There are exceptions, of course, such as Glenn Gould or Samson François.

21. Representatives of big international booking agencies (e.g., Sarfati, in France).

22. Here "good" means an instrument with which a soloist can show his or her mastery.

23. The value of a violin depends on several factors: its origin, the name of the violin maker, and the year of production (for example, Stradivari violins produced around 1715 are worth more than those from 1690). A violin's biography can also be a factor—prices rise for instruments that have been in the hands of famous players. Certain violins produced by Guarnerius del Gesù or Amati can sell for much more than a Stradivaris.

24. The situation of violinists is particular because their finest instruments cost so much more than others. Wind instruments and pianos must be acquired new, and in any case pianists play concerts and practice on different instruments. A "good" piano may cost from 100,000 to 150,000 euros; violin prices continue to climb, so that banks and investors now buy them as investments. In a transaction at Christie's on May 16, 2006, in New York, a Stradivarius sold for $3,544,000 after five minutes of bidding.

25. With the high prices of old violins and their limited number, violinists have great difficulties acquiring one.

26. The system of loaning these violins is very complex.

27. This student uses "us" speaking about her family, because she was the last to benefit from the support of this violin maker after her brother, a cellist, and sister, a violinist; both are professional musicians.

28. The maintenance and restoration of old violins is difficult. An article by Thomas Wagner of the Associated Press on February 14, 2008 ["Can his fractured fiddle—a million dollar Guadagnini—be fixed? It's too early to tell."] described a repair effort undertaken on behalf of virtuoso David Garrett, who tripped while carrying his eighteenth-century violin as he was leaving London's Barbican Hall after a performance. "I had it over my shoulder in its case and I fell down a concrete flight of stairs backward," Garrett said. "When I opened the case, much of my G. B. Guadagnini had been crushed." Garrett said he bought the 1772 violin for $1 million in 2003, and was hoping to get it repaired in New York, where he was based. "I hope and pray that it can be fixed, but if it can't, I hope my insurance policy will let me buy another great violin," the twenty-six-year-old musician said.

29. The hierarchy of tasks is observed in various occupational worlds (e.g., among bus drivers in Paris [Schwartz 2011], and cardiac surgeons [Peneff 1997]).

30. While the violinists may not own a violin, they have the responsibility for its care.

31. The majority of students have the same violin maker as their teacher.

32. Sometimes, this long relationship becomes a friendship.

33. Frequently, simple repairs are done in front of the violinist, because it is useful to test the instrument during such maintenance operations. This activity takes time and involves two people; it tends to engender long discussions.

34. Thibaud is the most important French competition.

35. This transaction took place in Hotel Druot in Paris and was announced in the press. The certificate of this transaction hangs on the wall of a violin shop in the rue de Rome.

36. Despite this, all violins made by Antonio Stradivari command a high price, though some are considered "deaf" or "dead" (and their value is much lower).

37. See, for sciences, Reskin (1979: 129–146).

38. Violinists are at times required to pay insurance or a part of it. The cost is generally about 0.8 percent of the violin's value for one year of coverage, but this varies depending on the violinist's country of residence (and the level of security there).

39. Old violins (and now all violins) need a "passport"—a certificate of authenticity—to pass through borders.

40. In rare cases, a violin teaching position could include this kind of deal, as is the case of the chief of the Strings Department in the Conservatory of Moscow.

41. Jacques Thibaud and Pawel Kochanski were concertmasters, but this position was not honored for a long period.

42. A Mericourt is a violin that is regarded as an instrument for studying and not for playing the soloist repertoire.

43. A seven-eighths-size violin is reduced version of a violin for a musician who has not yet grown into the adult-size violin.

44. Musicora—an important Parisian trade show.

45. School concerts, usually played by several students.

46. One thousand francs is about 150 euros.

47. A million francs is about 150,000 euros.

48. Five thousand francs is more than 750 euros.

49. Some violinists in my sample have violins valued between 30,000 and 70,000 euros; they may have been bought by grandparents, or through the pooled resources of a large family. A Ukrainian violinist who studied in Vienna received his violin from his parents, who sold their house in Lviv to pay for it.

50. Occasionally, violin makers are victims of criminal activity. In Amsterdam in 1990, a Dutch violin maker was killed in his atelier.

51. Violins (especially old ones) have a certificate of authenticity required by customs. In some countries, this document, prepared by the violin maker, must be validated by customs officials before any foreign trip.

52. See several cases in Brussilovsky (1999).

53. These practices were described among others by Reskin (1979).

54. Svengali, a musician with hypnotic power, is a character in the novel *Trilby*, by George Du Maurier.

55. Nathan Milstein provides several examples of this type of patronage of young musicians (Milstein 1990).

56. I show here the birth dates, in order to illustrate that these two paths of an international career are independent from the generation of virtuosos.

57. Of 122 students closely observed here, only 4 had never participated in an international competition.

58. The virtuoso violin world is similar to other highly competitive environments studied by Robert H. Frank and Philip J. Cook (1996) in the book entitled *The Winner-Take-All Society: Why the Few at the Top Get So Much More Than the Rest of Us*. The distribution of powerful positions in this professional world is reproducing inequality—all these processes take place in the name of the artistic based criteria selection.

59. M. Cresta and P. Breton, in the chapter titled "The International Competitions: Greatness and Thrall," state: "1950 was a decisive change. The competitions multiplied according to the proliferation of the young performers" in Paris (1995: 119); the *Guide for Competitions 1999/2000* announced a total of 85 competitions for violin, 245 for piano, 150 for singers.

60. For example, Queen Elisabeth of the Belgium Competition offers Belgian citizenship and a passport.

61. In the interview, pianist Piotr Andreszewski (2003) described how his failure (in the final stage of the Leeds competition) became a trampoline for his career.

62. At each stage of a competition, the violinist plays a different program and needs to prove the mastery of different musical forms (sonatas, virtuoso pieces, caprices, fugues, concertos) and various styles (baroque, classic, romantic, and modern music).

63. For detailed analysis of the criteria of scientific work quality and subjective criteria see Lemont 2010.

64. Every participant has a choice in each category of pieces. They choose according to their preferences among, for example, five sonatas, eight caprices, etc. In general, one modern piece written for the competition is selected and all participants are required to play it.

65. "Playing like Heifetz" or "playing like Oistrakh" are common expressions among soloist class participants.

66. The 1935 Wieniawski Competition was the first international competition for violin (a competition in Vienna created two years before was multidisciplinary).

67. She refers the following pieces: Chaconne, J. S. Bach; la Polonaise and la Tarentelle, H. Wieniawski; and la Tzigane, Ravel.

68. The organization of this activity was detailed in chapter 4, devoted to the analysis of parental activity inside a soloist class. The example of Madame Weber cited previously illustrates how these support groups function.

69. Festivals usually consist of a suite of concerts over a period of one or a few weeks, often during holidays at the seaside, in mountain villages, or in big cities.

70. A large number of concerts in Europe are organized by employees of public institutions (ministries or cultural departments of the regional or local administration).

71. Although one could compare soloists working in Germany, the Netherlands, or Great Britain, the noticeable stinginess of concert agencies and their inefficiency is peculiar to France and Poland.

72. During my study, it was too early to evaluate the impact of this kind of agency on the violinists' careers.

73. One of the amateur organizers responsible for several dozen concerts explained that despite his desire to hire young virtuosos, he did not engage any players younger than sixteen because of administrative constraints.

74. In her book *Les comédiens* Catherine Paradeise quotes an actor, who explained, "I go out in the evening frequently because my profession wants it, because it is necessary to go out, because it is necessary to be there, because it is necessary to remind them that we exist, because sometimes we may give some ideas. . . . In the movies, it is necessary that we seduce the film directors, they need to fall in love with us in the friend manner, that they have a desire to phone you, to see you, to go out with you, to have dinner, to speak, to produce you, to possess you, to do for you that, that and that. It is necessary to meet them, to see to it that they will say to [to directors] that they have met you in order for your name to come back" (Paradeise 1997: 86).

75. This violinist was not one of the soloist class students. Her reaction was similar to reactions of other young virtuosos.

76. Once, my presence attracted the attention of this violinist. But after a short talk in which he assured himself that I was not his peer and showed disappointment that I was not a concert organizer, but only the driver of a young violinist, he never spoke to me again.

77. Until 1980, certain artists (for example, soloists originating from the USSR) had only a local career—as a consequence of the division of the soloist market along political lines. Currently, the soloist market for CD sales, for example, is divided into three major parts: North America, Europe (including Eastern Europe and Israel), and Asia. The international soloist tries to be simultaneously present in at least two markets.

78. These may include playing twice in one season in a European capital, going on an Asian tour every three years, or playing each year during the same festival, etc.

CHAPTER 6   THE SOLOIST CLASS STUDENTS' CAREERS

1. This concept comes from B. G. Glazer (1964) in "Organizational Scientists: Their Professional Careers" (Glazer 1964: 127–136); for other authors analyzing that phenomenon see Faulkner (1971) and Hermanowicz (1998).

2. I heard of Svieta while doing research in a small music school in a provincial town. The children there viewed her as their idol, and the community accorded her the same position as Oistrakh and Perlman.

3. I am presenting this excerpt from Schwarz's book because Rabin's life fits well into my analysis of soloist education and the ambiance of the soloist world.

4. All three quotes in the Obituary section of the *New York Times*, January 20, 1972, in Schwarz (1983: 567–568).

5. In Schwarz (1983: 567–568).

6. Interview, Current Biography, April 1976, 12 (Schwarz 1983, 586–587).

7. See, for example, the salaries of violinists—the members of baroque orchestras (François 2000).

8. See, for example, Newman (1999: 77–82). This type of support is also practiced in physician's families. Hall (1949: 244) cited a medical doctor who showed how young graduates of medical school get physician jobs.

9. Final national French high school exam—science section, specialization biology.

10. See the autobiography of the French champion of ice dance, Sophie Moniote (1999).

11. "Evgueni Bareïev, champion d'échecs à l'ombre des géants," *Le Monde*, February 27, 2002.

12. The competition for amateur pianists in Paris is an excellent example.

13. After the war, Szeryng returned to his previous profession, and his international soloist career had a new, very successful period. Encyklopedia Muzyki (Warsaw, 1995), PWN, 874.

14. E. C. Hughes (1945: 353): "Now there may be, for a given status or social position, one or more specifically determining characteristics of the person. Some of them are formal, or even legal. . . . Neither the formal nor the technical qualifications are in all cases so clear. Many statuses, such as membership in a social class, are not determined in a formal way. Other statuses are ill-defined both as to the characteristics which determine identification with them and as to their duties and rights. There tends to grow up about a status, in addition to its specifically determining traits, a complexity of auxiliary characteristics which come to be expected of its incumbents."

15. My analysis is not exhaustive—I only focus on the characteristics pertinent for soloist education.

16. This indication, which is in the score, concerns the notes and also the manner of playing for the right hand.

17. This is the sociability proper to the bourgeois; see, for a French example, Pinçon and Pinçon-Charlot (2003), Monique de Saint-Martin (1993), and La Wita (1988).

18. In most sports, with the exception of figure skating, performance can be measured by objective criteria.

19. In fact, the stress on physical appearance has extended beyond stage occupations, for example, author photos are now frequently on book covers.

20. Women benefit from specific critical commentaries: Hillary Hahn is "angelic," Alina Pogotskina is a "charming Russian princess."

21. In France the physical presentation of artists has evolved over the past decade. In music magazines (*Diapason, Le Monde de la musique*) and on CD covers, the soloist is fashioned as an elite model (see, for example, the covers of Anne Gastinel's CDs, or the special edition of *Le Monde de la musique* devoted to Anne Sophie Mutter).

22. Leventritt is one of the most important competitions in the United States. The winners obtain a solo engagement with an important orchestra.

23. See the PhD dissertation of François (2000) about baroque musicians.

24. In his article, "Pourquoi les Japonais aiment-ils la musique européenne?" ("Why do Japanese like European music?"), M. Watanabe (1982) states that the main problem of Japanese music students is a lack of "artistic" personality.

25. For example, H. Szeryng, in addition to his language of birth—Polish—spoke Spanish, French, German, English, Yiddish, Russian, and Italian (Schwarz 1983).

26. It may take several years to conclude definitively how many participants of this study have accomplished their goal.

CONCLUSION

1. I am preparing a next book about this process occurring in other professional worlds.

2. Muchenberg (1991: 35) and Encyklopedia Muzyczna 2002: PWM, N-Pa, 264–265.

3. For the impact of Paganini's life on his time and upon history up to the present day, see Penesco (1997).

4. Muchenberg (1991: 33). During Paganini's life and for years after, some believed he had sold his soul to the devil.

5. "Chinese democracy" was before 2000 a common expression used in Eastern Europe for describing a totalitarian system.

Appendix   Difficulties and Limits

1. Jean Peneff remarks that "the observation method requires [from the researcher] considerable availability and a lot of time" (Peneff 1990: 49).

2. This section is based on the speech I gave at Ethnographical Conference at the University of Pennsylvania in November 2003 in Philadelphia. I'd like to thank Howard Becker, who gave me the opportunity to present my research to an American public.

3. This section was originally written in 2003.

References

Adler, Patricia A., and Peter Adler. 1991. *Backboards and Blackboards: College Athletes and Role Engulfment*. New York: Columbia University Press.

———. 1998. *Peer Power: Preadolescent Culture and Identity*. New Brunswick, NJ: Rutgers University Press.

Allen, Arthur. 2014. *The Fantastic Laboratory of Dr. Weigl: How Two Brave Scientists Battled Typhus and Sabotaged the Nazis*. New York: W. W. Norton.

Andreszewski, Piotr. 2003. "Talks 'Back Stage' about Music." *Gazeta Wyborcza* (22 December).

Barley, Nigel. 1992. *Un anthropologue en déroute*. Paris: Payot.

———. 1994. *Le retours de l'anthropologue*. Paris: Payot.

Becker, Howard S. 1951. "Role and Career Problems of the Chicago Public School Teacher." PhD diss., University of Chicago.

———. 1963. *Outsiders: Studies in the Sociology of Deviance*. New York: Free Press of Glencoe.

———. 1970. *Sociological Work: Method and Substance*. Chicago: Aldine.

———. 1982. *Art Worlds*. Berkeley: University of California Press.

———. 1983. "Mondes de l'Art et types sociaux." *Sociologie du travail*, no. 4. Paris: Dunod.

———. 1988. *Les mondes de l'art*. Paris: Flammarion.

———. 2002. "Les lieux du jazz." *Sociologies et Sociétés: Les territoires de l'art* 34, no. 2.

Becker, Howard S., and James W. Carper. 1956. "The Development of Identification with an Occupation." *American Journal of Sociology* 61.

Becker, Howard S., Blanche Geer, Everett C. Hughes, and Anselm L. Strauss. 1961. *Boys in White: Student Culture in Medical School*. Chicago: University of Chicago Press.

Becker, Howard S., and Anselm L. Strauss. 1956. "Careers, Personality, and Adult Socialization." *American Journal of Sociology* 52, no. 3.

Bera, Mathieu, and Philippe Lamy. 2003. *Sociologie de la culture*. Paris: Coll. Cursus, Armand Colin.

Bertaux, Daniel, and Isabelle Bertaux-Wiame. 1988. "Le patrimoine et sa lignée: Transmissions et mobilité sociale sur cinq générations," FRA, no. 4, Doc. IRESCO.

Bizeul, Daniel. 1999. "Enquête: Faire avec les déconvenues." *Sociétés Contemporaines* no. 1, 33/34. Paris: l'Harmattan.

Bourdieu, Pierre. 1979. *La distinction: Critique sociale du jugement*. Paris: Les Editions de Minuit.

———. 1995. *The Rules of Art: The Genesis and Structures of the Literary Fields*. Stanford, CA: Stanford University Press.

———. 1996. *The State Nobility: Elite Schools in the Field of Power*. Stanford, CA: Stanford University Press.

———. 1996, *The Rules of Art: Genesis and Structure of the Literary Field*. Trans. by Susan Emanuel. Stanford, CA: Stanford University Press.

Braude, Lee. 1961. "Professional Autonomy and the Role of the Layman." *Social Forces* 39, no. 4: 297–309.

Brussilovsky, Alexander, ed. 1999. *Yuri Yankelevitch et l'Ecole Russe du Violon*. Fontenay aux Roses, France: Suoni e Colori.

Campbell, Robert A. 2003. "Preparing the Next Generation of Scientists: The Social Process of Managing Students." *Social Studies of Science* 33, no. 6: 897–927.

Cameron, William Bruce. 1954. "Sociological Notes on the Jamsession." *Social Forces* 33.

Cantu, Alberto. 1997. "Portrait de Camillo Silvori." In Anne Penesc, *Défense et illustration de la virtuosité*. Lyon: PUL, 179–186.

Chapoulie, Jean-Michel. 1987. *Les professeurs de l'enseignement secondaire: Un métier de classe moyenne*. Paris: Editions de la Maison de Sciences de l'Homme.

———. 2001. *La tradition sociologique de Chicago*. Paris: Seuil.

Chin, Tiffany. 2000. "Sixth Grade Madness." *Journal of Contemporary Ethnography* 29, no. 2: 124–163.

Chua, Amy. 2010. *Battle Hymn of the Tiger Mother*. New York: Penguin.

Chylinska, Teresa, ed. 1967. *Dzieje przyjazni—korespondencja Karola Szymanowskiego z Pawlem i Zofia Kochanskimi*. Warsaw: PWM.

Cole, Stephen, and Jonathan R. Cole. 1967. "Scientific Output and Recognition: A Study in the Operation of the Reward System in Science." *American Sociological Review* 32.

Coulangeon, Philippe. 1998. "Entre tertiairisation et marginalisation subventionnée: Les musiciens de jazz français à l'heure de la réhabilitation culturelle." PhD diss., EHESS.

———. 1999. "Les mondes de l'art à l'épreuve du salariat: Le cas des musiciens de jazz français." *Revue Française de Sociologie* 40, no. 4 (Oct./Nov.).

Davis, Fred. 1974. "Stories and Sociology." *Urban Life and Culture* 3: 310–316.

Defoort-Lafourcade, Dominique. 1996. "L'insertion professionnelle des instrumentistes diplômés du Conservatoire National Supérieur de Musique et de Danse de Paris." Mémoire de Dea, EHESS, 231.

Dupuis, Xavier. 1993. *Les musiciens d'orchestre*. DEP, Ministère de la Culture.

Duret, Pascal. 1993. *L'héroïsme sportif*. Paris: PUF.

Durkheim, Émile. 1958. *Socialism and Saint-Simon, Routledge Revivals*. Edited with an introduction by Alvin W. Gouldner, trans. by Charlotte Sattler (French original, 1928).

Encyklopedia Muzyczna. 2002. Warsaw: PWN.

Encyklopedia Muzyki. 1995. Warsaw: PWN.

Erikson, Erik H. 1968. *Identity: Youth and Crisis*. New York: W. W. Norton.

———. 1980. *Identity and the Life-cycle: A reissue*. New York: W. W. Norton.

Faulkner, Robert R. 1971. *Hollywood Studio Musicians: Their Work and Career in the Recording Industry*. Chicago: Aldine-Atherton.

———. 1983. *Music on Demand: Composer and Careers in the Hollywood Film Industry*. New Brunswick, NJ: Transaction.

Ferrales, Gabrielle, and Gary Alan Fine. 2005. "Sociology as a Vocation: Reputations and Group Cultures in Graduate School." *American Sociologist* 36: 57–75.

Festinger, Leon, Henry W. Riecken, and Stanley Schachter. 1956. *When Prophecy Fails: A Social and Psychological Study of a Modern Group That Predicted the Destruction of the World*. New York: Harper Torchbooks.

François, Pierre. 2000. "Le renouveau de la musique ancienne: Dynamique socioéconomique d'une innovation esthétique." PhD diss., EHESS Paris.

Frank, Robert, and Philip J. Cook. 1996. *The Winner-Take-All Society: Why the Few at the Top Get So Much More Than the Rest of Us.* New York: Penguin.

Geertz, Clifford. 1996. *Ici et Là-bas: L'anthropologue comme auteur.* Paris: Métailé.

Gilmore, Samuel. 1987. "Coordination and Convention: The Organization of the Concert World." *Symbolic Interaction* 10, no. 2.

———. 1990. "Art Worlds: Developing the Interactionist Approach to Social Organization." In *Symbolic Interaction and Cultural Studies,* edited by H. S. Becker and M. M. McCall. Chicago: University of Chicago Press.

Gladwell, Malcolm. 2008. *Outliers: The Story of Success.* New York: Little, Brown and Co.

Glaser, Barney G. 1964. *Organizational Scientists: Their Professional Careers.* Indianapolis: Bobbs-Merrill.

Goffman, Erving. 1952. "On Cooling the Mark Out: Some Aspects of Adaptation to Failure." *Psychiatry* 15, no. 4: 451–463.

———. 1968. *Asiles.* Paris: Les éditions de Minuit.

———. 1973. *La mise en scène de la vie quotidienne: Présentation de soi.* Paris: Les éditions de Minuit.

Granovetter, Marc S. 1973. "The Strength of Weak Ties." *American Journal of Sociology* 78: 1360–1380.

Grazian, David. 2003. *Blue Chicago: The Search for Authenticity in Urban Blues Clubs.* Chicago: University of Chicago Press.

Gruzinski, Serge. 1999. *La pensée métisse.* Paris: Fayard.

Guide des concours de musique 1999/2000. 1999. Cité de la Musique.

Hall, Oswald. 1949. "Types of Medical Careers." *American Journal of Sociology* 55, no. 3: 243–253.

Hannerz, Ulf. 2002. *Transnational Connections: Culture, People, Places.* Abington, Oxon: Taylor & Francis.

Heinich, Nathalie. 1999. *L'épreuve de la grandeur: Prix littéraires et reconnaissance.* Paris: La Découverte.

———. 2000. *Etre écrivain: Création et identité.* Paris: La Découverte.

Hermanowicz, Joseph C. 1998. *The Stars Are Not Enough: Scientists—Their Passions and Professions.* Chicago: University of Chicago Press.

Horowitz, Joseph. 1990. *The Ivory Trade.* New York: Summit.

Hughes, Everett C. 1945. "Dilemmas and Contradiction of Status." *American Journal of Sociology* 50, no. 5 (March): 353–359.

———. 1971. *The Sociological Eye: Selected Papers.* Chicago: Aldine.

———. 1996. "Le regard sociologique." Paris: Edition EHESS.

Huston, Nancy. 2000. *Prodigy.* Toronto: McArthur.

Jelagin, Juri. 1951. *Taming of the Arts.* New York: Dutton.

Joachim, Joseph, and Andreas Moser. 1905. *Traité du violon.* Berlin: Simrock; Paris: Eschig.

Johnson, John M. 1975. *Doing Field Research.* New York: The Free Press.

Jouzefowitch, Wiktor. 1978. *David Ojstrach: Biesiedy z Igorem Oïstrachem.* Moscow. English trans. by Yuzefovich Viktor. 1979. *David Oistrakh: Conversations with Igor Oistrakh.* Worthing, West Sussex: Littlehampton Book Services.

Judy, Paul R. 2012. "An Interview with J. Richard Hackman: Life and Work in Symphony Orchestras." Harmony, no. 2 (April). http://www.polyphonic.org/wp-content/uploads/2012/02/Interview_Hackman_Judy.pdf.

Junker, Buford. 1980. *Field Work.* Chicago: University of Chicago Press.

Kuhn, Thomas S. 1962. *The Structure of Scientific Revolutions.* Chicago: University of Chicago Press.

La Wita, Béatrix. 1988. *Ni vue ni connu: Approche ethnographique de la culture bourgeoise.* Paris: Ed. de la Maison des sciences de l'homme.

Lehmann, Bernard. 2002. *L'orchestre dans tous ses éclats*. Paris: La Découverte.

Lemont, Michelle. 2010. *How Professors Think: Inside the Curious World of Academic Judgment*. Cambridge, MA: Harvard University Press.

Lepoutre, David. 1997. *Coeur de banlieue: Codes, rites et langages*. Paris: Editions Odile Jacob.

Levey-Freidman, Hilary. 2013. *Playing to Win: Rising Children in a Competitive Culture*. Berkeley: University of California Press.

Lourie-Sand, Barbara. 2000. *Teaching Genius: Dorothy DeLay and the Making of a Musician*. Portland, Oregon: Amadeus Press.

Masson, Philippe. 1996. "L'ordre scolaire dans l'enseignement secondaire au milieu des années 1990: Etude par observation des établissements d'une petite ville de l'Ouest." PhD diss., EHESS.

Menuhin, Yehudi. 1987. *La leçon du maître*. Paris: Buchet/Chastel. English edition. *Life Class*. London: William Heinemann, 1986.

Merton, Robert. 1968. "The Matthew Effect in Science: The Reward and Communication System in Sciences Are Considered." *Science* 156, no. 3810: 56–63.

———. 1984. "Socially Expected Durations: A Case Study of Concept Formation in Sociology." In *Conflict and Consensus: In Honor of Lewis A. Coser*. Edited by W. Powell and R. Robbins, 262–283. New York: The Free Press.

Milstein, Nathan, and Solomon Volkov. 1990. *From Russia to the West: The Musical Memoirs and Reminiscences of Nathan Milstein*. New York: Henry Holt.

Le Monde de la musique. Paris.

Moniotte, Sophie. 1999. *Les Patins de la colère*. Paris: Anne Carrière.

Monjaret, Anne. 1996. "Etre bien dans son bureau." *Ethnologie française* 26.

Muchenberg, Bohdan. 1991. *Pogadanki o muzyce*. Vol. 2. Krakow: Polskie Wydawnictwo Muzyczne.

Newman, Katherine. 1999. *No Shame in My Game*. New York: Russell Sage Foundation.

Padgett, John F., and Christopher K. Ansell. 1993. "Robust Action and the Rise of the Medici, 1400–1434." *American Journal of Sociology* 98, no. 6.

Padgett, John F., and Walter W. Powell. 2012. *The Emergence of Organizations and Markets*. Princeton, NJ: Princeton University Press.

Paradeise, Catherine, with Jacques Charby and François Vourc'h. 1998. *Les comédiens: Profession et marchés du travail*. Paris: PUF.

Pâris, Alain. 1995. *Dictionnaire des interprètes*. Paris: Laffont coll. Bouquins.

Pasquier, Dominique. 1983. "Carrières des femmes." *Sociologie du Travail*, no. 4.

Peneff, Jean. 1990. *La méthode biographique: De l'école de Chicago à l'histoire orale*. Paris: Armand Colin.

———. 1997. "Le travail du chirurgien." *Sociologie du travail* 39: 265–296.

Penesco, Anne, ed. 1997. *Défense et illustration de la virtuosité*. Lyon: PUL.

Peretz, Henri. 1998. *Les méthodes en sociologie: L'observation*. Paris: La Découverte coll. Repères.

Perron, Denis. 2001. *Ma vie est la musique: L'univers méconnu d'instrumentistes d'orchestres symphoniques*. Sainte-Foy: Les Presses de l'Université Laval.

Petit de Voize, Y. 1997. "Young, Gifted, Hardworking, They Are the Elite of French Instrumental Music." *Diapason*, no. 435 (March).

Pincon, Michel, and Monique Pincon-Charlot. 1997a. *Sociologie de la bourgeoisie*. Paris: La Découverte.

———. 1997b. *Voyage en grande bourgeoisie*. Paris: PUF.

Poupart, Jean. 1999. "Vouloir faire carrière dans le hockey professionnel: Exemple des joueurs juniors québécois dans les années soixante-dix." *Sociologie et sociétés* 31, no. 1 (Spring).

Powdermaker, Hortense. 1966. *Stranger and Friend: The Way of an Anthropologist.* W. W. Norton.

Quemin, Alain. 1997. *Les commissaires-priseurs: La mutation d'une profession.* Paris: Anthropos-Economica.

Raaben, Lev. 1967. *Zhizn' zamechatel'nykh skripachei* (The lives of famous violinists). Leningrad: Muzyka, Leningradskoe otd-nie.

Ravet, Hyacinthe. 2000. "Les musiciennes d'orchestre: Interactions entre représentations sociales et itinéraires." PhD diss., Université Paris X.

Ravet, Hyacinthe, and Phillippe Coulangeon. 2003. "La division sexuelle du travail chez les musiciens français," *Sociologie du travail* 45, no. 3.

Rawik-Rawik, Joanna. 1993. *Maestra—opowiesc o Wandzie Wilkomirskiej.* Warsaw: Twoj Styl.

Reif, Fred, and Anselm L. Strauss. 1965. "The Impact of Rapid Discovery upon the Scientist's Career." *Social Problems* 12.

Reskin, Barbara F. 1979. "Academic Sponsorship and Scientists' Careers." *Sociology of Education* 52 (July).

Rose, Arnold M. 1971. *Human Behavior and Social Processes: An Interactionist Approach.* London: Routledge & Kegan Paul.

Roth, Julius A. 1962. "Comments on 'Secret Observation.'" *Social Problems* 9 (Winter): 283–284.

———. 1974. "Turning Adversity to Account." *Journal of Contemporary Ethnography* 3. http://jce.sagepub.com/content/3/3/347.full.pdf (accessed 16 May 2012).

Roy, Donald. 2001. "Deux formes de freinage dans un atelier de mécanique: Respecter un quota et tirer au flanc." *Sociétés contemporaines,* no. 40. Original: "Quota Restriction and Goldbricking in a Machine Shop." *American Journal of Sociology* 57, no. 5 (1952).

Saint-Martin, Monique de. 1993. *L'espace de la noblesse.* Paris: Métailé, coll. "Leçons de choses."

Schnaiberg, Allan. 2005 "Mentoring Graduate Students: Going beyond the Formal Role Structure." *American Sociologist* 36, no. 2 (Summer): 28–42.

Schwarz, Boris. 1983. *Great Masters of the Violin.* New York: Simon & Schuster.

Schwarz, Olivier. 2011. "La pénétration de la 'culture psychologique de masse' dans un groupe populaire: Paroles de conducteurs de bus." *Sociologie* 4, no. 2. http://www.cairn.info/revue-sociologie-2011-4-page-345.htm (accessed 17 May 2012).

Slonimsky, Nicolas. 1997. *Baker's Biographical Dictionary of Twentieth-Century Classical Musicians.* Edited by Laura Kuhn. New York: Schirmer.

Soriano, Marc. 1993. *Secrets du violon: Souvenir de Jules Boucherit.* Paris: Des Cendres.

Spradley, James, and Brenda Mann. 1979. *Les bars, les femmes et la culture.* Paris: PUF.

Stephen, J., E. Fraser, and J. E. Marcia. 1992. "Moratorium-Achievement (Mama) Cycles in Lifespan Identity Development: Value Orientations and Reasoning System Correlates." *Journal of Adolescence* 15: 283–300.

Stern, Isaak, and Chaim Potok. 2001. *My First 79 Years.* Cambridge, MA: Da Capo.

The Strad. 2000. 111 (Dec.)

Strauss, Anselm L. 1959. *Mirrors and Masks.* San Francisco: Sociology Press.

Tedesco, Emmanuel. 1979. *Les familles parlent à l'école.* Paris: Casterman.

Thelot, Claude. 1982. *Tel père tel fils?* Paris: Dunod.

Thibaud, Jacques. 1947. *Un violon parle: Souvenirs de Jaques Thibaud.* Edited by J. P. Dorian. Paris: Du Blé qui Lève.

Traweek, Sharon. 1988. *Beamtimes and Lifetames: The World of High Energy Physicists.* Cambridge, MA: Harvard University Press.

Uzzi, Brian. 1997. "Social Structure and Competition in Interfirm Networks: The Paradox of Embeddedness." *Administrative Science Quarterly* 42, no. 1 (March): 35–67.

Villemin, Dominique. 1997. *L'apprentissage de la musique.* Paris: Seuil.

Wagner, Anne-Catherine. 1995. "Le jeu du national et de l'international: Les cadres étrangers en France." PhD diss., EHESS Paris.

Wagner, Izabela. 2004. "La formation de jeunes virtuoses: Les réseaux de soutiens." *Sociétés Contemporaines* 56.

———. 2006a. "Career Coupling: Career Making in the Elite World of Musicians and Scientists." *Qualitative Sociology Review* 2, no. 3.

———. 2006b. "La production sociale de virtuoses—cas de violonistes." PhD diss., EHESS soutenu 24 May 2006. EHESS Paris.

———. 2010. "Teaching the Art of Playing with Career-Coupling Relationships in the Virtuoso World." *Studies in Symbolic Interaction* (Oct.).

Waldemar, Charles. 1969. *Liebe, Ruhm und Leidenschaft.* Monachium: Moewig.

Watanabe, Michihiro. 1982. "Pourquoi les Japonais aiment-ils la musique européenne?" *Revue Internationale de Sciences Sociales* 34, no. 4.

Wax, Rosalie. 1960. "Reciprocity in Field Work." In *Human Organization Research: Field Relations and Techniques.* Edited by Richard N. Adams and Jack J. Preiss. Homewood, IL: Dorsey Press.

Westby, David L. 1960. "The Career Experience of the Symphony Musician." *Social Forces* 38.

Whyte, William Foote. 1955. *Street Corner Society: The Social Structure of an Italian Slum.* Chicago: University of Chicago Press.

Wprost. 2000. No. 32 (Aug.) Varsovie.

Wronski, Tadeusz. 1979. *Zdolni i nie zdolni o grze i antygrze na skrzypcach.* Kraków: PWM.

Znaniecki, Florian. 1937. "Rola spoleczna artysty" ("Rôle social de l'artiste"). *Wiedza I zycie,* nos. 8/9.

Zukerman, Ezra W., Tai-Young Kim, Kalinda Ukanawa, and James von Rittman. 2003. "Robust Identities or Nonentities? Typecasting in the Feature-Film Labor Market." *American Journal of Sociology* 108, no. 5.

Index

Prokofiev, Serge, 156
provenance of violin, 169

quality: ambiguity in selection criteria,
238n.75; peer recognition of, 50, 145; of performance, and growing body, 77
Queen Elisabeth competition (Brussels), 19,
237n.45, 245n.60

Rabin, Michael, 21, 194–195
racism, 240n.43
Rawik, Joanna, 49–50
recordings, 154, 155, 198; of lessons, for home
practice, 239n.18; video, required for international competition entry, 243n.15. *See
also* CDs
relationships: building of, and competition juries, 71; considered most important competition factor by parents, 70;
domestic instability among teachers,
114; informants' distorted memories of,
240n.41; master-disciple, 94–95, 111, 115,
142–147; with peers, eclipsing teachers,
135; soloist's cultivation of, and self-
promotion, 186–187; between teacher and
second-stage student (*see* career coupling); transformation of, with former
teacher, 143–144
relocation of family, 51–53
repertoire: distribution of pieces to be
played, hierarchy of, 64; large, for violinists, 27; of unpublished or forgotten pieces,
155–156, 243n.16
Repin, Vladimir, 43, 236n.19
reputation: and soloist's acquisition of
prestigious violin, 157; teacher's, 115, 116,
123–124
resistance: physical, to demands of career,
206–207; psychological, to career stresses,
207–208; to work, 48–49, 237n.35
Ricci, Ruggiero, 20, 43, 48, 236n.15
Richter, Sviatoslav, 62
Riecken, Henry, 216
Riepin, Vladimir, 146
Robillard, Virginia, 242n.73
Rogoff, Rony, 21
rosin, 235n.1
Roth, Julius A., 6, 226, 228
Roy, Donald, 226
Royal College of Music (London), 242n.73
Rubinstein, Arthur, 46, 171, 205, 233n.1, 242n.69
rudeness, 109
rupture of the student-teacher relationship,
124–126; and networking through new
teacher, 126–129
Russian tradition, in musical pedagogy, 15–
19, 55–56, 111–112, 140

"safety net" of ensemble-based career, 78. *See
also* ensembles: backup careers with
St. Petersburg Conservatory, 140
"St. Petersburg School" of violinists, 17
Salerno-Sonnenberg, Nadja, 21
Salle Pleyel (Paris), 190
Sanovsky, Berl, 21
Sarasate, Pablo, 13, 240n.44
Saslav, Isidor, 20
scale, musical, 235n.3, 242n.71
"scandals" at competitions, 1–2, 177,
216–221
Schacht, Liba, 22
Schachter, Stanley, 216
"school" as teacher-to-student lineage, 11–12
School of Young Virtuosos in Sion (Switzerland), 23
Schwarz, Boris, 10; on American school of
violinists, 19; on centers of virtuoso training in 1980s, 10; on Corelli, 11; on Flesch,
14; on Franco-Belgian school of violinists,
15, 62; on Haendel, 135; on Israeli violinists,
21; on Kreutzer's hands, 50; on "new style"
of virtuosos, 13; on Persiger, 19–20; on pri-
macy of Eastern European Jewish violinists, 16; on Ricci's parents, 48; on Russian
school of violinists, 21, 62
Schwarzberg, Dora, 22
secondary actors, role of, in third stage of
student soloist's career, 149–156
Seidel, Tascha, 17
self-control, 208
self-promotion, and sociability, 186–187,
203–204
Serkin, Rudolf, 233n.1
Sevcik, Otkar, 15
sexual attraction: and patronage, 173;
between student soloists, 114, 134–135
sexuality and gender, 113–114
Shaham, Gil, 21, 84, 135, 168, 171, 173
sight-reading, 236n.24
Sikorsky, Wladislaw, 200
Silverstein, Joseph, 20
Sitkovetsky, Dimitri, 21
sitting on the score, 102
Slonimsky, Nicolas, 10
soccer, 120
sociability, 202, 247n.17; and self-promotion,
186–187, 203–204
social capital, 153
socialization of the student soloist, 9; post-
education auxiliary characteristics of,
202; and third-stage networking, 186–187;
within the soloist class, 57–59
socially expected durations, 29
social position, and competitions, 69
Socrates exchange program, 241n.66

Western Europe, student soloists from, 55
Western tradition, in musical pedagogy,
    112–113
Whyte, William Foote, 228
Wienawski, Henryk, 13
Wienawski competitions, 65, 66, 135, 175,
    180–181, 182, 246n.66
Wilhelm, August, 13
Wilkomirska, Wanda, 49–50
work: discipline in, 115, 202; resistance to, 48–
    49, 202, 237n.35; rhythms of, 117, 119–121
"working" family paradigm, for soloist class,
    85–86
"work tool," violin as, 168
World Federation of International Compe-
    titions, 175
Wunderkind, 213. *See also* child prodigies;
    precocity

Yampolsky, Abram, 15, 18–19
Yankelevich, Yuri, 15, 19; as collector and
    donor of violins, 166, 169; evenings at his

apartment, 119; informal ties with former students, 143; on knowing students
outside music hours, 120; special relationship with his star students, 145, 169;
sponsors Belkin, 208; support foundation
created by former students, 137; teaching style, 85, 87, 109, 112; use of teaching
space, 62–63
Yehudi Menuhin School (Folkestone, UK),
    23, 80
Yiddish, 234n.15
YouTube, 205
Ysaÿe, Eugène, 13, 15, 20

Zazofsky, Paul, 21
Zeitlin, Zvi, 22
*Zhizn' zamechatel'nykh skripacheï i vio-
    lonchelstov* (Raaben), 8
Zimbalist, Efrem, 17
Znaniecki, Florian, 238n.69
Zukerman, Pinchas, 21, 22, 25, 57, 172
Zürich, conservatory at, 23

About the Author

IZABELA WAGNER was born in 1964 in Poland into a family of musicians. In 1983, after finishing her education at the Poznan music high school, she received the Award of Excellence and her teacher's diploma. She graduated from the University of Music in Poznan in 1987, receiving a master of arts with the Award of Excellence and First Prize with Honors. She emigrated from Poland to France in 1987, where she taught piano, music theory, solfège, and general music in the Conservatory of Music in Nanterre from 1988 to 2002.

In 1996, Wagner enrolled in the sociology doctoral program jointly offered by the Ecole Normale Superieur, the Ecole des Hautes Etudes en Sciences Sociales (EHESS), and University of Paris 8, and began her ethnographic fieldwork in the world of violinists. In 2006 she defended her PhD thesis "La production sociale des violonistes virtuoses" ("The Social Production of the Virtuoso") and received highest honors. Wagner has also studied the international mobility of life scientists and in 2010–2011 was a visiting scholar in the Department of the History of Science at Harvard University. She is the author of *Becoming a Transnational Professional— The Mobility and Career of the Young Elite of Polish Science.* She is also the author of several articles in scientific journals (*Qualitative Sociological Review, Studies in Symbolic Interaction, Societes Contemporaines*) and several chapters in scholarly books.

Since 2008, Wagner has been an associate professor at the Faculty of Philosophy and Sociology at Warsaw University in the Center for Sociology of Work and Organization. Between 2012 and 2014 she was the director of didactics at the Institute of Sociology at Warsaw University. She is a member of the European Sociological Association and a member of the board of Qualitative Network Section/ESA.